Google
for
Lawyers

Essential Search Tips
and Productivity Tools

Carole A. Levitt and Mark E. Rosch

ABA LawPractice Management Section
MARKETING · MANAGEMENT · TECHNOLOGY · FINANCE

Library of Congress Cataloging-in-Publication Data
Levitt, Carole A.
   Google for lawyers : essential search tips and productivity tools / by Carole A. Levitt and Mark E. Rosch.
       p. cm.
   Includes index.
   ISBN 978-1-60442-822-3
   1. Legal research–Computer network resources. 2. Google. 3. Web search engines. 4. Internet searching. 5. Internet research. I. Rosch, Mark E. II. Title.
   K87.L48 2010
   025.04252–dc22

                                                    2010016422

Contents

Chapter 1
Why Use the Internet to Locate Information?   1

Chapter 2
Introduction to Google   9

Chapter 3
Basic (And not so Basic) Google Search Strategies:
All You Need to Know to Become
a Good Internet Researcher   27

Chapter 4
Advanced Google Search Strategies:
All You Need to Know to Become
a Great Internet Researcher   39

Chapter 5
You've Got Your Search Results, Now What? Understanding and Manipulating the Displayed Search Results   51

Chapter 6
Google News   63

Chapter 7
Google Groups: Retrieving Information from Over
One Billion Publicly Archived E-mail Messages   79

Chapter 8
Google Image Search: Locating Photos
of Individuals, Products, and More   97

Chapter 13
Google Books: Quickly Locate Useful Books, Magazines, and Legal Treatises, Statutes, Opinions, and Legislative Histories   151

Chapter 14
Google Maps   165

Chapter 15
Location-Based Google Search via Your Non-Web-Enabled Telephone (GOOG-411)   181

Chapter 16
Free Knowledge-Management Tools from Google: Desktop Search   183

Chapter 17
Google Scholar: Locate Information from Academic Sources and Retrieve Free Case Law 203

Chapter 18
Google Apps: Free Collaboration Tools to Help Solos and Small Firms Compete with Big-Firm Technology Budgets 219

Chapter 19
Google Voice

319

Chapter 25
Advertising Services from Google 375

Chapter 26
Google's Web Browser: Chrome 391

Chapter 27
Google Knol: Experts Sharing Their Knowledge,
One Unit at a Time 401

Appendices   411

Index   499

About the Authors

Carole A. Levitt

Carole Levitt is a nationally recognized author and speaker on Internet research. She has over twenty years of experience in the legal field as a law librarian, legal research and writing professor, California attorney, and Internet trainer. She is a skilled online searcher, focusing on legal, public record, investigative, and business research. She is also coauthor of *The Cybersleuth's Guide to the Internet* (IFL Press, 2010) and *Find Info Like A Pro, Volume I: Mining the Internet's Publicly Available Resources for Investigative Research* (American Bar Association, 2010).

As President and founder of Internet For Lawyers (**www.netforlawyers. com**), she provides customized Internet research training to legal professionals (with continuing legal education credit). Ms. Levitt has presented at the ABA TECHSHOW; LegalWorks; LegalTech; the annual meetings of the American Bar Association (ABA), the National Association of Bar Executives, the Association of Continuing Legal Education, and the California State Bar Association; the worldwide Gibson, Dunn & Crutcher corporate attorney retreat; law firms, bar associations; and library associations throughout the country. Ms. Levitt serves on the Executive Council of the ABA's Law Practice Management (LPM) Section, and on the Section's Publishing Board. Previously, she was chair of the California State Bar's Law Practice Management and Technology Section and served on the Executive Board of the Los Angeles County Bar Law Practice Management Section, among various other professional association activities.

She was a regular contributor to the *Los Angeles Lawyer* magazine's "Computer Counselor" column for eight years and has also written for numerous magazines, newsletters, and Web sites such as *California Lawyer, Trial, The Internet Lawyer, Computer and Internet Lawyer, Research Advisor, Nashville Lawyer, FindLaw, CEB Case N Point,* and *LLRX.*

Ms. Levitt received her Juris Doctorate from the John Marshall Law School, where she graduated with distinction and was a member of the school's law review. She earned her BA in Political Science and her MLS at the University of Illinois. Ms. Levitt can be contacted at **clevitt@netfor lawyers.com.**

Mark E. Rosch

As Vice President of Internet For Lawyers (IFL), Rosch is the developer and manager of the Internet For Lawyers Web site. He writes and speaks about how to use the Internet for research and on technology implementation for the legal community. He is also coauthor of *The Cybersleuth's Guide to the Internet* (IFL Press, 2010) and *Find Info Like A Pro, Volume I: Mining the Internet's Publicly Available Resources for Investigative Research* (American Bar Association, 2010).

Mr. Rosch has also written about the application of computer technology in the law office for *California Lawyer, Law Technology News, Law Office Computing, Los Angeles Lawyer, Los Angeles Daily,* and other publications. Additionally, he has presented at the annual meetings of the ABA, the National Association of Bar Executives, the Association of Continuing Legal Education, the California State Bar, and in-house at various firms.

Mr. Rosch is a member of the ABA and served as a Vice Chair of its LPM Section education board. He is also a member of the Association of Continuing Legal Education (ACLEA), having served as chair of ACLEA's Entrepreneur's section and its Marketing section. He has also served on the Academy of Television Arts & Sciences' Public Relations Steering Committee, and the Television Publicity Executives Committee.

During his nearly twenty years of marketing experience, Mr. Rosch has developed and supervised the publicity, promotions, and marketing campaigns for numerous and varied clients, from legal portals to new media developers. He has also provided Web management consulting to the State Bar of California Law Practice Management & Technology Section's Web site and various law firms and solo practitioners.

He graduated from Tulane University, in New Orleans, with a BA in Sociology. Mr. Rosch can be reached at **mrosch@netforlawyers.com.**

Acknowledgments

We would like to thank and commend the ABA LPM Publications staff (Tim Johnson, Kimia Shelby, Trish Cleary, and especially Denise Constantine) for all their hard work in producing this book.

Carole would also like to thank Sharon D. Nelson, Esq., President of Sensei Enterprises, Inc., who first had the idea for this book when she chaired the ABA LPM Publications Board, and then asked us to write it. Sharon was an amazing Chair who worked tirelessly to improve LPM's publications by bringing many innovations to the publications department.

Finally, a thank-you to Rick Klau, Product Manager for Google Profiles, for graciously answering many of our Google questions and writing the foreword to this book.

Foreword

by Rick Klau, Product Manager, Google
Google Profile: http://profiles.google.com/rick.klau
Blog: http://tins.rklau.com/

Fifteen years ago I was part of a team of law students at the University of Richmond School of Law who published the first law journal to publish exclusively online. In those days, the Internet was very new, relatively unknown to the legal profession, and, truth be told, a bit of a novelty. Today more than one billion people (by some estimates, it's close to two billion) use the Internet regularly, and current estimates have mobile Internet usage surpassing desktop Internet usage within the next few years. It's exciting to work at a company in the center of this evolution, and I'm particularly pleased to see this book serve as such a comprehensive effort to document the many ways you can get more from Google's offerings.

Google's mission is simple, if ambitious: to organize the world's information and make it universally accessible and useful. While many know us for our search engine, far fewer know the full scope of what we've made available for free to users. Mark and Carole do a great job documenting many more of Google's products designed to deliver on our mission; our hope is that these applications will help *you* organize *your* information, and make it more useful in the process.

Looking at the tabs open in my Chrome web browser right now, I have no fewer than eight Google products open. In an average day, I write a blog post on Blogger, collaborate on documents with co-workers (and occasionally on personal documents with my wife) in Google Docs, update the Cub Scout website for my sons' scout pack using Google Sites, send e-mail and chat (both by voice and video) in Gmail, manage incoming and outgoing phone calls via Google Voice, organize information about me in my Google Profile, search for recent blog posts about topics I'm interested in in Google Blogsearch, share updates with friends via Google Buzz, and keep tabs on hundreds of websites in Google Reader. The list goes on . . . yet up until now, no single resource has existed to introduce professionals to these tools and get you comfortable with how they can improve your practice.

And with apologies to Mark and Carole, Google will continue to evolve. We've not yet completed our mission, nor do we expect to. One thing is certain, however: as we release new products, they will build on top of the foundation we've laid with the many applications covered in this book. Understanding and mastering these products now will hopefully benefit your practice today, and prepare you for what's on the way.

See you online!

Introduction

When people heard that our next book for the ABA Law Practice Management Section was about Google, many responded, "Google? Is there really enough for a whole book?" One look at the Table of Contents should answer that question.

Google for Lawyers is meant to be a practical guide for lawyers who want to know how to get the most out of Google for their research *and* their technology needs. It is designed to show lawyers how they can use free and low-cost tools available from Google to compete with large firms and their large research and technology budgets. These tools range from lesser-known resources such as Google Scholar's case law database and free office applications such as Gmail, Google Docs, and Google Calendar to services such as Google Voice, Google Wave, and Google Translate.

The time when lawyers could ignore the information on the Internet has passed. Legal professionals can use *Google for Lawyers* to become tech-savvy practitioners and gain the edge over other practitioners by learning how to use Google's advanced features for research and its free office applications to become more efficient in their practice. This book will be one of the most powerful weapons in your arsenal when it comes to sussing out information from the Internet and practicing more efficiently.

Google for Lawyers introduces novice Internet searchers to the diverse collection of information locatable through the Internet's most popular search engine. For intermediate and advanced users, the book unlocks the power of search strategies, functions, and services they are probably not aware of. The book discusses the importance of including effective Google searching as part of a lawyer's due diligence, and cites case law that mandates that lawyers should use Google and other resources available on the Internet, where applicable.

Google for Lawyers illustrates the reasons lawyers should use Google for research, from searching free case law and newspaper and magazine articles, to locating information about the opposition, expert witnesses, jurors, and existing and potential clients, to finding missing witnesses and missing heirs. The book also explains, step by step, how to use various Google tools and databases to get this information quickly and efficiently. "War Stories" from lawyers are also included to show how they have used Google to their advantage in their practice.

Conventions Used in This Book

Throughout the book we will use **boldfaced type** to indicate exact text that appears onscreen in links (URLs), buttons, drop-down menus, etc. for the services and tools we discuss (e.g, **More** or **Translate**).

Additionally, we will use *italics* to indicate exact text (search terms/ keywords) typed for sample searches we conducted to evaluate the Google services we discuss (e.g., *"Mark Rosch" OR "Carole Levitt"*).

Why Use the Internet to Locate Information?

1

1.1   The Lawyer's Duty to Google

Lawyers are fact finders, not just legal researchers. They often need to find that one fact to make or break a case or help complete a transactional matter. The Internet is filled with just that kind of factual information. This book will help you use Google more efficiently and effectively to locate the facts and manage that information.

Whether you need to find a weather Web site to prove or disprove that it really was a dark and stormy night on the night of the murder five years ago, or if there is a free Web site to full-text search public company filings, or you simply need to "Google" the contact information for a missing party, the Internet can often provide the answer . . . and Google can be your gateway.

In a number of recent cases, judges have told lawyers that they have a "duty to Google" as part of their due diligence procedure. In fact, lawyers may run the risk of competency claims if they do not have access to and make use of the Internet for research. At least one federal court has held that in order to avoid negligence, and to satisfy due diligence considerations, lawyers should be actively conducting research on the Internet.

As far back as 1995, some judges began to recognize the value of information's availability on the Internet and the importance of retrieving it. Seventh Circuit Judge Kanne held, in a Securities Exchange Act Rule 10b-5 securities fraud action, that nondisclosure of enacted or pending legislation and industry-wide trends is not a basis for a securities fraud claim" because the information was in the public domain and accessible to the plaintiff. "In today's society, with the advent of the information superhighway, federal and state legislation and regulations, as well as information regarding industry trends, are easily accessed. A reasonable investor is presumed to have information available in the public domain, and therefore Whirlpool is imputed with constructive knowledge of this information. *Whirlpool Financial Corporation v. GN Holdings, Inc.*, 67 F.3d 605 (7th Cir. 1995), *available at* http://scholar.google.com/scholar_case?case=7966566102163418003.

Reading this decision might make you think that this book should be more aptly titled "Be Sure to Use Google Before Filing Those Papers—Because the Judge Might Be." Almost ten years later, the Third Circuit agreed with *Whirlpool* in *In re: Adams Golf, Inc. Securities Litigation*, 381 F.3d 267 (3rd Cir. 2004), *available at* http://vls.law.villanova.edu/locator/3d/August2004/033945p.pdf. Not only do parties have a duty to search the Internet for legislation, regulations, and trends, but there is a duty to "Google" a missing party.

In an Indiana decision, the court was incredulous that the plaintiff failed to "Google" the missing defendant (Joe Groce) as part of his due diligence process. The court stated:

> We do note that there is no evidence in this case of a public records or Internet search for Groce . . . to find him. In fact, we [the judge] discovered, upon entering 'Joe Groce Indiana' into the Google™ search engine, an address for Groce that differed from either address used in this case, as well as an apparent obituary for Groce's mother that listed numerous surviving relatives who might have known his whereabouts.

The court upheld the defendant's claim of insufficient service of process and affirmed the dismissal of the case. *Munster v. Groce*, 829 N.E.2d 52 (Ind. App. 2005), *available at* http://caselaw.lp.findlaw.com/data2/indianastatecases/app/06080501mpb.pdf.

In a similar case, the court noted that the investigative technique of merely calling directory assistance to find a missing defendant has gone "the way of the horse and buggy and the eight track stereo" now that we have access to the Internet. *Dubois v. Butler*, 901 So. 2d 1029 (Fla. App. 2005), *available at* http://www.4dca.org/May2005/05-25-05/4D04-3559.pdf.

In a Louisiana case similar to *Munster*, a trial court judge nullified a tax sale after the judge conducted an Internet search and determined that the tax-delinquent owner (Dr. Weatherly) was "reasonably identifiable" and would have been locatable if the government had run a simple "Internet search" to locate the named mortgagee. The government claimed to have conducted a public-records search and a LexisNexis search. The appellate judge upheld the trial court's nullification of the government tax sale.

Part of the basis of the appeal was whether it was appropriate for the trial court judge to have conducted an Internet search. The Appeals court stated, "Nevertheless, we find any error the trial court may have committed by conducting the internet search is harmless, because the trial court's ultimate conclusion that the tax sale violated Dr. Weatherly's due process rights is legally correct." *Weatherly v. Optimum Asset Management*, 928 So. 2d 118 (La. App. 2005), *available at* http://www.la-fcca.org/Opinions/PUB2005/2005-12/2004CA2734Dec2005.Pub.10.pdf.

The court has gone on to admonish no less an institution than the FBI for not "Googling" to locate information on people. In *Davis v. DOJ*, 460 F.3d 92 (D.C. Cir. 2006), *available at* http://cases.justia.com/us-court-of-appeals/F3/460/92/580672/, the court found for the appellant Davis who had not received audiotapes he had requested under the Freedom of Information Act (FOIA) from the FBI. The FBI claimed they could not turn over the tapes because they could not determine whether the individuals on the tapes were living or dead. The court concluded "that the FBI has not 'made a reasonable effort to ascertain' whether the two speakers, on whose behalf it has invoked a privacy exemption from FOIA, are living or dead . . ." in part because "[the FBI] does not appear to have contemplated other ways of determining whether the speakers are dead, such as Googling them."

Lawyers have an obligation to clients (and to themselves, in order to remain competitive) to have access to the most comprehensive, cost-effective research resources. The Internet provides an unparalleled opportunity to find the facts relevant to legal issues, and Google can help you locate this information from obvious and obscure sources. Of course, not everything found on the Internet should be treated as fact.

1.2   Beware of the Reliability of Information on the Internet

With the openness of the Internet, however, comes the caveat that not all of the information you might find there is current or even credible (see the "Internet Source Credibility Checklist" later in this chapter and the associated Appendix B). Documentation is still somewhat lacking at many of the free sites on the Web. This is where pay databases can have an advantage over free Internet sites—you can rely on most pay sites' data to be credible and current without doing the extra checking you might need to do when using a free source. If you need documentation regarding the credibility or currency of the data found in pay databases, there's usually 24–7 customer service to provide the answers. The Web offers no such customer service.

A good researcher needs to be a sleuth, someone who specializes in finding facts, understanding why some facts can't be found, and figuring out which (if any) of the found facts are credible. Surrounded by today's ocean of information on the Internet, a lawyer now needs to be a "cyber-sleuth." Lawyers need to be able to look through endless reams of data to find the relevant pages. We are faced with so many data sources that simply keeping track of them, let alone vouching for their credibility, can be overwhelming. Google does a very good job of locating information on the Internet, but just because Google brings you back Web site results doesn't mean the information at the sites comes from credible sources or is necessarily quality information. Anyone can put up a Web site or Web log (blog), post to a newsgroup or an advice site, create a profile (even a false one) at a social networking site, or join an Internet mailing list, and say anything they want. Google has no stake in, or control over, the vast majority of Web sites displayed in its search results lists. And Google compiles its results list without any human intervention.

One tenet of sound research methodology is that a healthy ounce of skepticism is worth a pound of information. There is an adage in accounting that states, "Figures don't lie, but liars figure." The computer expert version is "Garbage in, garbage out." For most researchers, the adage can be stated even more simply: "Just because it's published doesn't mean it's true." Regular users of the Internet recognize that sentiment. The Internet puts a means of instantaneous worldwide publication at everyone's fingertips . . . from established commercial publishers to schoolchildren.

Case in point: In a two-week period, "Lawguy1975" dispensed 939 legal answers to 943 questions posed on AskMe.com (which was an advice site at the time). By mid-July, Lawguy1975 *aka* Billy Sheridan *aka* Justin Anthony Wyrick Jr. was the number-three-rated expert in criminal law on AskMe.com. Beneath him in the rankings were 125 licensed lawyers and assorted ex-cops and ex-cons. When asked why he hadn't answered four questions out of the 943 posed, he said, "I'm sorry, I don't know traffic law." Lawguy1975 finally came clean and admitted on AskMe.com that he wasn't a lawyer, but rather Marcus Arnold, a fifteen-year-old kid in Perris, California with an obvious penchant for Court TV. He didn't know about traffic law because, at age 15, he hadn't learned how to drive . . . yet. (Arnold's exploits were included in the book *Next: The Future Just Happened* by Michael Lewis, from which much of this account is paraphrased. In a BBC Television series based on the book, Lewis also related that Marcus's "ultimate ambition [was] to be a Supreme Court judge" *(available at* http://news.bbc.co.uk/hi/english/static/in_depth/programmes/2001/future/tv_series_1.stm). Arnold never had the chance to become a licensed lawyer. In the summer of 2004, he "went into a hospital with flu symptoms and never came out," according to a column in the *Los Angeles Times* that noted his passing *(available at* http://articles. latimes.com/2004/dec/19/opinion/op-lewis19). We know this because we located all of this information via Google searches, cross-checked it over multiple sources, and vetted the sources for reliability.)

So, your first job as an Internet-researching-lawyer is to evaluate a site's credibility before relying upon the information. How do you do this? There are a number of Web sites that offer advice on determining the credibility of sites returned in Google searches or that you find on your own. Consumer Union's Consumer WebWatch site offers a set of recommended guidelines for Web sites to follow (http://www.consumerwebwatch.org/consumer-reports-webwatch-guidelines.cfm and http://www.consumerwebwatch.org/web-credibility.cfm). The site also offers a report on its 2002 research survey, "A Matter of Trust: What Users Want From Web Sites" (http://www.consumerwebwatch.org/dynamic/web-credibility-reports-a-matter-of-trust-abstract.cfm). Another source of guidelines for testing Web site credibility is the University of North Carolina Health Science Library's Evaluating Online Information site (http://www.hsl.unc.edu/Services/Tutorials/eval/Index.htm).

We have also compiled a brief Credibility Checklist (below). A more detailed version, with specific resources for verifying information, can be found in Appendix B.

1.2.1 Internet Source Credibility Checklist

One way to verify a Web site's credibility is to develop a stringent review process. The following is an abbreviated version of an Internet Source Credibility Checklist we use when conducting research projects. A more detailed version that you can use to determine the credibility of sources you find in your own research is included in Appendix B.

1. Can you determine the site's owner, editor, or authors when you visit the site?
2. Determine the identity of the site's owner or sponsoring organization if it's not clear from the site itself.
3. Verify credentials by doing an independent search, not just by relying upon what is stated on the site.
4. Discover who else relies on a particular site by conducting a link search.
5. How fresh is the content?
6. What is the quality of the content?

7. Is the site missing any content? Is it as complete as its print version (if there is one)?
8. Verify all information by trying to find the same data at another site.
9. Ascertain the top-level domain (TLD) to help decide credibility.
10. Document your search.

With so many questions about the credibility of information found on the Internet, one might wonder whether judges will admit any of the information we find into evidence.

1.3 Case Law: Will Judges Admit Evidence from the Internet?

Just a little more than a decade ago, a district court cautioned against relying on data from the Internet as "voodoo information." *St. Clair v. Johnny's Oyster & Shrimp*, 76 F. Supp. 2d 773, 775 (S.D. Tex. 1999), *available at* PACER (subscription required). That court stated:

> While some look to the Internet as an innovative vehicle for communication, the Court continues to warily and wearily view it largely as one large catalyst for rumor, innuendo, and misinformation. . . . Anyone can put anything on the Internet. No Web site is monitored for accuracy and nothing contained therein is under oath or even subject to independent verification absent underlying documentation. Moreover, the Court holds no illusions that hackers can adulterate the content on any Web site from any location at any time. For these reasons, any evidence procured off the Internet is adequate for almost nothing . . .

Today, fortunately, as illustrated by *Munster* and *Weatherly,* judges are not only admitting information from the Internet into evidence, but they're the ones conducting the Internet research to help make judicial decisions. Getting Internet evidence admitted into evidence is no different than getting other traditional evidence admitted. Like traditional evidence, it too must be (1) relevant; (2) authentic; and (3) admissible.

As a lawyer attempting to authenticate information from the Internet for admission as evidence, it is important to prove when the research was done and what steps were taken to prove its veracity. This can be accomplished by having the researcher sign a declaration explaining how, and on what date, the researcher found the Web page evidence on the Internet. To further authenticate the evidence from a Web site, the Web page should be printed out—with the URL listed. It would also be advisable to print any page on the Web site that indicates who owns the site. This is usually found on the "About Us" page. (Searching a domain registry, such as Betterwhois.com, to verify ownership is not necessarily going to yield the true owner of the Web site because domain registries do not verify that real names are used.)

In addition to creating this paper record of the information as it appeared on the day your research was conducted, it can also be useful to create a PDF copy of the page(s) you're relying on. The ABA has published an excellent book, *The Lawyer's Guide to Adobe Acrobat* (www.abanet.org/ abastore/productpage/5110588), that details practical law-office uses of PDF documents, including techniques for creating and managing them.

Whether judges hearing matters you're handling will admit information you have found via Internet research into evidence remains to be seen. Generally, it will depend on the individual judge, their level of comfort with the Internet, and, in the end, the veracity of the information presented. Certainly, though, it is better to have a judge exclude information you might find than to have the court admonish you for not presenting information it has found.

1.4   War Stories: How Lawyers Have Used Information They Found on the Internet to the Benefit of Their Cases and Transactions

Impeaching the Opposition's Credibility

Indianapolis solo lawyer Marc Matheny (http://www.marcmathenylaw.com) used Google to quickly locate information online that directly contradicted statements of an alleged victim in a child molestation case. The information Matheny found saved his client from a reputation-destroying trial for a crime he did not commit.

> My client, a man in his mid-thirties, was accused of sexually molesting a sixteen-year-old girl. He adamantly maintained that he was innocent of the charges. In deposition, the sixteen-year-old repeated her claims against my client and portrayed herself as an "innocent," stating that she "was not sexually active" when asked directly.
>
> Among the results of a Google search for the sixteen-year-old's name was a link to her MySpace profile. The profile itself did not contain much in the way of contradictory information about her, but it did include a list of all of the other MySpace users she had designated as her friends— many of whom knew her "in real life." My investigator tracked down and interviewed these friends. The interviews revealed a very different image of the sixteen-year-old than the one she had portrayed. Her friends told the investigator about her various sexual relationships and a pregnancy she had medically terminated the previous year.

This new information seriously damaged the sixteen-year-old's credibility. By combining information we found on the Internet with old-fashioned investigative and interview techniques, I was able to get the charges against my client dropped.

A Google Search Leads to a Settlement

Charlie Cochran, a lawyer in Northern California, relates this story of how thinking outside the box allowed him to settle a case the day before the trial, for a fraction of the original settlement demand:

> [A]fter attending your seminar I tried to implement some of your research tools to a trial I had scheduled in March 2003. The Plaintiff was a well-known musician and producer who claimed he had [a] brain injury from an auto accident and could no longer play the piano. My search began with a Google I'm Feeling Lucky ["search"], which sent me to the Plaintiff's home page.
>
> On the home page he was selling an album that he had recorded after our auto accident. The Google search naturally hit many online sites where his albums were being sold. One of the Google hits had him giving an online interview with an entertainment reporter where he discussed his auto accident, that he could not play piano for a few months but after that he was back to playing and writing with a new spirit and inspiration. Google image hits are amazing. It's fascinating what people post on the Internet. One image of the Plaintiff was a concert he did about a year after the accident where he was shown playing piano in front of a class of graduate-level pianists. The look on their faces showed that they were really impressed with his abilities. We ended up issuing a trial subpoena to the woman that held the concert and the reporter who had interviewed the Plaintiff for the online interview. The case settled the day before the trial for a fraction of the original settlement demand because, in my opinion, we were going to confront the Plaintiff with the photo of him playing the piano, the words from his online interview, and albums that he was selling over the Internet.

The **I'm Feeling Lucky** search button returns one Web site only (see Section 3.11) and, as illustrated here, often it's the most relevant. Using Google's **I'm Feeling Lucky** search button quickly led lawyer Cochran directly to the plaintiff's own Web site. When it was clear that he wanted to see more results, Cochran returned to his original search page and merely clicked on the **Google Search** button for a complete list of search results. That expanded search led him to an online interview of the musician and to sites selling his recent albums, information that he probably would not have found without the Internet. Finally, using the Google Images feature (see Chapter 8), Cochran proved that a picture is indeed worth a thousand words.

Introduction to Google

2

2.1 What Is Google?

The name is a common misspelling of the mathematical term for a 1 followed by 100 zeroes—"googol."

Google started out life as a search engine. Its stated primary purpose has always been to help Internet users locate specific information stored on the untold billions of discrete pages on the Internet. Section 2.3 will discuss how Google does this in greater detail.

In the years since it was founded, Google has expanded the products and services it offers to include e-mail, office productivity/collaboration tools, desktop search capability, mapping, social networking, photo sharing, and video sharing, among others. These will also be discussed in subsequent chapters of this book.

In the "Corporate Information" section of the Google Web site (http://www.google.com/intl/en/corporate/index.html), the company indicates that its mission is "to organize the world's information and make it universally accessible and useful." Elsewhere (http://www.google.com/enterprise/end_user_experience.html), Google quotes cofounder Larry Page as saying that "the perfect search engine would understand exactly what you mean and give back exactly what you want." Based on our years of using, testing, and pushing Google to retrieve results from the Internet, we would have to say that Google comes as close to these goals as currently possible and that these goals apparently remain the guiding force that drives the online search innovations at the company.

▼▼▼▼▼

Google's company philosophy is clearly laid out online. It discusses the company's commitment to "research, development, and innovation" and includes a list of "Ten things we know to be true" in their quest for that goal (http://www.google.com/corporate/tenthings.html).

A shortened version of the company's philosophy is reproduced below.

Ten things Google has found to be true

1. Focus on the user and all else will follow.
2. It's best to do one thing really, really well.
3. Fast is better than slow.
4. Democracy on the web works.
5. You don't need to be at your desk to need an answer.
6. You can make money without doing evil.
7. There's always more information out there.
8. The need for information crosses all borders.
9. You can be serious without a suit.
10. Great just isn't good enough.

2.2 Where Did Google Come From?

Google was not the first search engine. But through its superior ability to categorize and rank its results based on relevance to the searched keywords, Google quickly surpassed now long-forgotten rivals like Snap, All the Web, InfoSeek, and others.

Google is now widely recognized as the world's most-used search engine. Recent statistics show that nearly two-thirds of Internet search queries in the English language are handled by Google.

Google began as a research project by two Ph.D. students at Stanford University—Sergey Brin and Larry Page. Their basic hypothesis was that the content of individual Web pages would be more valuable to you as a researcher if you knew what other pages relied on, or referenced, its content. Page and Brin surmised they could quantify that value by counting and analyzing the links into a particular Web page ("inbound links")—the notion being that the page with the most inbound links from other high-ranking Web sites would be the most valuable.

Essentially, this concept is similar to citations in case law. The more often a particular case is cited and the more influential those later citing cases are, the more influential that first (cited) case becomes.

At the time Page and Brin began their project, most search engines ranked their results primarily by the number of times a particular keyword appeared on the page. The more times a particular keyword was used, the higher a page would rank for that keyword, regardless of context, reliability of the source, etc.

To initially test their hypothesis, Larry Page built a Web crawler to locate Web pages that linked to other Web pages. The project, known as "BackRub," would follow these inbound links, branching backwards, to analyze which Web pages linked to which other Web pages. They then created a mathematical formula to calculate the relative value of all of those pages the crawler had found. This PageRank value is based on a number of factors, including how many (and which type of) sites linked to that particular Web page and in turn the number of (and which) sites linked to those sites, and so on.

In January 1998 Page applied for a patent based on his "method for node ranking in a linked database," based on his BackRub project. In September 2001, patent number 6285999 (http://tinyurl.com/PageRank-Patent) was granted to this PageRank method. While Larry Page is listed as the inventor, the patent is assigned to Stanford University. Google is reportedly the exclusive licensee of the technology covered by this patent. (Note: The "Page" in PageRank refers to Larry Page and not a Web page.)

In a current explanation of the PageRank technology posted on the Google Web site (http://www.google.com/corporate/tech.html), the company describes the technology this way:

> PageRank reflects our view of the importance of web pages by considering more than 500 million variables and 2 billion terms. Pages that we believe are important pages receive a higher PageRank and are more likely to appear at the top of the search results. PageRank also considers the importance of each page that casts a vote, as votes from some pages are considered to have greater value, thus giving the linked page greater value. We have always taken a pragmatic approach to help improve search quality and create useful products, and our technology uses the collective intelligence of the web to determine a page's importance.

2.3   How Google Works

Similar to the original BackRub project, Google still utilizes a Web crawler (Googlebot) to locate pages on the Web. Google stores a copy of these pages on its own indexing servers where it analyzes the content of those pages, those pages' inbound links, and employs a series of sophisticated mathematical formulas to determine the most relevant and reliable sources for a particular search. While there are numerous criteria that go into determining the final results, we'll focus on two distinct measures that are discussed most.

2.3.1   PageRank

The first measurement is the PageRank described in Section 2.2. It is a stand-alone measure of a page's trustworthiness or reliability (for lack of a better term). Each Web page in Google's index is assigned a PageRank of 0 to 10 based upon numerous criteria, including how many other sites rely on its content (or link to it), what those sites are (e.g., government-run, educational institution, and the linking site's own PageRank), how long the particular page has existed, etc. Different pages of the same Web site may have different PageRanks.

In an April 1, 2002 posting, Google poked fun at its own patented technology. The April Fool's Day posting (http://www.google.com/technology/pigeonrank.html) "explained" how its patented PigeonRank technology used a series of low-cost PCs (pigeon clusters) to return relevant results. Because of the pigeon's "unique capacity to recognize objects regardless of spatial orientation . . . [and] easily distinguish among items displaying only the minutest differences," the birds "could be used to compute the relative value of web pages faster than human editors or machine-based algorithms."

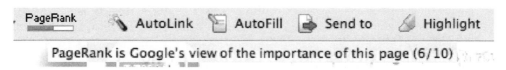

FIGURE 2.1

As important as PageRank is, PageRank is just one of the criteria used to determine the order of the search results list.

2.3.2 Relevance

The second most-discussed measure is how relevant a particular Web page is to the keywords searched for. The more relevant to the keywords Google determines a Web page to be, the higher Google places that page on the search results list. This relevance is also dependent on a large set of variables, the least of which isn't where and how often particular keywords appear on that page. So Google could rank a Web page with highly relevant content (e.g., an article on a specific topic) but a low PageRank in a higher position than a Web page with a higher PageRank but less relevant content (e.g., an article that only mentions your keywords in passing).

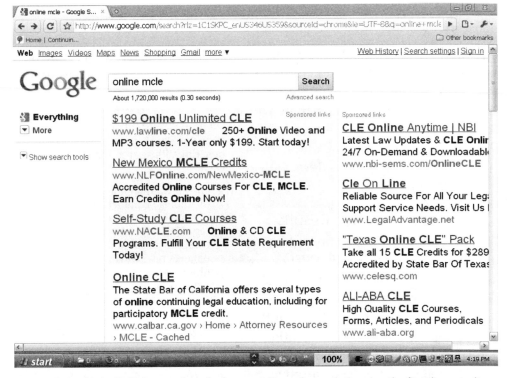

FIGURE 2.2 This is the first page of results for our *online mcle* search. Ignoring the first three results down the center and results down the left-hand side (because Web site owners pay to have that placement) we learn that the 3rd, 4th, and 5th most relevant of the organic (non-paid placement) results have a lower PageRank than the 6th most relevant organic result, confirming that PageRank and order of results are not directly correlated.

For example, when we clicked on each of the first ten results of a Google search for *online mcle* (pictured in Figure 2.2) their PageRanks were in the following order:

1st most relevant organic result	PageRank 6
2nd most relevant organic result	PageRank 5
3rd most relevant organic result	PageRank 3
4th most relevant organic result	PageRank 2
5th most relevant organic result	PageRank 4
6th most relevant organic result	PageRank 5
7th most relevant organic result	PageRank 2
8th most relevant organic result	PageRank 5
9th most relevant organic result	PageRank 4
10th most relevant organic result	PageRank 4

In this example, Web pages with a relatively high PageRank are returned as the first and second results. However, as we move down the list, notice that Web pages with PageRanks of 3 and 2 are returned higher than Web pages with PageRanks of 4 and 5. Even a Web page with a PageRank of 4 appears ahead of two others with a PageRank of 5.

2.3.3   Organic Search Results

This list of results is referred to as the "organic search results." They are determined completely automatically. There is no way to buy one's way in or otherwise guarantee a position on this list. There is no human intervention in determining inclusion or ranking.

Placement in the "sponsored links" that appear to the right and/or above the organic search results, however, can be purchased via Google's pay-per-click advertising program—AdWords. This program gives anyone with a Web site the ability to create text ads and

On its Web site (http://www.google.com/corporate/tech.html), Google describes its search technology this way:

The software behind our search technology conducts a series of simultaneous calculations requiring only a fraction of a second. Traditional search engines rely heavily on how often a word appears on a web page. We use more than 200 signals, including our patented PageRank(tm) algorithm, to examine the entire link structure of the web and determine which pages are most important. We then conduct hypertext-matching analysis to determine which pages are relevant to the specific search being conducted. By combining overall importance and query-specific relevance, we're able to put the most relevant and reliable results first.

have them displayed next to Google's search results (among other places). Users can select keywords important to their business and designate how much they are willing to pay each time someone clicks on their ad to link to their Web site. The more you bid (generally), the higher up your ad will appear. The minimum click/keyword bid is only $0.10. There is an innate capitalism built into the system, in that any other user who selects the same keywords for their ads can move up the sponsored links list by bidding more per click. The AdWords program allows advertisers to control their spending by setting a daily budget.

The AdWords program will be discussed in greater detail in Chapter 25.

2.3.4 Searching Google's Index, Not the "Live" Internet

Another important principal to note is that when you perform a search at Google, you are searching through the content the Googlebot has extracted from Web pages and has stored on Google's indexing servers—and not the "live" Internet. Creating a searchable index of Web pages is how Google can return its results more quickly than searching Web pages on their "home" servers.

In live seminars, we're often asked, "Why is my keyword displayed in the results list but isn't on the Web page when I click on the link?" The answer is usually due to Google searching Web-page content on its index servers rather than the "live" Internet.

Even though the Googlebot is working twenty-four hours a day, seven days a week to locate new and updated pages to add to its index, it does not visit every known page every day. It visits different pages/sites at varying intervals depending on the type of content and average update cycle for that site. For example, some news sites or blogs might be visited multiple times per day (in some cases in near-real time), while a law firm's site might only be visited once per day or per week, depending on the site's content and how often new material is posted there. This lag can create a situation in which a page (or content) that was located by the Googlebot on Monday is no longer the same as when you run a search and receive a link to that particular Web page on Friday because the Web site owner made a change to the page on Thursday. In Section 5.2, we'll discuss one way to locate the content of the page as it appeared when the Googlebot visited, even if a change has been made in the interim.

2.4   Personalizing Your Google Search Experience

Google allows you to "personalize" your search experience in two ways.

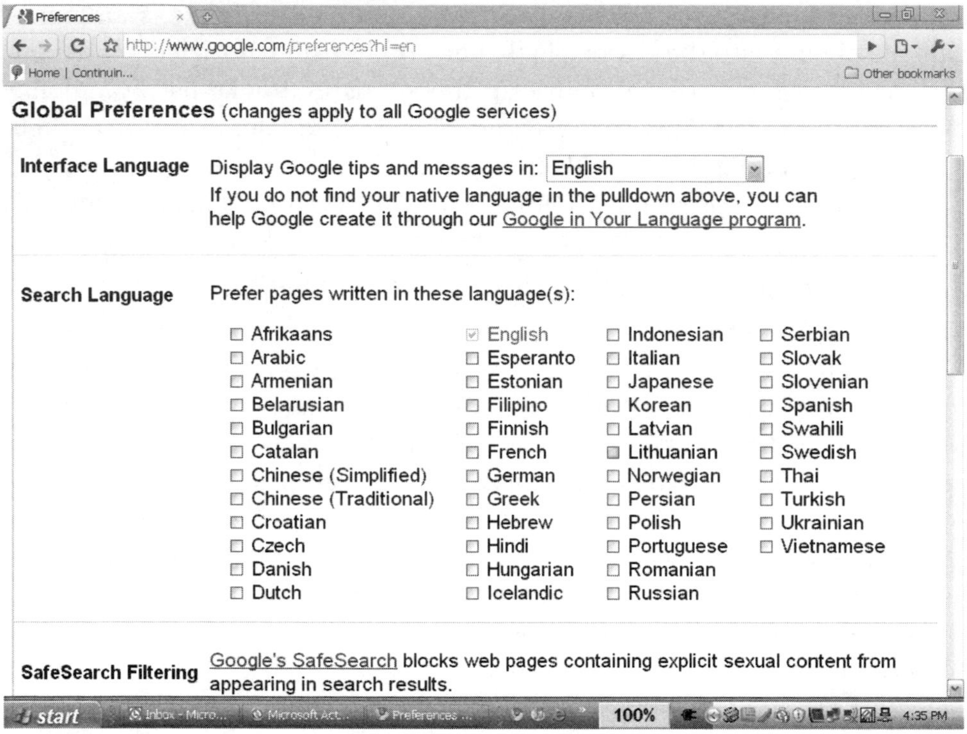

FIGURE 2.3   The first way to personalize your Google search experience is through the **SafeSearch** option on the **Settings** drop-down menu in the upper right-hand corner of the home page. On the Preferences page (http://www.google.com/preferences?hl=en), Google allows you to select the language of your search results, the language in which to receive Google tips and messages, the number of results you prefer displayed per page (10–100), and **SafeSearch Filtering** to minimize explicit content (e.g., adult-themed) in your results, among other features.

Similar preferences are also available for other Google search products, such as Google News (see Chapter 6), Google Scholar (see Chapter 17), and Google Apps (see Chapter 18).

2.4.1   Accessing Additional Features and Products via a Free Google Account

The second way to personalize your Google search experience (and gain access to many of the Google products and features we will discuss in upcoming chapters) is to create a free Google Account (https://www.google.com/accounts/NewAccount).

The form to create the Google Account is only one page long and pretty straightforward.

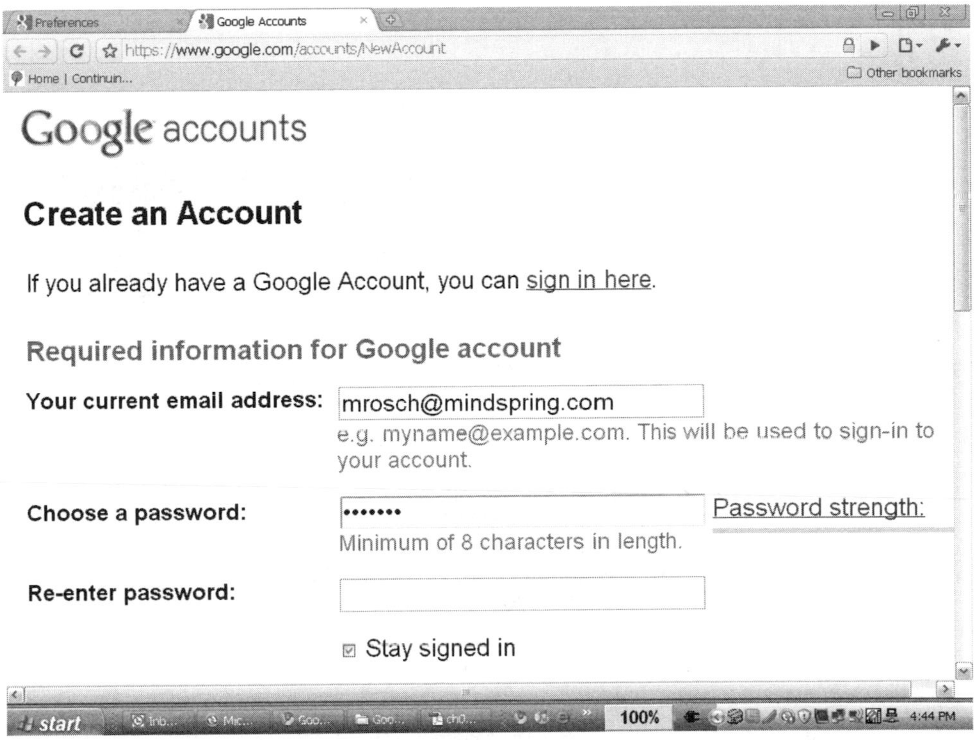

FIGURE 2.4   It is not necessary to tie your Google Account to a Gmail.com e-mail address—although this is the most common method for creating an account. You can use any existing e-mail address to create your account (e.g., *mrosch@mindspring.com* in this illustration) to create your Google Account.

One feature your Google Account gives you access to is a customizable iGoogle (Figure 2.5) start page (http://www.google.com/ig?hl=en). There you can add a variety of elements—some that are search-related (e.g., a list of your most recent Google searches, each a clickable link to quickly rerun the same search) and some that are not (e.g., local news, weather, RSS feeds from Web sites/blogs of professional or personal interest, etc.). iGoogle will be discussed in greater detail in Section 20.3.

A free Google Account is also required to access many of the collaboration tools discussed in Chapter 18.

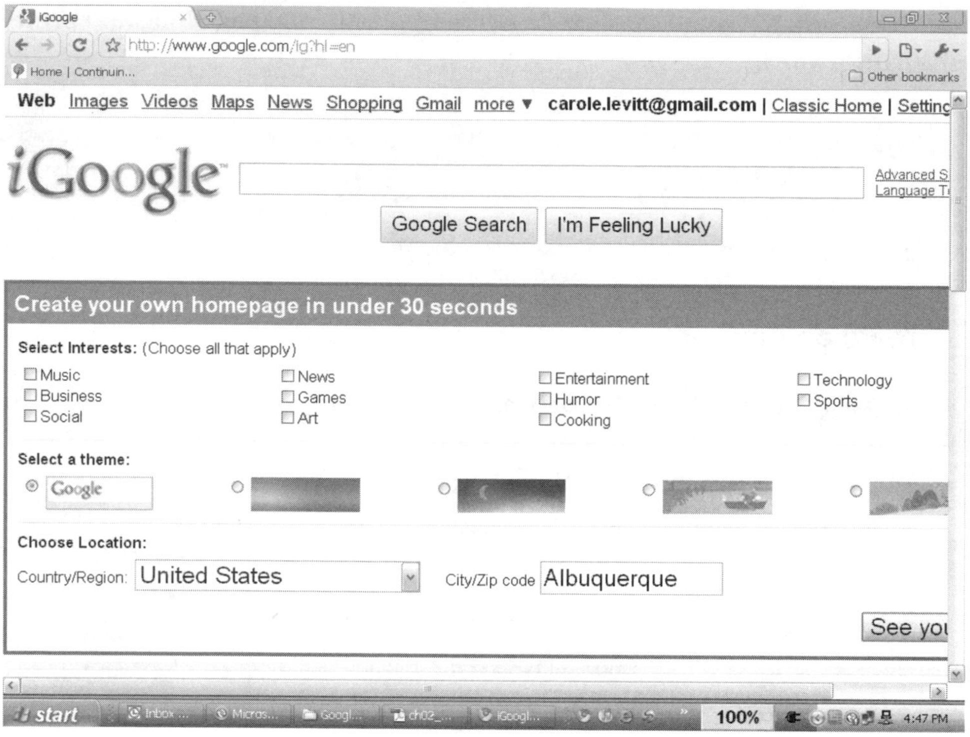

FIGURE 2.5

2.4.2   Create a Google Profile to Claim Your Identity Online

Google Profile, which is part of Google Accounts (see Section 2.4.1), allows you to place your biography and photo on Google and also allows you to link to your blog, your Web site, your Facebook or LinkedIn profiles, and

▼▼▼▼▼

PRIVACY ALERT

You are required to have a profile if you want to add content to some Google products. For instance, if you wanted to add a book review to Google Books (see Section 13.8), or write a Knol entry (see Chapter 27), or add content to Google Maps (see Figure 14-6) or Google Reader (see Chapter 9), you would need to first have a Google Profile. However, be aware that your profile will then be publicly displayed when search results include any of the content you have added.

online photos. If you enter your current location and places where you once lived, they will be displayed on your profile map.

When Google first launched Profiles in April 2009, once you placed your profile online and set your profile to show your full name publicly, anyone who searched your name (using Google's search engine) would find your Google profile (and photo) at the bottom of the first page of the results list.

Although both the authors of this book have a public Google profile and once saw them displayed at the bottom of the first page of the Google results list, their profiles were not displayed when they searched their names in January 2010. Upon further reading, they noted that Google states "a link to your Google profile *may* appear" (emphasis added). For those who absolutely want their profiles to appear in search results, Google suggests that you "verify" your name by using the verification procedure at Knol (see Section 27.2). (Note that the Google profiles for both authors returned subsequently and were visible in Google searches for their names as late as May 2010.)

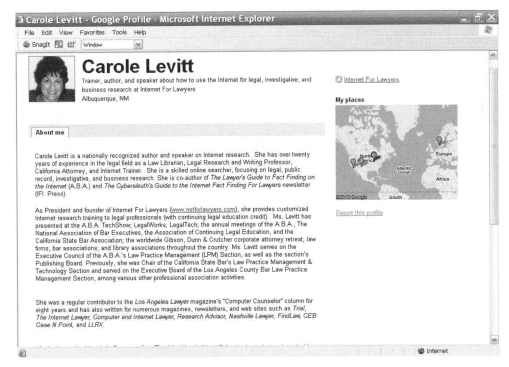

FIGURE 2.6   This is Carole Levitt's Google Profile. You should be able to reach this profile by searching *"carole levitt"* at Google.com, but as noted above, the profile is not always displayed at the bottom of the first page of the search results list. However, the profile will be displayed if you use this direct URL: http://www.google.com/profiles/carole.levitt).

2.4.2.1   Creating a Profile

To create your Google Profile, visit http://www.google.com/profiles and click the large blue tab to the right, which is labeled **Create my profile**.

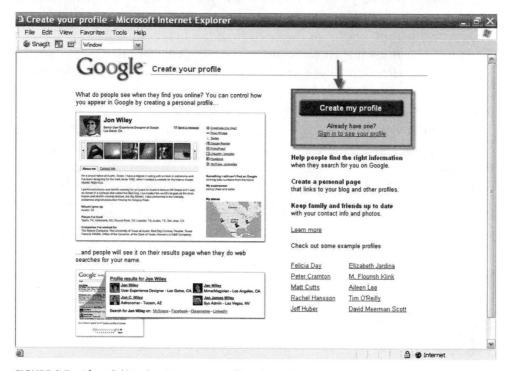

FIGURE 2.7   After clicking the **Create my profile** tab, a **Sign in with your Google Account** prompt will appear for you to enter your username and password. If you don't have a Google Account, click the **Create an account now** link (located below **Sign in with your Google Account**).

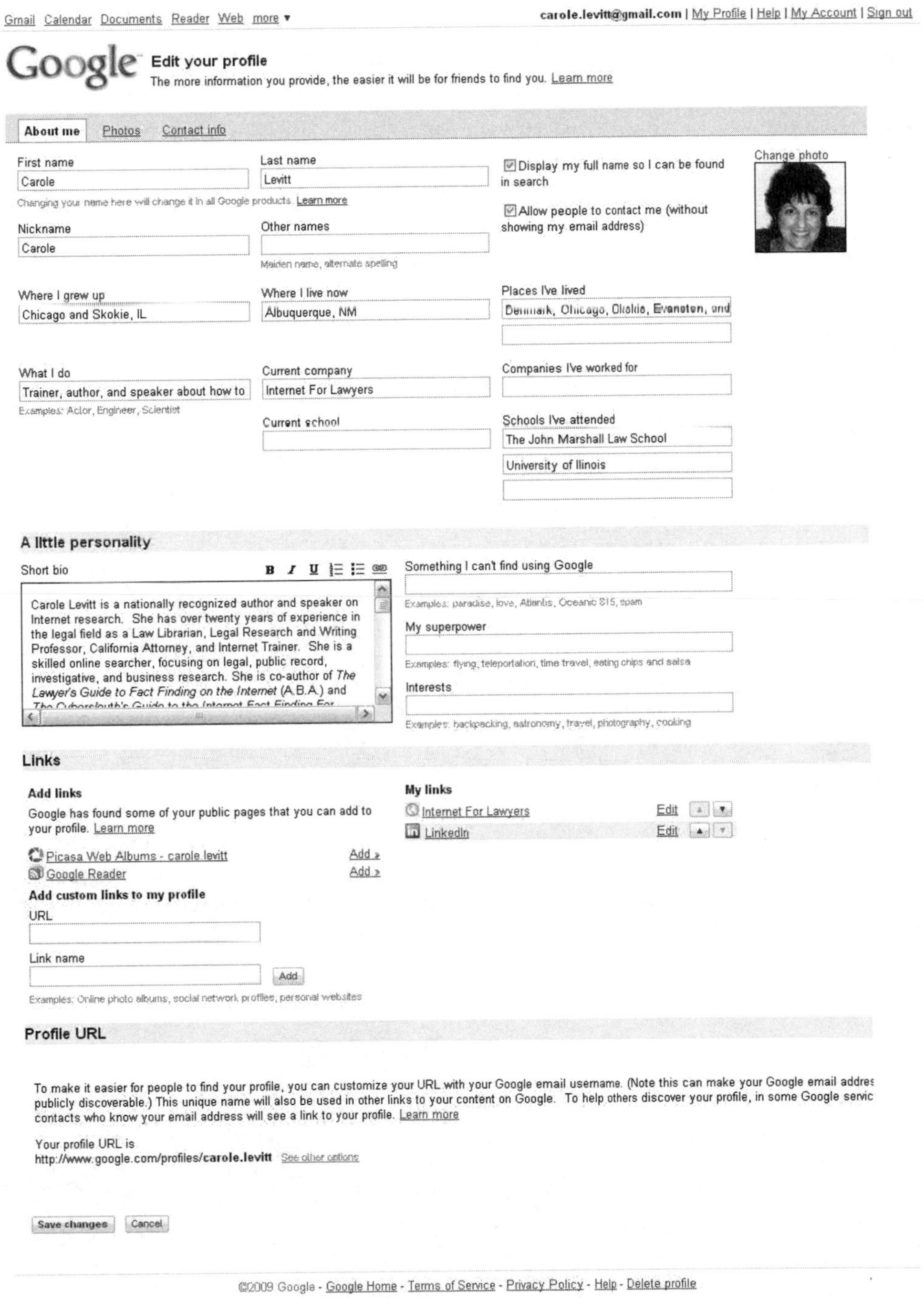

FIGURE 2.8   To create your profile, begin filling information into the blanks. Be sure to click **Save changes** when you are finished.

2.4.2.2   How to Access Your Existing Google Profile and Edit It

The easiest way to access your own profile is by visiting http://www.google.com/profiles/me. You will be prompted to sign into your account and then your profile will be displayed to you for editing.

FIGURE 2.9   This is how Carole Levitt's profile is displayed to her for editing. To edit the **About me** page of her profile (displayed here), she would click **Edit profile.** To edit the **Contact info** page of her profile, she would click the **Contact info** tab and then **Edit profile.**

▼▼▼▼▼

PRIVACY ALERT

Google generates a random Profile URL for you, but you can customize it with your Gmail username if you have Gmail. For instance, Carole Levitt's Gmail username is carole.levitt and her customized Google Profile URL is http://www.google.com/profiles/carole.levitt. While this makes it easier for people to find your profile, the partial e-mail address associated with your Google Profile URL becomes publicly discoverable. (Note: Even if you don't use Gmail, you can still sign up for a Google Account and create a profile. You would need to choose an available username for your Profile URL.)

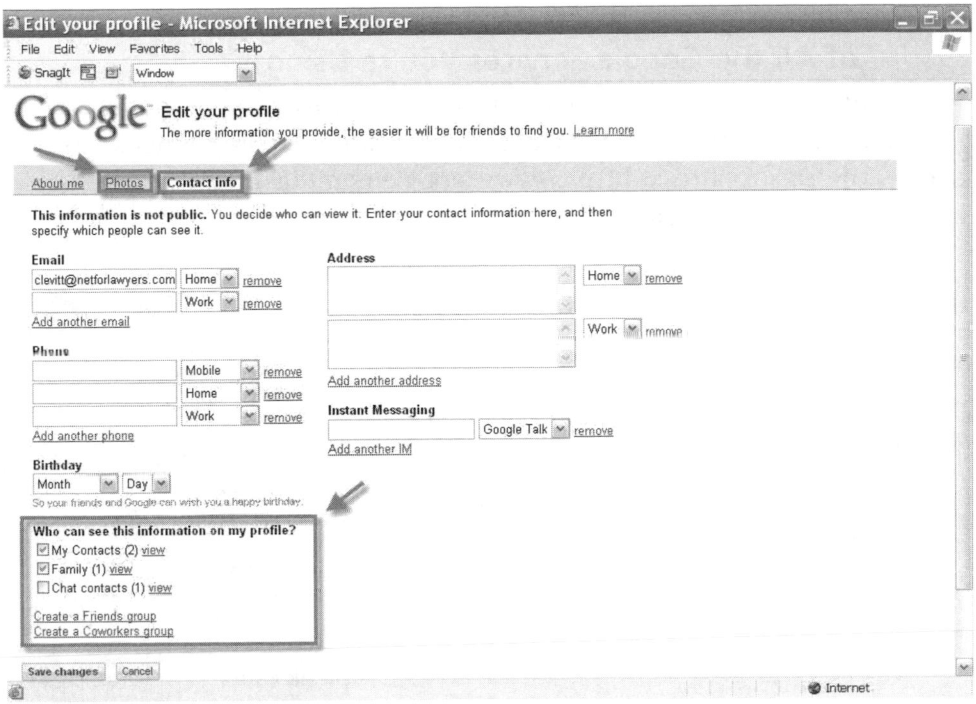

FIGURE 2.10   Clicking **Contact info** and then **Edit profile** displays a page on which you can add personal contact information to your profile. You decide how much information to add and who can see this information. Notice a new tab appears on this page, labeled **Photos**. Clicking on that tab allows you to link to photos at Flickr or Picasa (or another photo service).

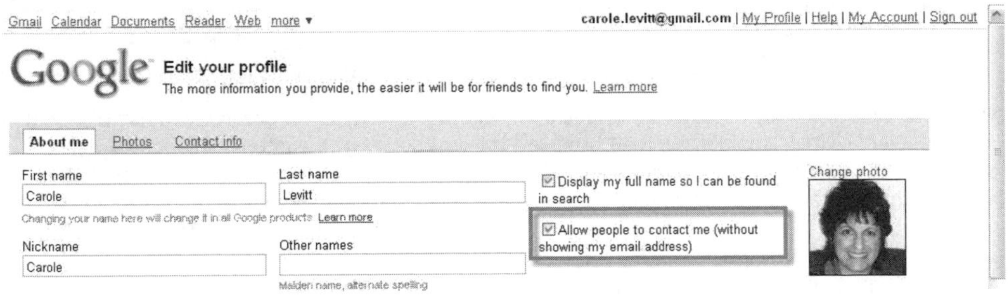

FIGURE 2.11   If you enable the **Allow people to contact me (without showing my email address)** feature, anyone with a Google Account can e-mail you via your profile page (without revealing your e-mail address to them). To enable this feature, you need to first click **Edit profile** and then **About Me**.

2.4.3 Google Dashboard Helps You Keep Track of All the Google Services You're Using

In the fall of 2009, Google created a Dashboard to compile details of the information you have stored in each of the various Google services. You can access the Dashboard at https://www.google.com/dashboard/ once you're logged into your account.

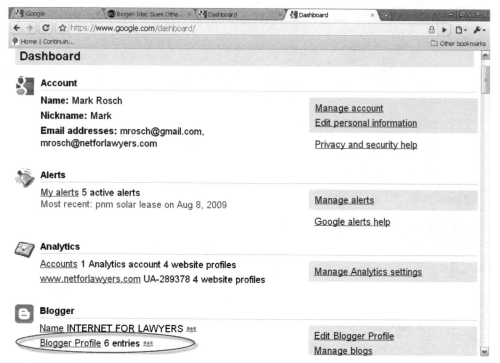

FIGURE 2.12 The Google Account Dashboard lists direct links to nearly a dozen and a half of Google's most popular services. Additionally, the Dashboard includes details of the information you've created or stored with each service along with an icon (that's supposed to look like three people next to one another) that indicates information that is public—such as the **Blogger Profile** in this illustration.

Note that not all available services are integrated into the Dashboard. Some, like FeedBurner and AdWords, only include a link you can use to manage the individual services.

You can also see all of the Google Services associated with your account by visiting the My Account page (https://www.google.com/accounts/ManageAccount?hl=en) once you're logged into your account.

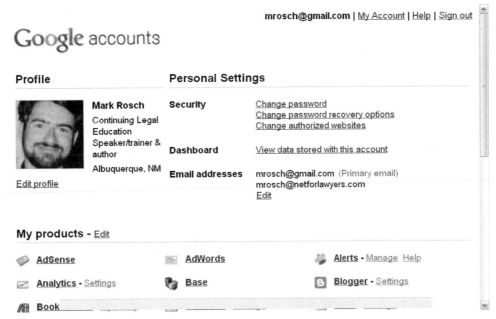

FIGURE 2.13   The My Account page lists the various services associated with your Google Account. (It does not include the same level of detail as the Dashboard.) Clicking any of the links takes you directly to that service, where you can manage your personal settings, etc.

2.5   Limitations of Google

Google is one of our favorite search engines. We have featured it in our live Minimum Continuing Legal Education presentations since shortly after its 1998 debut. Clearly, we think highly of its functions and search results or we wouldn't devote an entire book to it. That said, no search engine is perfect, and Google is no exception.

First, no search engine can currently index every page on the Internet. While this was possible when Google was first conceived (at that time it was estimated that the Web contained approximately 24 million pages), because of the Web's ever-expanding nature it is no longer possible to effectively index every page on the publicly available Internet.

Proximity Searching—Google does not offer the precise proximity searching that paid search products offer. There is no way to hone your search by requiring that a particular keyword be within 2 words of another keyword, for example. While Google does offer the asterisk as a *de facto* proximity indicator, it is imprecise—it is essentially a NEAR connector, standing in for one or more words. We'll discuss proximity searching in greater detail in Section 3.4.

Keyword Limit—For some, Google's limit of 32 keywords is a drawback. In reality, unless you are looking for a specific quotation (and there are times when you might be), 32 keywords should be more than sufficient. We'll discuss a work-around in Section 3.4 for some of those times when you do need to search for more than 32 keywords.

Grouping Keywords—Some search engines (e.g., Yahoo! and Bing) allow you to group keywords together with parentheses to help you better organize your query. For example, at Yahoo!, if you wanted Web documents that talked about George Bush and Dick Cheney but did not have anything to do with Iran or Iraq, you could structure your search like this: *"George Bush" "Dick Cheney" AND NOT (Iran OR Iraq)*. You can accomplish the same results at Google, but you have to use the exclusionary instruction before each term you want to exclude: *"George Bush" "Dick Cheney" -Iran -Iraq*. Boolean connectors and exclusionary connectors will be discussed in Section 3.1.

Basic (And not so Basic) Google Search Strategies: All You Need to Know to Become a Good Internet Researcher

3

3.1 Boolean Connectors

Boolean logic is a system developed by mathematician George Boole during the nineteenth century that utilizes a series of connectors to define relationships between objects. The best-known examples of Boolean connectors are AND, OR, and NOT. Their functions are (almost) self-explanatory. Using Boolean connectors to construc t a Google search helps you to create more precise searches for information.

Google's default Boolean connector is AND, which means that Google automatically adds an AND between each of the keywords you type into the search box. A search for *Mark Rosch* will return pages related to the keyword *Mark* AND the keyword *Rosch*. The results will not necessarily have those two keywords together, so you may also see results about *Mark Smith* AND *Ron Rosch*, as well as *Mark Rosch*.

You can override this default by substituting one of the other Boolean connectors.

A search conducted with the OR connector between keywords will return results that contain one keyword OR the other, as well as both keywords. (The OR connector actually functions as an AND/OR connector, so you might also get results that only contain *Mark*, or only contain *Rosch*, or contain both *Mark* AND *Rosch*.) The OR connector is most often used to search for synonyms. For example, a Google search for the keywords *divorce Chicago attorney OR lawyer* would return results that contain information about divorce lawyers in Chicago or divorce attorneys in Chicago. It is important to capitalize the OR connector when using it between keywords in a Google search. If you do not capitalize the OR connector, Google will ignore the lowercase "or" as a "stop word." ("Stop words" are discussed in more detail in Section 3.5.)

The NOT Boolean connector excludes a particular keyword from your search results. Using this Boolean connector in a Google search is not as straightforward as using OR. Rather than typing the word NOT, you type a hyphen to the left of the word (or phrase) that you want to *exclude* from your search. For example, if you wanted to search for information about RICO (the Act) but did not want information about traveling to Puerto Rico, you could search for *rico -puerto*. It's important to note that relevant information might also inadvertently get excluded from your results. While the *rico -puerto* search would exclude results that included "Puerto Rico," it could also exclude a result about someone named "Johnny Puerto," even if he was charged under the RICO Act.

3.2   Word Stemming

"Word stemming" usually refers to a search-engine feature that allows for the automatic extension of a particular keyword to search other forms of the word (e.g., extending the keyword *swim* to locate relevant results that include *swimming, swims*, etc.). Google seems to not only stem but to "un-stem" as well when retrieving results (e.g., reducing the keyword *swimming* to locate relevant results that include *swims* or *swim*).

Similarly, a search for *Carol Levitt* would return results for Rhode Island physician "Carol Levitt" and the co-author of this book, "Carole Levitt."

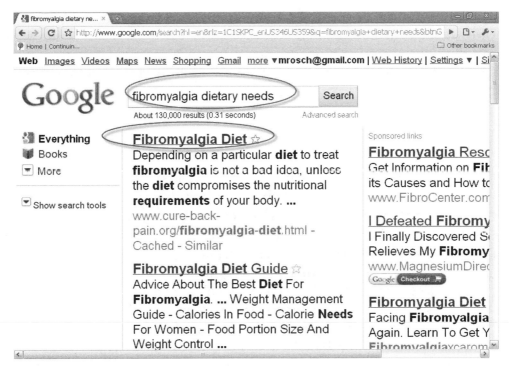

FIGURE 3.1 In our retrieved results for a search for *fibromyalgia dietary needs*, you can see by this illustration that Google left off the *"ary"* from the search term "*dietary*" when it retrieved results that include *fibromyalgia diet needs*. This is an example of how Google will un-stem (as well as stem) a search term.

3.3 Phrase Searching

Rather than searching for individual keywords, you can also search for exact phrases with Google. To do this you enclose your phrase in quotation marks. Phrase searching can be useful if you're searching for a term of art or a product name. A search for *"negligence per se"* returns results that contain those words in that exact order.

It is also common to search for people's names as exact phrases; however, there is the risk that doing so will omit important results if the individual uses a middle name or initial. It is often more productive to use a proximity search connector (see the following section) instead of phrase searching to link a first and last name—this way results that include a middle name or initial are also included.

NOTE: Enclosing search terms in quotation marks also eliminates the word stemming discussed in Section 3.2. So, a search for *"Carol Levitt"* will return results only for Rhode Island physician "Carol Levitt" (and others who spell their name the same way) but no results for the co-author of this book, "Carole Levitt."

3.4 Proximity Searching

Many paid search products such as LexisNexis and Westlaw offer the ability to search for keywords within a certain number of words from one another (a number that you define). Lexis, for example, allows you to search *w/* (within any number of words that you indicate, such as *w/2*), */s* (in the same sentence), and */p* (in the same paragraph).

Google does not offer this sophisticated search option. It does offer the asterisk (*) as a "wildcard"—taking the place of one (or more than one) word. It essentially acts as an imprecise proximity connector.

We have found using the asterisk in a Google search to be of limited value, as there is no way to define how many words the asterisk represents. For example, you might expect a search for *Carole * Levitt* to return results that include Carole's name whether or not it includes a middle name or initial since we're (essentially) asking Google to return results where *Carole* and *Levitt* are separated by one (or more than one) word. However, of the first ten results of that search, only one included information about the co-author of this book (including her middle initial). The rest of the results included the keywords *Carole* (or *Carol*) AND *Levitt,* but they were separated by as many as four other words, such as:

- *Carole Costanza, Marc Levitt*
- *Carole Gelfer-Katz, Harry Levitt*
- *Carol Huntington, SMP; Mitch Levitt*
- *Carol; Neuman, Arlene C.; Levitt*

The asterisk can be useful in locating the answer to specific questions. For example, the search *windshield wipers were invented by * returns results that include the name of the woman who invented windshield wipers in 1903, and the search ** clerked for Justice Souter* returns results that include the names of numerous individuals who did clerk (or are currently clerking) for Supreme Court Justice David Souter. While conducting these test searches without the asterisk did retrieve some of the same results as those searches conducted with the asterisk, using the asterisk put results that actually answered the question higher up on the results list.

3.4.1 Using More Than One Asterisk in a Search

While there is no way to define (or predict) how many words will be replaced by a single asterisk in a Google search, Google's own Web search help pages (http://www.google.com/support/websearch/bin/answer.py?answer=136861) indicate that you can use more than one asterisk as wildcards in a search. Google's own example, *Obama voted * on the * bill*, would seem to indicate that you would not put two asterisks adjacent to one another (e.g., *Lawyer's Guide * * Internet*), nor would you need to put your keywords and asterisks in quotation marks (*"Lawyer's Guide * * Internet"*).

If the asterisk stands in for one or more words, you may be wondering, "Why would it even be necessary to search with two asterisks adjacent to one another?" That would be a good question, and the answer would be an unenlightening "Because it works." Adding additional asterisks does change the search results. In some cases (e.g., long company names, product names, proper names, etc.), this can be a useful search strategy for retrieving information.

To test how the addition of multiple asterisks adjacent to one another affects search results, we conducted a number of test searches with none, one, or two adjacent asterisks separating our keywords, both with quotation marks around our keywords and asterisks and without. The individual searches were entered this way:

- *Carole Levitt*
- *Carole * Levitt*
- *Carole * * Levitt*
- *"Carole Levitt"*
- *"Carole * Levitt"*
- *"Carole * * Levitt"*

Unfortunately, two adjacent asterisks do not represent two words (or four words, as suggested by the Wikipedia entry). Even with the addition of adjacent asterisks, each asterisk still represents an undefined number of wildcard keywords.

As expected, the addition of adjacent asterisks pushed our keywords further apart, with each search yielding different results. Also as expected, the addition of quotation marks limited our results just to the spelling of "Carole" for which we searched. The most relevant results (for the co-author of this book) were returned for the *"Carole * Levitt"* search, yielding more results about her in the top twenty than in the other searches. All of those results included just her first and last name or her first and last name with middle name or middle initial as displayed in Figure 3.2. (Some of the other results had *Carole* and *Levitt* separated by two or more other words.)

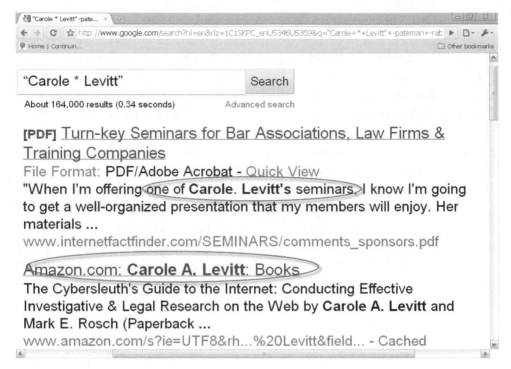

FIGURE 3.2

3.4.2 Using the Asterisk to Circumvent Google's 32-Keyword Limit

Using the asterisk can be one way around Google's 32-keyword limit (first discussed in Section 2.5). To test the search-terms limit, we entered 71 keywords into the Google Search box. (The search was for the exact phrase, *"term public record has always been VERY misleading. Even though a record is public and available for public scrutiny in the strictest sense, in reality it may not be readily available. The availability of numerous public records via the Internet has addressed some of the accessibility issues, but just as it's always been in the offline world, access to free public records via the web is a hit or miss proposition".*) These two sentences are contained in an article on our own Web site (http://www.netforlawyers.com/article_public_records.htm), which we knew had been indexed by Google. The search returned the Web page on which the text is contained, along with the notation by Google near the top of the results page that "'availability' (and any subsequent words) was ignored because we limit queries to 32 words."

FIGURE 3.3

We can use the asterisk to get around the 32-keyword limit by replacing some of the keywords in the two sentences with the asterisk. By altering our search to the exact phrase, *"* public record * always * * misleading. * though * record * public * available * * scrutiny * * strictest *, * reality * * * * readily *. * availability * numerous * records via * Internet * addressed some * * accessibility issues, * just * * * been * * offline *, access * free * records via * web * * hit * miss *"* we did not receive the " . . . ignored because we limit queries to 32 words" warning and still retrieved the exact Web page we had hoped to find. While this is an extreme example, we use it to illustrate how you are able to circumvent the 32-keyword limit. It can be extremely useful when you're trying to find an original source of information that has not been properly cited.

3.5   "Noise" or "Stop" Words

In most cases, Google treats many short or inconsequential words, single letters, and single digits as "noise" or "stop" words and ignores them. These include:

- I
- of
- am
- the
- where
- how
- who
- etc

We say "in most cases," because there are exceptions. By Google's own stated search rules, a search for *The Sound and the Fury* should search primarily for the two keywords *Sound* and *Fury*. However, because the novel *The Sound and the Fury* is heavily referenced on the Internet, this Google search will pick up a number of results for the book, as well as sources that contain only the keywords *Sound* and *Fury*. Google is also "smart" enough to recognize certain terms and phrases in context, so that a search for *The Who* will return results discussing that seminal English rock band and not treat *The* and *Who* as stop words.

There are two ways to force Google to search for "noise" words. The first is to conduct a phrase search and put all of your keywords in quotation marks. The second is to put a + directly before the term (without a space) for which you want to force Google to search.

So to conduct a targeted search for the first film in the latest *Star Wars* trilogy, you could conduct either of these two searches: *"Star Wars Episode I"* or *"Star Wars Episode" +I*. While the results of those two searches will be different, the first twenty results are very similar and the sources in both results lists include the Roman numeral I.

3.6   Punctuation in Searches

Google ignores most punctuation and "special characters" included in searches. These include periods; commas; exclamation points; question marks; and the @, <, and > signs. For example, Google treats a search for *Mark*

E. Rosch the same as a search for *Mark E Rosch*—returning the exact same results for each search (some results include the period but some do not).

Exceptions to this rule include apostrophes and hyphens. When searching for the book *The Cybersleuth's Guide to the Internet*, it is important to consider possible misspellings on the part of Web site owners. Google recognizes the apostrophe as a searchable character, so it returns different results for each of the following searches: *Cybersleuth's Guide*, *Cybersleuths' Guide*, and *Cybersleuths Guide*. While the first search (*Cybersleuth's Guide*) returns the most targeted results (for that book), it also includes some results with no apostrophe as we view some results much later in the results list (not shown in Figure 3.4). The last search example (*Cybersleuths Guide*) includes some results that do include the apostrophe.

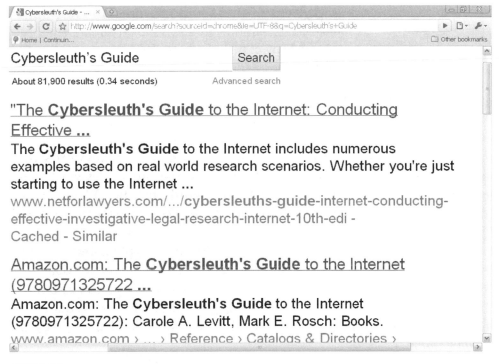

FIGURE 3.4

Google treats hyphens similarly. A search for *Cyber-Sleuth's Guide* yields different results from the search *Cybersleuth's Guide*. However, the results lists for both examples include sources that do use the hyphen and that do not use the hyphen (as seen in Figure 3.5).

FIGURE 3.5

To be as thorough as possible when searching for keywords that include apostrophes or hyphens, search for variations of keyword spelling and punctuation and separate the keywords by the OR connector (e.g., *Cybersleuth's Guide OR Cybersleuths' Guide OR Cybersleuths Guide OR Cyber-sleuth's Guide*).

You can force the inclusion or exclusion of a hyphenated or apostrophic spelling by using the + and the - described in Sections 3.5 and 3.1 (respectively) (e.g., *+Cybersleuth's Guide -Cybersleuths'*). You can also force the search to consider only the spelling you prefer by using quotation marks to indicate a phrase search as described in Section 3.3 (e.g., *"Cyber-sleuth's Guide"*).

3.7 Capitalization

Google searches are not case sensitive. Google does not consider capitalization of keywords when returning results. To Google, *Mark Rosch*, *mark rosch*, *MARK ROSCH*, and *MaRk RoScH* are all the same search . . . at least they're supposed to be. In a test search, the first three searches showed 189,000 results, but the last search showed 424,000 results. However, the first three pages of results for all four searches were identical. Since Google never actually displays all of those thousands of results before it shows the message "In order to show you the most relevant results, we have omitted some entries very similar to the [number of entries] already displayed. If you like, you can repeat the search with the omitted results included," the reported difference for the last search is actually meaningless.

3.8   I'm Feeling Lucky

We like to say that the **I'm Feeling Lucky** button on Google's home page stops obsessive-compulsive searchers from spending too much time looking at hundreds (or millions) of results, because it does not display a long list of results that you obsessively compulsively feel compelled to review, or even a link to one "lucky" site. When you enter your keywords into the Google Search box and click the **I'm Feeling Lucky** button, Google will take you directly to the Web page it has determined to be the most relevant to your search. If you find that the site doesn't have enough information for you, you can always hit your Web browser's **Back** button and click the **Google Search** button to retrieve the familiar list of search results.

FIGURE 3.6   After entering the phrase "*lottery winner*" into the search box and clicking the **I'm Feeling Lucky** button, we were brought to a story titled, "$266 million lottery winner is keeping her job."

Advanced Google Search Strategies: All You Need to Know to Become a Great Internet Researcher

4

Google's Advanced Search page offers a collection of form-based search options that allows you to easily create a more focused and sophisticated search. It can be reached using the **Advanced Search** link to the right of the search box on the home page or directly at http://www.google.com/advanced_search.

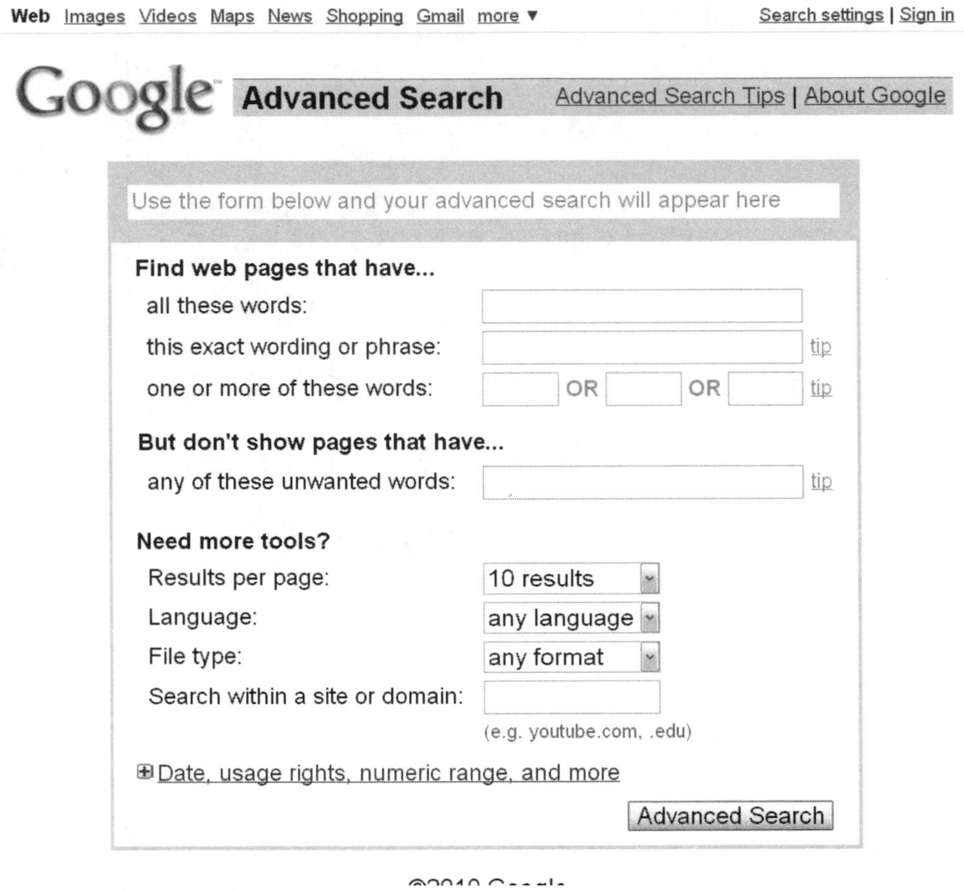

Web Images Videos Maps News Shopping Gmail more ▼   Search settings | Sign in

Google™ **Advanced Search**   Advanced Search Tips | About Google

Use the form below and your advanced search will appear here

Find web pages that have...

all these words: [   ]

this exact wording or phrase: [   ] tip

one or more of these words: [   ] OR [   ] OR [   ] tip

But don't show pages that have...

any of these unwanted words: [   ] tip

Need more tools?

Results per page: [10 results ▾]

Language: [any language ▾]

File type: [any format ▾]

Search within a site or domain: [   ]
                         (e.g. youtube.com, .edu)

⊞ Date, usage rights, numeric range, and more

                                    [Advanced Search]

©2010 Google

FIGURE 4.1 The Advanced Search page's form-based layout allows you to mix and match available search limiters to create more sophisticated searches.

At all of our live seminars, we ask for a show of hands from those people who use the Advanced Search page at Google to conduct their searches. The response varies, but it's usually less than half of those in attendance who are using these resources. At one live seminar we asked an attendee who had not raised his hand why he wasn't using the Advanced Search page. He answered, "Because I'm not an 'advanced searcher.'" Our response to him, and to anyone who is not already using the Advanced Search page, is "You don't have to be. In fact, using it will turn anyone into an 'advanced searcher.'"

4.1   Boolean Searches Using the Advanced Google Search Page

At the top of the Advanced Search page are four rows of options that represent the AND, EXACT PHRASE, OR, and AND NOT Boolean search connectors. Entering your keywords and phrases into the appropriate boxes allows you to define very specific criteria for your search.

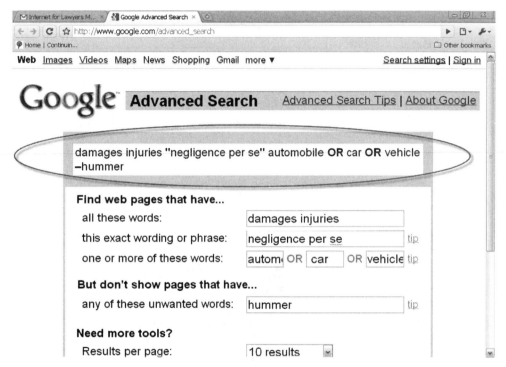

FIGURE 4.2   In this illustration, we've used the top section of the Advanced Search page to create a search that includes the keywords *damages* AND *injuries*; the EXACT PHRASE *negligence per se*; and *automobile* OR *car* OR *vehicle*; AND NOT *hummer*.

Using the **Find pages that have… one or more of these words** search boxes is one way to search for synonyms. If you want to search for more than three synonyms (as shown in Figure 4.2), you would have to return to Google's home page and enter each synonym (separated by the Boolean connector OR) into the search box.

It's important to note that you can only enter one phrase into the **Find web pages that have… this exact wording or phrase** box. If you want to search for two or more exact phrases, you would have to return to Google's home page and enter each phrase (enclosed in its own set of quotation marks) into the search box.

4.2 Limiting Results to Specific File Formats: Locating Unexpected Documents Posted to the Web (e.g., Opposing Experts' Prior PowerPoint Presentations)

Google's Advanced Search page also gives you the ability to limit your search results to a single type of document (e.g., Microsoft Word, Microsoft PowerPoint, Microsoft Excel, and Adobe Acrobat PDF, among others). To do so, you simply select the type of file you want to see in your results from the **File type** drop-down menu and then enter your keywords or phrases in the **Find web pages that have...** Boolean search boxes.

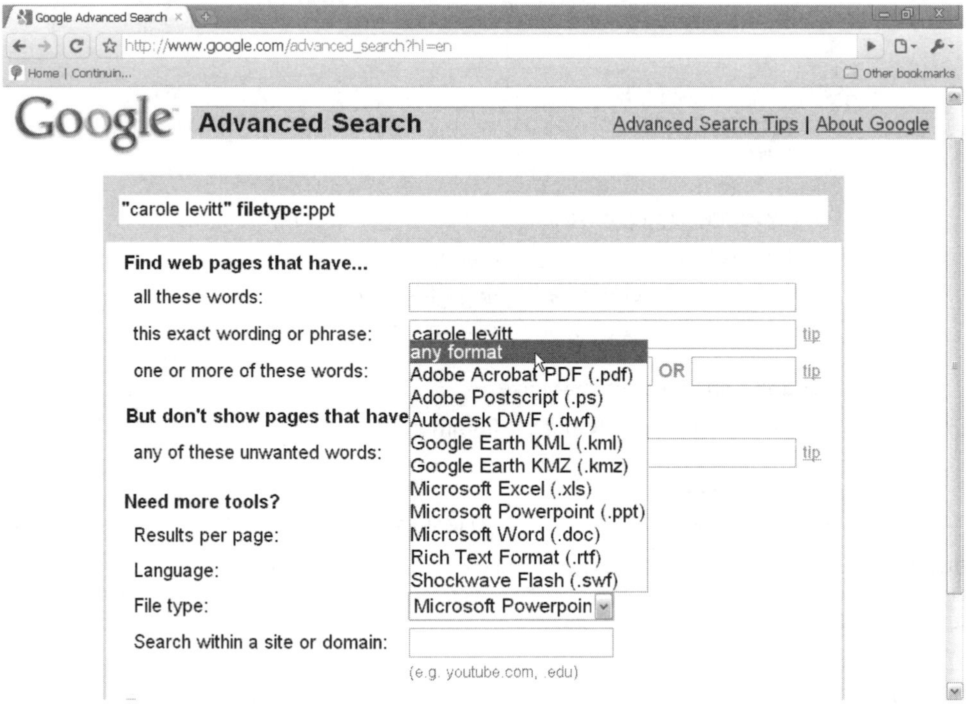

FIGURE 4.3   You can use the **File type** drop-down menu on Google's Advanced Search page to limit your results to a particular type of file. In this example, we're searching for **Microsoft PowerPoint** presentations that include the exact phrase *Carole Levitt*.

▼▼▼▼▼

Search Tip

Many expert witnesses post the PowerPoint slides from presentations they have made as one way to illustrate their expertise on their particular topic. Locating these presentations can be useful for two reasons. First, the presentations can be a useful educational tool for you to become informed on a particular topic. Second, locating previous presentations given by a specific expert witness can give you an indication of how they might testify in a matter. In some instances, there might even be indication that they had taken a contrary stand in the past to one they are presenting in your current matter.

Searching for the expert by name and limiting the results to **Microsoft PowerPoint** (as illustrated above) would return these presentations if they're posted on a Web server where the Google robot ("Googlebot") has located them.

For Windows users, left-clicking with your mouse button will open the presentation in your Web browser and allow you to view the individual slides as they would be viewed by an audience watching the expert in person. However, many PowerPoint presentations include more information than just what is visible in the slides. To access the entirety of the presentation, including any notes that the expert or presenter may have included in non-slide portions of the presentation, Windows users should right-click and select **Save Target as...** to save the presentation to their own computer hard drive. Opening the presentation gives you access to the slides as well as any notes or other metadata associated with the presentation. Note that you must have Microsoft PowerPoint installed on your computer to access this information.

4.3   Limiting Results to a Specific Web Site

A little bit further down the Advanced Search page is the **Search within a site or domain** box. This feature superimposes the power of Google onto any Web site, limiting your results to the one site you identify by entering its URL into this box.

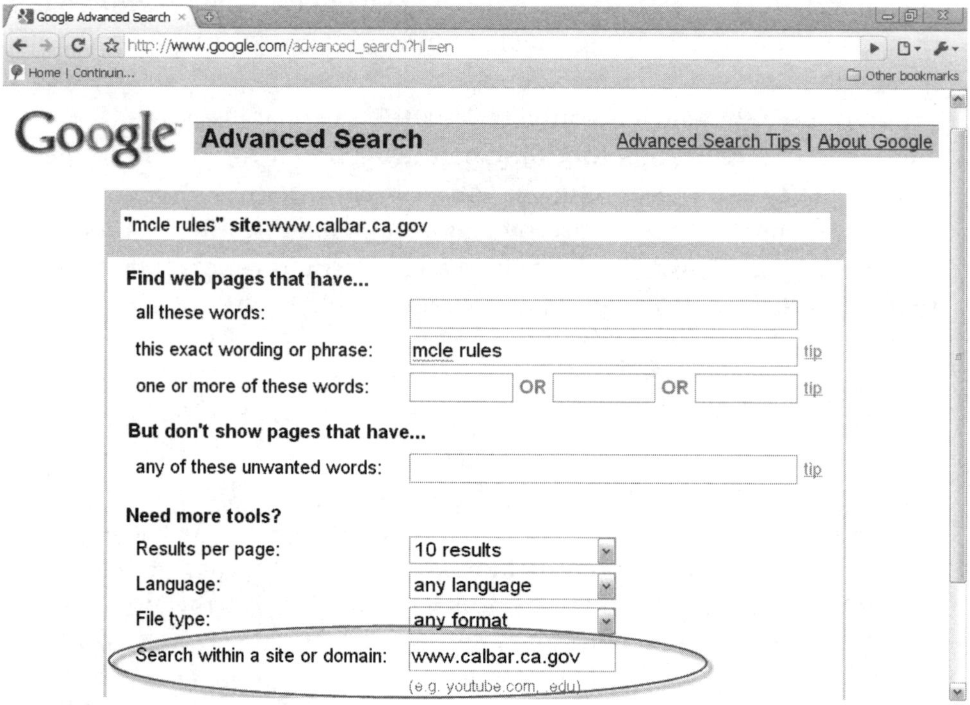

FIGURE 4.4   Entering a Web address in the **Search within a site or domain** box limits your results to just that site. In this example, we're instructing Google to return results that include the exact phrase *MCLE Rules* and are posted at the *www.calbar.ca.gov* Web site.

It's important to note that even when searching for results from a single site, Google is not reaching out to search "live" content on the Internet—it is still searching through the searchable index of Web pages its robot has compiled (as described in Section 2.3.4). When using the **Search within a site or domain** function, we're instructing Google to just search through the pages that come from the site we've identified.

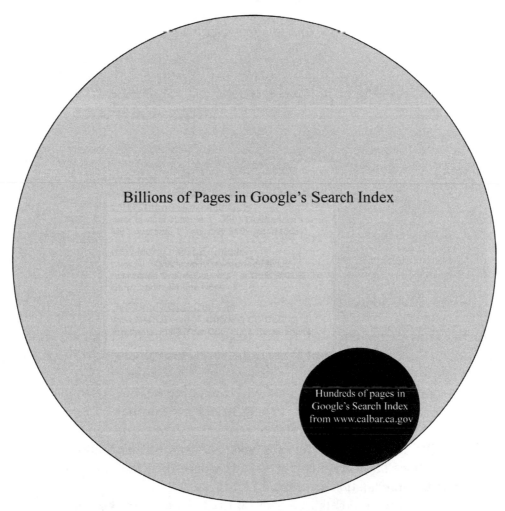

FIGURE 4.5   Entering a Web address in the **Search within a site or domain** box instructs Google to search for results from a subset of its entire index—just the Web site we have entered. In our example search (in Figure 4.4), Google would ignore the vast majority of pages in its index and search only for results from the *www.calbar.ca.gov* Web site.

Search Tip

Prior to a 2007 redesign of the Advanced Search page, Google also allowed you to omit a single domain from your search results— effectively the opposite of the current **Search within a site or domain** function. Even though Google removed this option from the Advanced Search page, we can still instruct Google to perform this kind of search. By typing *"MCLE Rules" -site:www.calbar.ca.gov* into the search box on Google's home page, Google will return results from all of the sites in its index except *"www.calbar.ca.gov"*.

This kind of search can be useful if you're looking for information about a particular person or product and want to omit results from their own Web site to see what other, unaffiliated sites have to say about your search target.

4.4   Who's Linking to Whom? Determining Possible Business or Personal Relationships

By learning who's linking to whom, we can sometimes determine business or personal relationships between individuals or companies. Typing a URL into the **Find pages that link to the page** box (located further down the **Advanced Search**), we can instruct Google to return a list of sites that link to the site we're interested in.

This can be also useful when we're evaluating a Web site for the first time. One criteria we use when trying to decide whether to rely on the information we find on a newly discovered site is what other Web sites cite back to it. If a lot of outside sites are linking back to this new site—and particularly if those sites are ones we already trust—then that is a vote for us to rely on the information on this new site.

The opposite could also be true—if the links back to the new site are accompanied by negative commentary, we might want to avoid relying on the site's information.

4.5   Hidden Features of the Advanced Search Page

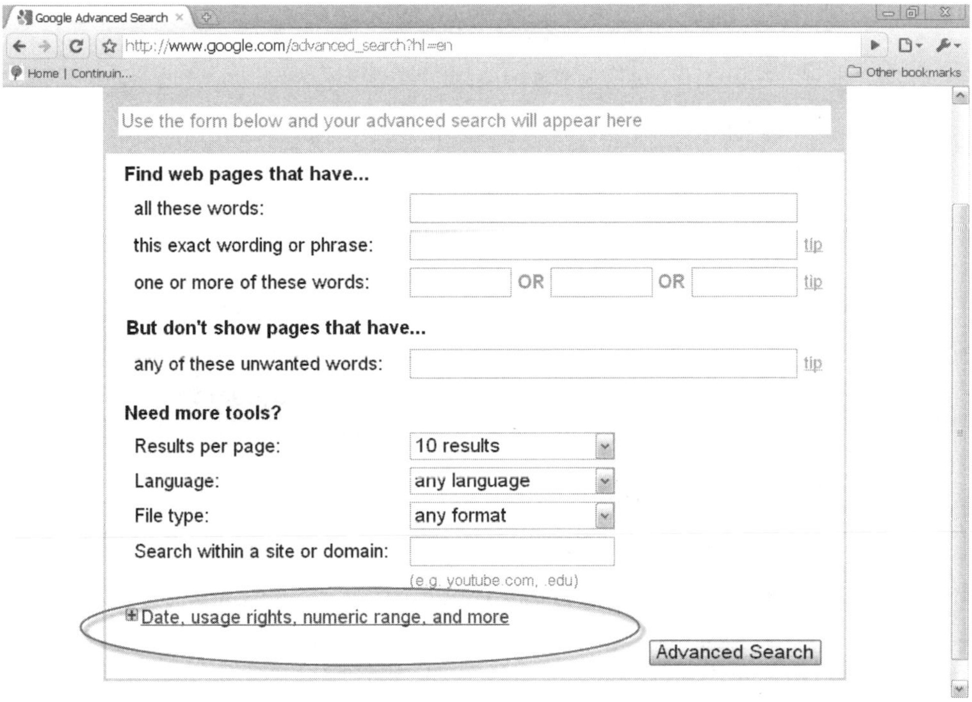

FIGURE 4.6   To view the features behind the **Date, usage rights, numeric range, and more** link, simply click on the link. For the "big reveal" see Figure 4.7.

So far, all of the features we've discussed on the Advanced Search page have been right out in the open where we can easily see them. While not initially described, a number of useful features are hidden behind the **Date, usage rights, numeric range, and more** link.

4.5.1   Date Search Restrictions

It's important to note that Google seems to base this date information on the date on which the page was first detected by its robot and added to its index. Minor subsequent edits to the page don't seem to affect this date. For example, our Web site (http://www.netforlawyers.com) has been online since 1999. However, we completely redesigned the site and in June 2009 migrated all of its pages to a new Web server, with new URLs for all of the pages on the site. Despite the fact that the original publication date was embedded in each page, Google's own datestamp on all of these pages indicates that they were "created" on June 9, 2009, a few days after the revised site went live—the date that Google's robot detected them.

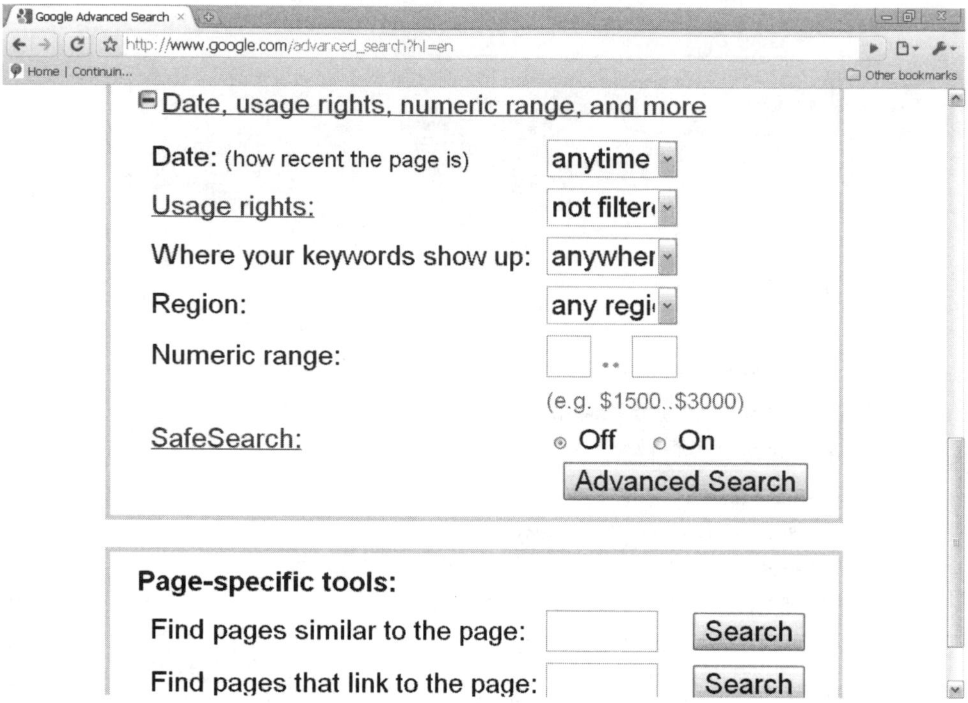

FIGURE 4.7   The **Date** limiter allows you to specify how recent or up to date you want your search results to be. Selecting **anytime** returns the widest range of results.

4.5.2   Usage Rights

The **Usage Rights** limiter allows you to filter results based on how a resource's creator will allow it to be used by you. The default selection is **not filtered by license**. If you're conducting your searches for background or investigative research purposes, you will want to keep this as your selection to get the widest range of information in your search results list. If you are searching for information to include in your own public presentations or articles that you are writing, you will want to limit your results to material that is **free to use or share, even commercially** or **free to use, share, or modify, even commercially**.

4.5.3   Pinpointing the Location of Your Search Terms

Also hidden behind the **Date, usage rights, numeric range, and more** link, the **Where your keywords show up** drop-down menu allows you to specify where on the Web page your keywords appear. Limiters include **anywhere in the page**, **in the title of the page**, **in the text of the page**, **in the URL of the page**, and **in links to the page**.

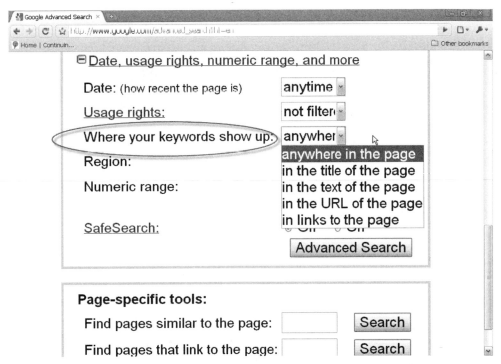

FIGURE 4.8   Limiting keywords or phrases to the title of a Web page is one way to try to find the pages that are most related to your search terms—although Google does a pretty good job of determining relevancy on its own.

You've Got Your Search Results, Now What? Understanding and Manipulating the Displayed Search Results

5

5.1   Indented Results

FIGURE 5.1

When a Google search returns multiple results from the same Web site, the most relevant result is listed first and other relevant pages from that same site are indented below it.

5.2 Google Cache

When Google's robot visits a Web page to add (or update) its content to the Google Search index, Google captures a copy of the page as it appeared at that moment and stores it on Google's own servers.

As discussed in Section 2.3.4, even though the Googlebot is working twenty-four hours a day, seven days a week to locate new and updated pages for its index, it does not visit every known page every day. This can create a situation in which a page (or some content on a page) that was located by the Googlebot on Monday is no longer the same as when you run a search and receive a link to that page on Friday if the Web site owner made a change to the page on Thursday. When you click on the big blue link, the information that the Googlebot originally found is no longer there because of the change the site owner made.

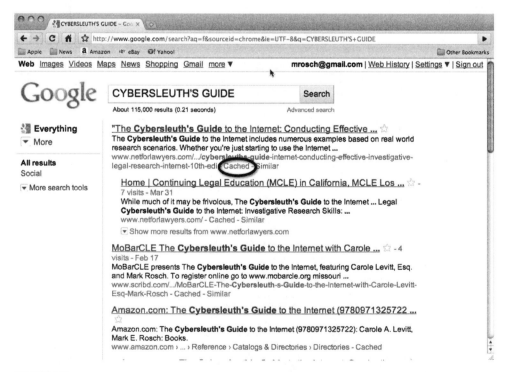

FIGURE 5.2

Clicking the **Cached** link will display the contents of the Web page as they appeared when the Googlebot last visited the site. The page displayed will then match your search results annotations, with your keywords highlighted.

5.3   Search Within Results

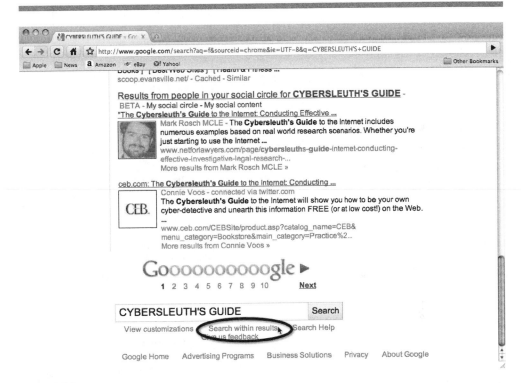

FIGURE 5.3

If you find that you have received too many results (as is often the case), you can narrow down your search by using the **Search within results** feature link at the bottom of each page of your search results. It allows you to add (or exclude) other keywords or phrases to your search using any of the search connectors discussed in this chapter. If you don't add a connector, it adds the default AND for you.

5.4   Narrowing Results by Information Type

In the spring of 2010, Google made a major alteration to the way it displays search results with the addition of the left-hand sidebar. This sidebar contains a variety of tools to narrow down your search results list.

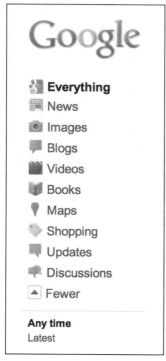

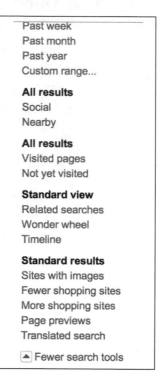

FIGURE 5.4   In the spring of 2010, Google added the left-hand sidebar to the search results list. This is the top half of the sidebar.

FIGURE 5.5   The bottom half of the sidebar gives you more choices for narrowing down the displayed list of results.

The first set of narrowing options, starting with **Everything**, allows you to narrow down your results list by the type of information returned, or the source from which the information comes. Options include **Videos**, **News**, **Blogs**, **Updates**, and **Discussions**, among others. Clicking any of those options reduces the results list to only those entries that come from the specific information source you've selected.

The most revolutionary addition to the Google search results list is hidden behind the **Updates** option. The **Updates** are the closest thing to "real-time" search currently available on the Web. They are drawn from a variety of sources such as Twitter, Facebook, MySpace, and FriendFeed updates, with the majority of them coming from Twitter. This is very different from the way other types of results are returned by Google. Another major difference is that Google continues to run your search and if it detects new **Updates** while you're browsing the results list, those new **Updates** are added to the top of the list.

FIGURE 5.6 Clicking the **Updates** link in the left-hand sidebar yields the closest thing to "real-time" Web search results currently available. **Updates** results, displayed in reverse chronological order, are drawn primarily from Twitter. Clicking anywhere along the timeline at the top of the results list displays only those results from the point in time you've selected. Clicking the month (**June** in this example) or the year (**2010** in this example) adjusts the timeline to access **Updates** for that time period. The **Top Links** column to the right lists the most popular (e.g., recurrent) resources cited (e.g., linked to) from within the **Updates**. (As of our Summer 2010 publication deadline, **Update** results were only displayed as far back as February 2010.)

Note that Google has created separate databases to search for some of these specific types of information (e.g., **News** and **Blogs**). We will discuss searching just those resources in subsequent chapters.

▼▼▼▼▼

Seeing Results Created by People You Know

Google's Social Search limits your results to pages and documents from people you know. First though, you have to tell Google where to find the people you know by including your Twitter and/or FriendFeed account information in your Google Profile (see Section 2.4.2 for more information on Profiles)—and you have to be logged into your Google Account (see Section 2.4.1 for more information on Accounts) so Google knows who you are. (Google also draws connections based on people in your Google contact list, as well as your Gmail/Google Talk chat lists.)

Using information about these connections, Google searches for content already available on the Internet, and accessible to search engines, created by those contacts or sites with which they are associated.

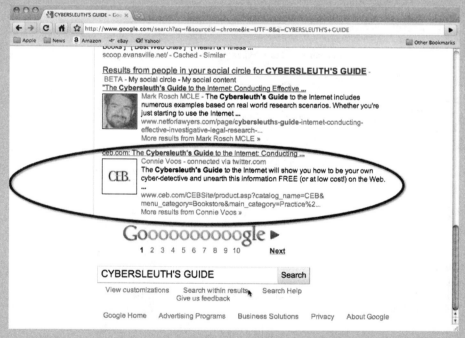

FIGURE 5.7

The content from those people you already know is displayed separately at the bottom of the regular search results list.

5.5 Narrowing Results by Currency

The next set of narrowing options, starting with **Any time**, allows you to narrow down your results list by the freshness of the information. A number of these options are similar to the Advanced Search page's date-limiting search feature discussed in Section 4.5.1 (specifically **past 24 hours**, **past week**, and **past year**). Date-limiting options offered here, not seen on the Advanced Search page, include **Latest**, and the ability to define a **Specific date range**. Selecting any of these limiting options also allows you to choose whether you want the new results displayed by date or by relevance.

Any time
Latest
Past 24 hours
Past 4 days
Past week
Past month
Past year
Custom range...

FIGURE 5.8   Clicking the **Latest** option narrows your list to the most recently-located results. Google also continues to run your search for the **Latest** results, adding any newly-located results to your list. Clicking the **Pause** link, located at the top of the search results list temporarily suspends this automatic updating.

▼▼▼▼▼

SEARCH TIP

You can customize the time frame of your displayed results beyond the options Google displays—by changing the date range parameter in the search's URL.

For example, the following URL displays search results from the **Past 24 hours** for the keywords *Barack Obama*. The *d* at the end (it stands for *day*) is what defines the date range as the **Past 24 hours**.

http://www.google.com/search?q=barack+obama&hl=en&tbo=1&prmd=nli&source=lnt&tbs=qdr:d

We can force Google to display search results from the past hour or minute by changing the *d* to an *h* or an *m*—like this:

http://www.google.com/search?q=barack%20obama&hl=en&sa=X&tbo=1&tbs=qdr:m

To display results from the past ten minutes, we would alter the URL this way:

http://www.google.com/search?q=barack%20obama&hl=en&sa=X&tbo=1&tbs=qdr:m10

To display results from the past three days, we would alter the URL this way:

http://www.google.com/search?q=barack%20obama&hl=en&sa=X&tbo=1&tbs=qdr:d3

Theoretically we could even instruct Google to display results from the past second by placing an *s* after the *qdr:* although we have never been able to generate any results trying this.

FIGURE 5.9 Clicking the **Specific date range** gives you the ability to enter a beginning and ending date to set your own date range for results.

As also noted in Section 4.5.1, Google seems to base this date information on the date on which the page was first detected by its robot and added to its index and not necessarily on the date that the information was first published.

5.6 Altering the Way Results Are Displayed

Search engine results have long been referred to, derisively, as "ten blue links," because the list format for search results (displayed ten to a page) has become a *de facto* standard. Google's Standard View is no different, but the options listed beneath **Standard View** give you a way to get beyond those ten links related to your keywords and expand your results to include **Related Searches** or a visual representation of the relationship between search terms and concepts with the **Wonder Wheel**.

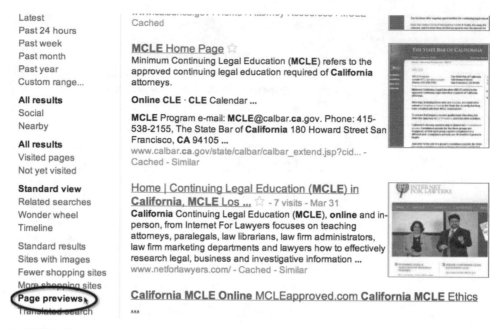

FIGURE 5.10 Clicking the **Page Previews** link adds thumbnail screenshots next to each of the sites on the results list.

FIGURE 5.11 At the bottom of the search results, the **Related searches** section displays a group of new search terms that are related to your original search. These new suggested searches sometimes narrow and sometimes broaden the scope of your original search. Clicking any of these **Related searches** links will display a new list of results based on the new link you have chosen.

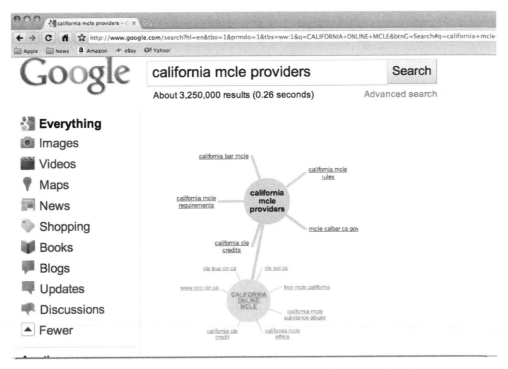

FIGURE 5.12 Clicking the **Wonder wheel** option gives you a visual representation of various key terms and topics that recur in the search results list and how they are related to your original search terms. Clicking any of the terms on the **Wonder wheel** itself allows you to drill down into these clusters of information to locate more and more specific information and links.

Further down the options list (see Figure 5.5), you can click **Sites with Images** to add images from the pages listed in the results list to the right of the descriptive text that accompanies each result.

You can also see an image preview of the sites containing the results by clicking the **Page previews** option (see Figure 5.10).

The **Fewer shopping sites** and the **More shopping sites** options reduce or increase (respectively) the number of online shopping sites included in your results.

Clicking the **Translated** search link automatically translates your search terms into **French**, **German**, **Italian**, and **Spanish**. You can also add additional languages using the drop-down menu. Additionally, Google displays selected results translated from each of those languages. See Chapter 12 for more information on Google's translation services.

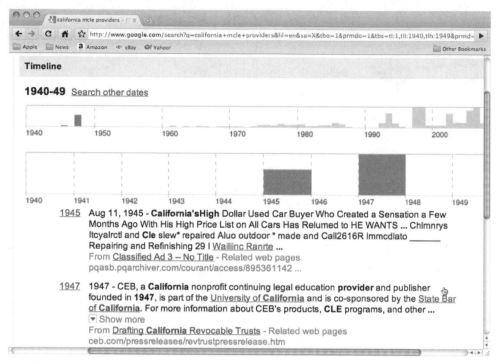

FIGURE 5.13 Clicking the **Timeline** link (as seen in Figure 5.10) generates a graphical representation of the date distribution of the results and reorders the results into "chronological" order. One drawback to the **Timeline** view is that the dates Google uses to create the chronological order are not necessarily the dates on which the documents in the results list were published/created—sometimes it's just a date that's included in the text of the document/page. For example, the first 1947 result is actually a press release from 2003. In that press release, there is a reference to CEB being founded in 1947 and that's apparently how Google decided the date origin of this particular document.

FIGURE 5.14 Clicking the **Nearby** link further narrows the results list either using the **Default Location** (automatically determined by your Internet connection) or a **Custom Location** you can define by clicking the **Custom Location** link and typing your selected location in the box.

Google News 6

Whether a lawyer needs to obtain recent background information about a potential client or an opposing party or simply needs to keep up to date about a particular client's business or industry, running a search through Google News (http://news. google.com) is a handy tool because:

- It's free.
- It's easy.
- It allows you to quickly hone in on *just* current news. (For older news, try Google News Archive, discussed later in this chapter.)
- It displays more news stories than you would see at a regular Google.com search.

6.1   What Google News Covers

Google News is a directory and a search engine devoted exclusively to the most recent thirty days of news articles retrieved from 25,000 news sources from around the world (ranging from the BBC, CNN, and the *Boston Globe* to press releases from selected companies). The news articles are updated continuously throughout the day. Articles are selected and ranked by Google's robot, based on "how often and on what sites a story appears online . . . [and] certain characteristics of news content such as freshness, location, relevance and diversity" (http://news.google.com/intl/en/about_google_news.html).

6.1.1   Google News Directory
The News home page is set up like a directory with various news categories, which Google refers to as "sections." The

Top Stories section is displayed first, with headlines and abstracts of what Google considers to be, as the label indicates, the top stories. You can either scroll down the page to view other sections (**World, U.S., Business, Sci/Tech**, etc.) or you can jump from one section to another by selecting from the sections listed on the left-hand side of the News home page.

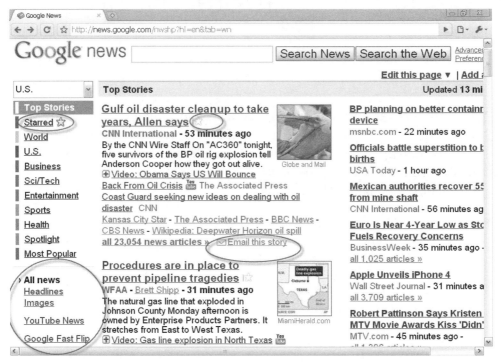

FIGURE 6.1   The layout of the News home page can be altered to display only headlines (or only images) by selecting **Headlines** (or **Images, video news stories stored on YouTube,** or Google's **Fast Flip** graphical view of news sources) from the column on the left-hand side of the News home page. (See explanation of **Fast Flip** that precedes Figure 6.7.) Notice the **Email this story** link and star icon that accompany each news story.

If you click on the **Email this story** link, you will be asked to sign in to your Google Account. (See Section 2.4.1 for more information on creating a Google Account.) After you sign in, a pop-up box with the headline and abstract

> **Practice Tip**
>
> What better way to stay in front of clients than by e-mailing them stories you know would interest them? The **Email this story** link makes it easy for you to accomplish this marketing task.

of the story will be displayed, along with a place to enter the recipient's e-mail address and your message. Clicking the star icon accompanying any story allows you to mark that story for later retrieval by subsequently clicking the **Starred** button, in the left-hand column.

Unfortunately, the link for the **News Alerts** (now referred to as an **email alert** or a **Google alert**) feature (discussed later in this chapter) has been removed from the home page entirely and the **RSS** link, once prominently displayed on the home page's left-hand column, has been relegated to the bottom of the home page, where it may easily go unnoticed by users. We say "unfortunately" because these two features are valuable for keeping up to date on any topic or person chosen by the user.

6.1.2   Personalize the Google News Directory Home Page

Google also offers you the ability to personalize the News home page so each time you visit Google News from your own computer, the news will be displayed to your specifications. To set up your personal page, scroll down to the bottom of the News home page and click on **Personalized U.S. Edition** (the default is **Standard Edition**).

FIGURE 6.2

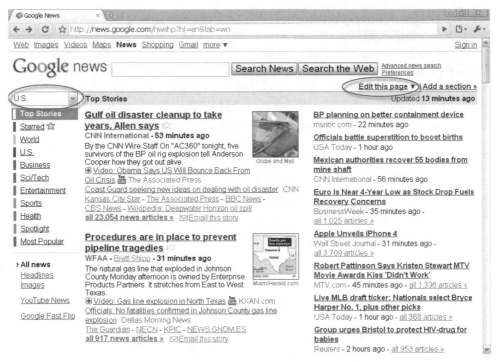

FIGURE 6.3 Personalizing your News page can help you to quickly keep abreast of the news that you're interested in. You can also change the language of the entire News home page by choosing a country from the drop-down menu on the left-hand side of the home page (above Top Stories). This illustration is set to U.S.

An **Edit this page** link on the top, right-hand side of the home page will then appear. Select that link for a drop-down menu that will allow you to personalize your News page by dragging and dropping the sections to rearrange their placement on the page. You can further customize your News page by clicking the **Add a section** link (to the right of the **Edit this page** link) to:

- Add a **standard section** (a country and a News category)
- Add a **local section** (Add a city, state, or ZIP code and choose the number of stories to be displayed from 1–9.)
- Add a **custom section** (Add keywords that the stories must contain and choose the number of stories to be displayed from 1–9. There is also an **Advanced** link to add a language and to label the custom section.)

Practice Tip

You can create multiple **custom sections.** They will appear after the standard sections listed in the left-hand column of the News home page. Your custom search can be quite sophisticated because Boolean connectors and phrases can be deployed. For example, to create a custom search to follow only the swine flu but not the avian flu, your search would look like this: **"swine flu" -avian.**

- Add a **recommended section** (Reportedly, "recommendations are based on what you have searched for and clicked on in the past, and they will improve over time as you use Google News." See the non-Google-affiliated blog "Inside Google" at http://linkon.in/c7dLxB.)

When you have completed personalizing the page, click on the **Save layout** button. This saves the settings to your computer. However, if you want to be able to access your personalized News home page from a computer other than your own, you must sign in to your Google Account and store your News settings. To later access your personalized News page from any computer (other than your own), you will need to first sign in to your Google Account.

After you have chosen the **Personalized U.S. Edition**, notice the down arrows that appear to the right of each section name (you will need to scroll past the **Top Stories** until you reach the first section, which in Figure 6.4 is the **World** section). If you click this down arrow, you are offered **more stories** or **fewer stories**. By clicking on either one, the user can view one more story or one less story in a particular section.

FIGURE 6.4   To continue adding more stories to a specific section, continue clicking on the **more stories** link and to delete stories from a specific section, continue clicking on the **fewer stories** link.

6.1.3   Google News Search Engine: Basic Search

Instead of viewing the news from the current day (in the Directory mode), users can use the search box near the top of the page to perform keyword (and/or phrase) searches for links to news stories about a topic or person of their own choice. All of the Boolean and Proximity features used in a regular Google search-engine search will also work here.

6.1.4   Google News Search Engine: Advanced Search

There is also an **Advanced news search** link (located to the right of the Google News basic search box at the top of the News home page). This link allows the user to limit the search by:

- **Date**
- **News source**
- **Source location** (It is important to take note of a story's source, because Google may also include company press releases in its News search results, which may at times be biased or include puffery.)
- **Location** (stories about a local area)
- **Authors**
- **Occurrences**

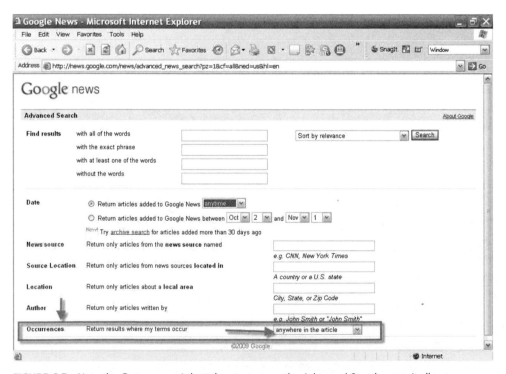

FIGURE 6.5   Note the **Occurrences**' drop-down menu on the Advanced Search page. It allows you to limit your results even further—to where your keywords appear **anywhere in the article, in the headline of the article, in the body of the article,** or **in the URL**.

In addition to the above, the Advanced Search page offers the same Boolean search menu (e.g., **with all of the words, with the exact phrase**, etc.) found on Google.com's Advanced Search page. There is also a link labeled **Try archive search for articles added more than 30 days ago** (to be discussed in Section 6.3) and a drop-down menu (to the right of the **with all of the words** search box) that allows the searcher to:

- **Sort by relevance**
- **Sort by date (newest first)**
- **Sort by date (oldest first)**
- **Sort by date with duplicates included**

6.1.5   Google News Search Engine: Results from Basic and Advanced Searches

News search results are displayed the same whether you have conducted a Basic Search or an Advanced Search. A headline and an abstract will be displayed for each story.

To alter the results display, you can select the following from the left-hand side of the results page:

- **All News**
- **Images**
- **Blogs**
- **Any recent news** (This is where you can select stories from the past hour, day, week, etc.)
- **Archives**
- **Sorted by relevance**
- **Sorted by date**

FIGURE 6.6 By selecting **Archives** (see Section 6.3), you can rerun the search at Google's News Archives to view older news stories.

At the bottom of each page of results, notice the various choices beneath the heading **Stay up to date on these results** (our search was for *public option health care*):

- **Create an email alert for public option health care** (to be discussed in the next section of this chapter)
- **Add a custom section for public option health care to Google News** (discussed in Section 6.1.2)
- **Search Google Fast Flip for public option health care** (Google partnered with three dozen publishers, from the *New York Times* to the *Atlantic,* to provide a way for the user to quickly view thumbnails of about a dozen stories at a time.)

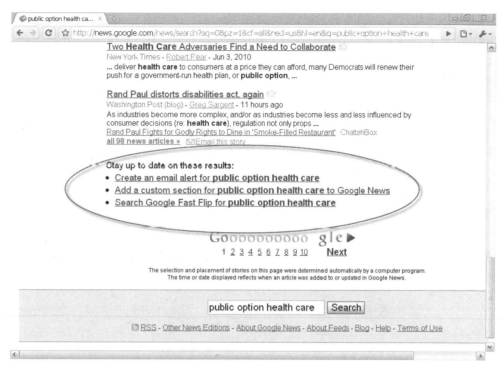

FIGURE 6.7   Use these features for an easy, automatic way to stay up to date about a client, a case, an industry, or even about yourself and your law firm.

6.2   Google Alerts (Formerly Known as Google News Alerts): Keeping Current with Information About Clients, Your Firm, the Opposition, or Even Yourself

Alerts are the Internet version of the old-fashioned clipping services, in which someone literally clipped out news articles on various topics and people and mailed them to the requestor. Although the Google Alerts home page states that this feature is in a beta stage, that doesn't mean it hasn't been around for a while or that it's not ready for prime time. We've used this feature from its 2003 launch and are quite satisfied with it. It's one of the few free alert services on the Internet.

6.2.1   What Google Alerts Covers

Google Alerts (http://www.google.com/alerts) takes the Google News personalization feature two steps further. First, instead of placing the burden on you to remember to visit your personalized news page on a regular basis, Google Alerts visits you by sending you e-mail alerts about the keywords you specify (such as a person's name or a topic).

> **Practice Tip**
>
> Consider setting up alerts with your name, your firm's name, a client's name, a client's industry, etc. to conveniently monitor what's important to your practice.

Second, the Alerts allow you to monitor more than just News. See Section 6.2.2 for details.

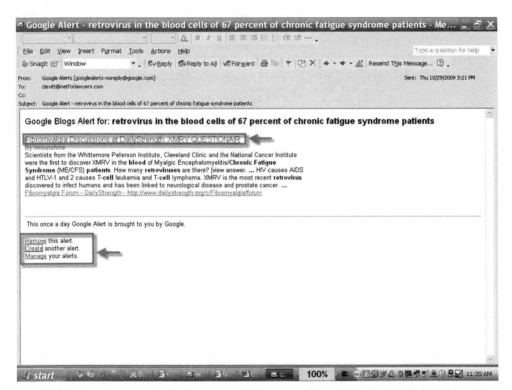

FIGURE 6.8   This is what an Alerts e-mail looks like when it is delivered to your inbox. To read the full story, simply click on the link that begins with the word "Fibromyalgia." At the bottom of the e-mail, you are offered three choices: (1) **Remove this alert**, (2) **Create another alert**, and (3) **Manage your alerts**. (See Section 6.2.2 for details on managing Alerts.)

6.2.2 How to Create a Google Alert

There are three ways to create an Alert.

First, as explained in Section 6.1.5, you can set up an Alert based on any News search you conduct by scrolling down to the bottom of your News search results and clicking on the link that begins with these words: **Create an email alert for...** (your keywords will already be inserted here).

Second, you can create a Google Alert by visiting the Alerts page directly at http://www.google.com/alerts and (1) entering your keywords into the **Search terms** box, (2) selecting **News, Blogs, Everything, Video,** or **Discussions** from the **Type** drop-down menu, (3) selecting **as-it-happens, once a day,** or **once a week** from the **How often** drop-down menu (to indicate you would like the alerts e-mailed to you), and (4) typing your e-mail address into the **Your email** box.

FIGURE 6.9 To create a sophisticated Alert, you can add Boolean connectors to your keywords and include phrases (as explained in Section 6.1.2's Practice Tip).

If you use either of these two Alert options, you will not be able to edit your Alerts. Instead, you will need to cancel the Alert entirely and create a brand new Alert to your new specifications. This cancellation option appears as a link at the bottom of all Alert e-mails.

Third, you can click the **sign in to manage your alerts** link that appears on the bottom left of the Google Alerts page at http://www.google.com/alerts. To use this management tool, however, you will need to sign in to your Google Account. (See Section 2.4.1 to learn how to set up a free Google Account if you don't already have one.) The benefit of this management tool is that every time you visit the Alerts page at http://www.google.com/alerts, you can click on the **Sign in** link on the top right-hand side of the page and view your list of Alerts, create new Alerts, easily edit or delete your existing Alerts, and select to have the Alert delivered to a feed or to your e-mail. (There is no need to type in your e-mail address, as you are already logged in with your e-mail address.)

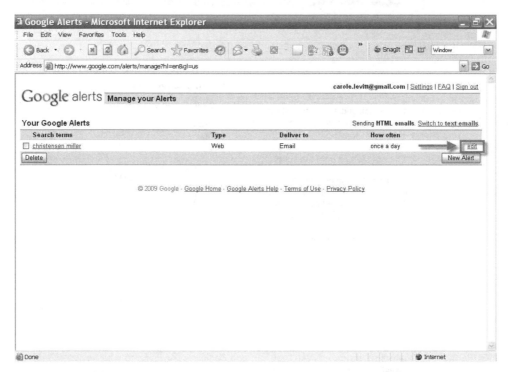

FIGURE 6.10   Click on the **edit** link to change any of your search criteria, from the search terms to the frequency of delivery.

For example, we originally created a **News Alert** to monitor the firm Christensen, Miller and requested a **once a day** e-mail Alert. Later, it was simple to revise our Alert to include **Everything** and to request that the Alert be sent **as it happens** instead of **once a day**. Later, when the law firm name changed to Glaser, Weil, Fink, Jacobs, Howard and Shapiro, we returned to our list of Alerts and easily edited the search terms.

> **Practice Tip**
>
> For those who can't wait to receive their automatic Alerts, the **Manage Your Alerts** page allows you to click on your Alert to immediately run your search, regardless of the frequency you originally set up.

6.2.3   How Setting Up Alerts with Your Clients' Names as Keywords (or Phrases) Might Help You Avoid a Conflict of Interest and Even a Malpractice Suit

Although setting up Alerts for all of your clients and cases, using their names as keywords (or phrases), is impractical, setting up Alerts for your major clients and important cases should be considered in light of the following malpractice case.

From 1993–2000, Weil, Gotshal & Manges represented the owners of Fashion Boutique of Short Hills against the fashion house Fendi. Fashion Boutique claimed that Fendi had used unfair business practices to destroy their business. In 1999, the firm began representing another fashion house, Prada (in unrelated matters). On October 13, 1999, unknown to the firm, Prada teamed up with LVMH Möet Hennessy Louis Vuitton to acquire a majority stake in Fendi. The *New York Times* and the *Wall Street Journal* had reported this venture, but the Weil attorneys who were working on the Fendi case apparently missed it. When they discovered this potential conflict, they did not immediately tell the owners of Fashion Boutique. In fact, it wasn't until 2000, when the jury was in the midst of deliberating Fashion Boutique's claims, seven months after Prada had become a Weil client, that Weil informed Fashion Boutique of the situation. When the owners of Fashion Boutique were disappointed by the amount of the jury award, they sued Weil for legal malpractice and breach of fiduciary duty. *Weil, Gotshal & Manges v. Fashion Boutique of Short Hills*, 780 N.Y.S.2d 593 (N.Y. App. 2004). If Google Alerts had existed back in 1999 and Weil had created Alerts for both Prada and Fendi, it might have learned that Prada had acquired a majority stake in Fendi, thus discovering the potential conflict early on. It could have either rejected Prada as a client or obtained informed consent, confirmed in writing, from each client, to proceed with the representation. (In 2006, Weil settled with Fashion Boutique days before the malpractice claims went to the jury.)

▼▼▼▼▼

GOOGLE ALERTS IN ACTION

William Rattner, the Executive Director of Chicago-based Lawyers for the Creative Arts (http://law-arts.org), a provider of pro-bono legal services for the arts, has put Google Alerts to work for his organization and his clients.

> We have created Google Alerts using the name of our legal service organization and every day I receive 2–3 updates. Usually the items are of no interest to me, but it only takes about one minute to read. I have occasionally found very useful information.
>
> When anyone in the world presents a play, it usually shows up on the Internet through a listing on the presenter's own website or a press release the presenter has sent out—so Google can find it. Setting up a Google Alert notifies the rights-holder of the usage so they can contact the presenter of the play to determine what action is necessary.
>
> We've had two recent instances where rights-holders have contacted our clients based on information those right-holders have located about their novels or plays using Google Alerts.
>
> First, our client, a small theater, presented a farcical parody of a famous Broadway show. The rights-holder contacted our client asking what they were doing and all details, etc. We explained the production and pointed out it was a parody, that it was for three nights only etc., and the matter was dropped.
>
> The second client was a larger theater that presented an adaptation of a novel written in the Middle East half a world away. The owner of the novel became aware of the play (which bore the same name as the novel!!) and delivered a cease and desist notice to our client, which was honored.
>
> Neither of these copyright owners would have known of the use of their materials without the monitoring provided by our Google Alert.

6.3   Google News Archive

While Google News provides full-text searchable access to current news sources, Google News Archive provides access to older news information. It also provides different ways to organize those results.

6.3.1   Find Older Documents Online (Even Pre-1940)

A link to the Google News Archive once appeared on the top right-hand side of the Google News home page. It has since been removed, so it's now a little trickier to find the Archive. Use the direct URL (http://news.google.com/archivesearch) or link to it from the Google News (the current News discussed earlier) Advanced Search page.

6.3.2 What Google News Archive Covers

In 2006, the Archive was launched to extend the date range of Google's News search to go further back in time. Instead of recent stories, this database retrieves major newspaper and magazine articles and news archives back to 1910 and earlier, primarily from U.S. sources (but also from international sources for more recent time periods). Google states that the purpose of the News Archive is to "[s]earch and explore historical archives" and to "[a]utomatically create timelines which show selected results from relevant time periods." Google is partnering with the copyright holders of various newspapers to scan newspapers that have not yet been digitized.

While access to many of the articles is free, the price to access other articles varies from source to source.

> **Practice Tip**
>
> Before paying for an article, check your public library to see if it's available free via their remote access service. (See Levitt and Rosch's other ABA book, *Find Info Like a Pro*, to learn more about free remote access to expensive pay databases via your public library.)

6.3.3 Searching Google News Archive: Basic, Advanced, and Timeline

The Google News Archive can be searched by entering keywords into the basic search box on the News Archive home page or by clicking on the **Advanced archive search** link and entering keywords there. After entering keywords into the basic search box, select either **Search Archives** or **Show Timeline**. After entering keywords into the **Advanced** search box, there is only one selection: **Search Archives**.

The Search Archives results are displayed by relevancy, but can be changed to a date range view by selecting the **Search other dates** link located on the top left-hand side of the results page. A date range covering the years represented on the results list will already be inserted into the **From** and the **To** date range boxes, but you can override them and change the beginning or ending date to any earlier or later date you prefer. However, the Timeline dates are spotty; they sometimes are treated as a keyword and don't relate to the date of publication while other times they do refer to the date of publication.

The **Show Timeline** results are shown in chronological order.

6.3.4   Limiting Results Using the Advanced Google News Archive Search

The Advanced News Archive Search (http://news.google.com/archivesearch/ advanced_search) is useful to limit your search by **Date**, **Language**, **Source**, **Price**, and **View** (the **View** feature allows you to select **Search articles, Show full timeline**, or **Show news timeline**).

6.3.5   Case Law Research Available for a Fee on Google News

The News Archive also indexes two case law databases (Loislaw and VersusLaw). However, when linking to results from these databases you'll discover there is a fee to retrieve full-text cases (which must be paid by credit card). (Google states that "We do not receive payment when users purchase articles." See http://news.google.com/ archivesearch/help.html.)

Practice Tip

Before paying for a case, see the discussion of Google Scholar's free case law search in Section 17.4. Also, check your state bar association to see if they offer free case law through Casemaker or Fastcase or visit the myriad of free case law databases such as the Public Library of Law at http://www.plol.org, Justia at http://www.justia.com, LexisONE at http://www.lexisone.com, or FindLaw at http://www.findlaw.com.

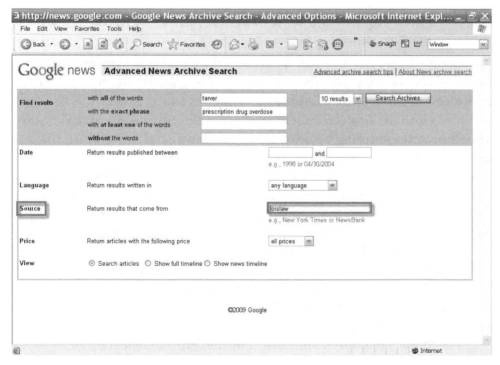

FIGURE 6.11   To limit your search results to case law only, enter *loislaw* or *versuslaw* into the **Source** search box on the Advanced News Archive Search page, in addition to your keywords.

Google Groups: Retrieving Information from Over One Billion Publicly Archived E-mail Messages

7

Whether you are trying to find a missing person or you need to obtain background information on a topic or a person, you can anonymously search through over one billion postings in Google Groups. Google Groups' full-text search capabilities (using keywords or names) makes the task easy. In addition, you don't even have to know to what group someone belongs in order to search; nor do you have to join their group (or any group). You can simply lurk . . . and learn.

7.1 What Google Groups' E-mail Archive Contains

Google Groups (http://groups.google.com) is one of the best-known online communities. It's a precursor to the more recent phenomena of social networking sites (such as Facebook and MySpace). Like social networking sites, Groups serves as a place where people of like minds share interests, similar to the way "friends" at various social networking sites combine into networks to share interests. However, users of Google Groups "share" via e-mail messages to their entire group instead of visiting a friend's social networking profile and leaving comments.

To create Google Groups, in 2001 Google purchased 500 million public discussion group e-mail messages dating back to 1995 from Deja.com, and messages from other groups dating back to 1981. Subsequently, Google Groups has added (and continues to add) millions (and possibly billions) of messages to the original archive of messages.

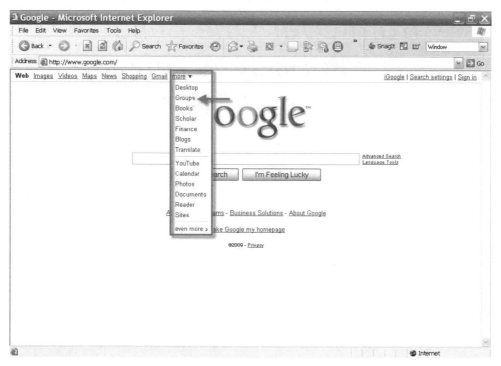

FIGURE 7.1 To visit the Groups database from Google's home page, select the **more** tab, which will reveal a drop-down menu with a link to **Groups**, or use this URL: http://groups.google.com.

It's important to note that these are not individual e-mail messages that were sent from person to person. These are not the e-mails we send to our clients, friends, family, etc. These discussion groups were always meant to be public. The difference now is that Google Groups gives us a one-stop search to access all of these public archives, rather than having to visit (and search) each one separately. People participating in these discussion groups in their earliest days couldn't have foreseen the ease with which we can now locate those old posts, because Google didn't even exist at the time.

Even though Google Groups messages are included in a regular Google Web search results list, they could be buried far down in the results list, so we recommend searching at the Groups database directly so you don't overlook them. Another reason to search Google Groups directly is to take advantage of some of the unique searches you can conduct using its Advanced Groups Search page (to be discussed in Section 7.3).

7.2 Basic Search Strategies

Although you can search Google Groups for information about a topic, we typically search Google Groups for information about a person. To do that, we conduct a keyword search or a phrase search using the person's name. Proper name searching is tricky because people some-

Ethics Alert

Be careful not to correspond directly with a represented party through Google Groups.

times use middle names/initials and sometimes they don't, forcing you to conduct multiple searches (with and without the middle name/initial). (See Chapter 3 to learn how to use Boolean and Proximity connectors and also phrases to create the best search.) If you know something about the person, add a descriptive keyword to the name search (such as the person's city, company, or profession) to narrow the search to the correct person. This may disclose messages authored by the subject of your search or other

FIGURE 7.2 This is the Google Groups home page, where you can enter a basic search such as *"john smith" elite* to find information about John Smith who works at Elite.com.

people's messages that contain your subject's name. You might learn someone else's opinion of your subject or the message may disclose some contact information for your subject. You can also attempt to e-mail the author of a message directly to learn more about their opinion of your subject.

One of this book's authors was looking for background information about the president of Elite. com because she had to introduce him at a conference. She decided to search Google Groups, and because he had a very common name, she searched using his name in conjunction with the name of his company. She came up with some interesting information, including his hobby—he's a Trekkie. Not being a Trekkie, she read a few of his postings to learn about Trekkies, and was able to slip the word "borg" into her introduction of him. (For a definition of "borg," now would be a good time to visit Chapter 11 to learn how to use Google to find definitions of words.)

Practice Tip

Groups might help you bond with a potential client or learn about a person you need to introduce.

Sometimes it's useful to discover whether a potential client or someone you need to introduce at a conference has a particular interest or hobby before your first meeting. Then you'll have something to talk to the client about right away or something to use in your introduction at the conference. You might obtain that information from a Google Groups search.

Practice Tip

Groups might help you bond with a deponent (or set them on edge).

According to Texas lawyer Craig Ball, he uses these tidbits of information from Google Groups at depositions to show the deponent that Craig Ball knows all! Ball swears deponents are more forthcoming when they think he already knows everything—even information about their hobbies. He also uses information found on the Internet about a deponent to "bond" with the deponent and help them feel more comfortable.

7.3   Advanced Groups Search Strategies

While the Google Groups full-text keyword search capability is helpful, there are even more useful features available on the Advanced Groups Search page (http://groups.google.com/advanced_search) to find information about a specific individual.

▼▼▼▼▼

**Google Groups can be an Excellent Source of Information
About Expert Witnesses—Yours or the Opposition's**

As a principal of the JurisPro Expert Witness Directory (www.JurisPro.
com) and the Expert Witness Profiler (www.ExpertWitnessProfiler.
com), attorney Jim Robinson is frequently called upon to research
expert witnesses.

The Advanced Search at Google Groups can be a gold mine
for finding information about expert witnesses. For example, when
researching a case involving an aquatics expert, we found a post on
Google Groups where the opposition's expert had contradicted himself regarding safety procedures in a public pool.

7.3.1 People-Finding Search Strategy Tips Using Advanced Groups Search: Search for a Message Authored by a Specific Person

The first useful Advanced Groups
Search feature allows you to search
for a message authored by a specific person by entering their name
or their e-mail address into the
**Return only messages where the
author is** field. Since many people
share the same name, searching by
a unique e-mail address might help
you verify that you've found the
correct person. After all, besides
a Social Security number, what
other identifier is more unique
than an e-mail address?

Practice Tip

*Because some people have more
than one e-mail address, try to
discover all of them to conduct a
complete search of their messages.*

There are various ways to discover
someone's e-mail address, from
simply asking them (whether
informally or through discovery)
to "Googling" their name through
Google and Google Groups,
unmasking it from another Google
Groups message (discussed in
Section 7.7), or searching social
networking sites.

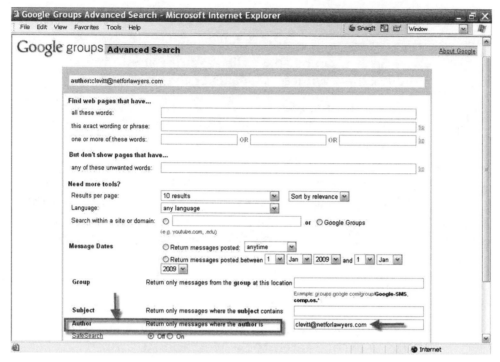

FIGURE 7.3   Although the Advanced Groups Search page allows you to search for messages sent by a specific author, keep in mind that some people surf anonymously (by using pseudonyms), so you may find nothing. That's another reason it might be better to search by their e-mail address.

7.3.2   Limiting Results to Specific Discussion Groups Using Advanced Groups Search

The second useful Advanced Groups Search feature allows you to search for a message by Group name. For example, entering *alt.med.cfs* into the **Return only messages from the group at this location** brings back 203 results. Some of these results contain multiple messages.

Usage Tip

You can mix and match the various search boxes on the Advanced Groups Search page to create a more targeted search.

For example, entering *alt.med.cfs* into the **Return only messages from the group at this location** search box and entering *levitt* into the **Return only messages where the author is** brings back only three results.

7.3.3   Limiting Results to a Specific Subject Using Advanced Groups Search

The third useful Advanced Groups Search feature allows you to search for a message by subject (the subject line in the message). Entering the keywords *a lot of messages on this thing* into the **Return only messages where the subject contains** search box brings back one message.

> **Usage Tip**
>
> Quotation marks (phrase searching) does not work. Strangely, when we placed quotation marks around our subject *"a lot of messages on this thing,"* we received no results.

7.3.4   Other Advanced Groups Search Features

There are other features located on the Advanced Groups Search page, so you can:

- Find messages posted on a certain date or during a certain range of time (by using the drop-down menu to choose **past 24 hours, past month**, etc. or use the other drop-down menu to select specific date ranges).
- Sort results by date or relevance.
- Limit results to a particular language.
- Search by the message ID (see Section 7.6).

7.4   Using Google Groups to Find or Background an Expert

Google Groups can also be used to search by topic to find experts in a certain specialty when you don't already have the name of an expert on a particular topic. For example, if you are representing a client who was seriously injured when the treads of his Firestone tires separated, causing his vehicle to overturn, searching Google Groups for the phrase *Firestone tires expert* might lead you to an expert who has testi-

> **Practice Tip**
>
> *Google Groups may help you undermine the opponent's expert or even evaluate your own expert.*
>
> Searching by an expert's name, you may come across a message sent by your own expert or your opponent's expert. This is an excellent way to attempt to undermine the opponent's expert and to evaluate your own expert. This search may also disclose other people's messages that contain their opinions about the expert.

fied in prior tread-separation lawsuits. Additionally, the same search may identify people who have also been seriously injured when the treads on their vehicles' tires separated. They might mention their expert's name or their lawyer's name (which can be a lead for you), or they may express their opinion about the expert.

A lawyer at one of our seminars told us he once searched the defendant's expert in Google Groups only to discover a message from that expert asking people in his group to bring him up to speed on a matter for which he had just been retained. You guessed it. It was the very same matter the lawyer was representing the plaintiff in.

7.5   The Anatomy of a Google Groups Message

As you are viewing a message, click the **More Options** link to reveal more information about the message.

FIGURE 7.4   Select the **More options** link to reveal more information about the message. You can also hide the options.

Under the subject line are various links, some of which (**Reply to author** and **Forward**) can only be deployed if you are logged into your Google Account (see 2.4.1). The other links can used by anyone (**Print, Individual message**, **Show original**, **Report this message**, and **Find messages by this author**).

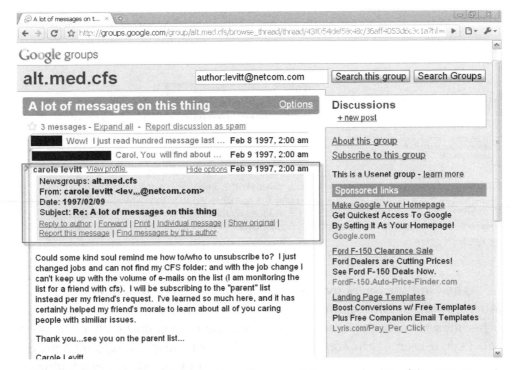

FIGURE 7.5   The author's partial e-mail address, the name of the group, the date of the message, and the subject line are revealed once you click on **More options**. (See the next paragraph to learn about the various links beneath the subject-line link).

If you click on the **Show original** link, the unique message ID is displayed. As noted in Section 7.3.4, it can be used to search for a specific message.

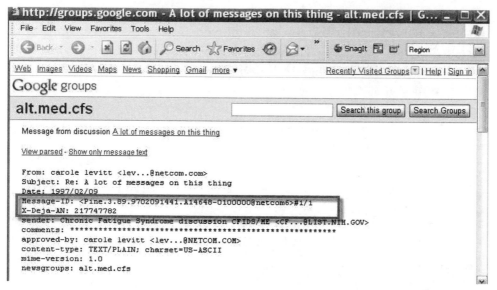

FIGURE 7.6 The **Message-ID** is a unique identifier for this particular message. We can direct colleagues to this exact message by copying only the numbers and letters in between the two chevrons ([...]) and pasting this ID into an e-mail. Our colleague can then paste the ID into the **Lookup the message with message ID** feature on the Google Groups Advanced Search page to locate the message themselves.

The **Find messages by this author** link that appeared after we clicked **More options** did not return other messages by the same author even though other messages by the same author do exist in the database. To accomplish this task, search by the author's e-mail address instead, as explained in Section 7.3.1. Read the next section to learn how to unmask an e-mail address from a Google Groups message.

7.6   How to Unlock an Author's E-mail Address

After performing a search through Google Groups and displaying results, the author's e-mail address used to also be displayed. Now, Google is masking the author's e-mail address. Although there is a work-around for unlocking the address, it takes several steps. First, click on the **More options** link (shown in Figure 7.4) on the message. A partial address will be displayed. It will have ellipses inserted between the first part of the e-mail address and the domain (*lev...@netcom.com*). Second, click on the ellipses to continue the unlocking process.

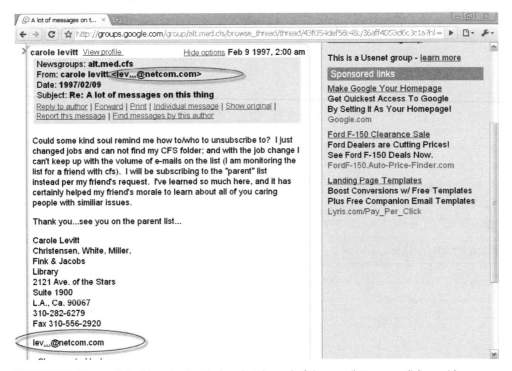

FIGURE 7.7   The partial address is also displayed at the end of the e-mail. You can click on either one to begin the unlocking process to display the full e-mail address.

Clicking the e-mail address opens an **Unlock email addresses** page. Enter the characters displayed into the captcha search box to "unlock" the full e-mail address.

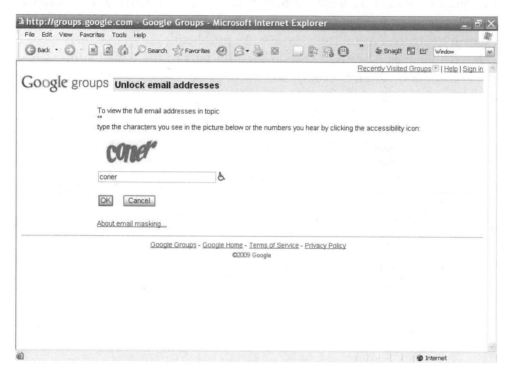

FIGURE 7.8 This is step three of the unlocking process, which will eventually reveal the full e-mail address to you so you can search for all of that author's messages by e-mail address.

Completing the captcha returns you to the message, but the e-mail address is still not displayed. Step four requires you to click **More options** (again) before the e-mail address will be unlocked.

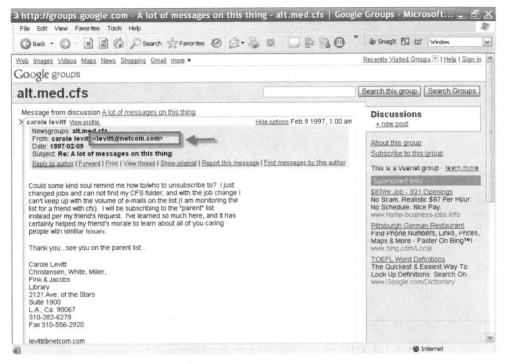

FIGURE 7.9   This is step four of the unlocking process, which finally reveals the full e-mail address. Now you can search for all of that author's messages by e-mail address.

A message found on Google Groups might reveal an unlisted phone number, a fax number, a cell number, or other hard-to-find contact information.

Practice Tip

Believe it or not, people do (sometimes purposely but other times inadvertently) post their unlisted or unpublished telephone numbers and addresses, cell numbers, or fax numbers to a public discussion message. For an example, see Carole Levitt's 1997 message in Figure 7.9. In 1997, Google Groups didn't even exist, so Carole didn't anticipate how easy it would be for anyone to search for this message and view her contact information.

7.7 How to Locate a Group to View Their Archives or to Join

To locate a group to view their archives or to join a group so you can participate, keyword search for the topic you are interested in or browse through the list of group categories.

FIGURE 7.10 We are searching for a group about truck accidents.

Once you find a group that interests you, you can join only if it is open to the public. If a group is not open to the public, you cannot participate or search its archives of messages.

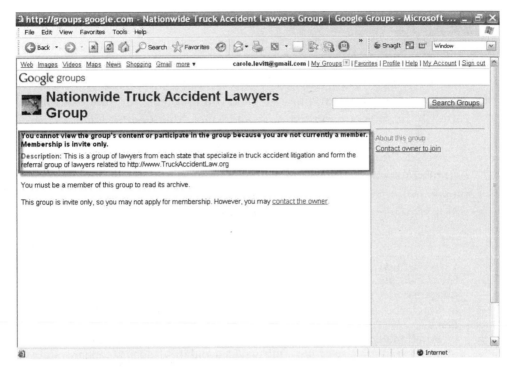

FIGURE 7.11   This group is by invitation only. Other closed groups allow interested nonmembers to contact the group's owners to request membership.

7.8   Creating Your Own Google Group

Many lawyers have created a Google Group to share information with others, including other lawyers or even potential clients. To create a group, first sign into your Google Account. To create a group, follow these easy steps:

- Name your group.
- Create a group e-mail address. (A group Web address will then be created for you.)
- Write a group description (in 300 characters or less).
- Choose an Access level.
- Click the **Create my group** link.

The following are the three access levels, as described by Google:

Public: Anyone can read the archives. Anyone can join, but only members can post messages and view the members list. Only managers can create pages and upload files.

Announcement-only: Anyone can read the archives. Anyone can join, but only managers can post messages, view the members list, create pages and upload files.

Restricted: People must be invited to join the group. Only members can post messages, read the archives, view the members list, create pages and upload files. Your group and its archives do not appear in public Google search results or the directory.

Ethics Alert

Lawyers must be mindful not to create a lawyer-client relationship (or the appearance of one) via their activity in groups they own or otherwise participate in. Be certain to read the ethics rules in all of the jurisdictions in which you are licensed and include the required disclaimers to avoid this issue.

Additionally, lawyers must be mindful of inadvertently engaging in the unauthorized practice of law. One way to avoid this issue is to clearly state in which jurisdictions you are licensed to practice and in which you are willing to accept/represent clients.

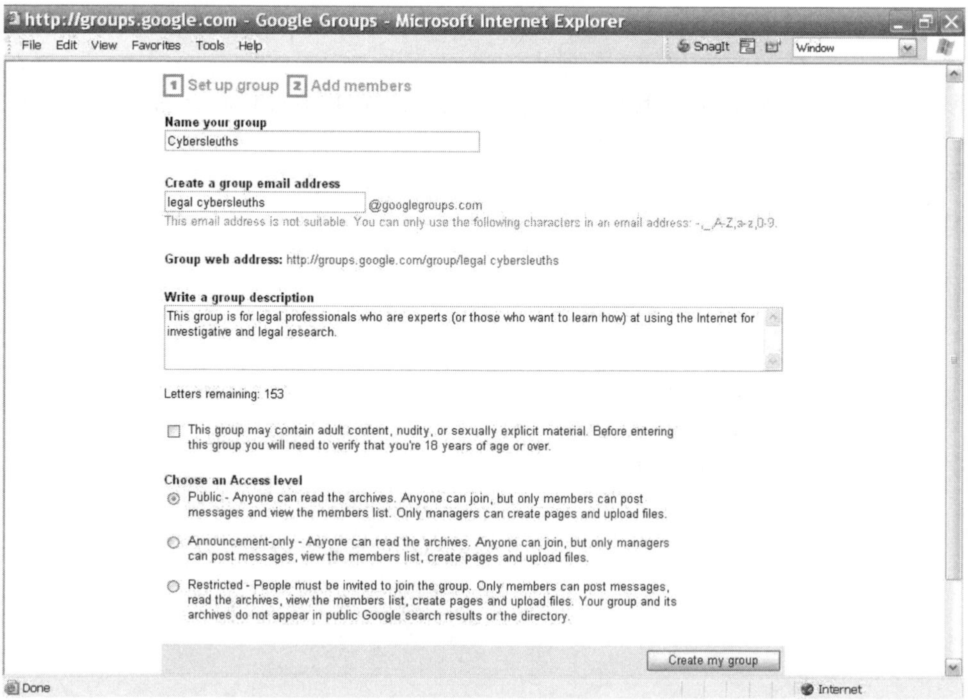

FIGURE 7.12   The Legal Cybersleuths group is open to the public.

After you create your group, the next step is to invite members.

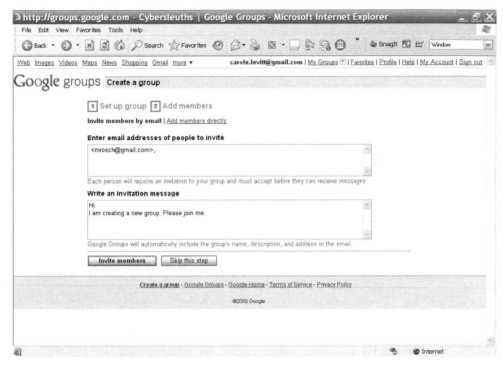

FIGURE 7.13   You can draft a customized invitation to send via e-mail to those who you would like to participate in your new group.

Once you have completed the creation of your group, click on **Visit your new group** to see how it looks.

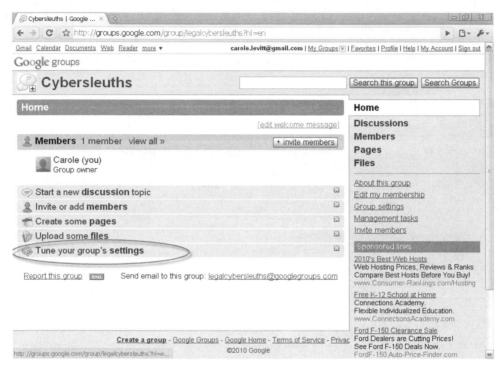

FIGURE 7.14 Now you are ready to start using your group to share information and/or to market yourself. You can change the look of your group by clicking on the **Tune your group's settings** link and selecting **Appearance.**

At this point you can do any of the following:

- **Edit welcome message and invite more members**
- **Start a new discussion topic**
- **Invite or add members**
- **Create some pages**
- **Upload some files**
- **Tune your group's settings**

Google Image Search: Locating Photos of Individuals, Products, and More

8

It's often useful to find out, in advance, what a person looks like, especially if you are investigating that person or need to identify someone you are meeting for the first time (such as a new client) at a public place. Entering the person's name into an image search engine can sometimes help you find his or her picture. In addition to finding images of people, you can also conduct an image search for places, concepts, or products by using the appropriate keywords to describe them.

8.1   How Google Images Works

To be able to return relevant images to you, Google must decipher the image by analyzing various factors about the image, such as its caption and other text information surrounding it. Google also applies algorithms to remove duplicate images and tries to display what it considers the highest-quality image first.

The Google Image Labeler is a feature to help Google improve image descriptions. While you probably don't have time to help Google, those who do are randomly paired with an online partner for two minutes to view the same images and describe them.

8.2   How to Access Google Images

Click the **Images** link on Google's home page or go directly to Google Images (http://images.google.com/) to search for images on the Internet. Once you are at the Google Images home page, you can enter your search into the **Search Images** box or you can create a more sophisticated search by clicking on the **Advanced Image Search** link to the right of the search box. The Advanced Image Search page can also be visited directly at http://images.google.com/advanced_image_search?hl=en.

8.3   Advanced Google Images Search Strategies

Five of the advanced search options found on the Advanced Image Search page are nearly identical to ones found at the Google Web Advanced Search page (the first four search boxes, which allow you to create Boolean keyword and phrase searches, are discussed in Section 4.1, and the Domain (third-to-last) search box, labeled **Return images from the site or domain**, is discussed in Section 4.3).

The other search options are unique to the Advanced Image Search and include the following:

- **Content types: Return images that contain: any content, news content, faces, photo content, clip art**, and **line drawings.**
- **Size: Return images that are: any size, medium**, and so on.
- **Exact size: Return images exactly the size:** (You would then add your width and height specifications.)
- **Aspect ratio: Return images with an aspect ratio that is:** (You would select from the drop-down menu: **Tall, Square**, etc.)
- **Filetypes: Return only image files formatted as:** (You would select from the drop-down menu: **JPG files, GIF files**, etc.)
- **Coloration: Return only images in:** (You would select from the drop-down menu: **any colors, black and white**, or **full color.**)
- **Usage Rights: Return images that are:** (You would select from the drop-down menu: **not filtered by license, labeled for reuse**, and so on.) For details about copyright issues and your right to use images found at Google Images, see http://www.google.com/support/websearch/bin/answer.py?answer=29508.

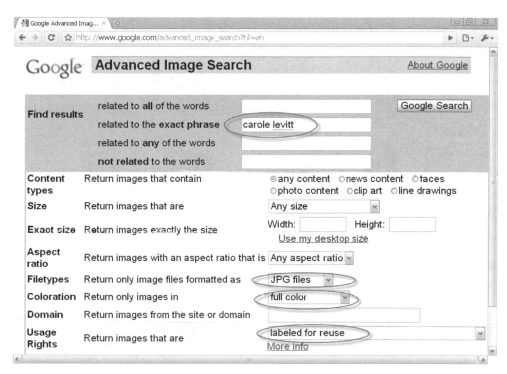

FIGURE 8.1   The Advanced Image Search page allows you to create a very narrow search. For example, you could limit your image request to a specific person, but the image would have to be a square-shaped JPG, in full color, and labeled for reuse.

8.4   Google Images Results

The results page will display thumbnails of images. Each image will be labeled (e.g., *Carole Levitt*), with the size and type of image (e.g., *217 x 147 - 59k - png*) and the source of the image (e.g., *scbar.org*). Some of the results may include images of more than one person if multiple individuals share the same name. In a personal name search, sometimes images other than a person will be displayed. For example, in our search for images of *Carole Levitt*, the image of a book cover with her name as the author is displayed, instead of an image of her.

FIGURE 8.2   In our search for images of *Carole Levitt*, in addition to images of her, the image of a book cover with her name as the author is displayed. Click on the image thumbnail to view more information about the image.

FIGURE 8.3   After clicking on one of the image thumbnails, the Web page that is the source of the image will be displayed. The page may include an article or other descriptive text about the image.

After clicking on one of the image thumbnails, notice the **See full size image** link (see Figure 8.3 just below the search box). Click on this link to view only the image, without the rest of the information from the page it derived from. You can right-click on the image to e-mail, save, or copy it (to paste the image into another document). You can even set it as your computer screen background.

On the thumbnail results page, notice the column on the left-hand side of the page, with links that allow you to limit the results by **Any size**, **Any type**, or **Any color**. For example, under **Any type**, you can select to limit your results to **Face**, **Photo**, **Clip art**, or **Line drawing**.

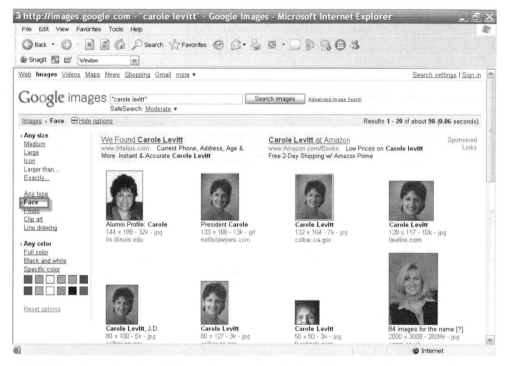

FIGURE 8.4 Choose **Face** to limit the results only to Carole's face. This removes the images of the book cover with Carole's name displayed and any other images that are not just of her face. If there are images of Carole with other people, these images will also be suppressed.

Images can also be displayed from a regular Google (Google.com) Web search by clicking on the **Show search tools** link located in the left-hand column on the results page and then selecting the **Sites with images** link, located in the left-hand column.

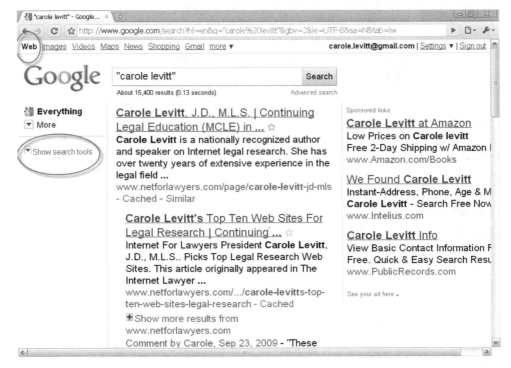

FIGURE 8.5 This is a regular **Web** search for *"carole levitt"* and from here we can change our search to find sites with images by first clicking the **Show search tools** link. See Figure 8.6 for the next step.

FIGURE 8.6 Click the **Sites with images** link to change your search results to show only sites with images.

FIGURE 8.7 If you choose to display images from a regular Google Web search, you won't have as many display options as you do when you search for images using the Google Images interface.

Google Blog Search

9

A blog (short for personal Web log) is a Web site that lists individual entries (called posts) in reverse date order. Posts can also be grouped into categories (tagged) so that posts on a particular subject can all be displayed together. Blogs also (usually) allow readers to comment back to the author/owner of the blog regarding these posts.

In part because of their chronological nature, blogs have been compared to an online diary. They are easy to create and to update. They can be educational, entertaining, or frivolous, depending on the person who set up the blog. Many lawyers have created blogs to share their opinions, publish information about current case awareness in their practice area, and other articles of interest to successfully display their expertise in their area of practice.

Because of the volume of information (both personal and professional) that people post on their blogs, they can be valuable sources of information. Blogs can be an excellent source of news (compiled from various sources by others), as well as commentary on hot topics, public opinion, or rumors regarding products or companies.

Google has created a separate search engine to locate information posted to blogs. Google's Web search results will include blogs, but to display blog-only results we use Google's Blog Search at http://blogsearch.google.com/. Google's Blog Search does a good job of keeping up with the frequently updated blogs it indexes. In test searches, we have found blog posts in Blog Search results within twenty minutes of their being posted.

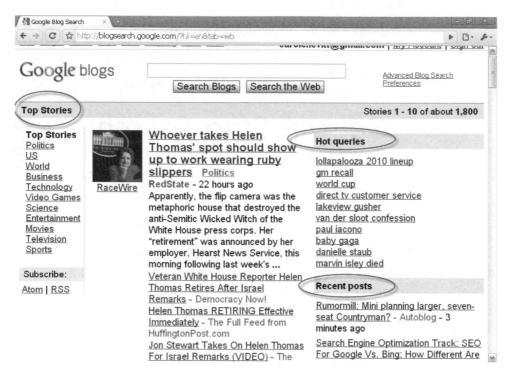

FIGURE 9.1 This is the home page of Google's Blog Search. Down the center it displays links to posts on **Top Stories**. Clicking any of the **Top Stories** links on the left displays only blog posts for that category. The **Hot queries,** on the right, link to the results of popular searches being run on Google's Blog Search. The **Recent posts** lists links to blog posts newly detected by Google's Blog Search. Note that some of these posts were located just minutes ago.

To search for information on a topic of interest, a product, or an individual, we can enter search terms into the search box on the Google Blog Search home page the same way we would on the Google Web search home page. All of the basic search strategies discussed in Chapter 3 (relating to Google Web search) are applicable to the Blog Search. One exception is the **I'm Feeling Lucky** button, which is not included in the Blog Search.

FIGURE 9.2   In this example, we have searched Google's collection of blog postings for the term *intellectual property*. Notice the links to **Related Blogs** above the results for individual blog posts. Rather than link to individual posts, those links lead to the home pages of various IP-related blogs. You can sort your results by relevance or date using the links on the right-hand side of the page. You can narrow down the time frame of your displayed results by clicking the **Last hour, Last 12 hours**, etc. links under the **Published** heading on the left-hand side of the results list. Clicking the **Choose Dates** link gives you the option of entering a date range (formatted MM/DD/YYYY).

Once you've reviewed your results, Google Blog Search also gives you options to be updated automatically about new results for your search terms. Clicking the **RSS** or **Atom** links, on the left-hand side of the search results, will generate a feed of the new results, which can be read with an RSS reader like Google Reader (see Section 9.2.1) or the customizable iGoogle page (see Section 20.3). Clicking the **Blogs Alerts** link sends you updates via e-mail. (See Section 6.2 for a detailed discussion of Alerts.)

Like all of Google's search databases, the Blog Search has an advanced search page (http://blogsearch.google.com/blogsearch/advanced_blog_search); access it by clicking the **Advanced Blog Search** link to the right of the search box on the home page. The Advanced Blog Search interface looks similar to the advanced search pages for other Google search databases (e.g., Web, Chapter 4; News, Section 6.1.4; Groups, Section 7.3).

FIGURE 9.3 Many of the search fields on the Advanced Blog Search page are self-explanatory and some are not so clear. See the next illustration for a diagram of which search fields to use to search for specific information.

FIGURE 9.4 The **Find posts with these words in the post title** option searches for your keywords only in this area marked **Post title** in the illustration. The **In blogs with these words in the blog title** option only searches for your keywords in the area marked **Post title** in this illustration. The **By Author...blogs and posts written by** option only searches for your keywords in the area marked **Author** in this illustration.

▼▼▼▼▼

SEARCH TIP: PHRASE SEARCHING

Google blogs **Advanced Blog Search**

Find posts	with **all** of the words	10 results Search Blogs
	with the **exact phrase**	
	with **at least one** of the words	
	without the words	
	with these words **in the post title**	
In blogs	with these words **in the blog title**	
	at **this URL**	
By Author	blogs and posts **written by**	mark rosch
Dates	⊙ posts written: anytime	
	○ posts written between 1 Jan 2000 and 8 Jun 2010	
Language	posts written in:	any language
SafeSearch	○ No filtering ⊙ Filter using SafeSearch	

FIGURE 9.5 Unlike a Google Web Search, multiple keywords are automatically treated as exact phrases if you type two (or more) words into Advanced Blog Search's **Find posts with these words in the post title**, **In blogs with these words in the blog title**, or **By Author...blogs and posts written by**. While these fields do recognize keywords separated by the OR Boolean connector to search for any (or all) of the terms, that is not a particularly effective search. This sample search will only return results where the author's name is Mark Rosch in that exact order.

9.1   Locate the Latest in Personal Opinion

People share a lot of information about themselves on their blogs; often this information includes their opinions about various products or services they have used, politics, or current events. Conducting keyword or topical searches can be an excellent way of "taking the pulse" of the public to gauge the opinions of many individuals. Similarly, blog searches for the names of clients

Practice Tip

Jurors

You can learn a lot about a person based on the topics they write about in their blog and the opinions they express. This information can be extremely useful in deciding which potential jurors to keep and which to challenge. This information can also be useful in predicting seated jurors' behavior/reactions to material presented at trial.

or their products that return a majority of negative opinions can be an early indicator of potential issues those clients might face. Proactive lawyers might be able to counsel those clients to keep those issues from "boiling over."

9.2   Keep Up to Date in Your Practice Area

As noted earlier, many attorneys have created blogs to publish their own articles online covering their area(s) of practice. Many of these blogs offer cogent commentary on current trends and/or decisions in their practice area(s). A targeted search can uncover a plethora of blogs on a particular topic. Reading posts on each blog will help you determine which are most trustworthy, up to date, and useful to you.

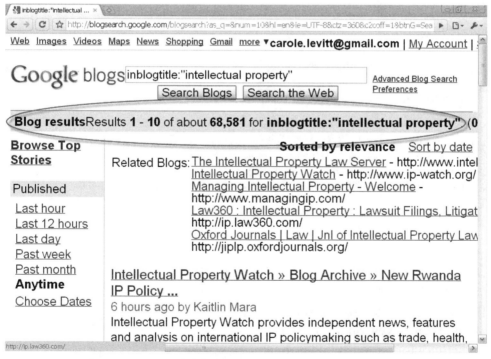

FIGURE 9.6   By searching for *intellectual property* using the **In blogs with these words in the blog title** option on the Advanced Blog Search page, we were able to generate a list of links to five **Related Blogs** and thousands of individual blog posts about intellectual property. Any practice area could be used as a keyword/phrase.

One way to keep up with the information in the useful blogs you find would be to bookmark each one and revisit them periodically to read new posts. This would be time-consuming. Almost all blogs utilize an RSS (Rich Site Summary or Really Simple Syndication) feed to send out a stream of information with summaries of new posts. Special RSS reader software is required to receive and display these RSS feeds—and Google makes one available for free.

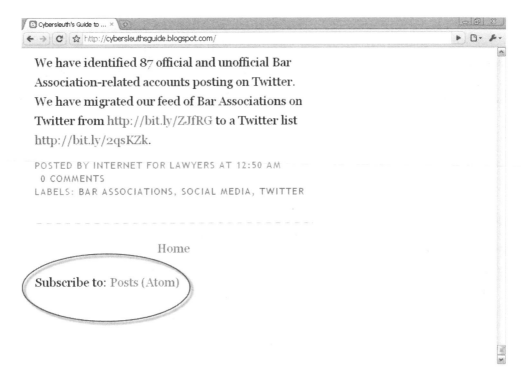

FIGURE 9.7   Here we see the link to our blog's RSS feed labeled **Subscribe to: Posts (Atom)**. (Atom is one format for RSS feeds.) Some browsers will indicate the availability of an RSS feed from a blog with an **RSS** notation in the address bar.

9.2.1 Receiving Automatic Updates from Useful Blogs You Find with Google Reader

The free Google Reader (http://www.google.com/reader) allows you to locate, subscribe, and read RSS feeds from your favorite blogs. You need a free Google Account (see Section 2.4.1) to access Google Reader.

FIGURE 9.8 Google Reader receives the RSS feeds from blogs you select and displays summaries of their recent posts in the center of the browser window. The **Subscriptions** section in the lower left-hand corner lists all of the RSS feeds you have chosen to receive. The **Recommended sources** section above **Subscriptions** are other blogs with content similar to the blogs you have subscribed to.

There are a variety of ways to locate new feeds to add to your Google Reader.

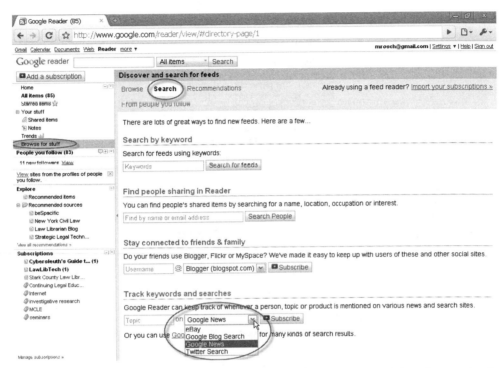

FIGURE 9.9   Clicking the **Browse for stuff** link on the left-hand side and then clicking the **Search** tab allows you to locate new RSS feeds via keyword searches. This search for *intellectual property* returned links to hundreds of individual RSS feeds on the topic. You can also use the **Track keywords and searches** section (at the bottom of the page) to continually feed **Google Blog Search**, **Google News**, or **Twitter Search** results to your Google Reader window.

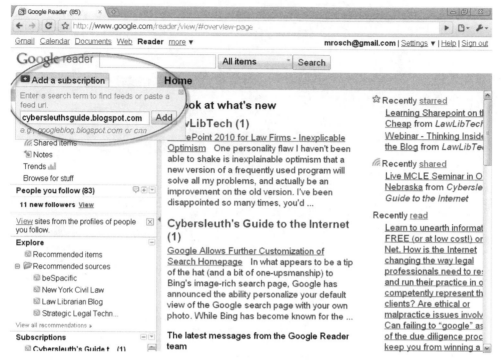

FIGURE 9.10 If you already know the URL for an RSS you would like to add to your Google Reader, you can click the **Add a subscription** button in the upper right-hand corner of the page and type the URL into the box that pops up. Clicking the **Add** button completes the process.

Google Reader lets you customize the way in which individual posts are displayed.

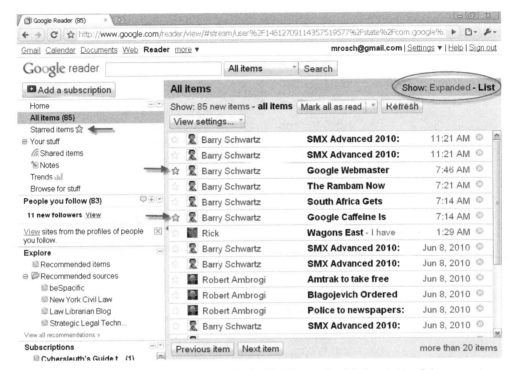

FIGURE 9.11   You can use the **Show: Expanded – List** links on the right-hand side of the screen to control the display format of the most recent posts in your Google Reader window. Here, the **List** view resembles an e-mail inbox. Similar to Google's Gmail (see Section 18.1), you can mark your favorite entries by clicking into the star to the left of any entry. (Clicking **Starred items** in the right-hand column displays only the posts you marked with the star.)

Google Reader offers a number of options to annotate, save, and share the posts you receive with others.

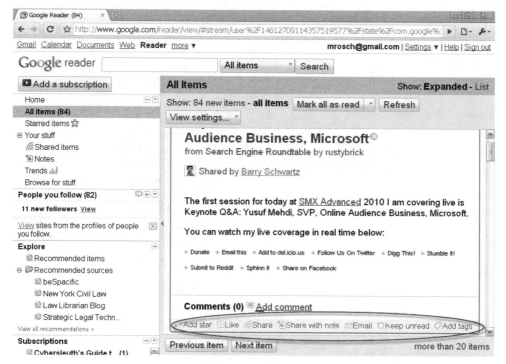

FIGURE 9.12   The **Expanded** view displays all of the posts' contents. Clicking the **Like** link informs anyone else who is also reading the same blog post in Google Reader that you like this particular post. Clicking the **Share** or **Share with note** link adds this particular post to a list of posts you can make available to other Google Readers you select. To share the post via e-mail with others who do not use Google Reader, click the **Email** link. You can also add your own descriptive keywords to make retrieving similar posts easier by clicking the **Add tags** link and typing your keywords into the box that pops up.

Google Reader also gives you a number of options for retrieving posts from your list.

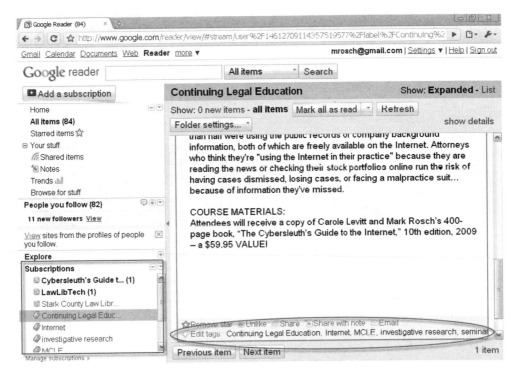

FIGURE 9.13   Using the **Add tags** link (described in the previous illustration) adds your keywords to the **Subscriptions** list in the lower left-hand corner of the Google Reader window. Clicking any of those keywords displays all of the posts you've annotated with that particular keyword. Clicking any of the blog names listed above the keywords displays only the posts from that blog.

9.3 Create Your Own Blog to Market Your Practice

Many lawyers have used their blogs to effectively market their law practices and establish themselves as knowledgeable in their particular practice areas. Google's Blogger (http://www.blogger.com) service allows anyone to create, publish, update, and host a blog for free—as long as you have a free Google Account (see Section 2.4.1).

FIGURE 9.14 Blogger.com allows anyone to easily create and maintain a blog for free.

FIGURE 9.15 The Blogger.com registration process is all form-based.

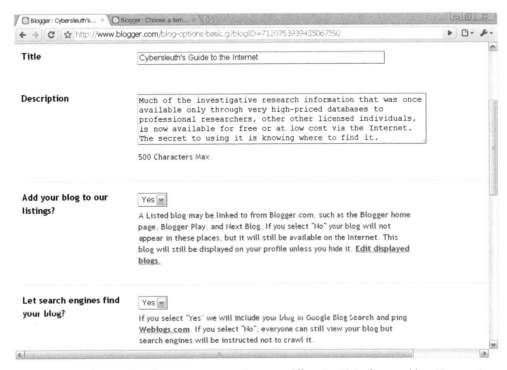

FIGURE 9.16 Blogger.com allows you to customize many different settings for your blog. Here, we're entering the **Title** and **Description** that visitors to our new blog will see. If you want to use your blog for marketing, then you'll want to be sure to answer **Yes** to the **Let search engines find your blog?** question.

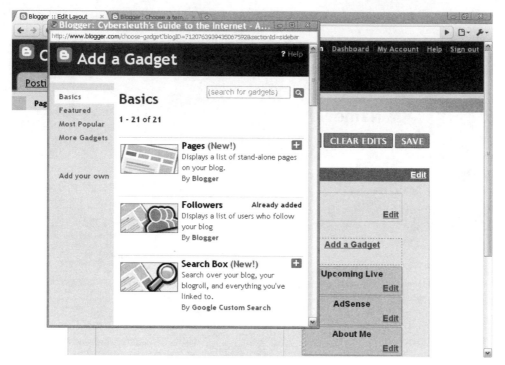

FIGURE 9.17 Blogger.com allows you to customize the layout of information on your blog. Here, we're adding a **Gadget** that automatically receives a feed of events entered into our Google Calendar and displays them in our blog. See Section 18.3 for more details about Google Calendar.

Always be sure to click the **Save Settings** button at the bottom of each page before moving on to another tab.

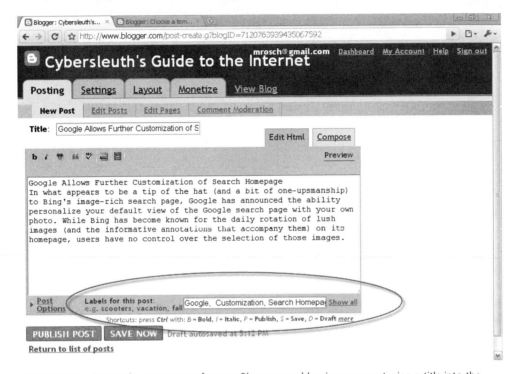

FIGURE 9.18   Composing a new post for your Blogger.com blog is as easy as typing a title into the **Title** box and the text of your post into the larger box beneath it. You can also organize your blog posts by typing categories into the **Labels for this post** box. Here, we've added the labels *Google, Customization,* and *Search Homepage.*

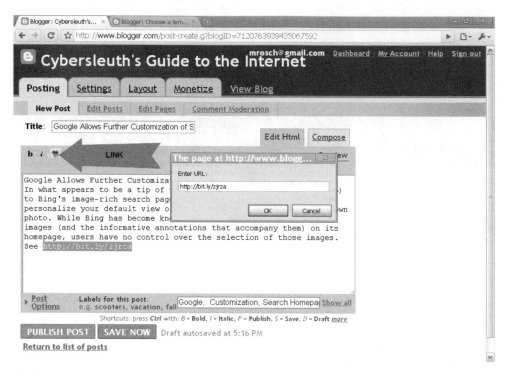

FIGURE 9.19 To add a link from our blog post to another Web site, we highlight the text that we want to be the link, click the link button, and type the Web address for the other Web site into the **Enter URL** box. Clicking the **OK** button saves this addition.

FIGURE 9.20 This is what the completed blog post would look like to a visitor. Note how all of the information we entered in the previous illustrations is integrated into the final blog.

Google Finance: Monitor Current Financial News on Public Companies and Market Trends for Due Diligence and a Competitive Intelligence Advantage

10

Google Finance provides information about stocks, mutual funds, and public companies by commingling licensed content from financial database companies with general content from the Web (primarily from Google News). Interactive charts, company searching, stock quotes, management of your own portfolio, and moderated discussion groups are also offered at Google Finance and will be discussed in this chapter.

10.1 How to Access Google Finance

To access Google Finance, click the **more** link on Google's home page and then click **Finance** (or go directly to http://www.google.com/finance).

How Lawyers Use Google Finance

As a lawyer, you probably have all sorts of reasons why you would use Google Finance. From a personal standpoint, it's an efficient way to track your own stock and mutual funds portfolio, using the My Portfolio feature discussed in this chapter. (But you'll need to be logged into your free Google Account. See Section 2.4.1 to learn how to create an account.)

From a business standpoint, it's an efficient way to conduct due diligence or track your client's business, assuming it's a public company. (Google states that Google Finance also includes private companies, but we have not found any in our test searches.) Google Finance can be useful for keeping up to date on the financial market in general and also on specific sectors in which you have clients, such as the Energy sector or the Technology sector.

By using the Trends, Related Companies, and Compare features (all discussed in this chapter), you can conduct "competitive intelligence" research for your clients to help them maintain a competitive edge over competitors.

10.2   The Anatomy of the Google Finance Home Page

The first thing you'll see on the Google Finance home page is the **Get quotes** search box (located toward the top of the page), where you can obtain a stock quote by entering either a company name or its ticker symbol. Depending on which exchange the stock is traded, stock quotes may be real-time or delayed up to twenty minutes. (See Section 10.03 for more information.)

As you scroll down the home page, you'll notice that Google Finance provides much more content than just stock quotes. Google refers to each content area of the home page as "sections."

Down the middle of the page, you can view the following sections:

- **Market summary:** As the section name implies, this is a brief, general summary of the market.
- **Top stories:** Only one tab—**Market**—is available if you're not logged into your Google Account. However, if you are logged into your Google Account, a second tab—**Portfolio related**—is available so you can view your personalized portfolio information.
- **Sector summary:** There are twelve sectors listed, such as **Energy**, **Technology**, **Services**, etc., but once you choose a sector, subcategories are then offered so you can hone in on narrower parts of a sector. For instance, after you choose **Services** a list of service subcategories, from **Advertising** to **Utilities**, is displayed.

- **Trends**
  - **Popular:** This refers to popular searches on Google. (See the more detailed explanation later in this section, labeled **Google domestic trends**.)
  - **Price:** This displays the top gainers and losers as it relates to the percent of a stock's price change compared to the prior day's official closing price.
  - **Mkt Cap:** This refers to "market capitalization" and shows the top gainers and losers as it relates to changes in absolute market capitalization compared to the prior day's official closing market capitalization.
  - **Vol:** This refers to stocks with the highest volume of shares traded.

From the right-hand column, you can view the following sections:

- **World Markets**
- **Currencies**
- **Bonds**
- **My Portfolio** (This section will only be displayed after you log into your Google Account.)

From the left-hand column, you can:

- Click on **News** to navigate to the **Top stories** section of the home page.
- Link to other services such as the following:

> **Usage Tip**
>
> **Customize the Layout**
>
> You can customize the layout of the Finance page by moving a section up or down (or even minimizing it). To move the Top Stories, Sector Summary, Trends, World Markets, Currencies, or Bonds sections, select the small drop-down arrow on the right side of that section's title bar. (After you log into your Google Account, the My Portfolio section will be also displayed and it too can be moved around the page or minimized.)

  - **Portfolios**: As noted above, you must be logged into your Google Account to create, edit, or view your portfolio.
  - **Stock screener**: As explained by Google, "Google Finance's stock screener allows you to search for stocks (currently US stocks only) by specifying a much richer set of criteria than a text search allows. For instance, if you wanted to look for bargain small-cap stocks, you could perform a search for stocks with a Market cap between 0 and $100M and a 52-week price change between −70 and −40%." (See http://www.google.com/support/finance/bin/answer.py?hl=en&answer=92883.)
  - **Google Domestic Trends:** As explained by Google, this service allows you to "track Google search traffic across specific sec-

tors of the economy. Changes in the search volume of a given sector on Google.com may provide unique economic insight. You can access individual trend indexes by clicking on the left-hand navigation. The indexes are currently calculated only for US search traffic. Note: the indexes measure relative query volume compared to the total number of searches on Google.com. Thus, an index that is decreasing does not imply that the total number of searches is decreasing; in fact the number of queries could be increasing, just not as quickly as overall search volume." (See http://www.google.com/finance/domestic_trends.)

Recent quotes, located in the left-hand column of the Google Finance home page, displays a list of stocks (and information) that you've recently viewed. To remove a stock from this list, mouse over the stock ticker symbol, and click the **X** that pops up to the right of the percent (%) column.

> **Usage Tip**
>
> **Financial Terms and Concepts Explained**
>
> For financial novices or even those just needing a refresher course in finance, we recommend a visit to Google's Finance Help page (http://www.google.com/support/finance). From explaining various financial concepts (including some financial concepts created by Google) to providing sample illustrations, the page offers invaluable help. We also recommend visiting Google's official Finance Blog (http://googlefinanceblog.blogspot.com) to learn about new features.

10.3   Stock Quotes

After entering a company name or ticker symbol into the **Get quotes** search box, the results page provides an inordinate amount of information, from the "usual" information about stocks (e.g., the opening and closing price, the volume traded, etc.) to unique interactive features, such as:

- **Watch this stock**: This feature allows you to add to your personalized portfolio any stock whose information you are viewing.
- **Compare**: This feature allows you to add one or more names of stocks into the **Compare** search box, so you can compare it to the stock you were originally viewing. (This will then alter the graph to display the comparisons.)

> **Usage Tip**
>
> **"Cross-Country" Stock Comparisons**
>
> Google Finance recently began supporting "cross-country" stock comparisons, so you can compare any public stock from one country to one or more other countries.

FIGURE 10.1 This is the top portion of the page displayed after we entered *Apple* into the **Get quotes** search box. Notice the letter **A** on the graph and the corresponding annotation labeled with the letter **A** on the right-hand side of the page ("52-Week High Companies: Microsoft Corp., Petrochina Company Ltd., Apple Inc. ..."). Clicking on the annotation to the right of the letter **A** will take you to this news story (from one hour ago).

- A graph that includes letters of the alphabet that correspond to news stories (labeled with the same letters), which might explain how certain news events affected the price of the stock on certain days.

The next portion of the page displayed after we entered *Apple* into the **Get quotes** search box (see Figure 10.2) shows you that the volume is delayed by 15 minutes, provides a list of related companies, and links to postings about Apple in several blogs and discussion groups. (To join a discussion group, you must create a Google Groups profile that contains, minimally, your name [or nickname] or

Real-Time vs. Delayed Time

It's important to keep in mind that while some stock quotes are displayed in real-time (e.g., Dow Jones Indices and the New York Stock Exchange), others could be delayed up to twenty minutes (e.g., American Stock Exchange). To learn which of the thirty exchanges delay quotes or offer them in real-time, see http://www.google.com/help/stock_disclaimer.html#realtime.

Usage Tip

a partial e-mail address and links to your most recent posts. Anonymous posting is not allowed.) (This is separate from your Google Account. See http://groups.google.com/support/bin/answer.py?hl=en&answer=46951.)

On the right-hand side of the page shown in Figure 10.2, notice the section labeled **Key stats and ratios**, which provides information such as the net profit margin and the number of employees, and also notice the section labeled **Address**, which provides the company's address and phone number.

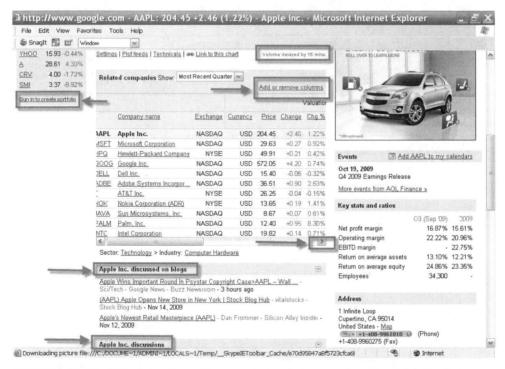

FIGURE 10.2 This is the next section of the page displayed after we entered *Apple* into the **Get quotes** search box. Notice the list of **Related companies,** with columns labeled **Company Name** through **Chg %**. There are nine more columns of information, but you will need to slide the scroll bar to the right (or click on the scroll bar's right-pointing arrow) to reveal the other columns.

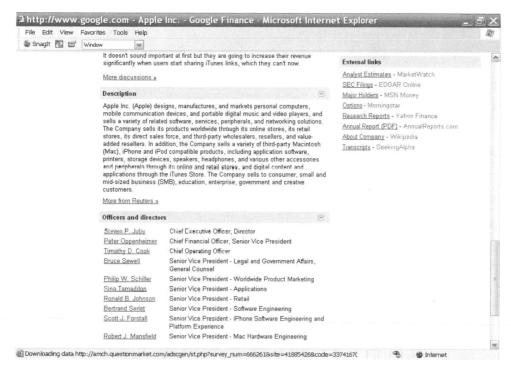

FIGURE 10.3   This is the last section of the page displayed after we entered *Apple* into the **Get quotes** search box. It provides a description of the company and a list of officers and directors. There are additional **External links,** which take you to useful documents about the company, such as **Analyst Estimates**, **SEC Filings**, and **Annual Report**.

10.4   Historical Stock Prices

Although it is not apparent from the home page, you can retrieve historical stock quotes, back to 1978 (for companies in existence that far back). This service isn't offered until after you enter a company name (or ticker symbol) into the **Get quotes** search box and retrieve a current stock quote results page, at which point a **Historical prices** link is provided on the far left-hand side of the page. After you click on this link, you must enter a date range. Both a chart and a graph will be revealed. The chart displays the **Date**, **Open**, **High**, **Low**, **Close**, and **Volume** for the stock. This information can be downloaded into an Excel spreadsheet by clicking on the **Download to spreadsheet** link (on the right-hand side of the page).

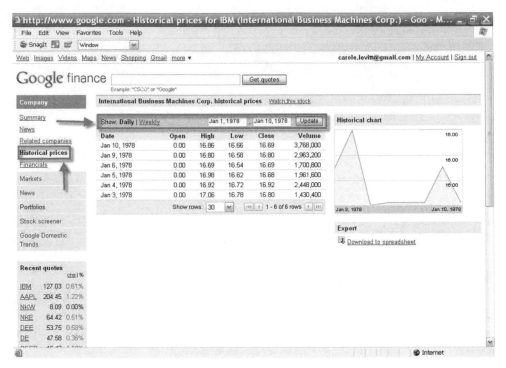

FIGURE 10.4   You can change the data in your historical stock quote chart to display a **Daily** view or a **Weekly** view.

10.5   My Portfolio

Google Finance allows you to track any stock you are interested in and to also personalize the tracking by allowing you to enter how many shares you own of a particular stock, its price, and the date of your stock transaction. To track and manage the information, you first must have a Google Account. After you have logged into your account, you can add a stock to your portfolio by selecting the **Portfolios** link (located on the left-hand column of the Finance home page) and then entering a company name or ticker symbol into the **Add Symbol** search box and clicking the **Add to portfolio** button. Another way to add a stock to your portfolio is when you are viewing your results from a Get Quotes search and clicking on the **Watch this stock** link (See Section 10.03).

When you visit your portfolio, you will first see an Overview of the portfolio. It will show you the current information about your selected stocks and will provide some links to news about your selected stocks (see next illustration).

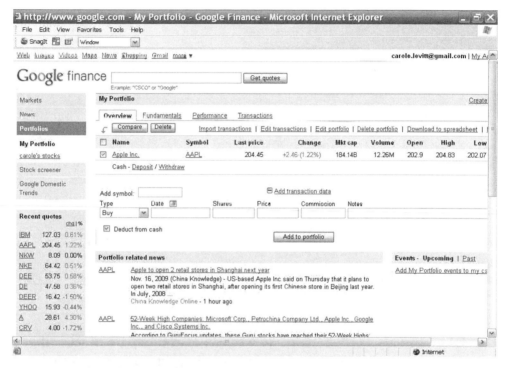

FIGURE 10.5 This is the **My Portfolio** page with the **Overview** option selected. The view can be changed to **Fundamentals**, **Performance**, or **Transactions**.

The view can be changed to:

- **Fundamentals:** Some historical information from the past year is displayed.
- **Performance:** The last price and percentage of change are displayed.
- **Transactions:** This is where you would add your personal information about your stock. (See the next illustration for details about the type of information you can enter.)

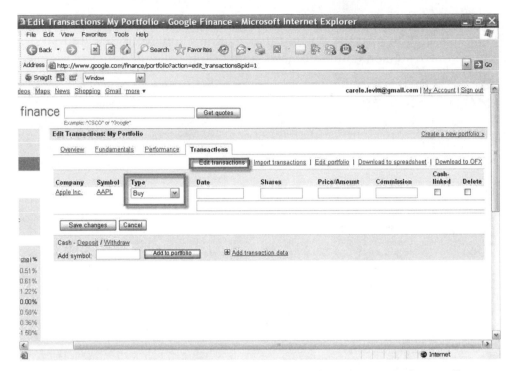

FIGURE 10.6 The **Edit transactions** menu allows you to describe your transaction by **Type** (from the drop-down menu, select **Buy**, **Sell**, **Buy to cover**, or **Sell Short**) and to add information into the following fields: **Date**, **Shares**, **Price/Amount**, **Commission**, and **Cash-linked**.

Using the My Portfolio service, you can also **Compare** stocks (if you have more than one stock in your portfolio), **Import transactions** (from an **OFX** or **CSV** file), **Edit transactions**, **Edit portfolio**, **Delete portfolio**, **Download to spreadsheet**, or **Download to OFX**.

Definition

OFX and CSV

OFX stands for Open Financial Exchange and is a format for exchanging financial information. CSV stands for Comma Separated Values and is the standard import/export format for Microsoft Excel and other applications.

Google Glossary 11

Before the easy availability of information via the Internet, the best way to get a definition for a word, phrase, or term of art you were unfamiliar with was to go to your bookshelf, pull down a specialized dictionary for the area covering your unknown word or phrase, and locate the definition. Of course, in the event that you didn't have that particular specialized dictionary, you would have to make a trip to a library that did.

All of this takes time. Google gives us a way to locate definitions from multiple sources simultaneously that takes hardly any time at all. In fact, there are two different ways to use Google as a replacement for these kinds of specialized glossaries and dictionaries. While both return definitions for the term(s) you type in, they handle the request and display those definitions differently.

The more informative of the two methods for retrieving definitions using Google is to structure the search in the following format: *define:keyword*. By doing so, you are instructing Google to return only definitions in the results list.

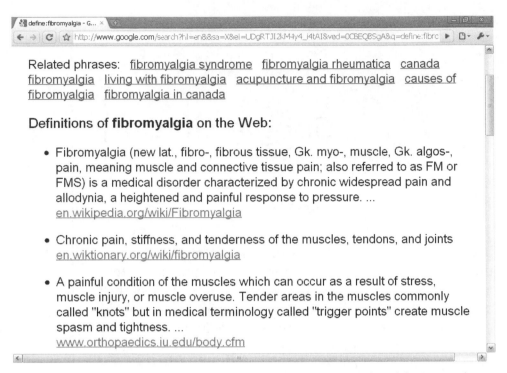

FIGURE 11.1 Pictured above are results for the search *define:Fibromyalgia*. These definitions are drawn from a variety of different types of sources, including a state government health department, a university hospital, a private rehabilitation institute, a pharmaceutical manufacturer, and Wikipedia.

The links to **Related phrases** that accompany the definitions in this search are not as useful as their label would imply. For example, clicking the **causes of fibromyalgia** link performs a new search in the format *define:causes of fibromyalgia*. The one result for that search is the same Wikipedia entry at the top of the original *define:Fibromyalgia* search. Conducting a Google Web search for the phrase *"causes of Fibromyalgia"* would yield more useful results.

The most common way we hear people use Google to retrieve definitions is to type the word *define* followed by the word they want to define. This is a less efficient and informative search than the one previously described.

FIGURE 11.2 Pictured above are results for the search *define Fibromyalgia*. This type of search retrieves one definition result that it pops up to the top of the search results list. Many of the subsequent search results also contain definitions for the term we entered (*Fibromyalgia*), but they were returned because they also contain some form of the word *define*. We have to sift through those subsequent search results to find the ones that do contain a definition of *Fibromyalgia*.

The **Definition in context** link that accompanies the **Web definitions for Fibromyalgia** result is not as useful as its label would imply. Clicking it just takes you to the Web page that contains the definition.

The more useful link is the **Web definitions for Fibromyalgia** link. Clicking that link reruns your search in the more effective format (*define:Fibromyalgia*) described earlier, displaying results like those shown in Figure 11.1.

Google Translate | 12

Google Translate is a service that translates text and Web pages into 52 languages. These languages cover 98 percent of the languages used by Internet users. What a boon for American lawyers who may not know any language but English. You can immediately understand what a document or Web page says, regardless of the language it is written in, without having to hire a translator.

12.1   How to Access Google Translate

To access Google Translate, click the **more** link on Google's home page and then click **Translate** (or go directly to http://translate.google.com).

12.2   The Anatomy of the Google Translate Home Page

On the Translate home page, you are offered three choices to begin your translation task. You can begin typing text to be translated (see Section 12.2.1); you can upload a document from your computer to be translated (see Section 12.3); or you can enter a Web site URL for a Web site to be translated (see Section 12.4).

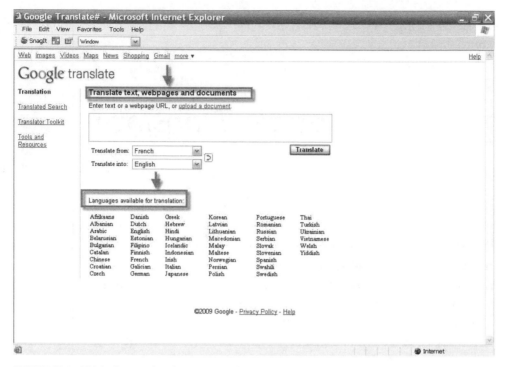

FIGURE 12.1 This is the Translate home page. Choose a translation task and then choose the languages to **Translate from** and **Translate into**. Be sure to review the available languages listed under **Languages available for translation**.

On November 16, 2009, Google launched a new look and feel for Google Translate and introduced three new features which we will discuss first (see Sections 12.2.1–12.2.3).

12.2.1 The First New Feature: Typing Text to be Translated ("Quick-and-Dirty" Document Translation "On the Fly")

Google Translate now translates text automatically as you type it. It's as close to simultaneous as you can get without the Translate feature reading your mind. Before you begin typing, choose the languages from the drop-down menus labeled **Translate from** and **Translate into**. You no longer have to click the **Translate** button. (However, if you are uploading a document or a Web page to be translated, then you will still need to click the **Translate** button as explained in Sections 12.3 and 12.4.)

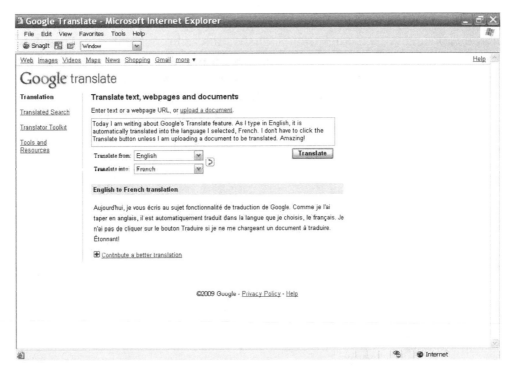

FIGURE 12.2   As I type in English, it is automatically translated into the language I selected, French. Amazing! Or, as Google Translate would say, *étonnant, surprenant stupéfiant, exceptionnel, incroyable, phenomenal, inouï, ahurissant,* and *soufflant.*

12.2.2   The Second New Feature: So What if You Can't Read the Language's Characters or Don't Have Them on Your Keyboard?

You can now read and write in any language . . . even if you can't read the language's characters. For example, if you can't read Han characters, you can click **Show romanization** to read the text phonetically in English. Currently, this works for many non-Roman languages with the exception of Hebrew, Hindi, Arabic, Yiddish, and Persian.

Even if your keyboard doesn't have Arabic, Persian, Hebrew, or Hindi characters, a new input transliteration feature (http://www.google.com/transliterate/) allows you to type the Arabic, Persian, Hebrew, or Hindi words as they sound to you and then converts them into Arabic, Persian, Hebrew, or Hindi native script.

12.2.3 The Third New Feature: Text-to-Speech

If you type a language other than English, such as French, into the **Translate text** box, and select French from the **Translate from** drop-down menu and **English** from the **Translate into** drop-down menu, you can hear the English translation by clicking the **Translate** button and then the speaker icon.

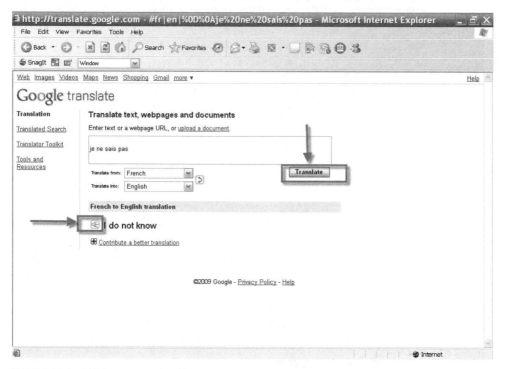

FIGURE 12.3 This is an example of how to convert from French language text to English language speech. Unfortunately, the speech portion only works for the English language. Notice the speaker icon to the left of the text translated into English. Click on it to hear the words spoken out loud.

12.3 Translate a Document from Your Computer (or Network, External Hard Drive, or Thumb Drive)

To translate a document from your computer (or network, external hard drive, or thumb drive), first simply click the **upload a document** link. Then, you can click the **Browse** button to browse through your folders to select the document to be translated.

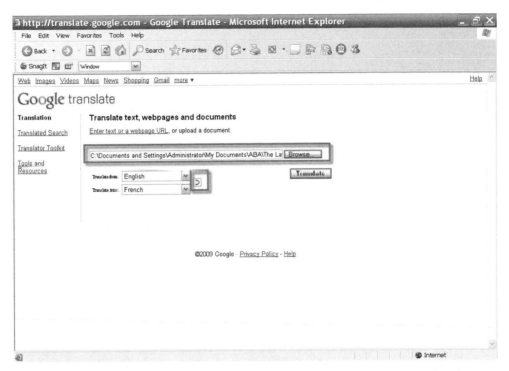

FIGURE 12.4 We selected to translate the document with the file name *C:\Documents and Settings\ Administrator\My Documents\ABA\The Lawyers Guide to Using Google\Chapter 12.doc*. Notice the curved arrow icon to the right of the language drop-down menus. If you hover over the icon, you will be offered the option to **Swap languages** (to reverse the languages currently displayed). You can also choose entirely different languages from the drop-down menu. The final step is to click the **Translate** button.

12.4 Translate a Web Site

If you need to translate an entire Web site into a particular language, enter its URL into the box located beneath **Enter text or a webpage URL, or upload a document**.

Practice Tip

You Might Still Need a Human Translator

The Google Translate feature is useful to provide you with the gist of a site created in another language, but it's no replacement for a human translator. To find a translator, you can search the Web either for a translation company or contact your local university's foreign language department.

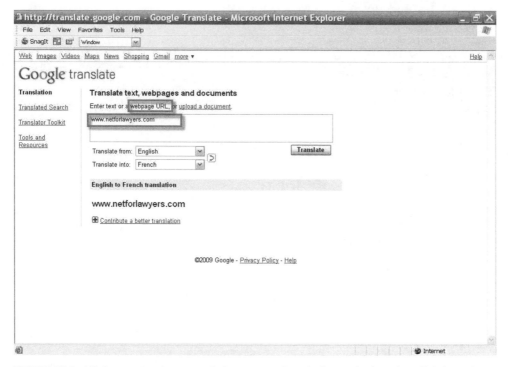

FIGURE 12.5 We have entered *www.netforlawyers.com* into the box and selected **English** from the **Translate from** drop-down menu and selected **French** from the **Translate into** drop-down menu. The next step is to click the **Translate** button.

FIGURE 12.6 Besides cutting off Mark's head from the *www.netforlawyers.com* home page and not having every single word on the page translated, Google Translate did a reasonable job. If you hover over any of the French text, a pop-up appears and displays the original English.

12.5 Translated Search: Locate Pages in Foreign Languages—While Searching in English

Translated Search is another nifty feature. Its link is located on the left-hand side of the Translate home page. It allows you to keyword search in your own language for Web pages written in a foreign language (that you specify), and then displays the results in *your* language.

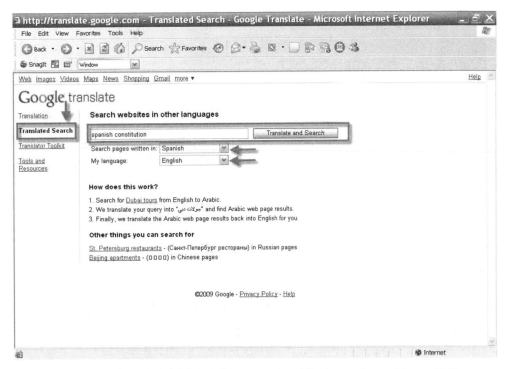

FIGURE 12.7   Using the Translated Search feature, we typed the keywords *spanish constitution* into the search box, selected **Spanish** from the drop-down menu labeled **Search pages written in**, selected **English** from the drop-down menu labeled **My language**, and then clicked on the **Translate and Search** button.

Usage Tip

Advanced Searching Not Available in the Translated Search Feature

Google's Translated Search feature does *not* support any advanced search operators, which means you cannot connect your words with the Boolean connectors OR and NOT. In addition, you cannot phrase search.

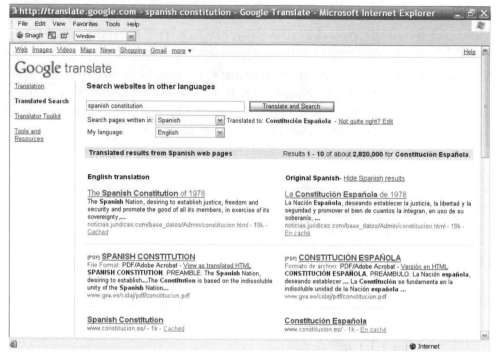

FIGURE 12.8 On the left-hand side of the page, you can view the English translations of the Web results for our search, *spanish constitution,* and on the right-hand side of the page you can choose to view the results in Spanish.

12.6 Allow Visitors to Translate Your Web Site Into Another Language "On the Fly"

Select **Tools and Resources** from the left-hand side of the Translate home page to make a translation of your Web site available in the browser of someone visiting your site. The foreign language translation of your Web site only appears "on the fly"—when a visitor visits your English-language site and deploys the banner on your site informing them of the ability to translate the site. (See the Usage and Practice Tip below, titled "How a Potential Client Will Find Your Translated Site," for an explanation about the banner and how the foreign-language site is actually created.)

Extend the Reach of Your Practice to Foreign-Language Speakers

Practice Tip

Do you speak a second or multiple languages? Would you like to offer your legal services to those who speak that language? Why not translate your site into that language by embedding a Web site translator into your site? Make sure that whoever speaks the foreign language in your office reviews the machine-generated Google translation of your site. If there are any issues, you may need to revise wording in your English-language site. You cannot revise the foreign-language translation because the foreign-language site only appears "on the fly."

But see Section 12.8 to learn how the Translator Toolkit's advanced tools could help you translate the content of your English-language site into another language by allowing you (or a professional translator) to edit the machine-translated content if you wanted to launch a separate translated site.

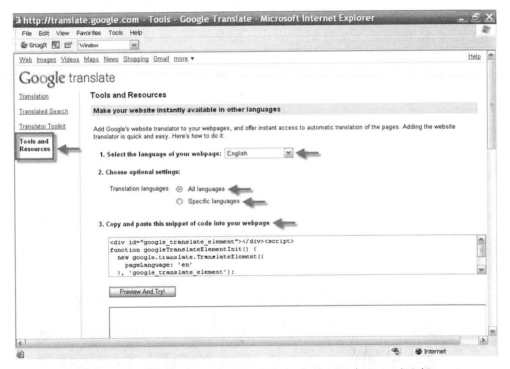

FIGURE 12.9   To allow visitors to translate your site into another language, select your site's language, choose one or more languages to translate the site into by clicking into the **Specific languages** button or the **All languages** button. Finally, copy and paste the snippet of code (shown in the box labeled as number **3**) into your Web site (this is something you will need to ask your Web manager to do, unless you are the Web manager). This will embed a Web site translator into your site.

Usage and Practice Tip

How a Potential Client Will Find Your Translated Site

Unfortunately, the translated version of your Web site will not be indexed by search engines. However, a potential client will know you have a translated Web site if they land on your English-language site and their browser interface language is different from the language found on your site. At that point, a banner at the top of the page will be displayed for them to click. If you have selected **All languages,** they will probably be able to view the site in their language, but we recommend you only select the language(s) in which you can offer legal services.

12.7   Word Translator: Translate from English to Your Language, One Word at a Time

To translate English words in a Web page, one word at a time, you can create a shortcut by adding a **Translate** button to your Google toolbar (see Section 20.1 to learn how to install the toolbar).

Once you have installed the toolbar, begin the process of adding the **Translate** button by clicking on the **Adjust Toolbar Options** icon (it looks like a wrench).

FIGURE 12.10   Click on the **Adjust Toolbar Options** wrench icon to add the **Translate** button to the toolbar (and to set up the WordTranslator feature).

After the **Translate** button has been added to the toolbar, the **Toolbar Options** menu will appear. See the next image to learn about several more steps you must take to set up the WordTranslator feature.

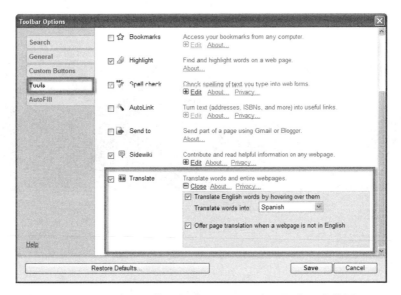

FIGURE 12.11   From the **Toolbar Options** menu, select **Tools** and click into the box to the left of the word **Translate**. Then, click on the plus sign to the left of **Edit**. A drop-down menu will appear from which you can select the language (e.g., **Spanish**) you want English words translated into.

You can turn the WordTranslator feature on by selecting the down arrow next to the **Translate** button and clicking into the **WordTranslator** box (this will add a check mark to the box).

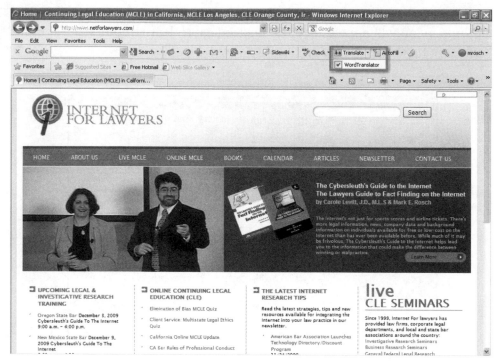

FIGURE 12.12   The WordTranslator feature is turned on in this image as indicated by the check mark shown in the box, but to turn the WordTranslator feature off, select the down arrow next to the **Translate** button and click into the **WordTranslator** box again, which will uncheck the feature.

Once your WordTranslator feature is turned on, the WordTranslator pop-up bubble will display the translation (in your chosen language) of any single English word you hover over.

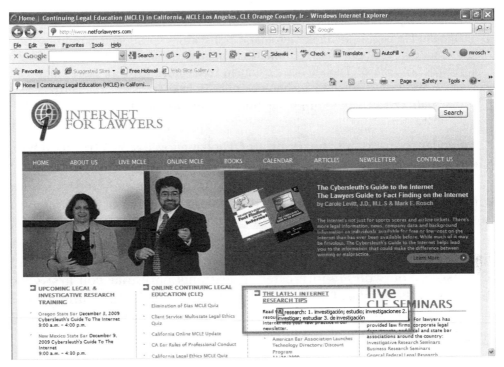

FIGURE 12.13 Notice when you hover over the word *Research*, the WordTranslator pop-up bubble displays several possible Spanish translations for the word.

12.8 Translator Toolkit

You can access a variety of advanced translating tools by selecting **Translator Toolkit** from the left-hand side of the Translate home page. You will then see a list of tools displayed:

- **Correct automatic translations in an easy-to-use editor.**
- **Search past translations to find words for new translations.**
- **Publish translations to Wikipedia or Knol.**
- **Collaborate with other translators.**
- **Use advanced tools like translation memories and multilingual glossaries.**

However, you will not be able to access these tools unless you log into your Google Account. (See Section 2.4.1 to learn how to create an account.)

Google explains how Translator Toolkit is different from Google Translate:

> Google Translate provides 'automatic translations' produced purely by technology, without intervention from human translators. In contrast, Google Translator Toolkit allows human translators to work faster and more accurately, aided by technologies like Google Translate. (See http://translate.google.com/support/toolkit/bin/answer.py?hl=en&answer=147809.)

Similar to Translate, the Translator Toolkit allows you to translate Web pages or documents from one language to another.

The Translator Toolkit stores these translations online and allows you to share these documents and collaborate with others similar to Google Docs (see Section 18.2). Because Translator Toolkit is geared to advanced translation users and probably will not be used by most lawyers, we won't go into detail about the tools, but we recommend to those of you who are interested in learning more that you first view the video about the Translator Toolkit at http://www.youtube.com/watch?v=C7W2NJFdoIg and review the help screens at http://translate.google.com/support/toolkit/bin/topic.py?topic=22236.

Practice Tip

Creating a "Permanent" Foreign-Language Site in Addition to Your English-Language Site to Attract Clients Who Speak That Language

If you really want to create a "permanent" foreign-language Web site and not rely upon the "on the fly" method discussed in Section 12.6 (which merely embeds a Web site translator into your English-language site), then you might want to explore the Translator Toolkit. Its advanced tools allow you (or a professional translator) to edit the machine-translated content of your English-language site to ensure that the translation is correct before you launch your new foreign-language Web site. You can then post this translated version of your site on the Web (in addition to your English-language site).

Unlike the "on the fly" version of your translated Web site, this separate foreign language Web site can be indexed by search engines (as long as you submit it for indexing, which you can do at http://www.google.com/addurl/?continue=/addurl).

Google Books: Quickly Locate Useful Books, Magazines, and Legal Treatises, Statutes, Opinions, and Legislative Histories

13

Google Books is a project launched by Google to scan books and magazines and then post them on the Web in a full-text searchable format (for free). As of October 2009, the full text of ten million books has been made available at Google Books. (Not all books are full-text. See Sections 13.4 and 13.5 for information about portions of additional books being made available at Google Books.) The books are in English and other languages.

Google explains the purpose for Google Books this way: "The aim of Google Books is to help you discover books and assist you with buying them or finding a copy at a local library." (See http://books.google.com/support/bin/answer.py?hl=en& answer=43729.)

Many of you might have heard of Google Books because of the copyright controversy and the ensuing class action lawsuit filed against Google. *The Authors Guild. v. Google Inc.*, Case No. 05 CV 8136 (S.D.N.Y.). On November 19, 2009, Google reported that the court granted preliminary approval of an amended settlement with authors and publishers (see http://www.googlebooksettlement.com/).

13.1   Where Does Google Books Acquire Books From?

There are two ways a book becomes part of Google Books.

- The first way is through Google's "Partner Program" (over 20,000 partners), in which authors and publishers decide how much of the book can be viewed. This could range from a few sample pages *to the entire book*.

- The second way is through Google's "Library Project," in which Google scans books from participating libraries and uploads them to Google Books. Some of the books are in the public domain (e.g., the copyright has expired or there has never been a copyright because the book is a government document). You can view the entire book online or download it to read offline. For books from participating libraries that are still under copyright and for which the publisher or author declines to be part of the Partner Program, the Google Books search result for those books display only basic bibliographic information (and possibly a few "snippets" to show a few sentences that include your keywords in context).

Privacy Tip

Is Google Tracking the Books You View at Google Books?

According to Google,

[to] protect copyrighted books, we only allow Google Books users to view a limited portion of the book we present. Enforcing these limits requires us to keep track of our users' page views. Before you log in, we don't associate your searches or the pages you view with any personally identifiable information about you, such as your name and address. Once you log in, however, to enforce limits on user page views, we do connect some information—your Google Account name—with the books and pages that you've viewed. As always, we strongly encourage you to read our Privacy Policy to be fully informed about how your confidentiality is protected. (See http://books. google.com/googlebooks/common. html - item 11.)

13.2   How to Access Google Books

You can access Google Books by clicking the **more** link on Google's home page and then clicking **Books** (or go directly to http://books.google. com/). There is also an Advanced Book Search (http://books.google.com/ advanced_book_search). For a list of scanned magazines currently available through Google Books, see http://tinyurl.com/googlemagazines. The titles range from the popular *Life Magazine* to the more esoteric *Timber Home Living* magazine.

It's Better to Be Logged Into Your Google Account When Searching Google Books (Or Is It?)

Because Google makes some pages of books available *only* after you log into your Google Account, if you want to see as many pages as possible, it's better to be logged into your Google Account when searching Books. But see the Privacy Tip in Section 13.1.

13.3   Advanced Book Search

The Advanced Book Search helps you search as narrowly or as broadly as you choose. The first four search boxes are very similar to those found on the regular Google Advanced Search page described in Section 4.1. For example, in the image below, we entered the keywords *california real property records* into the **with all of the words** search box, the phrase *los angeles* into the **with the exact phrase** search box, and the keyword *lane* into the **without the words** search box to exclude an author whose last name is Lane. We also selected *English* from the **Language Return pages written in** box.

You can also limit your search by entering information into one (or multiple) fields, such as **Title**, **Author**, **Publisher**, **Subject**, **Publication Date**, **ISBN (International Standard Book Number)**, or **ISSN (International Standard Serial Number)**. You can search only books or only magazines or both by clicking into the radio buttons labeled **All content**, **Books**, or **Magazines** adjacent to the **Content** search option.

Locate Books (and Magazine Articles) Authored by Expert Witnesses

You can search Google Books by author name to locate books or articles authored by your expert witness or the opposition's. Use the keyword search or the subject search to find potential expert witnesses with a certain expertise.

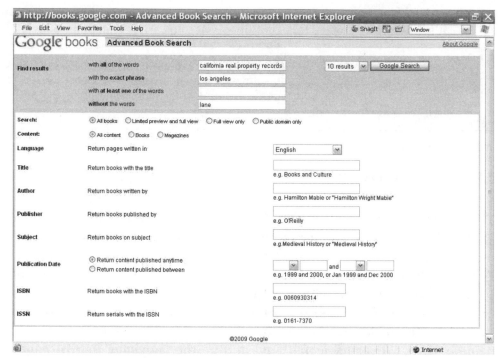

FIGURE 13.1 In the Advanced Book Search, you can also limit your search to **All books**, **Limited preview and full view**, **Full view only**, or **Public domain only**. The **Public domain only** books no longer have copyright protection (or never did—e.g., government documents), so they are displayed in full. Limiting a search to **Full view only** will often bring you back the same results as **Public domain only**.

13.4   Book Search Results

The types of books, the publication years, and the amount of displayed content will vary greatly in a Book Search results list as you can see in the image following this paragraph. The list of results ranges from a **Limited preview** of a 2006 A.B.A. book, *The Lawyer's Guide to Fact Finding on the Internet,* by Levitt and Rosch; a **Snippet view** of a 1978 CCH volume of *U.S. Tax Cases*; a **Limited preview** of a 2009 Nolo book, *How to probate an estate in California;* to a **Full view** of a 1910 volume of West's Pacific Reporter (containing individual court opinions). Some book results may indicate **No preview available**, in which case you will only be provided with bibliographic information. This could happen because the publisher or author of a book still under copyright is not a Google Books partner.

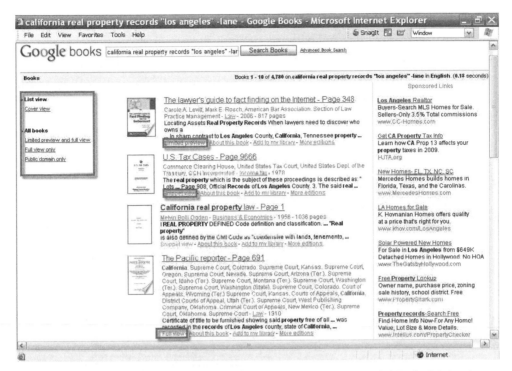

FIGURE 13.2 If you want to view only book covers, click on the **Cover view** link in the left-hand column on the results list page. If you conducted an **All books** search, but now want to narrow your search, select one of these options from the left-hand column on the results list page: **Limited preview and full view**, **Full view only**, or **Public domain only**.

After your search results list is displayed, you can click on any of the book title links to view the exact page where your keywords can be found (see Section 13.5 for further tips on navigating through a book) or you can click on the **About this book** link (see Section 13.6).

FIGURE 13.3 Notice that if you click the book title's link, you will be taken directly to page 348 of the book, but if you click **About this book**, you will be taken to an informational page about the book, not to the actual book.

13.5 How to Navigate Through a Book Result

After you have clicked on a specific book title link, you are presented with the exact page where your keywords can be found. To go to other result pages that contain your keywords, click the **Next** or the **Previous** links (see the next image).

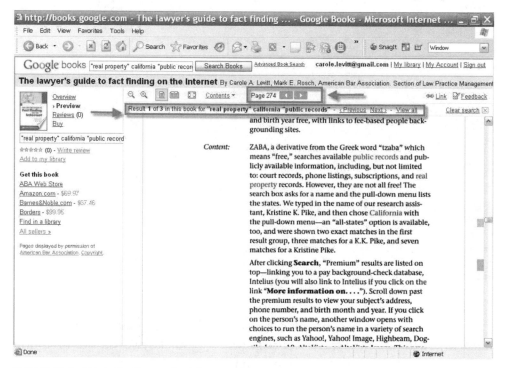

FIGURE 13.4 This is the first result of three results containing your keywords. If you want to continue to read this book in page order instead of reading only result pages containing your keywords, click the right-pointing arrow to go to the next page or the left-pointing arrow to go to the previous page.

The **View all** link in the prior image is misleading because it does not show you the entire book; instead, it shows you a list of snippets of all your search results.

Usage Tip

Why Can't You View the Next or Previous Page?

If you are viewing pages of a limited preview book, such as *The Lawyer's Guide to Fact Finding on the Internet*, you may not be able to actually go to the very next or previous page because, as the label indicates, you only get a limited preview of the book. For instance, when we were viewing page 71 of *The Lawyer's Guide to Fact Finding on the Internet*, we clicked on the right-pointing arrow to go to the next page, but received a message informing us that "Pages 72–162 are not part of this book preview."

To jump to another chapter of the book, click the **Contents** link (in the prior image) for a drop-down menu, which will display the book's table of contents, with hyperlinks to each available chapter.

Usage Tip

Google Books Is Not a Comprehensive Search of All Books

You might miss an important result if your keywords are contained only in the pages that are **not** part of the book preview of a limited preview book.

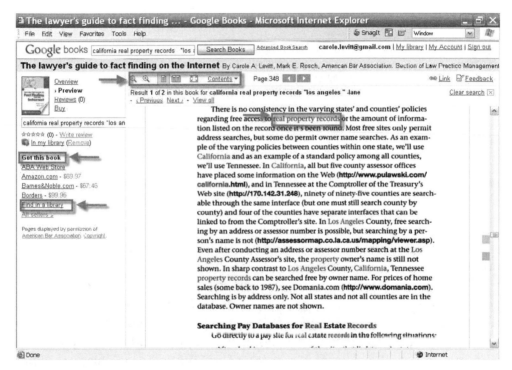

FIGURE 13.5   This is an image of the limited preview of *The Lawyer's Guide to Fact Finding on the Internet*. Our keywords are shaded in light yellow. To the left of the page number are icons. They can be used to decrease or magnify the text or change the view from one-page to either a two-page view or to a full-screen view. (A full-screen view differs from a one-page view by eliminating all the navigational links on the left-hand column of the Web page so you see only the book page.)

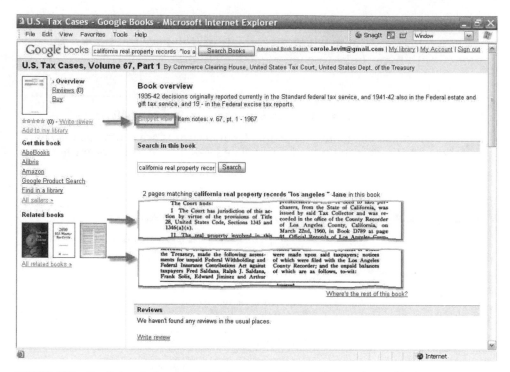

FIGURE 13.6 The **Snippet view** of a 1967 Commerce Clearing House volume of *U.S. Tax Cases* displays only a bit of text surrounding our keywords (shaded in light yellow) and not even the full page.

The public domain books and the full view books offer you features not available in limited preview books, such as the ability to download the entire book as a **PDF** or an **EPUB**, convert the book to **Plain text** (useful for copying and pasting the text into another document or e-mail, etc.), **Clip** (create a snippet to share), and create a **Link** to the book (this allows you to create a link to the entire book, not just a snippet, and to then paste the link into an e-mail or Instant Message). (The **Link** feature is also available when a limited preview book is displayed.)

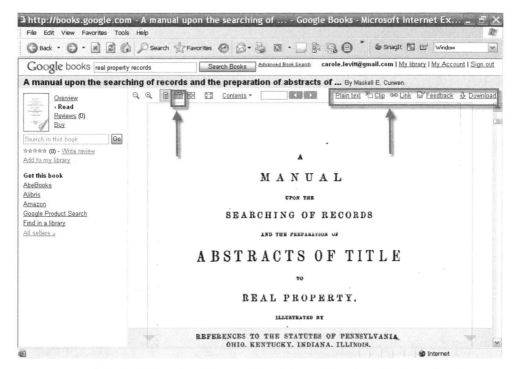

FIGURE 13.7 This is the display of a public domain book in Google Books' collection. Unlike the limited preview book, you can also view two pages of a public domain book at a time, just as you would if you had the physical book in your hands, by clicking the icon showing two pages side by side. See the next image to learn what happens when you click the **Clip** link.

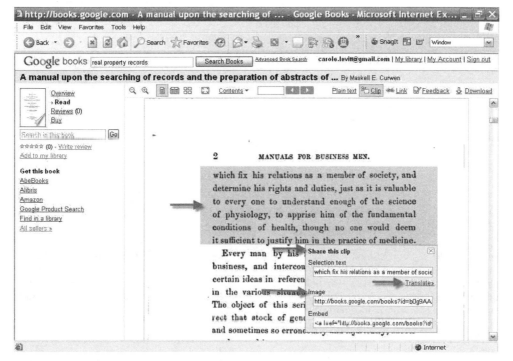

FIGURE 13.8 When you click the **Clip** link, you can create a snippet of any text by drawing a box around the text. A pop-up menu is then displayed with a box labeled **Image**, which provides a URL for just that snippet. You can copy the URL and paste it into an e-mail. The recipient would then be able to copy the URL and paste it into Google's address box to view the snippet. Notice that there is also a **Translate** link to translate the snippet into a different language.

13.6   About This Book, Search Within This Book, and Other Features

Instead of clicking the book title link from the results page, you can click **About this book**, which is located underneath the annotation of the book (*See Figure 13.2*). This presents you with the **Search in this book** feature, which allows you to conduct more keyword or phrase searches, within just this one book. Besides allowing you to search in the book, the About This Book page provides links to **Reviews** (we aren't convinced this feature works very well, as we know there are reviews of *The Lawyer's Guide to Fact Finding on the Internet,* yet they are not displayed). The **About This Book** page also includes other useful information about your book (See Figure 13.9).

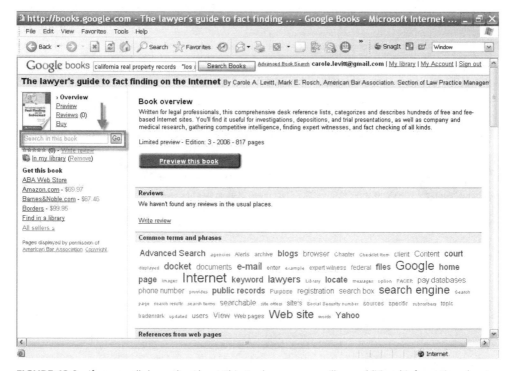

FIGURE 13.9   If you scroll down the About This Book page, you will see additional information about your book selection, such as **Common terms and phrases** (used in the book), **References from web pages** (about the book you selected), **Selected pages** (thumbnails of your book), **Places mentioned in this book** (pinpointed in a map), **Popular passages**, **Contents** (your book's Table of Contents), **Other editions**, and **More book information** (bibliographic information).

13.7 How to Purchase a Book You Find at Google Books or Locate a Library That Owns the Book

Whether you are viewing a page from a book or you are viewing an About This Book page, links to **Get this book** (purchase) and **Find in a library** are displayed in the left-hand column of the Web page. For an illustration of these links, see Figure 13.5. Selecting **Find in a library** will link you to your selected book's entry in WorldCat.org. (WorldCat.org, at http://www.worldcat.org/oclc, lets you search the online card catalogs of thousands of libraries around the world.) The entry will display a list of the libraries, beginning with the library closest to your location, that own your selected book (you can change your location if you prefer another location).

13.8 My Library

If you are logged into your Google Account, you will be able to add books to your own "personalized" library by clicking the **Add to my library** link (located to the right of the **About this book** link). The benefit of adding books to your library is fourfold: (1) to quickly return to the list of books you placed in your library, without rerunning your search; (2) to add notes, labels, and reviews about the books in your library; (3) to keyword search through books only in your library by clicking the radio button labeled **Search "[user name's] library,"**; and (4) to share your list of books with friends or colleagues by sending them your **My library** URL. (See Figure 13.11 for an illustration of Carole Levitt's library.)

Privacy Tip

My Library

Books in your My Library list, along with the notes, labels, and reviews you have added, are all "publicly available" according to Google and might be displayed when a searcher clicks **About this book**. However, in our test search, we did not find that the notes or labels that Carole had added to one of the books in her My Library list had become publicly available. But a review that Carole wrote about **The Lawyer's Guide to Microsoft Outlook** was displayed when we searched that book title in Google Books. Also, Carole's public Google Profile (see Section 2.4.2) is displayed if the searcher clicks on her name (which is displayed above the review).

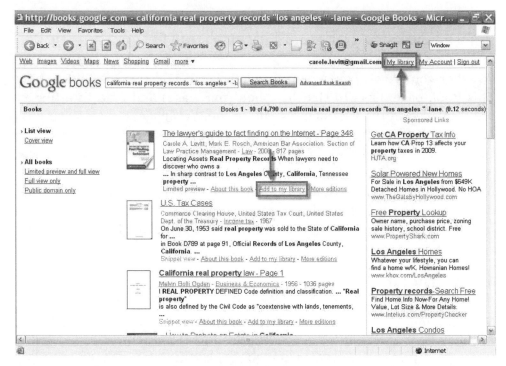

FIGURE 13.10 If you click the **Add to my library** link, the book you are currently viewing will be added to your list of books; this is akin to creating favorites in your browser. You access your personalized library by first logging into your Google Account, visiting the Google Books home page, and then clicking **My library** (located at the top right-hand side of the page).

FIGURE 13.11 Carole's **My library** list contains only two books so far. Beneath each book title are links that provide the following options: **Edit note**, **Write review**, **Add labels**, and **Remove book**. The **Edit note** option seems to be the most useful option. Using the **Edit note** option, Carole appended a note to *The Lawyer's Guide to Fact Finding on the Internet* stating that we are in the midst of updating the book and that it will be issued in several shorter volumes. Carole also added a label to the book (*Investigative research*). In the address bar, notice that Carole's **My library** has been assigned a URL so she can share her list of books with friends or colleagues.

You Have Reached a Page That Was Unavailable for Viewing or You Have Reached Your Viewing Limit

When Carole visited her My Library and conducted a keyword search of a limited preview book she had placed in her library, she limited the keyword search to **Search "[user name's] library"** and was informed that she had reached a page that was unavailable for viewing or that she had reached her "viewing limit" for this book. While you might receive this message with a limited preview book, you shouldn't have the same issue with a full view or public domain book. For more information about "viewing limit" and privacy issues, see the Privacy Tip in Section 13.1.

Google Maps | **14**

Whether lawyers are traveling to an unfamiliar courthouse for a hearing, or an unfamiliar office to take a deposition or meet a new client, Google Maps (http://maps.google.com) can make the travel easier. The free service provides directions, can show you what the building looks like, where it's situated on the block, and nearby landmarks. Google Maps can even help you find lodgings and restaurants in an unfamiliar town.

Google Maps allows you to search nearly any U.S. address and retrieve an aerial view of that location. You can also search for a business name coupled with a city (e.g., *Palmer House Hotel Chicago*) or a type of business coupled with a general location (e.g., *pizza 48th and 8th New York*).

Its maps are built through a combination of satellite imagery and on-the-ground photography. Maps can also include notations of points of interest in the area mapped (e.g., the legend *The Late Show with David Letterman* marks the location of the Ed Sullivan Theater on Broadway in the New York pizza search example above), public transportation routes and stations, or live traffic data, among other options.

The images used in the search results' aerial views are not real-time; in fact, they may be anywhere from "one to three years old," according to Google. Using images of houses we are familiar with, we've been able to determine that some photos are as old as four years based on the inclusion/exclusion of certain landscaping features, etc. (The images for that particular address have recently been updated, though.) Other images we've tested have been updated within the three-year time frame Google describes.

Google Maps has information for more than 218 countries, including:

- Australia
- Austria
- Belgium
- Brazil
- Canada
- China
- Czech Republic
- Denmark
- Finland
- France
- Germany
- Italy
- Japan

- Lichtenstein
- Netherlands
- New Zealand
- Norway
- Poland
- Russia
- Spain
- Sweden
- Switzerland
- Taiwan
- Thailand
- United Kingdom

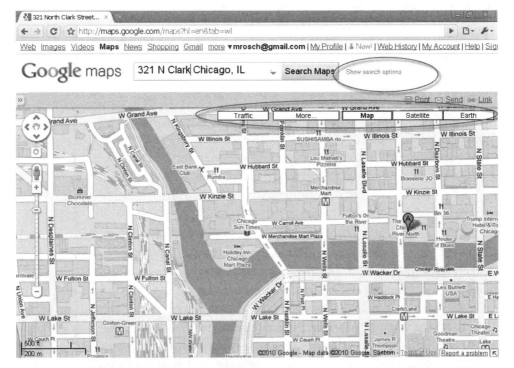

FIGURE 14.1 Google Maps displays a traditional, roadmap-like view of the area surrounding the address for which we searched. A "pin" (labeled **A**) marks our target address. We can add additional data to the map using the buttons in the upper right-hand corner of the map. Also note the **Show search options** to the right of the **Search Maps** button—it will be discussed in greater detail in Figure 14.3.

Use the slider on the left-hand side of the map results display to zoom in or out of your map.

Click the hand icon in the upper left-hand corner of the displayed map result and then place your cursor on the map, click and hold your left mouse button, and drag your mouse to drag the map around in the display window. You can also navigate to the North, South, East, or West using the arrow buttons that surround the hand icon.

There are a number of ways to add additional data to your Google Maps search results.

FIGURE 14.2 Clicking the chevrons (<<) on the left-hand side of the map opens a new information pane containing links to more information about the subject of our search on the left-hand side of the screen. Most of the links (**Directions**, **Search nearby**, and **Save to...**) are descriptive enough as to be self-explanatory. Some are not descriptive/self-explanatory, such as the **more** link. Clicking that link provides a drop-down menu where you can select **Zoom here**, **Street View** (see Figure 14.8), **Send** (see Figure 14.10), or **Move marker**. Clicking the **Street View** link displays a street-level image of the address in your search. You can click on arrows in the Street View images to navigate up/down the street (in successive images); you can left-click your mouse and rotate your mouse to virtually turn around within the image; or you can double-click to zoom into a portion of the image.

You can use the **Save to...** link to save maps you use frequently, or to create your own annotated maps using the **My Maps** link. (Both of these features require a Google Account and profile as discussed in Section 2.4.1 and 2.4.2.)

Clicking the **Show search options** link (circled in Figure 14.1) next to the search box gives you a drop-down menu (circled in Figure 14.3) from which you can choose different types of information to add to your map results.

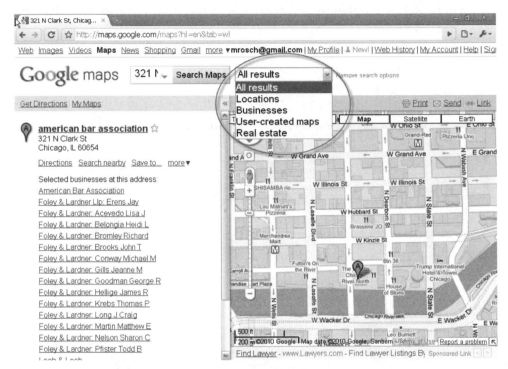

FIGURE 14.3 Selecting **Businesses** from the **Show search options** drop-down menu displays a list of businesses at and near the address of your search (in the left-hand information pane). The **Real estate** option pinpoints the locations of real estate for sale, rent, or in foreclosure on the map and adds additional information and links in the left-hand information pane. We have found the **Related maps** and **Mapped web pages** options less than informative. Also, the **User-created content** option displays less content than the photos, videos, etc. displayed when using the **More...** button discussed later in this introduction.

The **Satellite** button is probably the most popular option for customizing Google Maps search results. Clicking it overlays satellite photographic imagery of the area. You can then use the slider on the left-hand side of the map to zoom in and out.

FIGURE 14.4 This is the Google Maps search result for *321 N. Clark Chicago* (as seen in the previous illustration) with satellite photo imagery added by clicking the **Satellite** button. The button also gives us the option of checking the **Show labels** box, which adds the names of streets, points of interest (e.g., hotels, restaurants, shops), highways, and public transportation stations. These labels are also illustrated here.

The **Traffic** button overlays color-coded traffic data for the major streets/highways displayed on your map. Green indicates fast-moving traffic, yellow indicates slower-moving traffic, red indicates still slower traffic, and dashed red and black indicates the slowest (probably stopped) traffic.

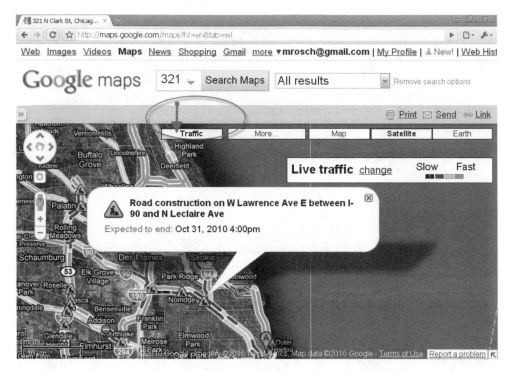

FIGURE 14.5   In this illustration, we've clicked the **Traffic** button to add **Live traffic** data to our map of results for *321 N. Clark Chicago*. We could also choose to add predictive **Traffic at day and time** by selecting a day of the week from the drop-down menu (at the right) and a time of day from the slider below it. "Data is predicted based on past conditions."

The **Traffic** button also overlays major road construction information onto the map results. In the above illustration, we were able to click on the red-and-white caution sign on Interstate 90/94 to open the information bubble (seen on the left-hand side of the illustration above) regarding the six-month-long construction project scheduled for that stretch of highway.

Just about every Google application, database, or feature has a drop-down menu (or two) with a vague label like **More...**, and Maps is no exception. In Maps, the **More...** button allows you to add more layers of information to the map by checking the associated boxes.

> **Practice Tip**
>
> The **Traffic at day and time** function of Google Maps could be useful in determining how long it will take to get through a particular stretch of road(s) if you're traveling to an unfamiliar area for a deposition or hearing.
>
> See Section 14.1 for more information on getting directions to unfamiliar locations.

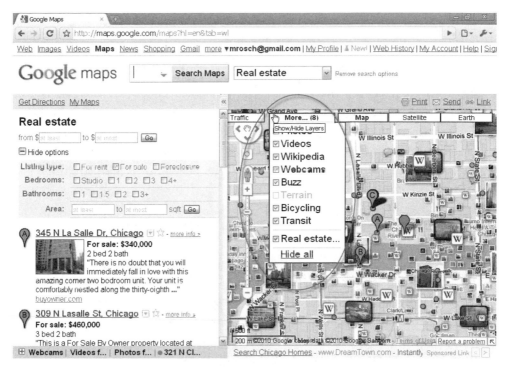

FIGURE 14.6   In this illustration, we've clicked the **More...** button and chosen to add various user-generated content that has been associated with areas on our map of results for *321 N. Clark Chicago*. We have added the maximum amount of additional data by checking the **Photos**, **Videos**, **Wikipedia**, **Webcams**, **Transit**, and **Real estate** boxes. Clicking on any of these allows you to see a larger version of the referenced photo/video/etc. Checking the **Real estate** box functions the same way as selecting the **Real estate** option on the drop-down menu described earlier. You could choose to add just one of these options or any combination to your search results.

The **Terrain** button is the least interesting in most city map results. It changes the Google Maps search results display to a topographical-type map showing features in the terrain, changes in elevation, etc. (For our *321 N. Clark Chicago* search, it's all flat.)

Clicking the **Map** button at any point gets you back to the roadmap-like view seen in the first illustration.

14.1   Getting Directions to Far-Flung Deposition Locations

Directions between addresses are available in more than 150 countries.

Clicking the **Get Directions** link in the left-hand information panel opens up the directions search interface, where you can enter the starting and ending address for your trip. If you have already run a search for a specific address, Google Maps will fill that address in as your destination.

▼▼▼▼▼

PHANTOM TOWN ON GOOGLE MAPS?

On October 31, 2009, the U.K.'s *Telegraph* newspaper reported on the "town" of Argleton in England's northwest county of Lancashire. Argleton search results "brings up a series of home, job and dating listings for people and places 'in Argleton,' as well as websites which help people find its nearest chiropractor and even plan jogging or hiking routes through it," according to the report. The only problem is that the town does not exist. "The businesses, people and services listed are real, but are actually based elsewhere in the same postcode area," the report continued.

The report also noted that "so-called 'trap streets' are often inserted by cartographers but are, as their name suggests, usually far more minor and indiscreet that [sic] bogus towns." However, neither Google, nor its map supplier, know where the town came from.

The report noted that the map's supplier Tele Atlas "would now wipe the non-existent town from the map."

The article originally appeared online at http://bit.ly/mYlX0.

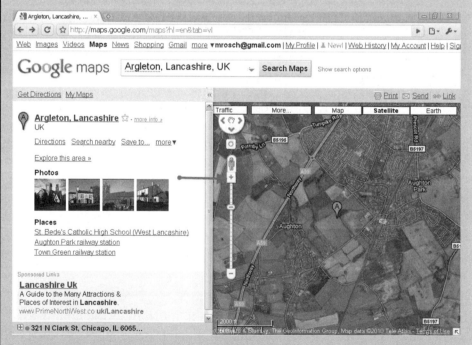

FIGURE 14.7 Zooming into the "town" of Argleton in Google Maps search results shows that it is just a series of empty fields. To zoom in, move the slider bar up toward the plus sign. The slider bar is located on the left edge of the map. (We added the arrow pointing towards the slider bar.)

Once you've filled in both addresses, you can click the two-headed arrow at the right of the address boxes to switch the addresses in the event you need directions *from* the address you searched rather than *to* it.

Clicking the **Add Destination** link adds another box, where you can add a third address. You can add more address boxes if you plan to have multiple stops on your trip.

Once all your addresses are entered, click the **Get Directions** button to generate your results.

> **Practice Tip**
>
> In addition to driving directions, Google Maps also offers **Walking** directions, as well as **By public transit.** These two options can be very useful if you have traveled to an unfamiliar city for a conference and you do not have a car.

FIGURE 14.8   This image illustrates the different methods by which we can view the directions Google Maps has generated. The most familiar will probably be the turn-by-turn directions in the left-hand information panel and the map on the right showing the route from point A to point B. However, clicking on the camera icon to the right of each line of those directions shows the Street View image for that location and the directions for that portion of the trip at the top of the image. You can manipulate the Street View images as described in Section 14.3, or you can click the right-pointing arrow next to the directions to see the next segment of the trip. (Clicking the left-pointing arrow goes back one segment in the trip.) Clicking the hollow box (not visible in this illustration but you would see it if you replicated this search—it would appear under the word **Link** at the top right of the street view) in the upper right-hand corner of the image expands the Street View to full screen. Clicking the **X** in the upper right-hand corner of the image closes it, reverting to just the text directions and the map.

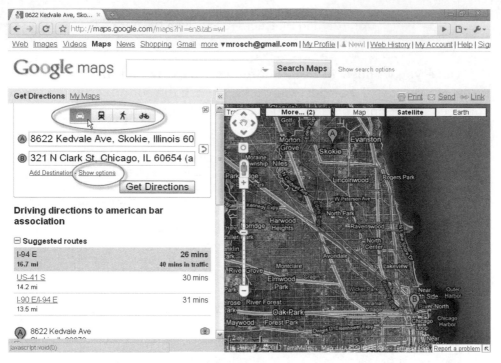

FIGURE 14.9 Notice the four icons (a car, public transportation, a person walking, and a bicycle) displayed above the addresses entered into the Get Directions search boxes. After selecting one of the icons, you can then click the Show options link to add more details to your search. For example, after selecting the **car** icon from the drop-down menu, you can also indicate whether you want directions that **Avoid highways** or **Avoid tolls**. If you select **By public transit**, you're prompted to enter a date and time you want to **Depart at** or **Arrive by**. If you select **Walking** or **Bicycling** directions, you can choose to have distances displayed in miles or kilometers.

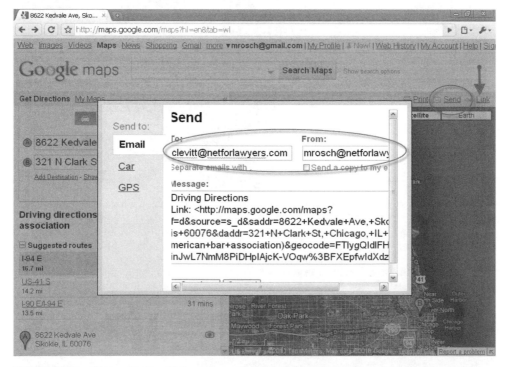

FIGURE 14.10 Clicking the **Send** link opens up a window that allows you to send information about your directions/results to whomever you designate by entering their e-mail address in the **To** box. Enter your e-mail address in the **From** box and click the **Send** button to send your recipient a message containing a link to display the same results page you've retrieved with your search and the list of turn-by-turn directions.

Practice Tip
Clicking the link labeled **Link** (seen to the right of the **Send** link in Figure 14.10) generates a URL that you can embed into any Web site to display a map and/ or directions to the location for which you've searched. This can be a useful addition to your practice's Web site. Search for your office address and embed a map and directions to make it easy for potential clients to find your office.

14.2 Local Searching: Find Restaurants and Hotels Near Far-Flung Deposition Locations

If you travel with any regularity, you know how nice it can be to get out of the hotel and eat in a local restaurant. It's also nice to have some idea where you'd like to go, particularly if the hotel staff is less than knowledgeable.

Similarly, if you're traveling for a hearing, to meet a client, or to take a deposition in an unfamiliar city, you might need to locate a hotel close to the courthouse or meeting location. Google Maps also allows you to locate businesses near a particular address.

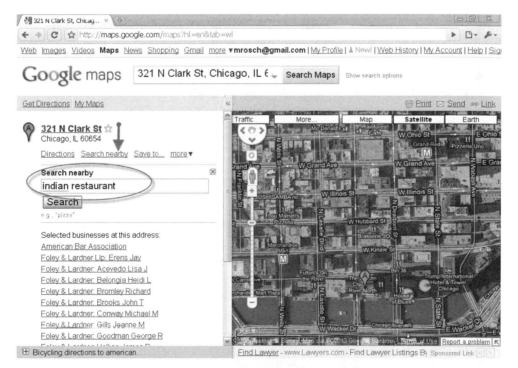

FIGURE 14.11 Clicking the **Search nearby** link in the left-hand information panel opens the **Search nearby** box. In this illustration, we're searching for an *Indian Restaurant* near the *321 N. Clark* address we had searched for previously in *Chicago*.

FIGURE 14.12   Individual *Indian restaurant* results are displayed in a list in the left-hand information pane along with their respective distance from the address we indicated. On the right, push pins corresponding to each result are placed on the map. An arrow indicates the location of the address we searched (*321 N. Clark*).

You can search for any type of business (e.g., *electronics*, *florist*, *caterer*, *office supplies*) near your selected address.

14.3   Street View

Google launched Street View in May 2007 as what the company describes as "the last zoom layer on the map." They meant that "when you've zoomed all the way in you find yourself virtually standing on the street." Street view uses "360° horizontal . . . panoramic street level views" to allow you to virtually turn around in a location you've found using Google Maps. The 290° vertical panoramic street level views allow you to (virtually) look up at skyscrapers and down to the street.

> **Usage Tip**
>
> Use the Street View to find landmarks that will help guide you to your destination.

Google has created specialized vehicles to collect these images. (For streets not accessible by automobile, Google created camera-equipped tricycles in 2009.) Images are matched to specific locations using GPS data and then "sewn" together to create the panoramic effect.

"Faces and license plates are blurred before the panorama images are served and become viewable in Google Maps," according to Google.

As of Spring 2010, Street View is available for:

- Australia
- Canada (Calgary, Ontario, Ottawa, Montreal, Nova Scotia, Toronto, Quebec, Vancouver)
- Canary Islands
- Denmark
- Finland
- France
- Germany (portions)
- Hong Kong
- Italy
- Japan
- Macau
- Netherlands
- New Zealand
- Norway
- Portugal (portions)
- Singapore
- South Korea
- Spain (portions)
- Sweden
- United Kingdom
- United States

Street View can be used in conjunction with Google Maps directions (as discussed in Section 14.1) or to view a single location.

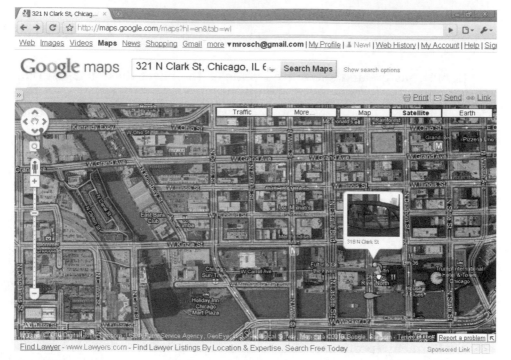

FIGURE 14.13 When looking at a Google Maps search result, you can grab the orange "Pegman" icon located on the left-hand side of the map (above the zoom in/out slider) and place him anywhere on the map to see the Street View for that location. Here, we are dragging Pegman close to the *321 N. Clark Chicago* address we had searched for previously.

FIGURE 14.14 This is the Street View image associated with the location on the map (close to *321 N. Clark Chicago*). You can click on arrows in the Street View images to navigate up and down the street (in successive images); you can left-click your mouse and drag your mouse to virtually turn around within the image; you can tilt up to see the height of the skyscraper in the image; or you can double-click to zoom into a portion of the image.

Note that not every street or address that includes an aerial view in Google Maps is available on Street View.

Prior to launching Google Maps, Google had a stand-alone local search site located at http://local.google.com. That local search has pretty much been integrated into Google Maps. In fact, the http://local.google.com URL redirects to the Google Maps search page.

Usage Tip

If you click the zoom-out (–) button, you will return to the aerial view of the Street View location. This is the same aerial view available in the regular zoomed-in Maps view. Conversely, if you are looking at an aerial view, clicking the zoom-in (+) button after you've zoomed in to the closest image automatically displays the Street View for that location.

Google's 800-GOOG-411 telephone information service (Chapter 15) and its Google SMS (information via text messages; Chapter 21) are also good sources of localized information.

Location-Based Google Search via Your Non-Web-Enabled Telephone (GOOG-411)

15

For those times when you're not near a computer or Web-enabled cellular phone, Google offers a free telephone-based 411 service that delivers localized information about businesses based on your voice request. (Information about residential phone listings is not available and the service cannot accept calls from pay phones.)

To access the service, simply dial 800-GOOG-411 (800-466-4411). You will be prompted for the type of business, city and state. Here you can speak the answer to those questions. You may also be asked to narrow down the search radius by saying a nearby intersection or entering a ZIP code. (The ZIP code must be keyed in from your phone's keypad. In our tests, GOOG-411 did not recognize spoken ZIP codes.)

Once your request is processed, you will be told the number of results for your request. Results are numbered 1-X, with each result's assigned number spoken before the business name and address. You can say the number of any result to be connected to that particular business.

If you are calling from a cellular phone, you can also say *text message* and GOOG-411 will send you a text with additional information about the business, or you can say *map it* and GOOG-411 will text you a link to a map of the area where the business is located.

Regardless of the type of phone you're calling from, saying *details* instructs GOOG-411 to give you additional details regarding the business you've selected. Saying *help* at any time takes you directly to the service's help menu.

Google's SMS text messaging/search service (discussed in Chapter 21) can also be useful for locating localized results or residential phone listing information on your phone.

Free Knowledge-Management Tools from Google: Desktop Search

16

We've talked a lot about locating information on the Web, but what happens when you need to find something that is stored on your computer (at least you *think* it's stored on your computer)?

Google's Desktop Search (available as a free download at http://desktop.google.com) puts the power of a Google Web search right onto your own computer. It's like installing your own personal Google robot onto your computer to index, full-text search, and return the information you've saved on your hard drive in a fraction of a second. On installation, it will begin to index the contents of your computer's primary hard drive (usually C:). Right out of the box, it does not index external (USB) hard drives, network attached hard drives, or file servers. (It does, however, index individual documents that you access from those drives using the computer on which the Desktop Search application is installed.) We discuss how you can modify Desktop Search to include these other sources of files in Section 16.6.1.4.

Desktop Search uses the familiar Google interface, including many of the search features and strategies we discussed in Chapter 3 to conduct searches. For example, when using Desktop Search, phrases can be searched by enclosing them in quotation marks; you can limit your results to a particular type of file with the instruction *filetype:pdf* (PDF in this example); you can omit a term by preceding it with a minus sign (-). However, Desktop Search does not recognize the OR Boolean connector or the wildcard (*) to take the place of search terms.

Desktop Search also recognizes a number of unique search instructions such as *to:*, *from:*, *cc:*, and *subject:* to locate e-mail messages to a particular person, from a particular person, carbon copied to a particular person, or that contains specific keywords in the subject line (respectively).

Additional search operators recognized by Desktop Search can be found at http://desktop.google.com/support/bin/answer.py?hl=en&answer=10111.

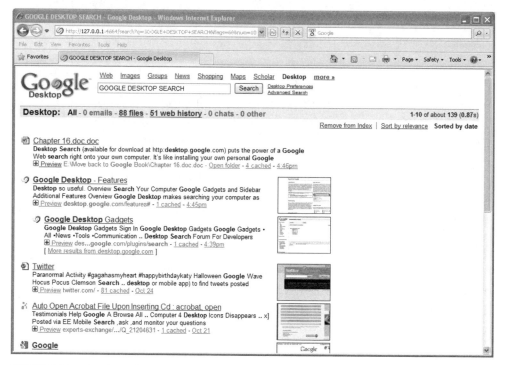

FIGURE 16.1 Google Desktop Search results look very similar to Google Web search results, except that all of the documents on the list are located on your computer. You can also choose to add results from a Google Web search to the search results of information found on your own computer.

Google's Desktop Search is available for Windows (XP, Vista, 7) and Mac (10.4, 10.5) operating systems.

On installation, the Windows version indexes the following file types:

- Word
- Excel
- PowerPoint
- PDF
- TXT
- HTML
- Zip (compressed)
- Outlook E-mail
- Outlook Express E-mail
- Music
- Images
- Video
- MSN Instant Messenger
- AOL Instant Messenger
- Google Talk

Using options found on the Desktop Preferences pages (discussed in Section 16.6.1.2), you can add additional types of information to the index to be retrieved in a Desktop Search.

Plug-ins are also available to extend Desktop Search's capabilities to include WordPerfect files and Gmail messages, among other file types. Plug-ins can be located and downloaded at http://desktop.google.com/plugins/c/index/search.html?hl=en.

On installation, the Mac version indexes the following file types:

- Word
- Excel
- PowerPoint
- PDF
- TXT
- HTML (including the text of Web pages you've visited)
- E-mail from Apple Mail, Microsoft Entourage, and Gmail (even if you're not online)
- Address Book contacts, system preference panes, and file names for most other files including applications
- metadata for audio and video files (e.g., artist and album information contained in iTunes)
- IChat

On the Mac, Google's Desktop Search is built to function "as a companion" to the Mac's built-in Spotlight search application, even sharing some components. Because of this, the Mac version of Desktop Search can also index and retrieve other file types for which there is an existing Spotlight plug-in such as WordPerfect or Corel Painter, among numerous other file types. The complete list of those available for download can be seen at http://www.apple.com/downloads/macosx/spotlight/.

If you work in an office large enough to have an IT department, discuss the Desktop Search feature with them (and any program that you're considering downloading) before you download or install it—they will definitely have an opinion about whether they want this (or any) new software installed on the company's computers (and if so, how).

Once installed, the Desktop Search's local robot will begin building its index of your files. The more files you have stored on your hard drive, the longer this process will take. Initially, you may see "partial results" displayed for a search until all of your files have been indexed. Once the initial indexing process is completed, the local robot will always be running in the background indexing your files.

Since there's a better than 90 percent chance that you are using some flavor of the Windows operating system, the following sections illustrate features of Desktop Search for Windows.

16.1 Advanced Search

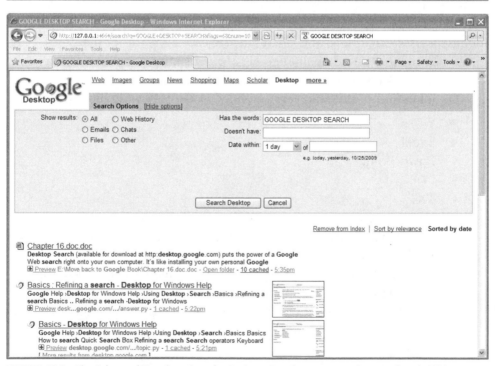

FIGURE 16.2 The Advanced Search options for Desktop Search are not as robust as Google Web search's. It does not offer the **Find pages that have... one or more of these words** or **this exact wording or phrase** options we discussed in Chapter 4. (Note that you can use the OR Boolean connector or enclose exact phrases in quotation marks to achieve the same results.) It does give you the ability to limit your search by date or to certain types of files, e.g., **Emails**, or **Web History**. See the previous section for details on how to search more precisely for specific file types like PowerPoint or PDF files.

16.2   Cache

As with Google Web search, Google Desktop Search creates cached copies of your files each time you view them. These cached versions are stored on your computer's hard drive.

Practice Tip

If you have accidentally deleted a file, there's a possibility that you might be able to retrieve a previously cached version by running a Google Desktop Search for keywords found in the document.

FIGURE 16.3   The **cached** link beneath a Google Desktop Search result indicates that prior versions of the document have also been saved by Desktop Search.

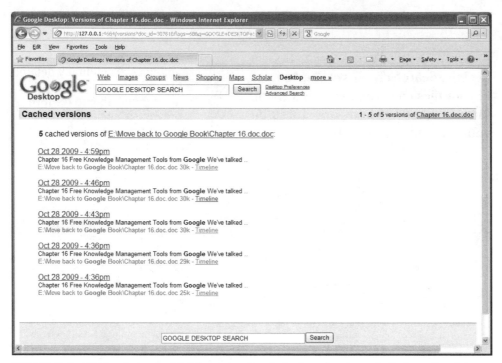

FIGURE 16.4 Clicking the **cached** link beneath a Google Desktop Search result displays a list of the available versions of the file. In this illustration, we could view any of the five previous versions of the document **Chapter 16.doc**.

16.3   Previewing the Content of Documents the Desktop Search Returns

You don't have to click the blue link at the top of a Google Desktop Search result to open the file and see its contents. Desktop Search gives you the ability to preview most of the file types it retrieves right in the browser.

FIGURE 16.5 Clicking the **Preview** link beneath a Google Desktop Search result displays a plain-text version of the file's contents right in the browser window. Clicking **Hide preview** closes it.

16.4   Removing Files from the Desktop Search Index

Google Desktop Search also gives you the ability to remove items from its index, as shown in Figures 16.6 and 16.7 on page 190.

FIGURE 16.6 Click **Remove from index** to begin the process of removing selected files from the Desktop Search index.

FIGURE 16.7 After clicking the **Remove from index** link, you can check the individual items you want to remove. The final step is to click the **Remove** button.

16.5   The Quick Search Box

Desktop Search's Quick Search Box offers a fast, no-frills method of locating files on your computer. To open it, simply click the *Ctrl* key twice. Just type a few letters or words into the Search Box and your top results pop up instantly. You can also use it to launch applications without having to surf the Start menu; for example, you can launch Microsoft Word by typing *wor* into the Quick Search Box and selecting *Microsoft Word* in the list of results that appears. Or simply type in your search term and press *Enter* to search the Web.

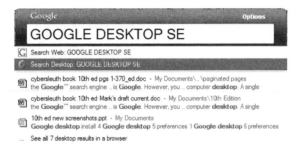

FIGURE 16.8   To open Desktop Search's Quick Search Box, simply click the *Ctrl* key twice. As you type your search terms into the box, the top results matching what you type are displayed below. Clicking on any result opens that file. You can also opt to see the results in a browser, as we have seen in the previous examples.

16.6   Using Desktop Preferences to Control Desktop Search's Functionality

So far we've looked at the visible features and functions of Desktop Search, but there are others located behind the **Desktop Preferences** link. How these preferences are set can make a big difference in the kinds of results Desktop Search returns.

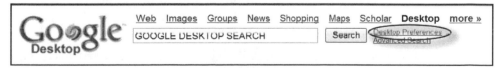

FIGURE 16.9   A number of options are available to extend (or limit) some of Desktop Search's functionality. They are accessible via the **Desktop Preferences** link, located to the right of the search box.

The preferences are broken down into four tabs. We'll look at what each tab contains.

16.6.1   The Desktop Search Preferences Tab

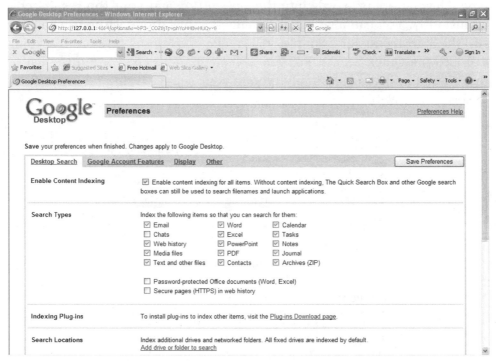

FIGURE 16.10   The first tab, labeled **Desktop Search,** exerts the most control over what kinds of files are included in the index, where they're retrieved from, and how they're treated.

16.6.1.1   Enable Content Indexing

This first preference is the master "on/off switch" of Desktop Search. Unchecking this box stops your personal Google robot from building the index from which it retrieves the results we've been talking about in this chapter. With this box unchecked you can still use Google Desktop Search to search all of the information in files created or edited prior to turning off the indexing. For documents created or edited after the indexing was turned off, though, only the file or application names are searchable, not text that appears in documents. Cached versions of those newer documents are also not available.

16.6.1.2   Search Types

In this section you can dictate what file types from your hard drive you want Google Desktop Search to include in its index, including **Contacts**, **Calendar** entries, **Tasks**, or **Notes**. Checking any of the boxes includes the corresponding file type in the index.

You can also opt to include certain categories of files—**Password-protected Office documents (Word, Excel)** or **Secure pages (HTTPS) in web history**. The password-protected documents are self-explanatory. **Secure pages (HTTPS) in web history** could include anything from messages sent via Web-based e-mail (e.g., Gmail, Yahoo! Mail) or online shopping and banking transactions. Including these categories of files in the index would make them available in the Preview mode, as well as making cached versions of the files available after they've been deleted from your hard drive.

> **Practice Tip**
>
> If you use a shared computer, or someone else has access to your computer (e.g., temporary staff, night cleaning crew), you will want to omit **Password-protected Office documents (Word, Excel)** and **Secure pages (HTTPS) in web history** from the Google Desktop Search index.

16.6.1.3   Indexing Plug-ins

This section provides a link to the helper applications we discussed at the beginning of the chapter.

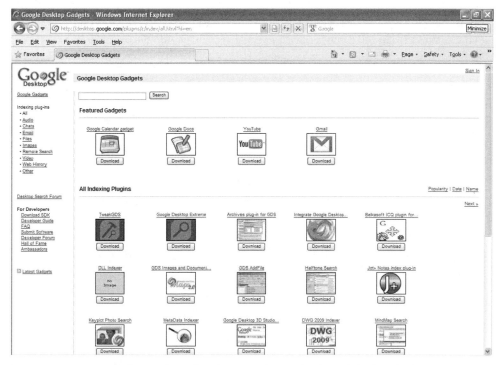

FIGURE 16.11   You can keyword search or browse to locate plug-ins to help Google's Desktop Search index additional file types, such as WordPerfect.

16.6.1.4 Search Locations

This section allows you to select additional, external hard drives or file servers to include or exclude from the index.

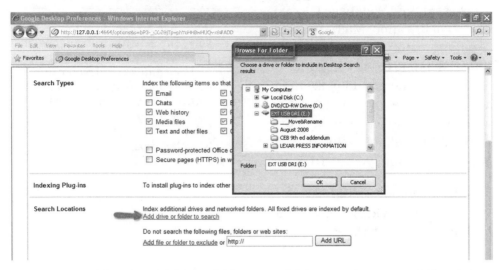

FIGURE 16.12 Clicking the **Add drive or folder to search** link opens a **Browse For Folder** window in which you can **Choose a drive or folder to include in Desktop Search results**. In this example, we've selected **EXT USB DRI (E:)** to include. Conversely, clicking the **Add file or folder to exclude** link pops up a similar **Browse For Folder** window.

16.6.1.5 Google Integration

This section allows you to include results from your Google Desktop Search index in the same browser window as results from your Google Web search (when files on your computer match your keyword search).

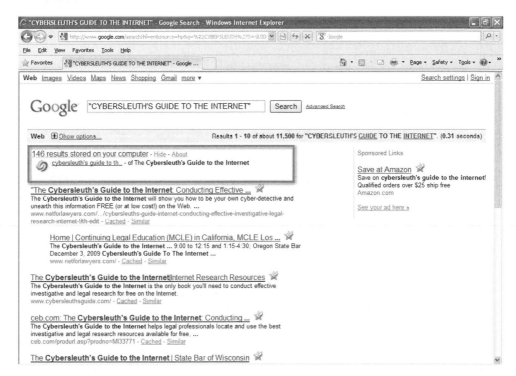

FIGURE 16.13 In this example we've conducted a Google Web search for *"The Cybersleuth's Guide to the Internet."* Above the results drawn from the Web, this integrated search also shows that there are **146 results stored on [my] computer**. Clicking the **146 results stored on your computer** link will display the entire results list from my computer or we can browse and click on the Web links as usual.

16.6.1.6 Encrypt Index

This section allows you to add a layer of security to protect the information within Desktop Search's index. Encrypting the index can make the data in the index unreadable to someone who steals or otherwise copies it from the machine on which it is installed. However, as long as your computer is turned on, anyone sitting in front of it could run a search and retrieve information from the index. Encrypting the index will also slow down all of your searches.

16.6.1.7   Remove Deleted Items

This section allows you to instruct Desktop Search to remove files from the index once they're deleted from your computer. This would seem like a logical step . . . for the documents you intentionally delete and really want to get rid of. However, selecting this option would eliminate your ability to retrieve cached versions of documents you delete by accident, as described in Section 16.2. On the other hand, lawyers must consider their firm's document-retention policies for information that may be covered under HIPAA, Gramm-Leach-Bliley, or Sarbanes-Oxley legislation.

16.6.2   Google Account Features Tab

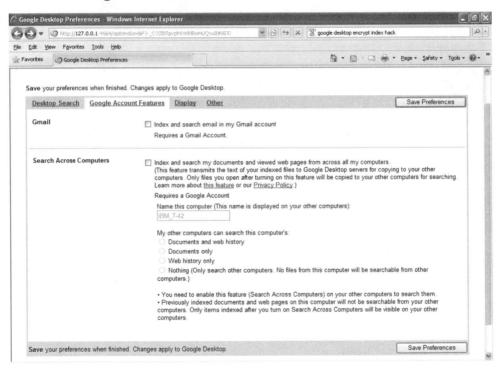

FIGURE 16.14   The second Desktop Search Preference tab allows you to define how Desktop Search interacts with other Google services like Gmail.

16.6.2.1   Gmail

Checking the box in this section instructs Desktop Search to index messages sent and received via your Gmail (Google's online e-mail service) account. (See Section 18.1 for more details on this service.)

16.6.2.2   Search Across Computers

Activating this feature lets you access your Desktop Search index from multiple computers. (A Google Account is required.) For example, you might enable this feature to search your home computer from your work computer or vice versa. To do this, Search Across Computers uploads your index to servers controlled by Google.

Practice Tip

The Search Across Computers feature is one of the frequent causes of security concerns we hear related to Google's products and applications—after all, information about your documents and their contents is being transmitted and stored on computers controlled by Google.

Google Desktop's Privacy Policy (http://desktop.google.com/privacypolicy.html) explicitly states that Google will "securely transmit copies of your indexed files to Google servers in order to provide the [Search Across Computers] feature." It also refers back to Google's General Privacy Policy (http://www.google.com/privacypolicy.html) for more detailed information about how Google works to safeguard this kind of personal information. It reads, in part:

> We take appropriate security measures to protect against unauthorized access to or unauthorized alteration, disclosure or destruction of data. These include internal reviews of our data collection, storage and processing practices and security measures, as well as physical security measures to guard against unauthorized access to systems where we store personal data.

> We restrict access to personal information to Google employees, contractors and agents who need to know that information in order to operate, develop or improve our services. These individuals are bound by confidentiality obligations and may be subject to discipline, including termination and criminal prosecution, if they fail to meet these obligations.

Most of these restrictions deal with our names, e-mail addresses, and other personal information we willingly provide to Google. Their Privacy Policy indicates that Google categorizes the Desktop Search index as "personal information," so these two paragraphs are a good indication of the lengths Google will go to to shield these indices from unauthorized access. However, because lawyers are dealing in confidential client information, they may be right to be wary of *any* service that stores their documents (or information about their documents) remotely.

For this reason we would not recommend enabling this feature.

Note that this feature can search only your Web search history; Microsoft Word, Excel, and PowerPoint; text; and PDF files in your My Documents folder across multiple machines. It cannot include the multitude of file types discussed at the beginning of this chapter.

The Search Across Computers feature was discontinued as of January 20, 2010. It is not available in versions of Desktop Search downloaded and installed after that date. It may, however, still be available in older versions of the Desktop Search already installed before that date. To completely avoid this feature be sure to update the version of Desktop Search installed on your computer.

16.6.3   The Display Preferences Tab

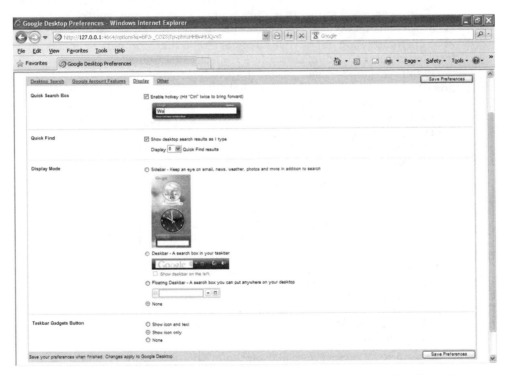

FIGURE 16.15   This section allows you to vary how and where on your computer's desktop the Desktop Search box is displayed.

16.6.3.1   Quick Search Box

Checking the box in this section enables the Quick Search Box described in Section 16.5. (The option of enabling/disabling the Quick Search Box is not included in versions of the Google Desktop Search installed/updated in 2010. However, the Quick Search Box still functions as described in Figure 16.8 in Section 16.5.)

16.6.3.2   Quick Find

Checking the box in this section enables the Quick Search Box results as illustrated in Figure 16.8 in Section 16.5. The drop-down menu allows you to select the number of results that are displayed in this view, ranging from 1 to 10.

16.6.3.3   Display Mode

This section allows you to place a "permanent" Desktop Search box on your computer's desktop. These options would be in addition to the Quick Search Box discussed in Section 16.5. **The Deskbar** ("A search box in your taskbar") and the **Floating Deskbar** ("A search box you can put anywhere on your desktop") are the least intrusive or distracting. The **Sidebar** (which allows you to "keep an eye on email, news, weather, photos and more in addition to search" in a panel running vertically down one side of your desktop) is the most distracting.

For productivity purposes, and to keep our computer's desktop as uncluttered as possible, we opt for **None** of these and call up the Quick Search Box only when we need it.

16.6.3.4   Taskbar Gadgets Button

This section allows you to select Desktop Search's Taskbar display format (the Taskbar is located in the lower right-hand corner of Windows operating system computers). You can opt to **Show icon and text**, **Show icon only**, or show **None**.

FIGURE 16.16   The Desktop Search icon is seen (lower right) in a Windows XP Taskbar. Clicking on the icon opens up the menu seen at the left.

16.6.4 Other Preferences Tab

For some reason, Web designers and site builders (apparently) love to put important, useful, or otherwise helpful information and features behind vague links labeled **More**, **Links**, or **Other**—and Google is no exception. The actions covered by the following Google Desktop Search Preferences are very important, but are accessed by clicking a tab simply labeled **Other**.

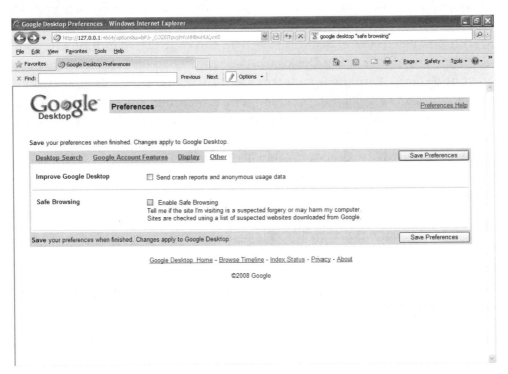

FIGURE 16.17 The **Send crash reports and anonymous usage data** option, hiding behind the innocuous **Other** Preferences tab, is very important.

16.6.4.1 Improve Google Desktop

In its efforts to locate, track, and repair bugs in its Desktop Search software, Google has created a way for it to "phone home" to let Google know about any problems the software encounters. The list of Google Desktop Search Privacy Policy frequently asked questions (http://desktop.google.com/privacyfaq.html) describes this information as "non-personal information about things like the application's performance and reliability"; this would include matters like conflicts with other programs and crash reports. Checking the box in this section enables this communication from your computer back to Google.

As mentioned earlier in this chapter, if you work in an environment large enough to have an IT department, they will have an opinion on whether they want this kind of outbound stream of communication on your network. The opinion is often "no."

While we ordinarily like to be participating members of the online community and share information back with the developers of software we find useful (especially when it is free like Google Desktop Search), for network security reasons we recommend not enabling this feature.

16.6.4.2 Safe Browsing

This section is an attempt to help you avoid potentially fraudulent or malicious Web sites.

Checking the box in this section instructs Google Desktop to download a list of Web sites that are suspected of being a "forgery or may harm [your] computer" and to compare sites that appear in your Google Web search results against that list.

Security and privacy advocates have expressed concerns about the way this feature communicates information about users' surfing habits (checking the sites they visit against the known list of malicious sites), the way the feature shares information with Google servers, and the retention of user data by Google (at only two weeks, the retention period is shorter than for other types of data Google gathers about search and other activities). For these potential issues, we recommend not enabling this feature.

(In the late summer of 2009, Google indicated that they would stop supporting this feature. If you have recently updated your computer, operating system, or browser, you may no longer see this option.)

Google Scholar: Locate Information from Academic Sources and Retrieve Free Case Law

17

Google Scholar (http://scholar.googlc.com/) is a specialized search that retrieves results from a separate database than the regular Google Web search. It includes "articles, theses, books, abstracts and court opinions, from academic publishers, professional societies, online repositories, universities and other web sites," (see http://scholar.google.com/intl/en/scholar/about.html). The most important distinction is that much of the content listed in the search results list is not available for free, except for the free case law added to Scholar on November 17, 2009 (see Section 17.4). While some of the results do link to PDF or Web versions of the articles, many more link to an abstract or some other type of descriptive page that includes the ability to purchase access to the article. They are offered for sale by the publishers of the journals in which the articles appear—not by Google.

> **Practice Tip**
>
> Scholarly journals can be excellent sources of information about expert witnesses. Google Scholar can help you locate experts on a particular topic, or search by author's name to locate articles written by your own or the opposition's expert to see if the opinions they've expressed in prior articles matches the testimony in the matter you're handling.

FIGURE 17.1 Google Scholar draws its results from different sources than the more-familiar Google Web search. These results might be drawn from electronic versions of print publications "from a wide variety of academic publishers and professional societies, as well as scholarly articles available across the web" (http://scholar.google.com/intl/en/scholar/help.html).

17.1   Anatomy of the Search Results Page

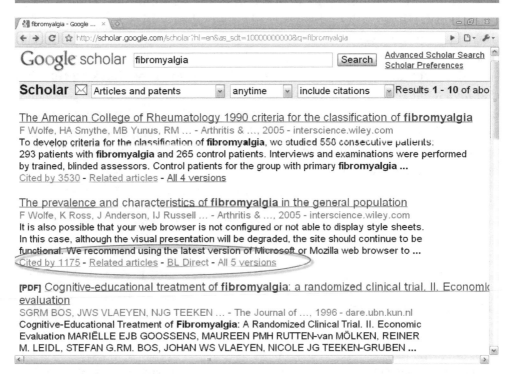

FIGURE 17.2   In some ways Google Scholar search results resemble Google's Web search results, but there are numerous elements displayed in addition to the blue link and the text abstract describing the page.

There are a number of unique elements to Google Scholar's search results.

Beneath each result is a notation labeled **Cited by [XX]**, where [XX] represents the number of other scholarly publications that Google Scholar has detected citing back to the article in that particular result. As in case law, the more citations to an article the more authoritative it becomes. Clicking on this link brings up a new results list of those articles that cite to the article in the result you were originally looking at.

> **Practice Tip**
>
> You can use the citation information provided in the search result to locate a copy of the article in which you're interested from a library or other "real world" source.
>
> Also see the description in Section 17.3 of how you might be able to use the Library Links preference to help locate a local library with a copy of one of the articles that is listed in your search results list.

The **Related articles** link can be useful for locating articles from different experts and different publications on the same topic.

The **BL Direct** link routes you to British Library Direct, "a new service that allows you to search across 20,000 journals for free and order full text using your credit card."

Many results include a link labeled **All [X] versions**. Clicking this link displays a list of links to alternate sources of the same article or "preprints, early drafts, and other versions of the article" (http://scholar.google.com/intl/en/scholar/help.htm). Be aware that these preprints and drafts may not be identical to the final version. They can undergo significant changes before final publication.

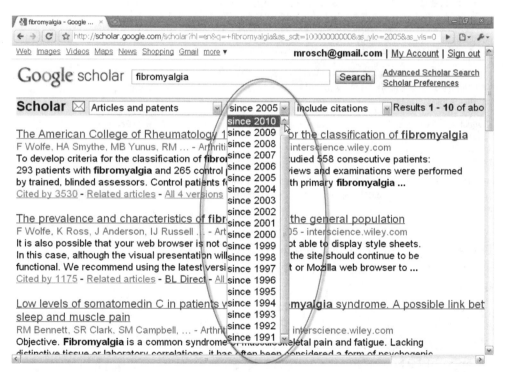

FIGURE 17.3 The drop-down menu at the top of the search results allows you to limit your results (somewhat) by date. In this illustration, we've used the drop-down menu to limit our results to articles **since 2005**. Google Scholar allows us to limit results to the current year or as far back as 1991.

Some results are accompanied by a green triangle that points to a secondary link for a particular search result. In our test searches, this secondary link is often a review of a book listed in the main search results (but not the book itself) or it might be a link to a free copy of the full-text article listed in the main search results from some source other than the original.

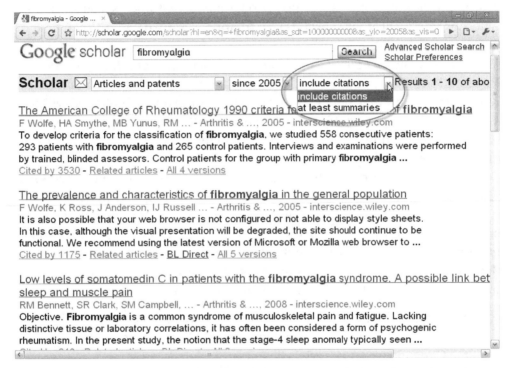

FIGURE 17.4 Some of the articles that Google Scholar returns in results do not have a description or a link—they are only citations to articles. These citations are added to the Google Scholar index when they are cited in an article that the Scholar robot has indexed, but a version of which has not been located online. Selecting **at least summaries** from the right-hand drop-down menu eliminates these citation-only results from your list.

17.1.1 Google Scholar Alerts

See Appendix J on page 493 for this topic.

17.2 Advanced Search

The Advanced Scholar Search page (http://scholar.google.com/advanced_
scholar_search) is divided into 4 segments (the 4th segment will be discussed in Section 17.4). The first segment (that begins: **Find articles with
all of the words**) is similar to Google Web search's Advanced Search page.
The primary difference is the drop-down menu that allows you to dictate
whether you want your search terms to appear **anywhere in the article** or
just in the title of the article.

The second segment of the Advanced Scholar Search page (**Author,
Publication, Date**) lets you search for articles by author's name, limit
results to a particular publication, or search for articles published within a
specific date range (e.g. *1996–2001*). Note that this date range limiter offers
more precision than the date drop-down menu (discussed earlier) located
above Scholar's search results.

The third segment of the Advanced Scholar Search page (**Collections,
Articles and patents**) allows you to target your results to articles on a particular topic or subject area. The default setting is to **Search articles in all
subject areas (include patents)**. However, you can opt to exclude patents
from the articles search by unchecking the box and you can also opt to
Search only articles in the following subject areas to select as few or as
many of the following subject areas from which to limit your results:

- Biology, Life Sciences, and Environmental Science
- Business, Administration, Finance, and Economics
- Chemistry and Materials Science
- Engineering, Computer Science, and Mathematics
- Medicine, Pharmacology, and Veterinary Science
- Physics, Astronomy, and Planetary Science
- Social Sciences, Arts, and Humanities

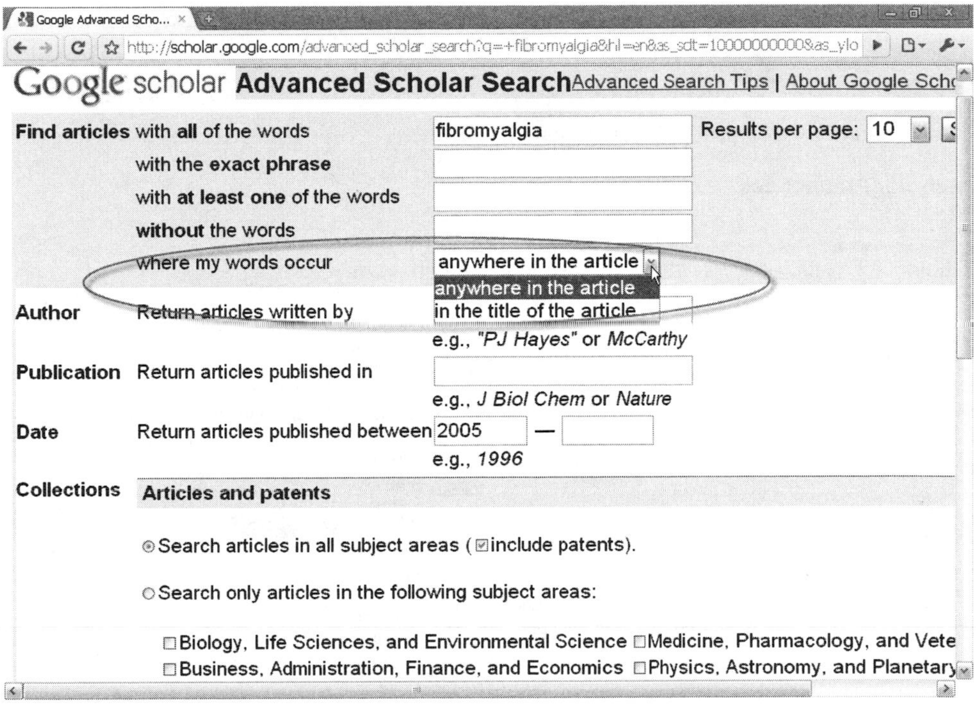

FIGURE 17.5 This illustration shows the first 3 segments of the Advanced Scholar Search page.

17.3 Preferences

Google Scholar's Preferences page (http://scholar.google.com/scholar_ preferences) allows you to customize the look of the search and results interfaces, as well as information about the potential sources for and availability of the articles listed in your search results.

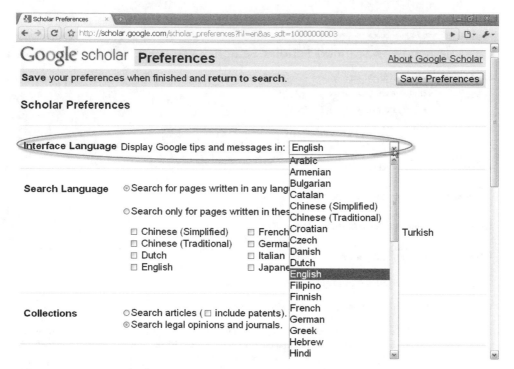

FIGURE 17.6 Among the features you can customize using Google Scholar's Preferences page is the language used to label the search boxes and buttons on the search page. Pictured here is the list of nearly four dozen languages that can be chosen as the default.

If you are looking for source material written in a particular language, you can limit Google Scholar's results to any of nine available languages. The default setting is to **Search for pages written in any language**. (If you do retrieve results in languages that you do not read, see Chapter 12 for information about using Google Translate.)

> **Practice Tip**
>
> Some academic libraries (e.g., UCLA, UC Berkeley), for a fee, will fax or e-mail articles to anyone who requests them.

The **Library Links** feature will be of limited use to most lawyers. It allows you to search for and select up to three (mostly academic) libraries. If any of those libraries offer access to an article in your results list, a **Find it @ [XXX]** link (where [XXX] is the name of your preferred library) will accompany the search result. To access the document electronically, you must have electronic access to that library's system—which usually means you are a student or faculty member. However, some institutions grant electronic library access to their alumni. Additionally, you might select nearby institutions in the event you would want to visit their libraries in person to retrieve a copy of an article in a Google Scholar search result.

The **Number of Results** preference allows you to change the number of results displayed on a single page from the default *10* to *20, 30, 50,* or *100.*

The **Results Window** preference allows you to dictate whether links to articles you click on from the results list open in the same browser window or a new window. Opening results in a new window can be useful because it allows you to keep the window open and return to your results list in its separate window. This preference can make comparing different articles and sources much easier.

Unless you are conducting academic research, the **Bibliography Manager** preference will be of little use to you. It instructs Google Scholar to make bibliographic reference information available, formatted in one of five citation standards. One of these, RefMan, is compatible with Thomson Reuters's $299 Reference Manager software. Most lawyers can select the **Don't show any citation import links** option.

Clicking the **Save Preferences** button binds your newly selected preferences to all of your future Google Scholar searches.

17.4 Free Legal Opinions and Journals

On the evening of November 17, 2009 Google fired (arguably) the loudest and certainly most recent salvo in the battle for free access to case law . . . and it apparently came as a tweet. Google launched a database of federal and state case law and legal journal articles available via its Google Scholar search. The announcement was made by lawyer-turned-Google-product-manager Rick Klau on Twitter. Google later posted a more "official" announcement on its blog about the availability of free case law via Google Scholar.

Tim Stanley, founder of Justia.org, points out that Google links to alternate sources for some cases (in addition to Google's own database version), such as Cornell's LII, Justia, and Public.Resource.org.

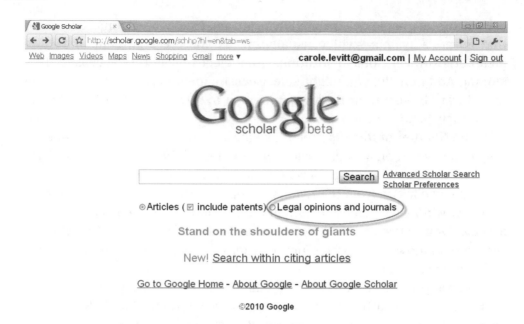

FIGURE 17.7 Note that the Scholar home page now includes a **Legal opinions and journals** radio button to click into for those who wish to search free (full-text) case law and articles from legal journals.

17.4.1 Advanced Scholar Search for Free Legal Opinions and Journals

On the Google Advanced Scholar Search page, you can limit results to:

- **all legal opinions and journals:** You cannot limit your search to just journals or just legal opinions.
- **only US federal court opinions:** You cannot limit your search to just one type of federal court (such as U.S. Supreme Court).
- **only court opinions from the following states:** You can select any combination of the fifty states and the District of Columbia.

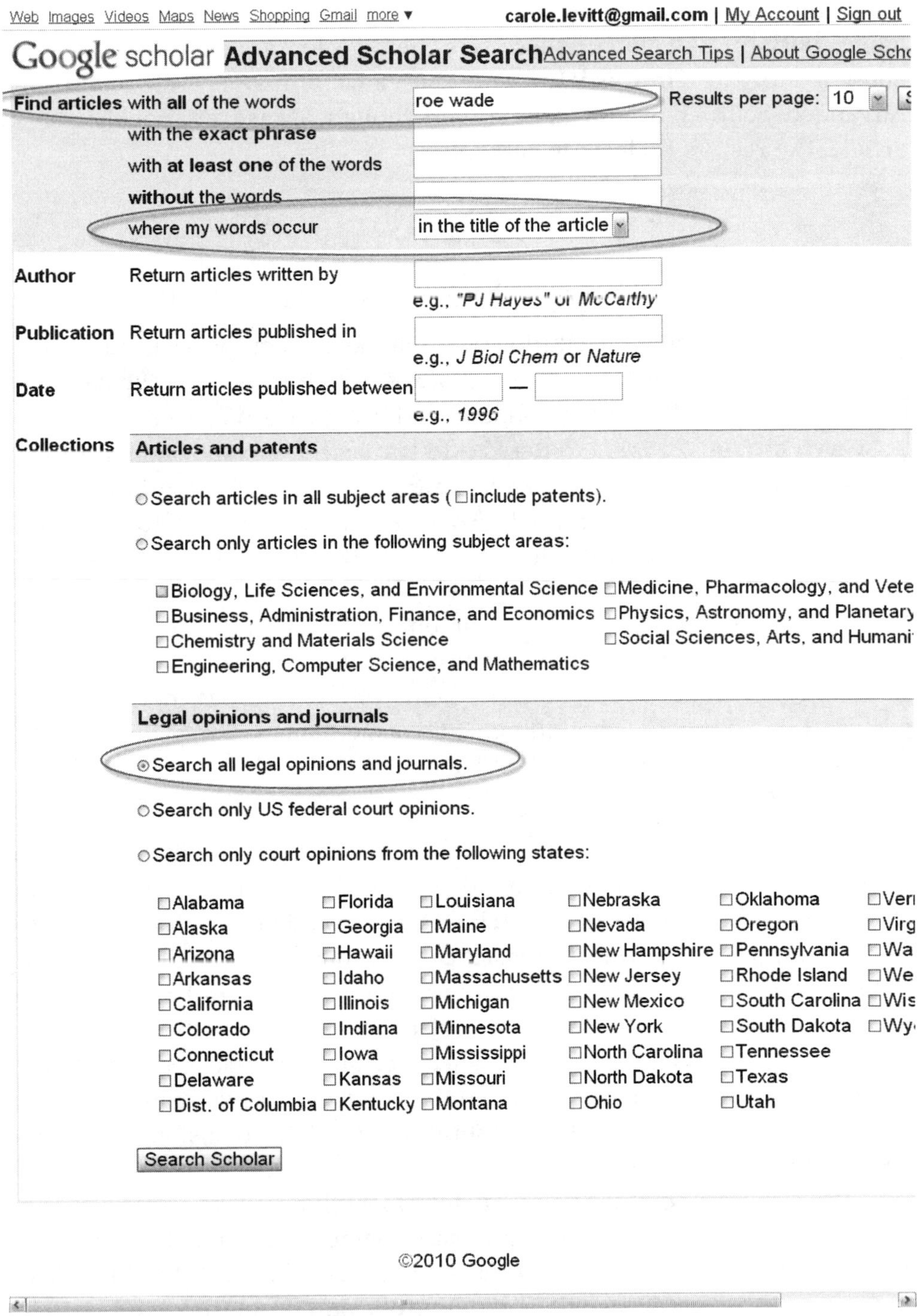

Web Images Videos Maps News Shopping Gmail more ▼   carole.levitt@gmail.com | My Account | Sign out

Google scholar **Advanced Scholar Search** Advanced Search Tips | About Google Scho

Find articles	with **all** of the words	roe wade	Results per page: 10 ▾
	with the **exact phrase**		
	with **at least one** of the words		
	without the words		
	where my words occur	in the title of the article ▾	

| **Author** | Return articles written by | |
| | | e.g., *"PJ Hayes"* or *McCarthy* |

| **Publication** | Return articles published in | |
| | | e.g., *J Biol Chem* or *Nature* |

| **Date** | Return articles published between | — |
| | | e.g., *1996* |

Collections   **Articles and patents**

○ Search articles in all subject areas (☐ include patents).

○ Search only articles in the following subject areas:

☐ Biology, Life Sciences, and Environmental Science ☐ Medicine, Pharmacology, and Vete
☐ Business, Administration, Finance, and Economics ☐ Physics, Astronomy, and Planetary
☐ Chemistry and Materials Science ☐ Social Sciences, Arts, and Humani
☐ Engineering, Computer Science, and Mathematics

Legal opinions and journals

◉ Search all legal opinions and journals.

○ Search only US federal court opinions.

○ Search only court opinions from the following states:

☐ Alabama	☐ Florida	☐ Louisiana	☐ Nebraska	☐ Oklahoma	☐ Ver
☐ Alaska	☐ Georgia	☐ Maine	☐ Nevada	☐ Oregon	☐ Virg
☐ Arizona	☐ Hawaii	☐ Maryland	☐ New Hampshire	☐ Pennsylvania	☐ Wa
☐ Arkansas	☐ Idaho	☐ Massachusetts	☐ New Jersey	☐ Rhode Island	☐ We
☐ California	☐ Illinois	☐ Michigan	☐ New Mexico	☐ South Carolina	☐ Wis
☐ Colorado	☐ Indiana	☐ Minnesota	☐ New York	☐ South Dakota	☐ Wy
☐ Connecticut	☐ Iowa	☐ Mississippi	☐ North Carolina	☐ Tennessee	
☐ Delaware	☐ Kansas	☐ Missouri	☐ North Dakota	☐ Texas	
☐ Dist. of Columbia	☐ Kentucky	☐ Montana	☐ Ohio	☐ Utah	

Search Scholar

©2010 Google

FIGURE 17.8   This is the 4th segment of the Google Advanced Scholar Search page where you can now search for **Legal opinions and journals**.

There are no search boxes to search by citation, party name, or judge name, but you can "force" these searches. To force a search by citation, enter it into the **Find articles with the exact phrase** search box on the Advanced Scholar Search page. (Even though a case citation is not an article, the results do include cases.)

▼▼▼▼▼

Get Out Your Bluebook to Search by Citation

When you search for a citation, you will need to enter it in Bluebook style. A search for *100 Federal Supplement 1* (entered into the search box labeled **with the exact phrase**) will bring back no results, while a search for *100 F Supp 1* (entered into the search box labeled **with the exact phrase**) will bring back that exact case *and* any other later case that has cited to *100 F Supp 1*. (Note: Google ignores punctuation, so there is no need to place the period after the "F" when searching for *"100 F. Supp 1"*.)

You can search by official or unofficial citations. For example, our search for the unofficial citation *22 L Ed 158* brought back four versions of *Burke v. Miltenberger*. Some of the versions included the 22 L. Ed. 158 unofficial citation, while some included only the official citations for the case (86 U.S. 519 and 19 Wall. 519).

To force a search by party name, you must first decide whether you want to bring back narrow or broad results. For example, in a search for *Roe v Wade*, the most narrow search strategy would be to enter *Roe v Wade* into the **Find articles with the exact phrase** search box, limit your results to **Search only US federal court opinions**, and from the **Find articles where my words occur** drop-down menu, select **in the title of the article** (this search will bring back cases, not articles, because you selected **Search only US federal court opinions**). This search brought back two results (the U.S. Supreme Court decision and the Federal District Court decision). Be sure to use "v" and not "versus" or "vs."

The most broad search strategy for research about *Roe v Wade* (using Scholar) would be to enter the two party names, *Roe* and *Wade,* into the **Find articles with all of the words** search box, click into the **Search all legal opinions and journals** radio button, and from the **Find articles where my words occur** drop-down menu, select **anywhere in the article** (this search will bring back both cases and articles). This search brought back 31,900 results, from the *Roe v Wade* case to state and federal cases and articles citing to *Roe v Wade*. (Searching *Roe* and *Wade* at Google.com brought back over 17 million results.)

To force a search by judge's name, first enter the judge's last name into the search box labeled **Return articles written by** and then either click into the radio button labeled **Search only US federal court opinions** or **Search only court opinions from the following states** (and then choose a state). At the U.S. Supreme Court level, this search will bring back any case in which the specified judge delivered the opinion, concurred with it, or dissented from it. If you want only cases in which a specified U.S. Supreme Court judge *delivered* the opinion, for example, you could try entering the judge's last name and the word *delivered* into the phrase box. This is very hit-or-miss. It's possible that a result (or results) could include cases in which someone else delivered the opinion but the specified judge was mentioned regarding his or her delivery of another opinion cited to in the case you are viewing.

17.4.2   Google Scholar Case Coverage

"Currently, Google Scholar allows you to search and read opinions for U.S. state appellate and supreme court cases since 1950, U.S. federal district, appellate, tax and bankruptcy courts since 1923, and U.S. Supreme Court cases since 1791 (please check back periodically for updates to coverage information). In addition, it includes citations for cases cited by indexed opinions or journal articles which allows you to find influential cases (usually older or international) which are not yet online or publicly available" (http://scholar.google.com/intl/en/scholar/help.html).

"Legal opinions in Google Scholar are provided for informational purposes only and should not be relied on as a substitute for legal advice from a licensed lawyer. Google does not warrant that the information is complete or accurate" (http://scholar.google.com/intl/en/scholar/help.html).

17.4.3   The Anatomy of a Google Scholar Legal Opinions and Journals Results List

The next illustration is a results list for our Figure 17.8 search of *Roe* and *Wade* (entered into the **Find articles with all of the words** search box), in which we clicked the **Search all legal opinions and journals** radio button, and selected **in the title of the article** (from the **Find articles where my words occur** drop-down menu). In most of our searches of **all legal opinions and journals**, it seems that the first result is to the actual case (versus an article or a case citing the actual case). The first result is typically to the official version (see Figure 17.9).

FIGURE 17.9 The first result is to the official U.S. Supreme Court opinion of *Roe v. Wade.* To the right of the case name, note the **How cited** link (see Figure 17.11 for an explanation). Beneath the case name you will find (1) one official and two unofficial citations to the case, (2) a brief case annotation, and (3) links to **Cited by 23572, Related articles**, and **All 4 versions.** Clicking the case name link will bring you to the full-text of the case (see the next illustration). The third result is to a *Yale Law Journal* article and beneath the article title and brief annotation you will find **Cited by 1501, Related articles**, and **All 5 versions**.

In Figure 17.9, **Cited by 23572** refers to how many books, cases, and articles cited to *Roe* and *Wade.* If you click **All 4 versions**, you will find the text of *Roe v. Wade* (from up to four different sources). In this particular search, however, there seems to be three sources: two versions were from Cornell, one was from bulk.resource.org (a project of Public.Resource.Org), and one was probably from the U.S. Supreme Court's official site.

17.4.4   The Anatomy of a Google Scholar Case

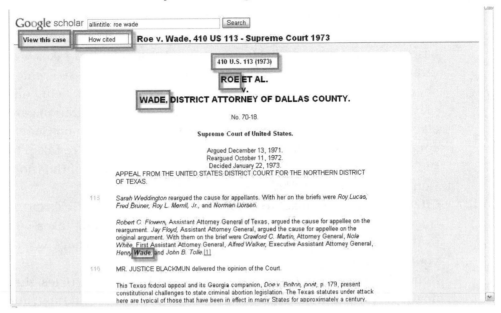

FIGURE 17.10   After clicking the first *Roe v. Wade* result, we are taken to the **View this case** mode (as indicated by the tab on the top left-hand side of the page), where the full-text of the case is displayed (in this result, it is the official version, and only the official citation is displayed therefore). Each of our keywords is highlighted in different colors. Notice the **How cited** tab (see below for an explanation) to the right of the **View this case** tab.

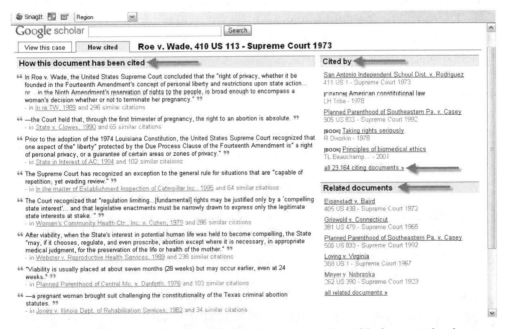

FIGURE 17.11   The **How Cited** page is divided into three sections, **How this document has been cited**, **Cited by**, and **Related Documents**. To view a list of all citations, you would need to click the **all 23,164 citing documents** link in the **Cited By** section.

The How Cited page includes the following sections:

- **How this document has been cited:** a snippet of text is displayed that attempts to show how your case was treated in the citing case or journal article. Clicking on one of these snippets takes you directly to the location of the snippet in the citing case—which should be the location of your cited case—if the case is being displayed from Google's collection of free cases. Journal citations are also included in this list. Some journals coming from non-Google sources are in the form of PDFs. In those instances, you're taken to the beginning of the article or to a log-in/payment page of the [non-Google] database vendor.
- **Cited by:** lists (and links) to cases, books, and journal articles citing the case you're reading. (Clicking on a case citation link takes you to the first page of the case, not to the exact pinpoint page where your case is cited.)
- **Related documents:** lists related cases and journal articles that might have similar fact patterns (or could be a countersuit, for instance).

Nowhere does Google explain the difference between **How this document has been cited** and **Cited by**. From what we can tell, there are more documents in the **Cited by** section and, as noted above, **How this document has been cited** takes you to pinpoint pages while **Cited by** does not.

There will be, no doubt, many who point out inadequacies of the search and coverage of the Google Scholar case law database, but remember that this is *free* case law research.

For more information on locating other free and low-cost case law databases (and investigative and legal research resources) on the Internet, see the oft-revised and updated treatise *The Cybersleuth's Guide to the Internet*—also authored by Carole Levitt and Mark Rosch.

▼▼▼▼▼

Research Alert: Does Google Scholar's Case Law Database Include Shepard's or West's Key-Cite?

No. The **How this document has been cited** and **Cited by** features are Google's attempt to update the case you are reading, but there is no editorial treatment to tell you how the citing cases treated the case you're reading—that determination is up to you. The **How this document has been cited** and **Cited by** features are definitely a step in the right direction.

Google Apps: Free Collaboration Tools to Help Solos and Small Firms Compete with Big-Firm Technology Budgets

18

Google has created a set of Web-based tools that allow you to create, share, and store documents on the Internet and communicate online—Google Apps (http://www.google.com/apps). These Apps include e-mail (Gmail), word processing (Google Docs), an appointment calendar (Google Calendar), spreadsheets (Google Spreadsheets), and slide presentations (Google Presentations).

Using Google Apps, you can draft documents online and share them with clients or co-counsel for comment. Online storage eliminates the need to attach documents to e-mails. Google's tracking of the changes made to these shared documents makes viewing revision histories easier, with each contributor's changes datestamped. So the concern of whether or not you're working from the most recently revised version of a document is precluded. As the owner of the document, however, you have final say over which changes are included in the final document.

There are three (generally available) versions of Google Apps. Two versions are free.

The first, and most common, version comes with your free Google Account (see Section 2.4.1). All e-mail and documents created in these types of accounts are connected to a generic *your_selected_username@gmail.com* address (e.g., mrosch@gmail.com or other e-mail address you used to create your Google Account).

▼▼▼▼▼

RUNNING A PRACTICE WITH GOOGLE APPS

Kevin Thompson, founder of The Advocate Group, a solo law practice and consulting firm focused on multilevel-marketing issues (http://www.theMLMattorney.com/), has put Google's Apps to work in his practice.

> With so many great applications from Google, it's hard to write about just one. I've built my entire law practice on the services provided by Google. I use Google for e-mail, instant messaging, calendaring, document collaboration, Web analytics, pay-per-click ads, and video blogs. But if I had to choose one application to write about, I'd write about Google Docs. The most obvious benefit of Google Docs is the ability to share documents with clients and collaborate in real-time without having to manage several attachments. But a not-so-obvious benefit that's equally as valuable is the ability to easily create a "Form" and collect data from multiple people. With the "Form" feature, it's easy to create a question-and-answer survey and share it via e-mail or on a Web site. When people submit their information, the data is automatically populated into a Google Spreadsheet.
>
> I've found this tool to be invaluable for class action attorneys who want to collect and organize information from potential class members. When I filed a class action lawsuit against a pyramid scheme in 2009, I simply created a WordPress Web page and embedded a "Request for Information" form I created in Google Apps on the site. Class members flooded the site! Instead of me having to collect phone numbers and chase down leads, it was incredibly easy for class members to tell me their stories and give me their contact information. We were able to obtain several key affidavits from great witnesses we identified this way.
>
> Although the vast majority of the business world is still stuck on Microsoft Word, Google Docs is evolving into a viable alternative to Word. And as our culture gets more comfortable with Web-based applications, I would imagine that all of Google's Apps will see more adoption.

The second free version allows you to customize these tools for your own Internet domain name (e.g., *netforlawyers.com*). This Standard Edition lets you create up to 50 users with customized *username@yourdomain.com* e-mail addresses.

The third version is similar to the second but adds greater storage capacity, additional security features, dedicated technical support, and certain service guarantees. This Premiere Edition costs $50 per user per year.

A free version is also available to educational institutions. A reduced-price version is available to nonprofit organizations ($30 per user per year for organizations with over 3,000 users) and government agencies ($50 per user per year).

Throughout this chapter we will use our own free Standard Edition account to illustrate how a law firm might integrate Google Apps into its practice.

18.1 Gmail

The most familiar of the Google Apps is the Gmail e-mail service. Gmail can be accessed either via its robust Web-based Inbox interface or through your favorite e-mail client, such as Microsoft Outlook. If you use Google Apps for your practice and have multiple e-mail users, they can each choose how they want to access their messages. For example, Carole prefers to receive her messages in Outlook, where she takes advantage of some of Outlook's organizational features to keep track of her messages, projects, appointments, etc. Mark prefers to receive his messages in Gmail's Web-based Inbox because he can access his e-mails (and any attachments) from anywhere he can get an Internet connection. If you prefer to receive your Gmail messages in Outlook or some other e-mail client, Google has created a step-by-step guide to set up your e-mail client at http://mail.google.com/support/bin/topic.py?topic=12912.

If you're already using an e-mail client such as Outlook, and then opt to receive your Gmail messages there, you will find no differences in how you send, receive, and search those messages. For this reason, we'll focus on Gmail's Web-based Inbox, which operates differently from Outlook.

18.1.1 Advantages of Gmail

Gmail offers a number of advantages over conventional e-mail providers, the biggest of which is its price. The free Standard Edition will fit the needs of many solo and small firms. Even with its $50 per user per year price tag, the Premiere Edition can be a big cost-saver for larger firms and even government agencies. (See Section 18.8.3 for some examples of governmental legal departments switching to Gmail.)

Some of Gmail's other advantages include its large storage space for messages, superior search capabilities (via the Web interface), large file-attachment limits, and strong spam-filtering regardless of how you access it.

Free Gmail and Standard Edition accounts (*username@yourdomain. com*) come with a little over 7 gigabytes (GB) of storage space for e-mail messages and attachments. Premiere Edition accounts come with 25 GB of storage space.

Another advantage is Gmail's ability to search and retrieve messages. Because Gmail is a Google service, it has powerful search and retrieval capabilities.

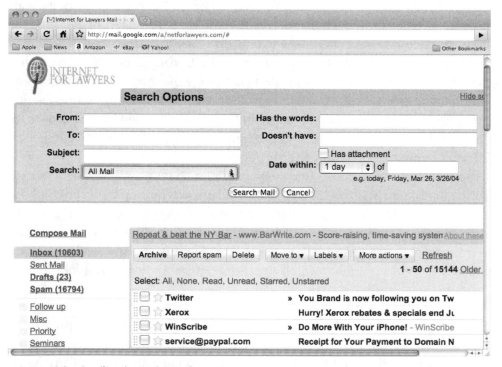

FIGURE 18.1   Like most of Google's services, Gmail offers both a "simple" search (accessed by typing search terms into this box at the top of the Gmail Web interface) and a set of more advanced search features (accessed by clicking the **Show search options** link to the right of the search box).

FIGURE 18.2   Gmail's advanced **Search options** menu allows you to search through your Gmail messages **To** or **From** specific individuals; that contain your keywords in the **Subject** line; that you have already read; or that are stored in specific folders (e.g., **Trash** or **Follow up**). Additionally, you can limit your search results to messages sent or received during a specific time frame (e.g., **Date within**).

One more advantage Gmail has over other e-mail services is its **Undo** feature. If you have ever sent an e-mail message and regretted it immediately after hitting the send button, or realized that the e-mail message you just sent was addressed to the wrong "Mike" from your contact list, then this is the feature for you. See Section 18.1.3.8 for more information on enabling the **Undo Send** feature in your account.

Your message has been sent. Undo View message

FIGURE 18.3   After you click the send button on a Gmail message, you get a chance to "unsend" the message. This is an illustration of the message that appears at the top of your Gmail Web interface after you send the message. You have up to 20 seconds to click the **Undo** link—and it's like the message was never sent. Clicking the **Undo** link pulls the message from your outbox and places it in your **Drafts** folder. Unlike the Recall Message feature in Microsoft's Outlook, which works only if the recipient is also on a Microsoft Exchange e-mail server, Google's Undo feature will work for any e-mail you send—but you must act quickly.

Gmail can also prompt you to add an attachment if you've obviously forgotten one.

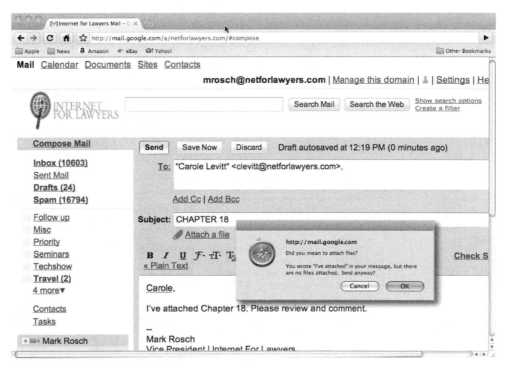

FIGURE 18.4   You can instruct Gmail to recognize phrases such as *I've attached*, *I'm attaching*, *attached is*, etc., as being related to the presence of a file attached to an e-mail. If Gmail detects one of these phrases in a message, but does not detect a file attached to the message when you click the **Send** button, you will be prompted with the pop-up box pictured here. You can then select **Cancel** to attach the missing file or **OK** to send the message without an attachment. (See Section 18.1.3.8 for information on how to turn this feature on.)

18.1.2   Gmail's Web-based Inbox Interface

In many ways, Gmail's Inbox is similar to other stand-alone and Web-based e-mail software. In the center section, it displays e-mail messages in reverse chronological order, with the most recently received message displayed at the top of the list. Unread messages are denoted by their display in a bold typeface, and read messages are not bolded.

☆ ABA-CLE Announcement	»	Inbox	Digital Platforms 101 |
☆ ABA-CLE Announcement	»	Inbox	The Ins and Outs of Pu
☆ ABA-CLE Announcement	»	Inbox	Hollywood Calling: Tra
☆ ABA-CLE Announcement	»	Inbox	Patent Licensing for St
☆ ABA-CLE Announcement	»	Inbox	Death of Major Label D
☆ ABA-CLE Announcement	»	Inbox	Creating a Culture that
☆ ABA-CLE Announcement	»	Inbox	Hollywood Calling: Tra
☆ ABA-CLE Announcement	»	Inbox	Death of Major Label D
☆ ABA-CLE Announcement	»	Inbox	Managing Stress in the
☆ ABA-CLE Announcement	»	Inbox	The Ethics of Starting '
☆ ABA-CLE Announcement	»	Inbox	CLE at a Glance - ... a

FIGURE 18.5   The identity of the message's sender and a snippet of text from the beginning of the message, along with the time of receipt (if received today) or date (if not received today), are displayed in the Inbox. The chevrons to the left of the subject line are "personal level indicators." Two chevrons, as shown in this illustration, indicate a message that was sent only to your e-mail address. One chevron indicates a message that was sent to your e-mail address, among others (e.g., you are cc'd, but the message is not from a mailing list). These indicators can be turned on by clicking the **Settings** link in the upper-right hand corner of the Inbox, then clicking the **General** tab, and then scrolling down to the **Personal level indicator** section to make your selection.

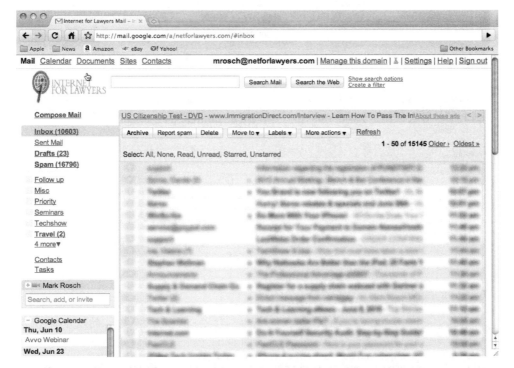

FIGURE 18.6   The Gmail Web interface includes numerous tools to manage and display your e-mail messages. These include the links to the left of the message list and buttons and links above the message list. (The contents of this Inbox are blurred to preserve the anonymity of the correspondents and to shield proprietary information displayed in some posts.)

One major difference between Gmail and most e-mail software is the way Gmail groups messages with the same subject line into "conversations." As a new message is added to the conversation, the sender's name, subject line, etc. are boldfaced (indicating that the message is unread) and the message moves to the top of the reverse-chronological list of messages.

| ☐ ☆ Denise .. Tim, Edward (31) | Inbox | [ACLEA-General] CLE Registrat | 11/5/09 |

FIGURE 18.7 The "conversation" (an exchange of messages taking place on a professional e-mail discussion group) in this illustration contains 31 separate e-mail messages from different individuals. Clicking the subject line displays each of the messages in a reverse-chronological list. You can opt out of reviewing new messages in a specific conversation by clicking the checkbox to the left of the conversation and clicking the **More actions** button (see the next illustration) and selecting **Mute**. Note that messages in muted conversations are not deleted, they are just moved from your Inbox to your All mail folder—and any subsequent messages in that conversation are automatically routed to the All mail folder without appearing in your Inbox. Muted conversations can still be retrieved in searches of All mail.

18.1.2.1 The Area Above Gmail's Message List

Above the message list are tools to help you manage your messages, as well as some other information.

FIGURE 18.8 At the top of the message list are three rows of information. The first, the blue "Learning Management" row in this illustration, is a Web Clip that may display a **Sponsored Link**—a paid advertisement based on keywords that appear in your e-mail messages (or news and information from some third-party Web source). These ads can be turned off or replaced with your own customized information by clicking the **Settings** link in the upper right-hand corner of the screen and then clicking the **Web clips** tab and unchecking **Show my web clips above the Inbox** on the subsequent page. (See Section 18.1.3.7 for more information on these ads and Section 18.8 for privacy concerns related to Gmail.)

The second row (the buttons below the blue banner ad) allow you to organize and manage your e-mail messages. For example, clicking the **Archive** button cleans up your Inbox by moving selected messages from your Inbox to your All mail folder (which contains all of the e-mail messages you've received, even those in your Trash folder); the **Report spam** button moves selected messages to the Spam folder and automatically sends future messages from the same sender to the Spam folder; and the **Move to** and **Labels** buttons allow you to group selected messages into default categories such as **Follow up**, **Misc.**, and **Priority**, or any other labels you create by clicking **Labels** and then **Manage labels**. The **More actions** button allows you to mark selected messages as **Read** or **Unread**; **Filter** selected messages; or **Mute** a conversation, among other actions.

☆ **LPM Publications**　　　　　» Inbox　**Lawyers: Find Info |**

FIGURE 18.9　You can mark any message in your Inbox for easy retrieval by clicking the star icon to the left of the message you want to select. Doing so will turn the star from clear to yellow. Subsequently clicking the **Starred** link in the column to the left of the message list will display only those messages that you have previously marked with a star.

The third row (labeled **Select**) contains contains links that allow you to mark the checkboxes next to **All, Read, Unread, Starred,** or **Unread** messages. Once you've made a selection in this row, you can use the buttons in the second row to organize or manage all of the displayed messages that meet the criteria you selected. Subsequently, clicking the link None unchecks all of the messages.

18.1.2.2　The Left-hand Column of Gmail's Web-based Inbox Interface

The tools in Gmail's Web-based Inbox interface that get the most use are in the left-hand column.

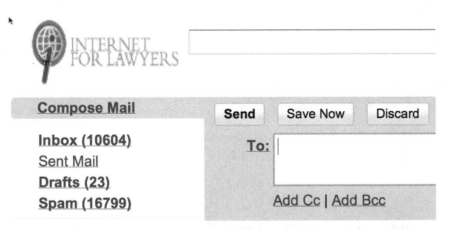

FIGURE 18.10　The **Compose Mail** link at the top of the column to the left of the message list opens a new, blank e-mail message. (Holding down the *Shift* key on your keyboard while clicking the **Compose Mail** link opens the new, blank e-mail message in a new Web browser window—instead of navigating away from your Inbox.) The rest of the links at the top of the column to the left of the message list lead to individual folders where mail is stored. The **Inbox** folder is the first stop for a message after it's received. The **Sent Mail** folder contains all of the messages sent from your account. The **Drafts** folder contains e-mails in progress (clicking the **Save Now** button while you're composing an e-mail saves the contents of the message to the **Drafts** folder for later retrieval).

In the Spring of 2010, Google made it even easier to add attachments to the e-mails you send in Gmail.

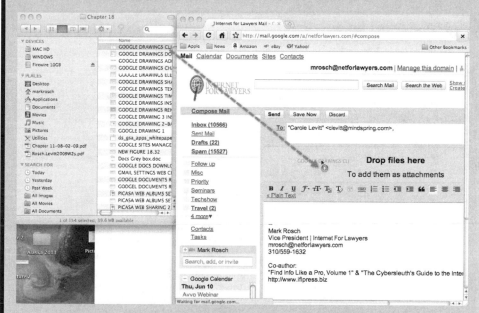

You can now easily attach any file on your computer to a Gmail message by selecting it, and then dragging and dropping it into the area underneath the To section of your message. The file is then automatically attached to the message.

As of our publication deadline, this feature works only in the Firefox and Chrome Web browsers for both Windows and Mac Operating Systems.

18.1.2.3 Spam

The last link in this section leads to your **Spam** folder. Gmail does a very good job of blocking spam from getting into your Inbox.

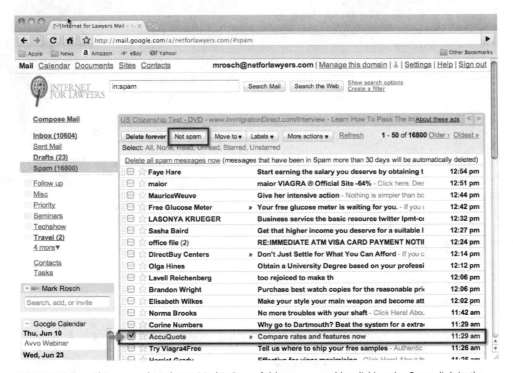

FIGURE 18.11 This screenshot shows Mark's Spam folder—accessed by clicking the **Spam** link in the left-hand column. Sometimes Gmail does too good a job filtering messages into this folder. Clicking the checkbox to the left of the message and then clicking the **Not spam** button near the top of the window instructs Gmail not to treat future messages from the sender of this message as spam and automatically moves the selected message to the **Inbox** folder.

18.1.2.4 Additional Tools in the Left-hand Column of Gmail's Web-based Inbox Interface

The next section of links in the left-hand column lists Labels you can assign to the messages you receive. Clicking any of these links displays all of the messages you have assigned that label. (Labels are assigned using the **Labels** button described in Section 18.1.3.3). You can create your own labels by clicking the **Create new label** link and typing the name for your new label into the pop-up box that subsequently appears. Clicking the **OK** button adds your new label to the list.

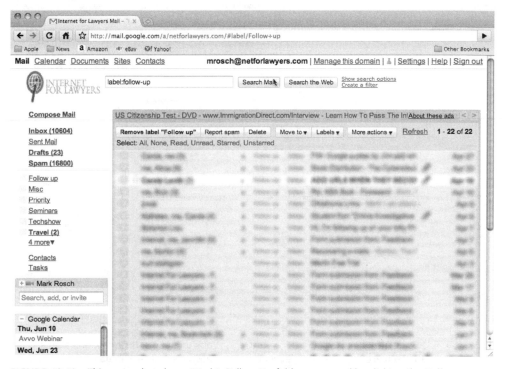

FIGURE 18.12   This screenshot shows Mark's Follow Up folder—accessed by clicking the **Follow up** link in the left-hand column. Any messages he has marked with the **Follow up** label will appear here. (The contents of this folder are blurred to preserve the anonymity of the correspondents and to shield proprietary information displayed in some posts.)

FIGURE 18.13   This is a detailed screenshot of a message in Mark's Follow Up folder (as seen in Figure 18.12). Once the follow-up is completed and the project or task is completed, you can click the **X** next to the **Follow up** label to remove the **Follow up** label—which removes the message from the Follow Up folder. The message would still remain in the Inbox.

18.1.2.5 Contact Manager

Gmail also has an integrated Contact Manager. You can import contacts from other e-mail software such as Outlook (using a CSV file), or you can enter individuals into the contact list one at a time. Gmail also builds a *de facto* list of contacts for you automatically from the e-mail addresses with which you frequently correspond.

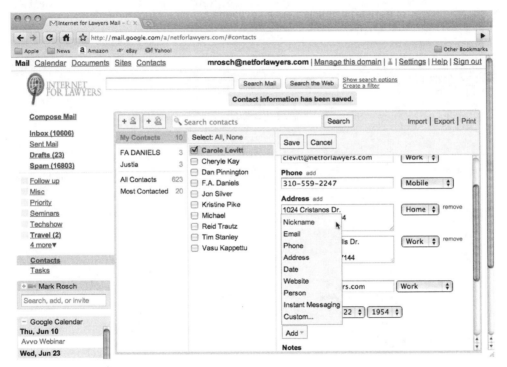

FIGURE 18.14 Clicking the checkbox to the left of any name and then the **Edit** button (visible in the illustration below) allows you to add information about the contact you've selected, including **Title**, **Company**, additional **E-mail** addresses, mailing **Address**, **Website** address, **Birthday**, and **Notes**. Clicking the **Add** menu allows you to enter additional information such as **Nickname** or custom fields you can define.

Gmail also allows you to create groups of multiple contacts so you can send e-mails to all members of that group simply by typing the group's name into the message's To box.

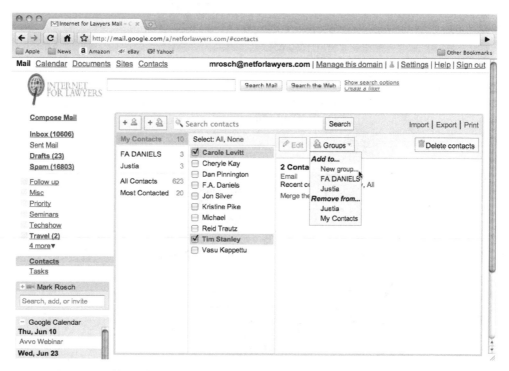

FIGURE 18.15   To add contacts to a group, click the checkbox to the left of any name you want to add and then click the **Groups** drop-down menu. Selecting an existing group from the drop-down menu adds the selected contact(s) to that group. You can also select **New group** from the drop-down menu to create a new group to which to add your selected contacts.

18.1.2.6 Task Manager

Gmail also has an integrated Task Manager that allows you to list and track tasks you must complete. You can access it by clicking the **Tasks** link in the left-hand column.

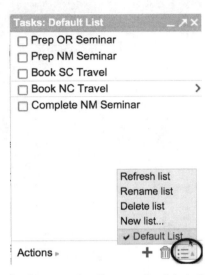

FIGURE 18.16 This screenshot illustrates the default Gmail **Tasks** list. You can **Rename** any list or create a **New list** by clicking on the menu in the lower right-hand corner. Clicking the trashcan icon would delete the selected task (**Book NC Travel** in this illustration). Clicking the plus sign adds a new item to the list.

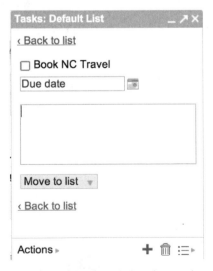

FIGURE 18.17 Clicking the right-pointing chevron that appears next to any task after selecting it allows you to add a **Due date** or other notes to the task.

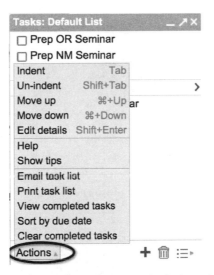

FIGURE 18.18 Clicking the **Actions** menu in the lower left-hand corner of the **Tasks** list allows you to manipulate the list (e.g., **Move up**, **Move down**, **Sort by due date**). You can also view all past completed tasks or clear the list of completed tasks. Detailed **Help** and usage tips can also be accessed from this menu.

18.1.2.7 Additional Useful Elements of Gmail's Web-based Inbox Interface

Google allows you to add additional "gadgets" to the your Gmail Inbox interface. These are accessible by clicking the **Settings** link in the upper right-hand corner, then clicking the **Labs** tab, and then scrolling through the list and clicking **Enable** for any of the features listed there. Subsequently clicking **Disable** turns the feature off. Mark has enabled the Google Calendar gadget which adds information from his Google Calendar (see Section 18.3) to the left-hand column of his Gmail Web interface (see Figure 18.15).

Above the Google Calendar gadget is the Google Chat gadget. (Marked only with the user's name until expanded by clicking the plus sign to the left of that name—see Figure 18.15.) Google Chat allows you to send messages back and forth instantly to other Gmail users. You can even integrate voice and video chat by activating/installing Google Talk (see Section 18.6).

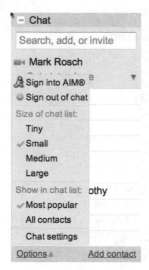

FIGURE 18.19 Before you can start chatting with other Gmail users, you must invite them to chat, by clicking the **Add Contact** link, and they must accept. Google Chat also interacts with Google Voice (to add video and voice chat; see Section 18.6) and the popular AOL Instant Messenger application AIM so you can use Google Chat to communicate through an existing AIM account by using the **Sign into AIM** selection located on the Options drop-down menu.

18.1.3 Gmail Settings

You can customize the look and feel of your Gmail account with the controls you'll find by clicking the **Settings** link in the upper right-hand corner of the Web interface. After you click the **Settings** link you'll see eight tabs: **General**, **Accounts**, **Labels**, **Filters**, **Forwarding and POP/IMAP**, **Chat**, **Web Clips**, and **Labs** (see the upcoming sections for more details).

18.1.3.1   Gmail General Settings

The **General** tab contains settings that control much of the look and feel of your Gmail Web interface, as well as some of its special features. While settings like **Language**, **Maximum page size, Signature,** and **Vacation responder** are pretty self-explanatory, some of the others may not be so clear. For example, Gmail has a number of **Keyboard shortcuts** that allow you to invoke many of the service's features and functions with predetermined keystroke combinations, rather than clicking buttons and icons in the Web interface. You can see the full list of these shortcuts at http://mail. google.com/support/bin/answer.py?hl=en&ctx=mail&answer=6594.

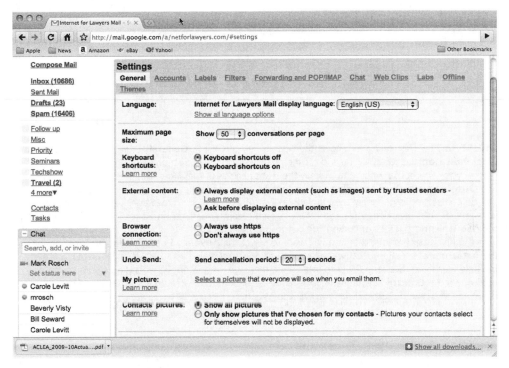

FIGURE 18.20   This screenshot illustrates the top half of Gmail's **General** settings tab. In the **External content** section you can determine whether you want to display externally linked content in messages you receive, such as images. When you receive a message with such content, Gmail will not display it in the message, but will include two links at the top. Clicking the **Display images below** link will approve the display of the content in that one message. Clicking the **Always display images from sender@sender.com** link at the top designates that sender to be a "trusted sender." To always display images in messages from these trusted senders, click the **Always display external content (such as images) sent by trusted senders** option. You can use the drop-down menu in the **Undo Send** section to designate the 5- or 20-second time limit for the Undo Send feature discussed in Section 18.1.1. The **My picture** section allows you to select a photograph that will be displayed to other Gmail users with whom you make contact. The **Contacts' pictures** section lets you choose whether to display other Gmail users' chosen pictures in your Gmail Web interface (not pictured).

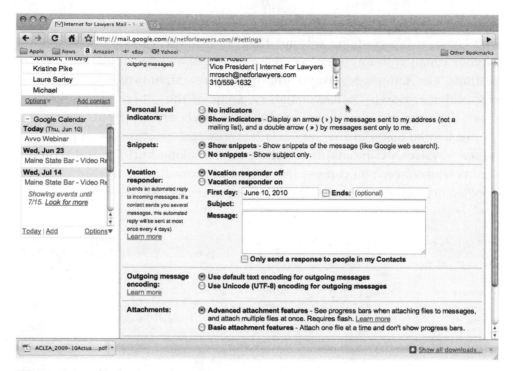

FIGURE 18.21 This illustration shows the bottom half of Gmail's **General** settings tab. The **Personal level indicators** section turns on and off the feature discussed in Section 18.1.2. In the **Snippets** section you can choose whether to display the text previews of messages, described in Section 18.1.2. The **Outgoing message encoding** section controls the encoding of messages transmitted to recipients. The default setting is generally acceptable; however, if you're sending messages to foreign-language speakers, or your recipients inform you that they are receiving garbled messages, you might want to try the **Use Unicode (UTF-8) encoding for outgoing messages** setting. If you send a lot of messages with multiple attachments, then you will want to select the **Advanced attachment features** option in the **Attachments** section because it allows you to select multiple files to attach all at once. (To select multiple files from the same folder to attach to a message on a Windows operating system computer, hold down the **Control** key and left-click each file you want to attach; on a Mac OS computer, hold down the ⌘ key and click each file you want to attach.

18.1.3.2 Accessing Multiple E-mail Accounts Through Gmail

Gmail allows you to consolidate multiple e-mail accounts you might own into the Gmail Inbox. The **Accounts** tab allows you to add and control the influx of mail from these other accounts.

FIGURE 18.22 This illustration shows Gmail's **Accounts** settings tab. The **Send mail as** section allows you to identify messages that you send via the Gmail Web interface as coming from other e-mail accounts you might own such as *mrosch@mindspring.com* or *mrosch@earthlink.net*. You can also use the **edit info** link to the right of this section to change the identifier associated with your outgoing Gmail (e.g., *Mark Rosch – Vice President, Internet For Lawyers* or *Mark Rosch – Author* instead of just *Mark Rosch*). You can use the **Get mail from other accounts** setting to receive messages from other e-mail accounts you might own such as *mrosch@mindspring.com* or *mrosch@earthlink.net*.

18.1.3.3   Creating and Managing Labels for Your Gmail Messages

As discussed in Section 18.1.2.1, your Gmail account comes with a standard set of folders in which messages are stored, but it also allows you to create **Labels** to group associated messages together.

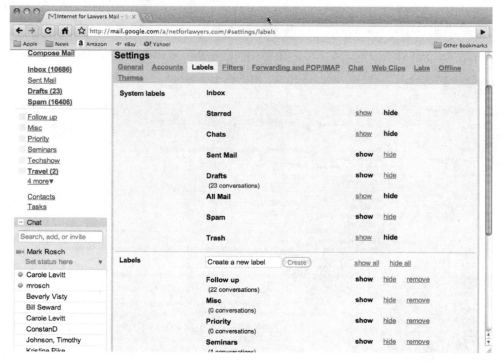

FIGURE 18.23   This illustration shows Gmail's **Labels** settings tab. Opting to **show** any of the labels makes links to them appear in the left-hand column of the Gmail Web interface. Opting to **hide** any of the labels groups them under the **[X] more** drop-down menu in the left-hand column (**4 more** in this illustration). You can create new labels using the **Create new label** link in that drop-down menu or by using the **Create a new label** box in the lower portion of this screen.

18.1.3.4 Creating Filters to Manage the E-mail Messages You Receive

Similar to Outlook and other e-mail software, Gmail allows you to set up **Filters** to automatically categorize/sort your messages as they are received. (In Outlook this feature is called "Rules.")

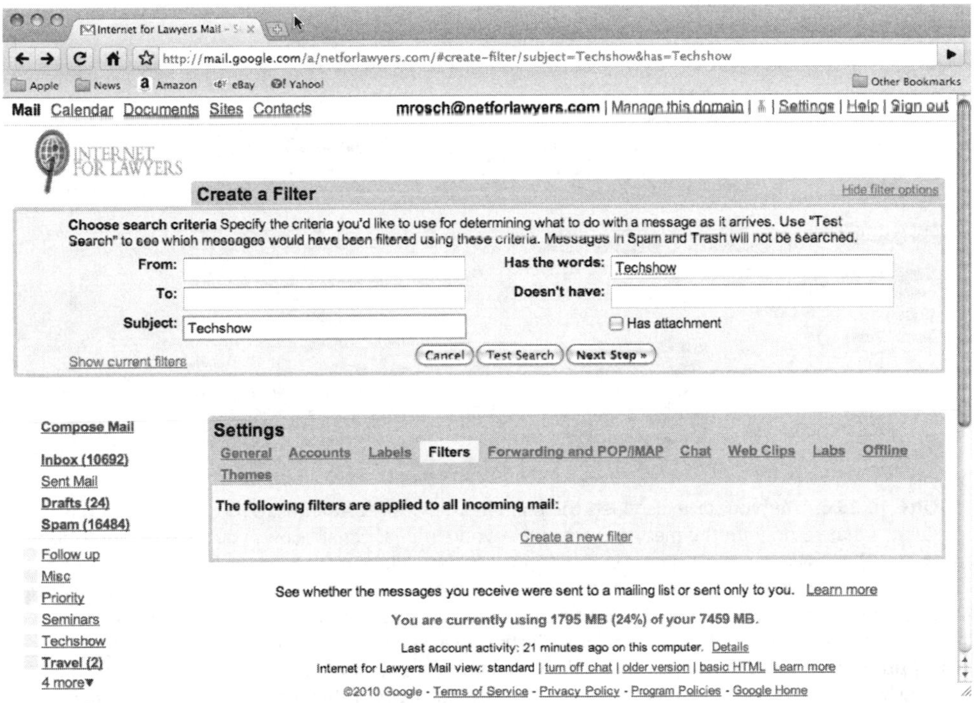

FIGURE 18.24 Click the **Filters** tab and then the **Create a new filter** (not pictured) link to initiate the process of creating a new filter (seen here) to organize your incoming messages. In this example we want to group any messages that include the word *Techshow* anywhere in the message, including in the subject line or the body of the message. Once we've entered the criteria we want to use to categorize mail, we click the **Next Step** button to continue. (Clicking the **Test Search** button searches through your previously received messages to show how many messages would be effected by this new filter.)

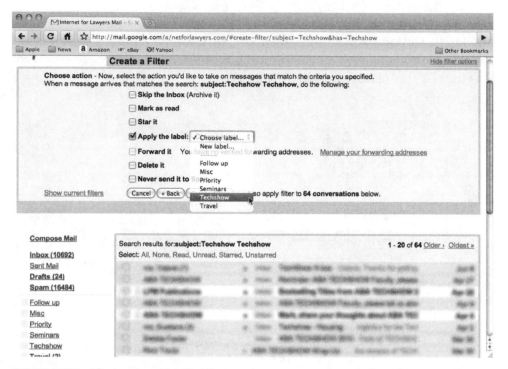

FIGURE 18.25   After you have identified the content you want to categorize/sort, the next step is to tell Gmail what to do with the messages that meet your criteria. Gmail allows you to **Skip the Inbox (Archive it)** (messages would appear in the All mail folder), **Mark as read**, **Star it**, **Apply the label** (that you select from the drop-down menu), **Forward it to** (the e-mail address you designate), **Delete it**, or **Never send it to Spam**. In this example, we've chosen to **Apply the label Techshow** to all incoming messages that include the keyword *Techshow* anywhere in the message. By marking the **Also apply filter to 29 conversations below** checkbox, we've also chosen to apply this filter to all previously received messages currently stored in this Gmail account that include the keyword *Techshow* anywhere in the message. (Note that portions of the contents of this Inbox are blurred to preserve the anonymity of the correspondents and to shield proprietary information displayed in some posts.)

18.1.3.5   Accessing Gmail Messages from Other E-mail Accounts or Software

Gmail offers a great amount of flexibility for viewing and retrieving messages received in your Gmail account. You can consolidate your e-mail messages into one place by forwarding all of your Gmail messages to another e-mail account you own. Also, as discussed in Section 18.1, Gmail allows you to retrieve your messages using your favorite e-mail software including Microsoft Outlook, Eudora, and Apple Mail.

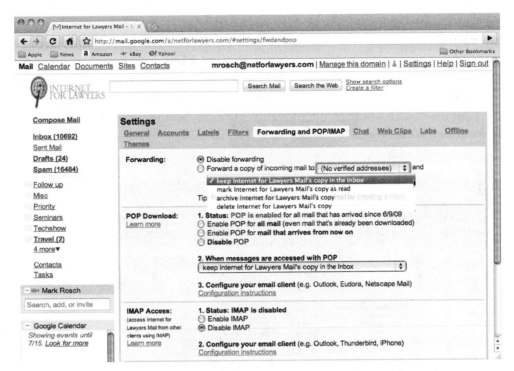

FIGURE 18.26   Gmail will forward all of your incoming messages to another e-mail account you own if you select **Forward a copy of incoming mail to** and designate another e-mail address to which the messages should be sent. You can also use the drop-down menu (next to the **email address** box) to instruct Gmail how to handle messages (on Gmail's own servers) after they've been forwarded. You can select from **keep [e-mail sender's] copy in the inbox**, **archive [e-mail sender's] copy**, or **delete [e-mail sender's] copy**. To receive Gmail messages in your favorite e-mail software, you must **Enable POP for all mail** in the **POP Download** section. If you want to stop receiving Gmail messages in your favorite e-mail software, you can **Disable POP**. You can also use the drop-down menu in the **When messages are accessed with POP** section to instruct Gmail how to handle messages (on Gmail's own servers) once you have downloaded those messages to your e-mail software. The options on this drop-down menu are the same as on the previous drop-down menu. (See Section 18.1 for a link to detailed configuration instructions.)

IMAP Access allows you to access messages similar to the way you can if you **Enable POP**. IMAP Access offers greater synchronizing capabilities between the Gmail settings and your e-mail software. Google offers a detailed discussion of the benefits of IMAP Access versus POP at http://mail.google.com/support/bin/answer.py?hl=en&ctx=mail&answer=75725.

18.1.3.6 Customizing Your Google Chat Experience

As discussed in Section 18.6, Gmail has integrated an instant messaging/chat feature into the Web-based interface. The **Chat** settings tab allows you to customize the Chat feature. You can even integrate voice and video chat by activating or installing Google Talk (see Section 18.6).

Some of the settings on this tab, such as **Sounds** and **Auto-add suggested contacts,** are self-explanatory.

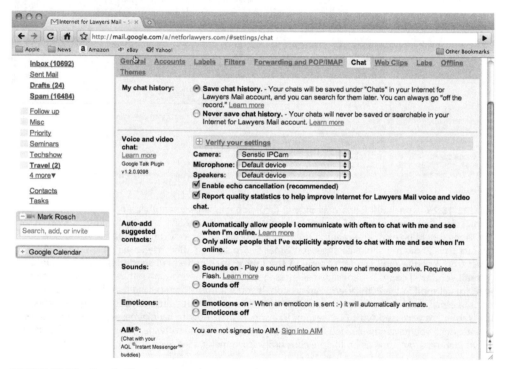

FIGURE 18.27 Google Chat gives you the option of saving the transcripts of your chats to your Gmail account, where they can be searched and retrieved like e-mail messages using the Web-based interface. (A **Chats** label is created.) On the **Chat** settings tab you can opt to **Save chat history** or **Never save chat history**. Note that even if you are saving your chat history, you can stop recording any chat by selecting **Off the record** from the chat conversation **Options** menu (not pictured). Note, too, that once you take a chat conversation with someone "off the record," all future chat conversations with that individual are off the record until you unselect that option.

18.1.3.7 Customizing or Removing Web Clips and Ads from the Top of Your Gmail Web-Based Interface

As discussed in Section 18.1.2.1, Gmail places sponsored links and/or news and information from outside sources into a bar above your message display in Gmail's Web-based interface.

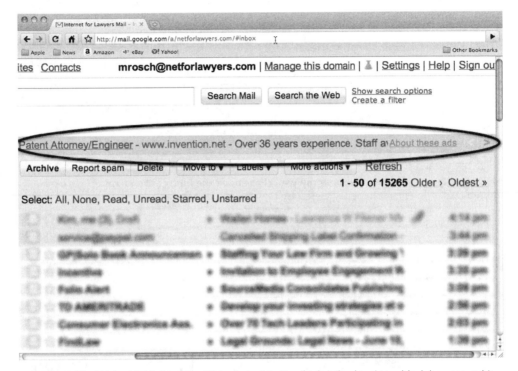

FIGURE 18.28 We've highlighted the Web clip in this Gmail Inbox by drawing a black box around it. In this example, the Web clip is a paid advertisement. Clicking the right-arrow button (on the right side of the boxed Web clip) will display a different Web clip.

You can customize these Web clips to a degree, or if you prefer not to see them, you can turn the Web clips off entirely.

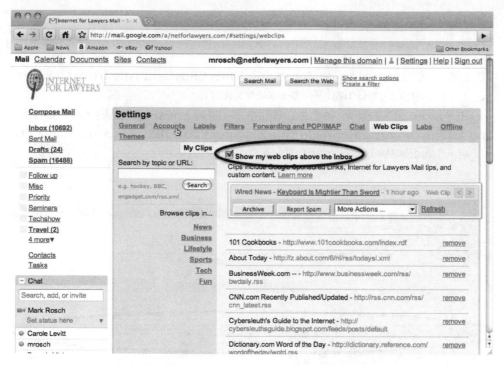

FIGURE 18.29 Unchecking the **Show my web clips above the Inbox** option turns off the display of Web clips. If you prefer to display these Web clips, you can customize the sources for the news and information (but not the ads) by clicking the **remove** link to the right of any of the included sources you want to eliminate.

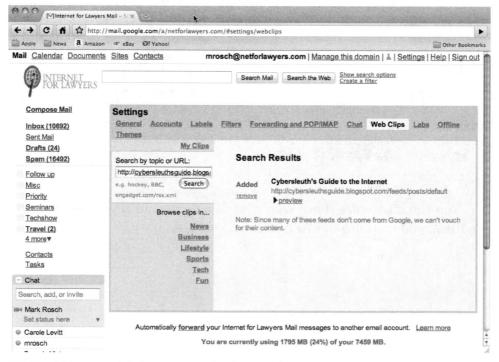

FIGURE 18.30 You can further customize the Web Clips feature by entering the URL for an RSS feed that you find interesting. Then, instead of drawing information from sources selected by Gmail, you can select the sources yourself. (Removing all of the default sources provided by Gmail, as discussed in the previous illustration, and leaving only your own makes Web Clips more useful. In this illustration, we are adding the RSS feed from the "Cybersleuth's Guide to the Internet" blog to the Web Clips sources.

TURN YOUR GMAIL INBOX INTO A CURRENT AWARENESS READING ROOM

Usage Tip

As discussed in Section 9.2, reading relevant blogs can be an excellent way to keep up to date with developments in your practice area.

You can add the RSS feeds from multiple blogs you find useful to the Web Clips sources (see Figure 18.30). Then headlines from those blogs' posts will appear in the space above your Inbox in the Gmail Web-based interface. Clicking on any headlines that interest you will take you directly to the blog post where the information is located.

18.1.3.8 Add Experimental Features and Functions to Your Gmail Web-Based Interface

Gmail development teams and other engineers periodically create new add-on tools for Gmail. These experimental features are available behind the **Labs** settings tab.

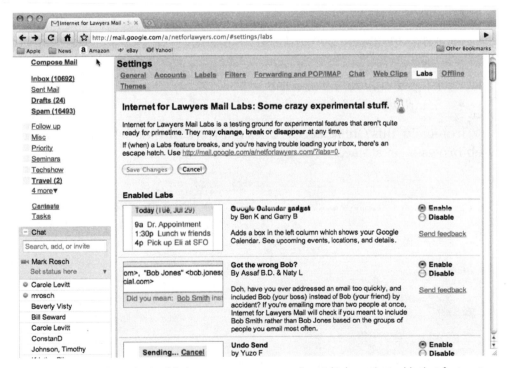

FIGURE 18.31 Clicking the **Enable** button next to any experimental Labs project adds that feature to your Gmail account. Some useful Labs experiments include Forgotten Attachment Detector (discussed in Section 18.1.1), Google Calendar gadget (discussed in Section 18.1.2.7) and Undo Send (discussed in Section 18.1.1).

18.1.3.9 Accessing Your Gmail Messages Without an Internet Connection

One concern many people have about using an online storage system for their e-mail messages is the inability to access those messages in the absence of an Internet connection. Gmail solves this problem by giving you offline access to your messages stored on Google's servers even when you're not connected to the Internet.

The Offline feature is only available for use with certain Web browser/ Operating System combinations—with the addition of a free helper application available from Google (Google Gears available for download and installation at http://gears.google.com).

Google Gears allows Offline access to your messages on your Windows computer with:

- Windows XP, Windows Vista, or Windows 7
- Firefox version 1.5 or newer
- Internet Explorer version 6.0 or newer
- Chrome (pre-installed)

On Mac computers Google Gears requires:

- OS 10.4 (Tiger) or 10.5 (Leopard) and a G4 (or newer) or Intel CPU
- Firefox version 1.5 or newer
- Safari version 3.1.1 or newer

Ironically, this Offline access does not work with Google's own Chrome Web browser on a Mac.

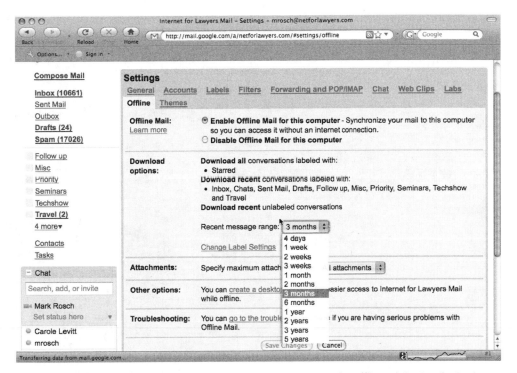

FIGURE 18.32   Once you've installed Google Gears, you can access the Offline tab in Gmail's Settings. The Download options section allows you to control which messages and attachments are downloaded to your computer so you can access them when you do not have an Internet connection.

18.1.3.10   Customizing Your Gmail Interface

You can customize the color scheme (and other elements) of your Gmail Web-based Inbox.

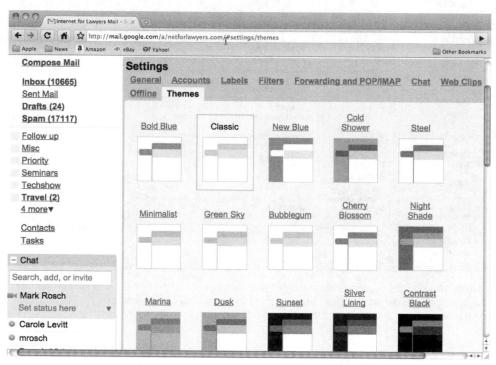

FIGURE 18.33   Clicking the Themes tab in Gmail's Settings section allows you to select from a number of preset color schemes for your Gmail Inbox. At the bottom of the list (not pictured) is an option to select your own custom colors.

18.2   Google Docs

The "Google Docs" name can be a bit confusing. When most people hear it they think only of word processing documents (like the ones we're all used to creating in Microsoft Word or Corel WordPerfect). While this service does create documents like those (see Section 18.2.1), it also offers the ability to create, edit, store, and share spreadsheets (Section 18.2.2), presentations (Section 18.2.3), and forms (Section 18.2.4).

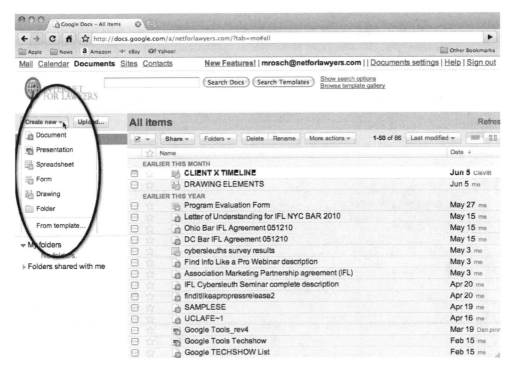

FIGURE 18.34   Some of the confusion over the type of documents you can create in Google Documents is Google's own fault. The name "Google Docs" is used to cover the entire service (i.e., all of the spreadsheets, presentations, forms, and word processing documents you can create with the service), not just the word processing Documents. In this illustration, the **Documents** link in the upper left-hand corner accesses all of the files, regardless of type, stored online in Mark's account, while the **Document** selection on the **Create new** drop-down menu opens a new word processing Document (as opposed to another type of document; e.g., **Presentation**, **Spreadsheet**, **Form**, or **Drawing**).

The **Upload** button, next to the **Create new** button, allows you to upload an existing document from your own computer to Google Docs' online storage, where you can securely share it with others. You and all of your invited collaborators can edit these documents with Google Docs' tools.

You can upload the following file types:

- documents up to 500 kilobytes (KB) in size; there is a limit of 500 Documents in a Docs account; acceptable file types are .doc, .docx, .html, plain text (.txt), .rtf, .odt
- spreadsheets up to 256 columns wide; there is a limit of 1,000 Spreadsheets in a Docs account; acceptable file types are .xls, .xlsx, .ods, .csv, .tsv, .txt, .tsb
- presentations up to 10 megabytes (MB) in size or containing up to 200 slides; there is a limit of 500 Presentations in a Docs account; acceptable filetypes are .ppt, .pps
- .pdf files up to 10 MB in size can be uploaded and viewed but not directly edited; there is a limit of 100 .pdf files in a Docs account

DOWNLOAD YOUR DOCUMENTS FROM GOOGLE DOCS IN BATCHES

In October 2009, Google introduced an easier way to download your documents from Google Docs storage to your own computer.

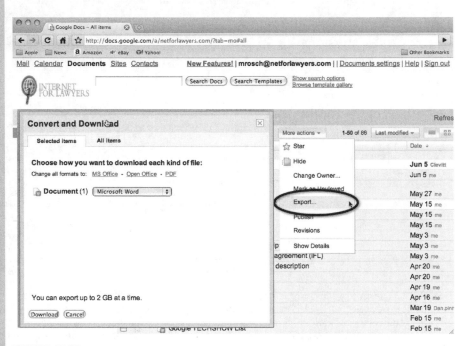

FIGURE 18.35

You can download one file or multiple files simultaneously. To download multiple files simultaneously, check the boxes next to the files you want to download, then click the **More actions** drop-down menu (not shown) and then click **Export** (not shown). The Google document(s) you have chosen are automatically converted to Microsoft Office file types (e.g., Google word processing Documents are converted and saved as Microsoft Word files by default). You can also select other file types (e.g., Open Office, Plain text) to convert your files into, if you prefer, from another drop-down menu that appears after you've made your file selections. Also after you've made your file selections, you can choose the **All items** tab to download all of the documents you've stored in your Google Docs account. Google even compresses ("zips") the files so they take less time to download. There is a 2 GB limit per download.

Regardless of whether you uploaded a Google Document from your computer or created a new one online, Google Docs includes editing and formatting tools that will look very familiar to you if you are a regular user of Microsoft Office, Corel WordPerfect Office, OpenOffice, or Apple's iWork productivity software.

When files are uploaded to Google Docs, the formatting in the original document is *usually* preserved; however, formatting is occasionally lost in the translation. In the Spring of 2010, Google launched a series of upgrades to Google Docs—one of which was aimed at reducing these formatting errors. If they do still occur, you can use the editing tools available in Google Docs to restore the original formatting.

You can also add files to your Google Docs collection by e-mailing them to a special e-mail address Google creates for your account. Clicking the **Show information on emailing in your documents and files** on the Upload page will reveal your special, personalized e-mail address to which you can send files to be added. Note that this feature is meant for text in the body of your e-mail message or for .txt, .rtf, .html, .odt, or .doc file attachments. It will not work with spreadsheets, .pdf files, or files saved in Microsoft Office 2007 and 2010's .docx format.

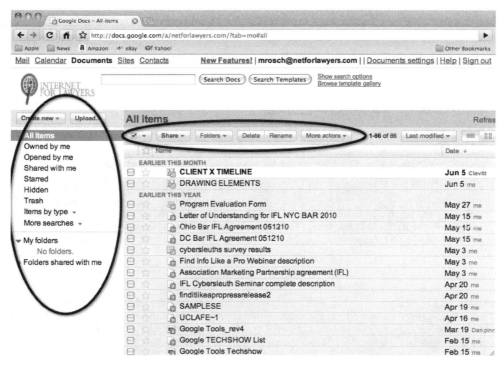

FIGURE 18.36   Links in the left-hand column of the Google Docs storage interface allow you to select specific categories of documents, such as those **Owned by me**, **Opened by me**, or **Shared with me**. Other functions in this section are similar to Gmail functions discussed in Section 18.1.2, such as **Starred** and **Trash**. The **Hidden** category in Docs is similar to the Archive category in Gmail. The **Items by type** drop-down menu lets you display just the **Documents**, just the **Presentations**, or just the **Spreadsheets**. (The **Files** option on this drop-down menu displays any files that do not fall into the three previous categories.)

18.2.1 Google Documents

Google Documents is an online word processing documents creation and sharing service. It allows you to create word processing documents similar to the way you would with Microsoft Word, Corel WordPerfect, or Apple Pages.

Google Documents started out life in August 2005 as Writely, an independent service. Writely was purchased by Google in March 2006.

An April 2010, redesign made Google Documents function even more like a commercial word processor, with the addition of rulers, tab stops, spell-check as you type, and the ability to better manipulate images you insert into your Documents.

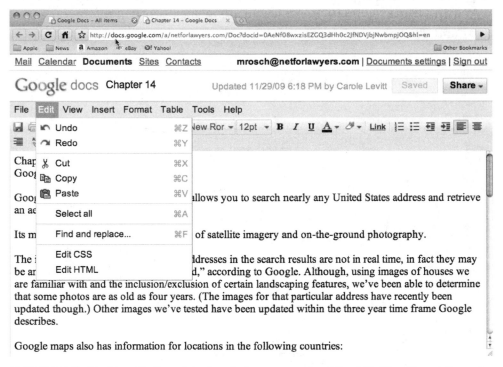

FIGURE 18.37 The Menu Toolbar of the Google Documents editor (**File**, **Edit**, **View**, **Insert**, **Format**, **Table**, **Tools**, **Help**) will look familiar to regular users of commercial word processing software like Microsoft Word. Even familiar keyboard shortcuts like *Control+C* (for copy) and *Control+V* (for paste) work in Google Documents. (Mac OS users would substitute the for the *Control* key.)

18.2.1.1   Sharing Documents in Google Docs

You can share documents that you create or edit in Google Docs with everyone on the Web or you can share and collaborate on these documents with select individuals.

FIGURE 18.38   As the label suggests, the Google Docs **Share** pull-down menu allows you to share your document with everyone on the Internet by selecting the **Publish as web page** option or to share more selectively by selecting the **Invite people** option. You can also **Email as attachment** to share the document the "old fashioned" way (but then you can't collaborate on the document online through Google Docs).

FIGURE 18.39   Selecting the **Get the link to share** option (seen in the preceding illustration) displays this dialog box with two options. Both generate a URL that you can paste into an e-mail so others can view and/or edit the document. One (seen in this illustration) is only for registered users of Google Apps in your domain (**Internet For Lawyers users only** in this example). The other is for anyone to whom you can send an e-mail. You could even embed that URL into a Web page if you wanted to share the document with anyone who has Web access.

You can also invite others to read and/or edit your documents by selecting the **Invite people** option (seen in the first illustration in this section). Regardless of their e-mail address, collaborators must have a Google Account to access these documents.

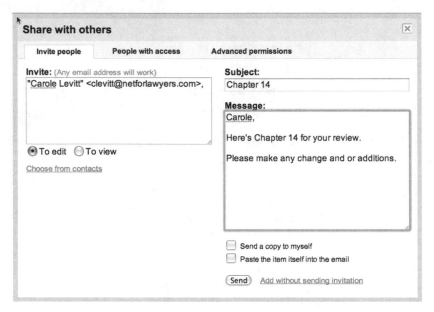

FIGURE 18.40 Selecting the **Invite people** option (seen in the first illustration in this section) allows you to enter the e-mail addresses of anyone you want to have access to the document. Beneath the **Invite** box, you can choose whether the people you've listed have access **To edit** the document or just **To view** it. The document name is automatically filled into the **Subject** box, but you can change it. You can also type a **Message** to the individuals who you invite. Clicking the **Send** button sends the invitation message (which includes a link to the document). The **People with access** tab lists the individuals who can already access this particular document. The **Advanced permissions** tab lets you control how much access the people you invite to edit the document have and whether they can invite others, or if invitations can be forwarded to other people.

Note the **Add without sending invitation** link. This option is not preferable, as the people you invite would have to log into their own Google Account before they could access the document you've shared with them.

18.2.1.2 Tracking Changes to Google Documents

An important element of online collaboration is the ability to track the changes made by others with whom you are collaborating on documents. This is the feature that makes services like Google Documents superior to e-mailing documents back and forth for revisions (especially when more than two people are revising the document).

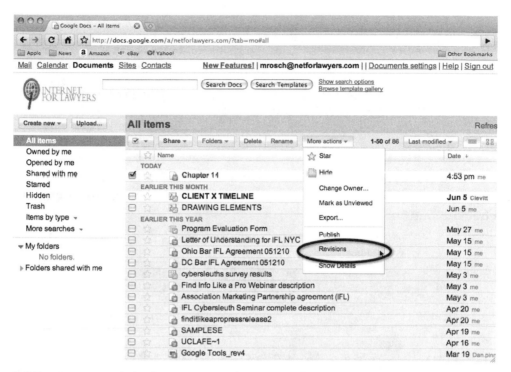

FIGURE 18.41   To track the changes to a Google Document, first click into the checkbox to the left of the document in the **All items** folder and then select the **Revisions** item from the **More actions** drop-down menu.

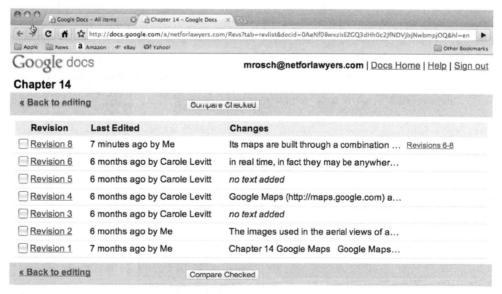

FIGURE 18.42   Selecting the **Revisions** option from the **More actions** drop-down menu in the Google Docs **All items** folder displays all of the revisions made by various collaborators for the selected document. Clicking the **Revision 4** link, for example, will show only the changes made to the document up until that point in time. Clicking the **Revision 6** link would show all revisions to date.

In the Spring of 2010, Google made a number of changes/upgrades to Google Docs. One of those made it possible for those collaborating on a document at the same time to see the revisions made by other collaborators in real time—as they are being typed.

This is a feature that originated in Google Wave (see Section 18.5). It can be quite distracting—if not downright disconcerting.

You can see the changes made from one revision to another by marking the checkbox next to specific revisions and clicking the **Compare checked** button.

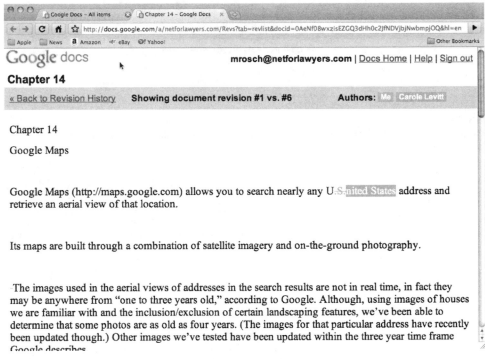

FIGURE 18.43   In this illustration, we are comparing **Revision 1** with **Revision 6**. Google Docs assigns a different color to changes made by each particular collaborator (from one revision to the other). In this portion of the Document we can see that Carole changed the text *U.S.* to *United States*.

As the owner of a Document being shared in Google Docs, you have the power to reject changes made by any collaborator.

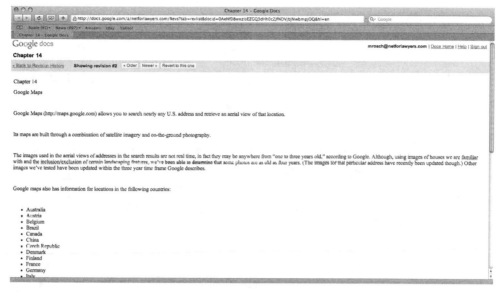

FIGURE 18.44   In this illustration, we are looking at **Revision 2**. As the owner of the Document, we can look at **Older** or **Newer** revisions, or **Revert to this one** to ignore any changes made in subsequent revisions.

18.2.2   Google Spreadsheets

Like Google Documents, Spreadsheets was born as part of the previously independent company Writely before it was acquired by Google. Also like Google Documents, the Menu Toolbar of the Google Spreadsheet editor (**File**, **Edit**, **View**, **Insert**, **Format**, **Form**, **Tools**, **Help**) will look familiar to regular users of commercial spreadsheet software like Microsoft Excel. Google's April 2010 redesign of its Apps made its Spreadsheets even more like commercial software with the addition of features like auto-complete, the ability to drag-and-drop columns, and a formula bar for cell editing.

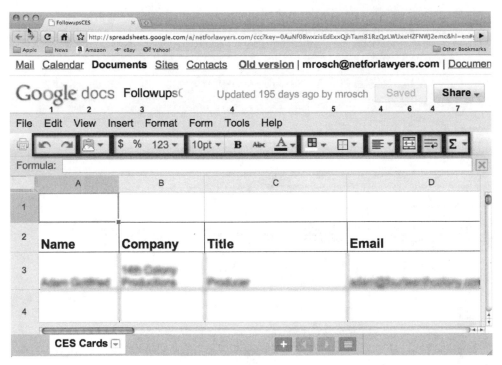

FIGURE 18.45 Beneath the Menu Toolbar are tools to format the contents of the spreadsheet's cells; these tools will also be familiar to Excel users. You can (1) undo or redo a change you've made, (2) copy and paste data to Google's web-based Web Clipboard to make it accessible in other Google Docs files (e.g. Spreadsheets, word processing Documents, Presentations), (3) format numbers in cells you've selected, (4) format text in cells you've selected, (5) format the cells themselves (e.g., add background colors, borders), (6) merge cells you've selected in the same row, (7) or format a formula in a cell you've selected. One (slightly) hidden feature can be found by hovering over the row between the labels (**A**, **B**, etc.) and row **1**. Doing so will present an option to sort the entire spreadsheet based on the content of the column you have chosen (either from **A→Z** or **Z→A**). (The contents of this spreadsheet are blurred to protect personal contact information displayed in some of its fields.)

FIGURE 18.46 One (slightly) hidden feature can be found by hovering over the row between the labels (**A**, **B**, etc.) and row **1**. Doing so will present a drop-down menu of options to manipulate the column selected or the layout of the spreadsheet in the vicinity of the column selected. You can **Cut** or **Copy** a column or **Paste** a previously copied column; **Delete**, **Clear**, **Resize**, or **Hide** a column; **Insert** a new column; or **Sort** the entire spreadsheet based on the content of the column you have chosen (either from **A→Z** or **Z→A**). The **Validate Data** option allows you to define the type of information to be contained in the cells of the column you've selected (e.g. **Numbers** within in a certain range, particular **Text**, or a **Date**). If you are sharing a Spreadsheet, this limits the type of information your collaborators can enter.

18.2.2.1 Sharing Google Spreadsheets

The process for sharing spreadsheets in Google Docs is similar to the process described for sharing word processing Documents in Section 18.2.1.1—with one exception.

FIGURE 18.47 The **Share** pull-down menu for spreadsheets includes one option not on the menu for Documents—**Set notification rules**.

The process of reviewing changes in spreadsheets is very different than the process of reviewing changes in Documents. With spreadsheets, you are notified when all or even specific changes occur.

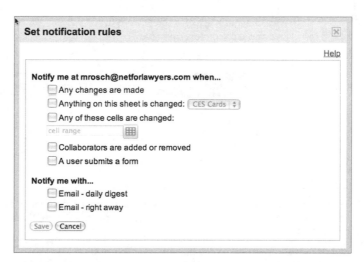

FIGURE 18.48 Selecting **Set notification rules** from the Spreadsheets **Share** pull-down menu opens the options box seen in this illustration, with which you can instruct Google Docs to e-mail you when certain changes are made to the spreadsheet, including when **Any changes are made** or only **Any of these cells are changed**. You can opt to receive individual e-mails for each change (**right away**) or just once per day (**daily digest**).

18.2.2.2   Tracking Changes Made to Google Spreadsheets

The **Set notification rules** option described in the preceding section only alerts you that changes were made to a spreadsheet. To view the actual changes made by individual collaborators, you must return to the spreadsheet itself.

FIGURE 18.49   Selecting **See revision history** from the Spreadsheets **File** pull-down menu allows you to access the changes made to a spreadsheet by various collaborators over time.

Previous version by:	10:03 AM mrosch ▾	« Older | Newer »	Revert to this one		Changes are	highlighted
		3:19 PM clevitt				
		10:03 AM mrosch				
		11/29/09 mrosch sorted				
		11/29/09 mrosch sorted				
		11/29/09 mrosch deleted				
		11/29/09 mrosch				

FIGURE 18.50   Google Spreadsheets' revision history allows you to view changes made by a particular collaborator on a particular date—using this drop-down menu. You can use the **<<Older** or **Newer>>** button to see more revisions.

The tracking of revision history in Google Spreadsheets is not as useful or precise as the tracking of revisions in Google Documents. You can only view the changes one revision at a time. You cannot compare revisions side by side, the same way you can in a Google Document (see Section 18.2.1.2). Google Spreadsheets' autosave feature can create multiple (five-minute increment) revisions from one (thirty-minute) editing session. Additionally, only revisions made on the current day carry a timestamp; all others carry only a day stamp (but are listed in reverse chronological order).

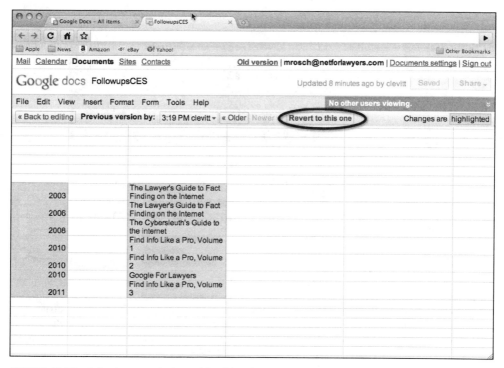

FIGURE 18.51 Selecting a particular revision from the Google Spreadsheets' revision history displays the changes made during that revision and highlights them in a colored box. Clicking the **Revert to this one** button eliminates any changes made to the spreadsheet since the revision you're viewing.

18.2.3 Google Presentations

Google Docs also includes a slide presentation editor and creator similar to Microsoft PowerPoint, Corel's Presentations, or Apple's Keynote.

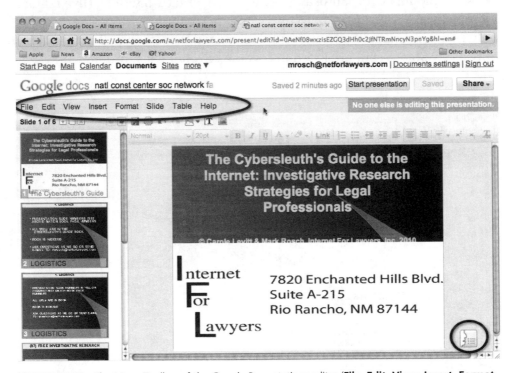

FIGURE 18.52 The Menu Toolbar of the Google Presentations editor (**File**, **Edit**, **View**, **Insert**, **Format**, **Slide**, **Table**, **Help**) will look familiar to regular users of commercial presentation tools like Microsoft's PowerPoint. Clicking the icon in the lower right-hand corner of the editing window opens up a pane containing any speaker's notes contained in the original PowerPoint presentation. This presentation in this illustration was originally created in PowerPoint and was imported into Google Presentations. You can see from the (mis)placement of the text in the slide that the conversion is not perfect.

One shortcoming of Google Presentations is that it does not support the animation of text, images, or other elements that are supported in commercial presentation software. Any animations contained in presentations imported into Google Presentations will not be active.

FIGURE 18.53

Beneath the Menu Toolbar are tools to create, format, and navigate through the slides in the presentation. You can:

1. Insert a slide, duplicate the current slide, or delete the current slide.
2. Retreat or advance one slide at a time.
3. Save or print the presentation.
4. Undo or redo changes.
5. Copy and paste data to Google's web-based Web Clipboard to make it accessible in other Google Docs files (e.g. Spreadsheets, word processing Documents, Presentations).
6. Insert a text box or image into the current slide.
7. Select a fill color for shapes on the current slide.
8. Format selected text in the current slide.
9. Add a link to selected text.
10. Format selected paragraphs in the current slide.
11. Clear the formatting of selected text in the current slide.
12. View and edit the speaker's notes for the current slide.

18.2.3.1 Sharing Google Presentations

The sharing process for Google Presentations is exactly the same as the process described for Documents in Section 18.2.1.1.

In addition to sharing your presentations with other collaborators, you can make your slide presentations available to the public on the Internet.

FIGURE 18.54 You can make your presentations available to view by anyone on the Internet by selecting **Publish/embed** from the **Share** drop-down menu. You can also opt to publish only to other registered users of Google Apps for your domain (e.g., all *username@netforlawyers.com* users), or **Email as attachment** to anyone.

18.2.3.2 Tracking Changes to Google Presentations

Tracking changes in Google Presentations is not as straightforward as it is in Google Documents (as described in Section 18.2.1.2). It is also not nearly as useful.

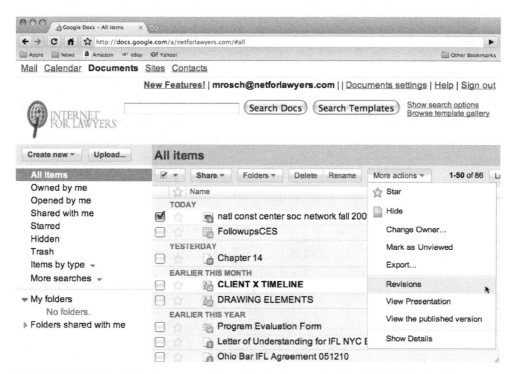

FIGURE 18.55 To track the changes made to a Google Presentation, first click into the checkbox to the left of the presentation in the **All items** folder and then select the **Revisions** option from the **More actions** drop-down menu.

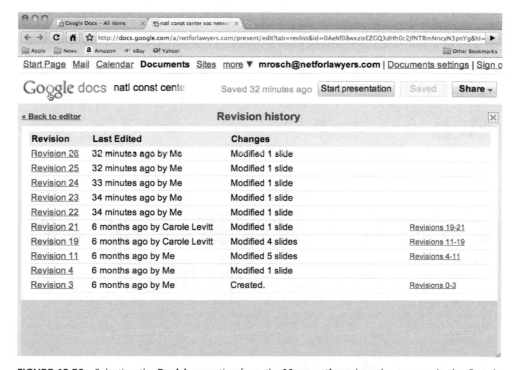

FIGURE 18.56 Selecting the **Revisions** option from the **More actions** drop-down menu in the Google Docs **All items** folder (see Figure 18.55) displays all of the revisions made by various collaborators for the selected document. Clicking the **Revision 4** link, for example, will show only the changes made to the document up until that point in time. Clicking the **Revision 26** link would show all revisions to date.

Unfortunately, you cannot compare one version of the presentation to another to ascertain what changes were made. Additionally, note how each revision carries an annotation as to how many slides were modified (because of Google's autosaving feature, all of these revisions encompass only one slide modification). When you click on any of the revisions, you see all of the slides in the presentation—there is no mark-up to indicate what changes have been made, either to the slide(s) or to the speaker notes.

18.2.4 Google Forms

Google Forms allows you to create forms and surveys that you can post online to collect information from others. Google Forms also allows you to receive, review, and analyze the results in your Google Account.

18.2.4.1 Creating Google Forms

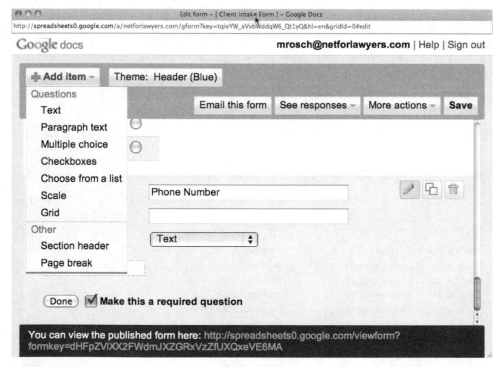

FIGURE 18.57 When creating a Google Form, click the **Add item** button to add questions and other elements to the form. You can create questions that require many different types of answers, like single-line **Text**, multi-line **Paragraph text**, **Multiple choice** (one answer), **Checkboxes** (multiple answers), **Scale** (rating from *0* or *1* up to *10*), or **Grid** (several multiple-choice questions grouped together). A check box is available as you edit each question to **Make this a required question**. You can also add a **Section header** or **Page break** to organize the form. You can view the form anytime during the creation/editing process by clicking the link at the bottom of the screen.

18.2.4.2 Distributing Your Forms Publicly

Once you have created all of your questions, you can distribute your form using the **Email this form** button or by selecting **Embed** from the **More actions** drop-down menu. (The button to access the **More actions** drop-down menu can be seen in Figure 18.57.)

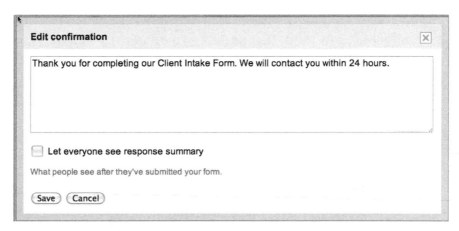

FIGURE 18.58   You can customize the message your respondents see after they click the **Submit** button on your form by selecting the **Edit confirmation** option from the **More actions** drop-down menu. Note the **Let everyone see response summary** checkbox. While this option wouldn't be appropriate for a Client Intake Form, it might be appropriate for some types of survey.

Your completed form will look something like Figure 18.59. We selected this layout and color scheme, called Header (Blue), by clicking the **Theme** button and choosing **Header (Blue)** from the list of nearly 100 Themes.

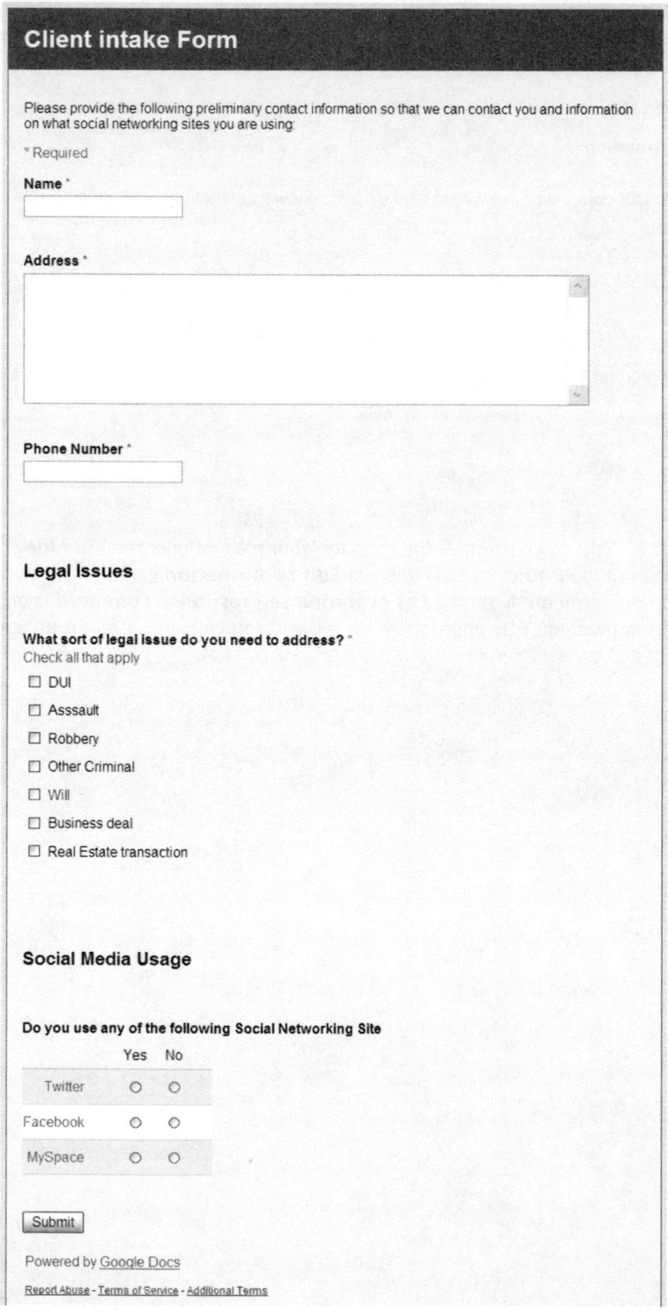

Client intake Form

Please provide the following preliminary contact information so that we can contact you and information on what social networking sites you are using.

* Required

Name *

Address *

Phone Number *

Legal Issues

What sort of legal issue do you need to address? *
Check all that apply

☐ DUI

☐ Asssault

☐ Robbery

☐ Other Criminal

☐ Will

☐ Business deal

☐ Real Estate transaction

Social Media Usage

Do you use any of the following Social Networking Site

	Yes	No
Twitter	○	○
Facebook	○	○
MySpace	○	○

Submit

Powered by Google Docs

Report Abuse - Terms of Service - Additional Terms

FIGURE 18.59 This is a sample Client Intake Form created in Google Forms. It includes **Text** ("Name"), **Paragraph text** ("Address"), **Checkbox** ("What sort of legal issue..."), and **Grid** ("Do you use any...") questions and two **Section header(s)** ("Legal Issues," "Social Media Usage"). Required questions are marked with a red asterisk. A **Submit** button is also included at the bottom.

18.2.4.3 Viewing the Results of Your Forms' Submissions

The responses from submissions of your form are automatically posted to an untitled spreadsheet in your Google Docs account.

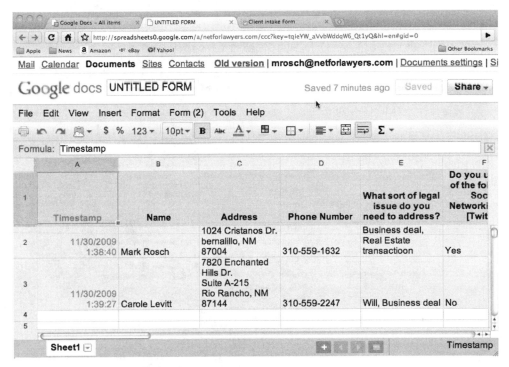

FIGURE 18.60 In this illustration we see the responses from the two form submissions (to date), as well as the date and time on which the forms were completed. To name the spreadsheet, click **Untitled form** and then type your preferred title in the box that pops up.

18.2.4.4 Sharing Forms with Collaborators

Because of the way Google Forms automatically creates an accompanying spreadsheet to hold submitted data (see Section 18.2.4.3), Forms are linked to and accessible (for editing purposes) only through those respective spreadsheets.

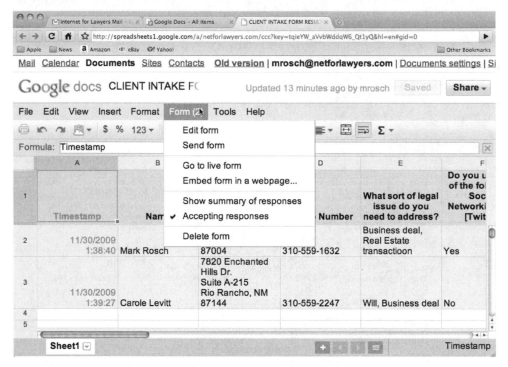

FIGURE 18.61 Forms, like the one we created in Section 18.2.4.1, do not appear in the Google Docs storage interface. To access a form for editing, we must open the spreadsheet in which the form's data is stored, and then select the **Edit form** option from the **Form** menu item.

18.2.5 Google Drawings

See Appendix K on page 495 for this topic.

18.3 Google Calendar

Google Calendar is a full-featured appointment calendar. You can add appointments, events, reminders, etc. and access them anywhere you have an Internet connection—including Web-enabled cellular phones.

You can also sync your Google Calendar with Microsoft Outlook, Apple iCal, and Mozilla Sunbird by clicking the **Sync** link in the upper right-hand corner of the calendar. One advantage Google Calendar gives you over these stand-alone products is the ability to share your calendar with others on the Web. As with Gmail, however, you can also store your Google Calendar information on your own hard drive to access your events and appointments when you do not have an Internet connection.

Because Google Calendar is integrated with the rest of the services in Google Apps, you can also access the Tasks list (discussed in Section 18.1.2.6) and attach any of your Google Docs to an event.

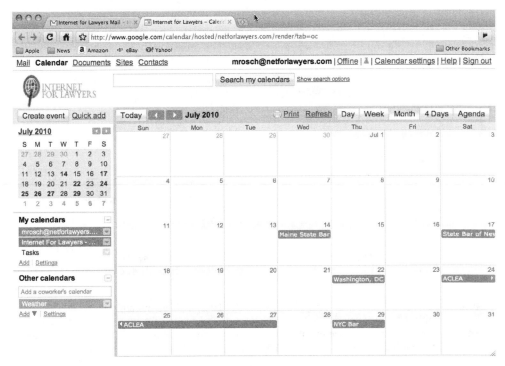

FIGURE 18.62   This is an illustration of the authors' public Google Calendar. It shows Google Calendar's one **Month** view of our events and appointments. Calendar allows you to select different views of your events and appointments, including **Day**, **Week**, **4 Days**, and **Agenda** (which is a list view.)

You can quickly scroll through the months to get to a particular date using the arrow buttons in the upper left-hand side of the calendar or above the smaller calendar in the left-hand column.

18.3.1 Adding Events to Google Calendar

There are three ways to add new events to your Google Calendar.

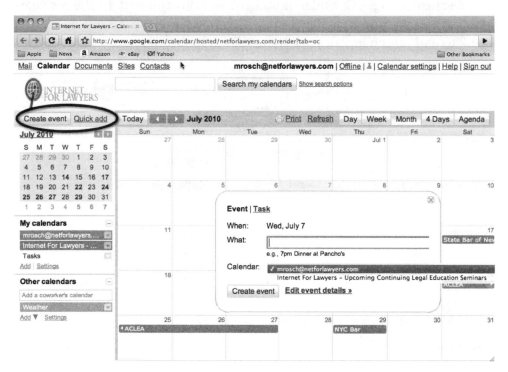

FIGURE 18.63 You can add events to your Google Calendar by clicking into any date on the calendar, as shown in this illustration. You can add an event/appointment name and time. Clicking the **Create event** button adds the event/appointment to your calendar. You can also create events by clicking the **Create Event** or **Quick Add** links in the left-hand column.

Clicking the **Create Event** link in the left-hand column gives the most options for entering information about your event/appointment.

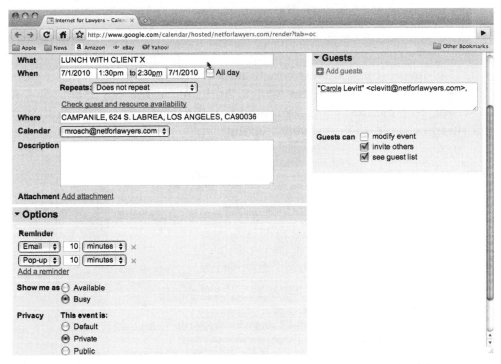

FIGURE 18.64 Clicking the **Create Event** link in the left-hand column gives you the ability to enter a large amount of information about your event/appointment. You can enter an event name (**What**), beginning and ending times (**When**), location (**Where**), and a **Description**. Because the event in this illustration is with a client, we've marked it **Private**. You can invite other guests to the event using the box on the right-hand side. Clicking the **Check guest and resource availabilty** link allows you to better coordinate your invitations to your new Google Calendar event with the schedules of other Google Calendar users who you invite to the event. You can also set reminders to **E-mail** you or open a **Pop-up** on your computer at set times (**weeks**, **days**, **hours**, or **minutes** before the event).

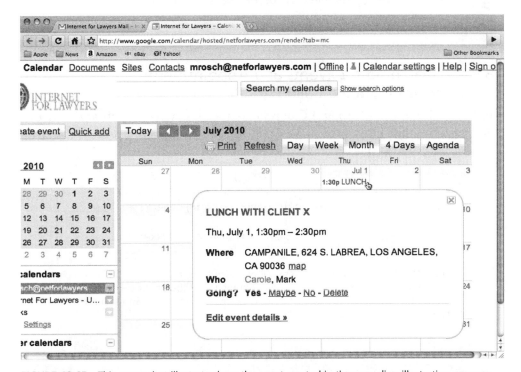

FIGURE 18.65 This screenshot illustrates how the event created in the preceding illustration appears on the authors' Google Calendar.

The quickest and easiest way to add events or appointments to your Google Calendar is to use the **Quick Add** link in the left-hand column. However, this method limits you to adding the least amount of identifying information about the new event/appointment.

FIGURE 18.66 Clicking the **Quick Add** button opens the dialog box illustrated here. You can type in the event/appointment with a fixed date (e.g., *4/21*) or you can use a relative date as illustrated here (e.g., *next Wednesday*). Google understands both. Clicking the **Add** button (or your computer's *Enter* key) adds the event/appointment to your calendar.

18.3.2   Searching for Events and Appointments in your Google Calendar

Another advantage of Google Calendar is its ability to search and retrieve messages. Because Calendar is a Google service, it has very powerful search and retrieval capabilities.

FIGURE 18.67 Like most of Google's services, Calendar offers both a "simple" search (accessed by typing search terms into this box at the top of the Calendar Web interface) and a set of more advanced search features (accessed by clicking the **Show Search Options** link to the right of the search box).

TRACK PERSONAL AND PRIVATE EVENTS ON SEPARATE CALENDARS

You can create separate Google Calendars to list your professional and your personal events, engagements, etc. Each can be managed separately.

FIGURE 18.68 Google Calendar's advanced **Search Options** menu allows you to search through your calendar events/appointments for keywords and phrases in **What** (event names), **Who** (specific individuals), and **Where** (specific locations) fields to target your search results. Additionally, if you have more than one Google Calendar (e.g., one personal and one professional), you can expand your search to **All Other Calendars** or focus just on one of them. You can also limit your search results to appointments set during a specific time frame (**Date from**).

18.3.3 Customizing Your Calendar with Settings

Like the other Google Docs services we've examined in the this chapter, Google Calendar offers a collection of settings to customize the display of information in the calendar. You can access them by clicking the **Settings** link in the upper right-hand corner.

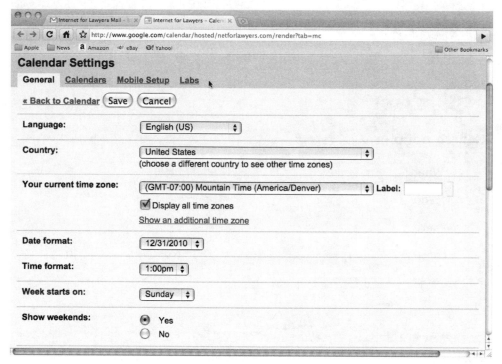

FIGURE 18.69 Google Calendar's **General** settings allow you to set your preferred **Time format**, **Date format**, etc.

The **Calendars** settings tab allows you to give your calendar a name and description, as well as determine how widely you want to share the calendar with others.

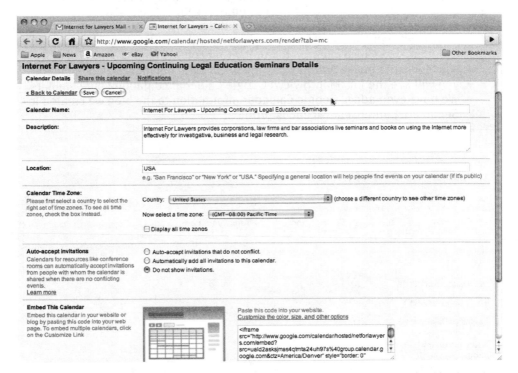

FIGURE 18.70   In addition to designating a **Calendar Name** and **Description**, Google Calendar will generate HTML code for you to **Embed This Calendar** into your existing Web site. You can also click any of the buttons in the **Calendar Address** section to get a Web address that you can share with others to access the calendar. The **XML** button (not pictured) will generate code to the RSS feed of events in the calendar. This feed can be used to add calendar information to any Web page. Clicking any of the buttons in the **Private Address** section (also not pictured) generates a web address that will show visitors all of the events—public and private—on your calendar. (From your calendar, click **Calendar Settings** then **Calendars** then **Your Calendar Name** to get to this view.)

On the **Share this calendar** tab you can indicate whether you want all Internet users to be able to see your calendar or just other registered users of your domain's Google Apps.

If you have authorized multiple people (e.g., other lawyers at your firm) to post and edit events on the calendar, you can use the **Notifications** tab (as seen in Figure 18.70) to opt into notifications by e-mail or SMS text message from the calendar of new, changed, or cancelled invitations. You can also request the calendar to send you an e-mail with your **Daily agenda** each morning at 5:00 A.M. local time from the **Notifications** tab.

ADDING GOOGLE CALENDAR TO AN EXISTING WEB SITE

Usage Example

We have been using Google Calendar to share our schedule of live MCLE seminars around the country for about five years. By using Google Calendar, we can update information on upcoming events in one place and have it automatically update in other places on the Web.

For example, if you visit our Web site (http://www.netforlawyers.com), on the left-hand side of the home page you will see XML data from our calendar's RSS feed integrated into the first column (about one-third of the way down the page). Additionally, if you click the **Calendar** link on our site you will see the full (**Month** view) Google Calendar containing our seminars. We have even added Google Calendar information to the blog we created in Section 9.3 and to our Facebook profiles.

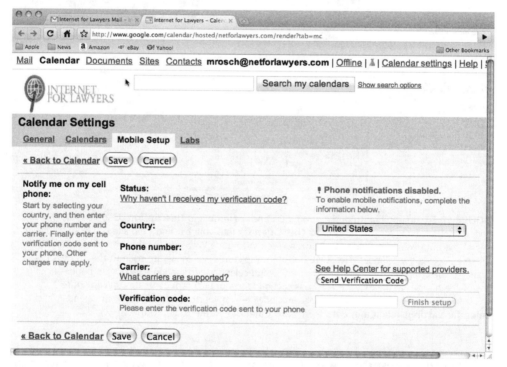

FIGURE 18.71 Google Calendar can be configured to send you alerts about upcoming events and appointments via text messages to your cellular phone. Google does not charge for this feature, but your regular phone company rates for receiving text messages will apply. The feature works with most major U.S. cellular carriers, but does not work with pre-paid phones. A complete list of compatible phone companies is available at http://www.google.com/support/calendar/bin/answer.py?answer=37226&ctx=tltp.

Google development teams and other engineers periodically create new add-on tools for Google Calendar (and other Apps services). These experimental add-ons are available behind the **Labs** settings tab.

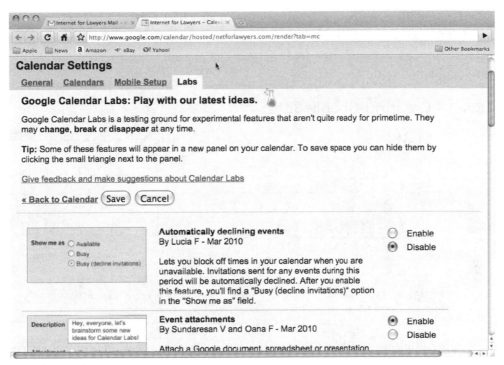

FIGURE 18.72 Clicking the **Enable** button next to any experimental Labs project adds that feature to your Google Calendar. One useful Labs experiment is **Attach Google Docs** (not pictured), which allows you to attach one of your Google Documents to an event on your Google Calendar.

18.4 Google Sites

Google Sites is one more way you can post and share information online for a selected group to review, edit, or just comment. The group can be as large or as small as you like. The service allows you to access elements from many of the other Google Apps services (e.g., Google Docs, Google Calendar, etc.) through a Web interface you can customize.

You might choose to create a "private" Google site to organize documents, comments, and events for a working group or practice area within your firm; to update and/or collaborate with clients about their case; or to share documents and update co-counsel on a particular case.

You might choose to create a "public" Google site—available to everyone on the Internet to market a particular area of your practice, or gather information, or locate potential plaintiffs for a potential class action lawsuit.

Note that the information shared through Google Sites would be subject to all of the same privacy concerns discussed in Section 18.8.

Google Sites began as an independent product called JotSpot in February 2006 and was purchased by Google in October 2006. The service was relaunched as Google Sites in February 2008, replacing the then-available Google Page Creator.

18.4.1 Creating Google Sites

FIGURE 18.73 Creating a new Google Site is as easy as clicking the **Sites** link that appears in the upper left-hand corner of any of your Google Apps pages.

After clicking the **Sites** link in the preceding illustration, click the **Create site** button on the subsequent page (seen in the background of the next illustration).

FIGURE 18.74 After you've clicked the **Create site** button, you can select a design on which to build your site from Google's available templates. One of the **Business collaboration** templates would be most appropriate for the types of lawyer-related sites mentioned in Section 18.4.

Once you have selected your template, Google Sites will display your new site.

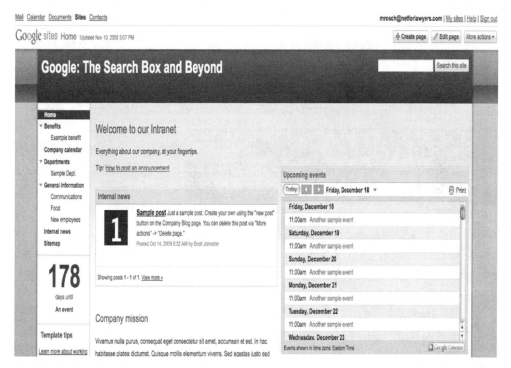

FIGURE 18.75 This is the new Google Site we created (in the process showed in the preceding two illustrations). Each area of content contains placeholder information. These placeholders are completely editable and customizable.

18.4.2   Creating and Editing Google Sites Pages

Once you've created a Google Site, you can edit any of the default pages included in the site and create new pages to add content to the site.

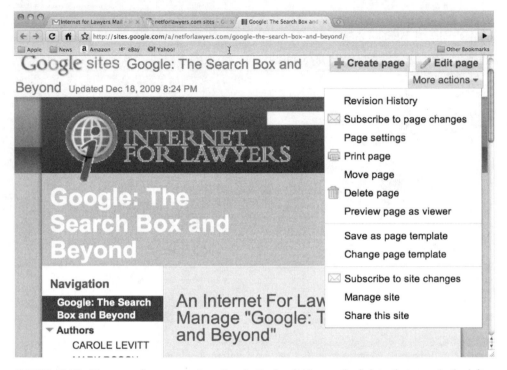

FIGURE 18.76   You can edit any page in a Google Site by clicking on the link to that page in the left-hand column and then clicking on the **Edit page** button in the upper right-hand corner. To delete the entire page you're viewing, select the **Delete page** option from the **More actions** drop-down menu.

The tools used to edit Google Site pages are similar to the Google Docs editing tools discussed in Section 18.2.1.

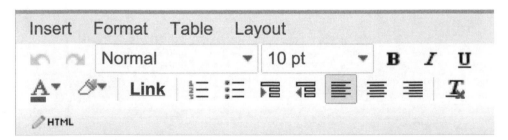

FIGURE 18.77   The editing toolbar for pages in Google Sites looks similar to the editing toolbars of many commercial word processing programs.

The **Layout** menu item is particular to the Google Sites editing toolbar. It allows you to select different layout characteristics for individual pages of the site you're creating.

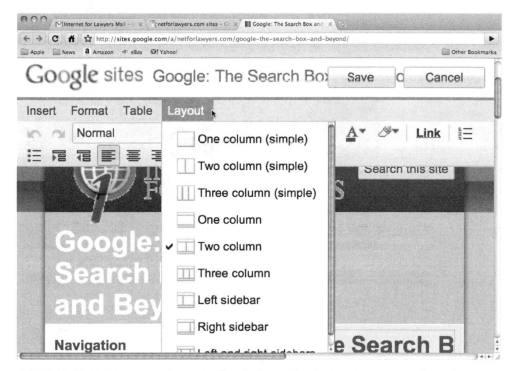

FIGURE 18.78   The **Layout** option on the Google Sites editing toolbar allows you to select a layout format for the page you're editing, including **One column (simple)**, **Three column**, and **Right sidebar**. We've selected a **Two column** format for the page being edited in this illustration.

In addition to text, you can also embed information from your other Google Apps into Google Sites' pages.

FIGURE 18.79 Use the **Insert** option on the Google Sites editing toolbar to embed files from other Google Apps into your site. You can select a Google **Document**, **Presentation**, **Spreadsheet**, or **Spreadsheet form**, among other information.

Practical Note	Documents, Spreadsheets, etc. embedded in this way are for display purposes only (on the site's page). They cannot be edited as described earlier in this chapter. To collaborate on the content of those individual documents, you would have to share them in Google Docs as described in sections 18.2.1.1, 18.2.2.1, and 18.2.3.1.

To create a new page, click the **Create page** button in the upper right-hand corner (see Figures 18.76 and 18.80).

FIGURE 18.80 Clicking the **Create page** button in the upper right-hand corner allows you to create and organize new pages within the Google Site.

There are a number of different types of pages you can add to your Google Site. They are:

- **Web page**—allows you to enter text (including bulleted lists and numbered lists), images, and tables; embed spreadsheets, presentations, and videos; and easily link to other pages in your site. You can even attach documents from your computer to the bottom of the page.
- **Announcements**—allows you to post chronological information such as news, project status updates, or notable events.
- **File Cabinet**—allows you to upload multiple documents to a single page for collaborators to download and view. These files cannot be edited directly online like Google Docs.
- **Lists**—allows you to post a list of information (e.g., action items) that includes assignments for collaborators/team members to complete. Items can be edited/updated by any collaborator—and marked as **Complete** when done.
- **Start Page**—allows each viewer to add their own personalized set of gadgets (similar to the Gmail **Labs** add-ons discussed in Section 18.1.3.8). These pages include information that all collaborators will see and some that each can personalize.
- **Department Page**—a preformatted page using the **Right sidebar** layout, it includes pre-defined areas into which you can enter content (e.g., **Department Resources**, **Key Contacts**, and **Important Links**). (These pages are similar to the **Dashboard** page type that was available to Google Sites users until October 2009.)

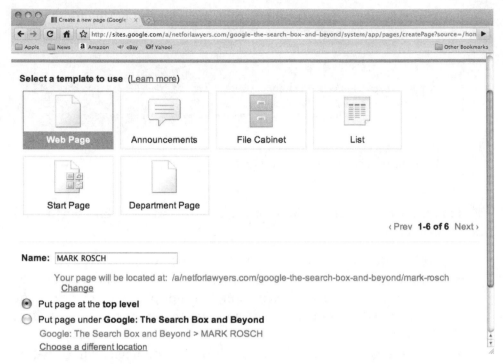

FIGURE 18.81 After clicking the **Create page** button (see preceding illustration), you can choose which page type you want to create. The **Name** you enter in the box at the center will appear at the top of the new page when viewed in a Web browser. It will also become part of the page's URL. Use the **Change** link in the center to customize the new page's URL. You can also use the radio buttons in the lower section of this illustration to indicate where in the site's organization the new page should appear or use the **Choose a different location** link to select a different organizational location for the page within the site.

18.4.3   Sharing Sites

Sharing Google Sites is pretty straightforward.

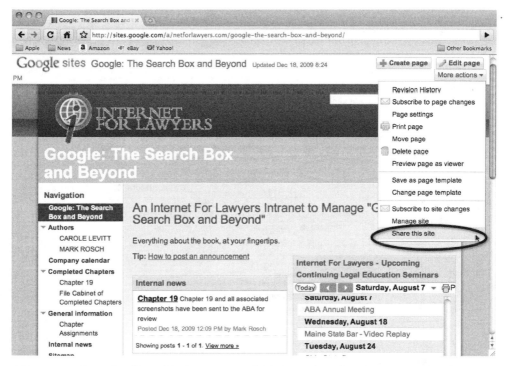

FIGURE 18.82   Use the **Share this site** option on the **More actions** drop-down menu to share your site with other viewers and/or collaborators.

You can control how open or closed you want your site to be, setting permissions for **collaborators** or **viewers** whom you identify.

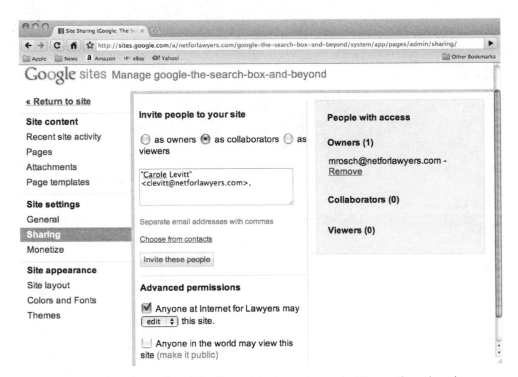

FIGURE 18.83 After you've selected the **Share this site** option on the **More actions** drop-down menu, the page that displays (illustrated here) allows you to invite specific individuals to collaborate or view your site by entering their e-mail addresses into the large box. (You can also add people to this list from your Google Contacts by clicking the **Choose from contacts** link. (Note that you can invite only 50 people at a time this way.) In the **Advanced permissions** section you can include all registered members of your hosted apps domain (netforlawyers.com in our case) to **view** or **edit** the site or you can make the site completely public so that **Anyone in the world may view this site.** Still, only people who you designate can edit the site.

Anyone you have invited **as collaborators** or have indicated can **edit** the pages will have access to all of the editing tools discussed in the preceding section—including the ability to create and delete pages. As with Google Documents, however, as the owner of the site, you can track which collaborator has made changes and disapprove any of those changes. Changes would be visible to anyone you have designated can view the site. Disapproved changes would disappear immediately after their removal. (See the next section for more information about disapproving or restoring changes.)

You can also enable site viewers to leave comments that do not edit the primary content of a page by selecting the **Page settings** option from the **More actions** drop-down menu.

FIGURE 18.84   After selecting the **Page settings** option from the **More actions** drop-down menu, checking the **Allow comments** box enables individuals you have authorized only to view your site to add comments at the bottom of the particular page you've so-enabled.

18.4.4   Tracking Revisions to Sites

You have three ways to track changes made to your Google Site. You can view a list of changes made to the entire site; view a list of revisions made to the page you're viewing; or receive e-mail updates whenever changes are made to a particular page or anywhere on the site.

First, you can view a list of changes made to the entire site.

FIGURE 18.85   Use the **Manage site** option on the **More actions** drop-down menu to see a list of changes made to the site.

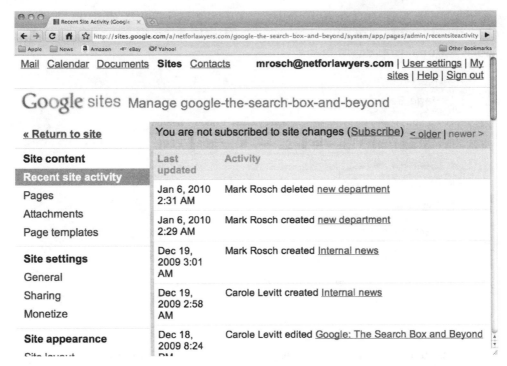

FIGURE 18.86 After selecting the **Manage site** option from the **More actions** drop-down menu, you will see a reverse chronological list of changes made to all of the pages of the site. In this view, however, there is no way to manage or reject any of those changes.

Second, you can view a list of revisions made to the page you're viewing.

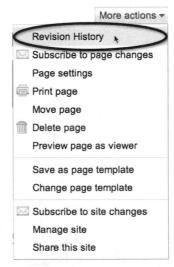

FIGURE 18.87 Use the **Revision History** option on the **More actions** drop-down menu to see a list of changes made to the page you're viewing.

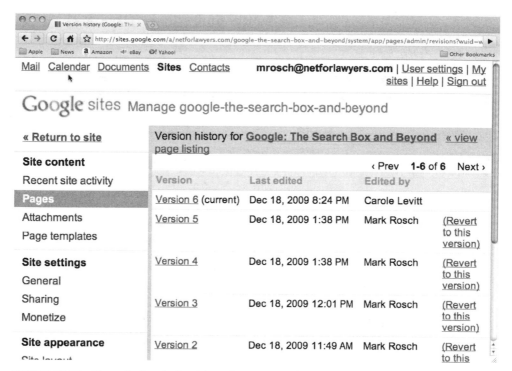

FIGURE 18.88   After selecting the **Revision History** option from the **More actions** drop-down menu, you will see a reverse chronological list of each of the changes made to the page you were viewing. Clicking the **Version [X]** link allows you to read that particular version. Clicking the **Revert to this version** link allows you to disregard any subsequent changes.

When viewing a version of a document in the **Revision History**, Google Sites gives you the ability to compare versions by clicking the **Compare two versions** link at the top of the version you're reading and then selecting another **Version** to compare the current version to. Unfortunately, in our tests we have found this comparison is unreliable.

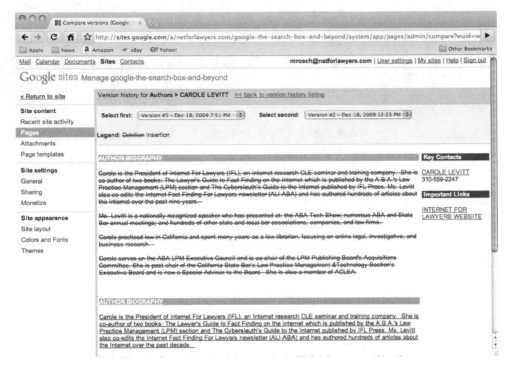

FIGURE 18.89 This illustration is a comparison of **Version #5** and **Version #2** of the page revisions seen in the last illustration. In theory, the comparison should show any changes made in context (additions, deletions, etc., similar to the feature described for Google Documents; see Section 18.2.1.2). However, Google Sites did not recognize edits to individual words/sentences/paragraphs; instead it marked the complete text of **Version #2 Deleted** and marked the entire text of **Version #5** as an **Insertion**—even though only minor text edits were made between these versions.

> **Usage Note**
>
> Google Sites tracks and keeps all of the changes made to your site. Even if you revert to **Version #2** (as shown in Figure 18.89), Google Sites does not discard the changes made in **Version 3, 4,** and **5**—they are just ignored. At some point in the future, you (or another collaborator) could decide to revert to **Version #5** and the changes in that version would still be available.

The third way to track changes made to your Google Site is by receiving e-mail updates whenever changes are made to a particular page or anywhere on the site.

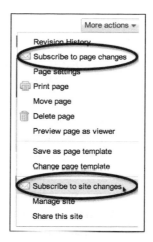

FIGURE 18.90   Use the **Subscribe to page changes** link on the **More actions** drop-down menu to receive an e-mail message that updates you to changes to a particular page—with the insertions/deletions/etc. marked. Similarly, selecting the **Subscribe to site changes** option further down the drop-down menu alerts you via e-mail to changes made to any page on the site.

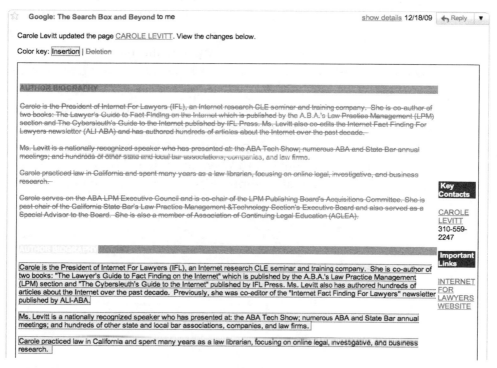

FIGURE 18.91   This is a sample e-mail message alerting Mark to changes that Carole made to her biography page on the Google Site. Unfortunately, in our tests, these e-mail alerts suffered the same weaknesses noted for the **Compare two versions** feature discussed in Figure 18.89—even though only minor text edits were made, the entirety of the text of the previous version is marked as deleted.

18.5   Google Wave

Google Wave is an online communication and collaboration tool. One element that can be a bit confusing is that "Wave" (with a capital "W") is the name of the service, and "wave" (with a lowercase "w") is the name used for an individual conversation created in Wave.

In one online explanation of the service, Google describes it this way: "a wave can be both a conversation and a document where people can discuss and work together using richly formatted text, photos, videos, maps, and more" (http://wave.google.com/about.html).

Like Google Docs, any wave participant can add or edit content anywhere in the conversation.

A wave is live. Unlike Google's other collaboration services we have discussed in this chapter, Wave is meant to work in real-time. When multiple collaborators are online simultaneously, the wave is updated in real-time. As you type edits or additions, other participants on a wave can see what you're typing *as you type it.* A wave can also be viewed or edited by one collaborator at a time if others are offline at any particular moment.

> **Practical Tip**
>
> Lawyers might find Google Wave useful to collect documents for a presentation from co-presenters or co-counsel, or to collect information from multiple sources to create exhibits for a trial.

Wave's Playback feature lets collaborators rewind the wave to see who said what and when.

At the time of this writing, Google Wave is very much in the alpha phase—meaning that it's even more experimental than a beta-phase service. Currently it is more of a concept than a mature service. Because of this, we expect to see many changes to Wave over time. So this section will provide an overview of Wave and some of its currently available features, but will not be as detailed as other sections of this chapter.

18.5.1 Anatomy of Wave

The Wave interface encompasses many of the features of other Google services we've examined in previous sections of this chapter.

In the upper left-hand corner is the **Navigation** panel.

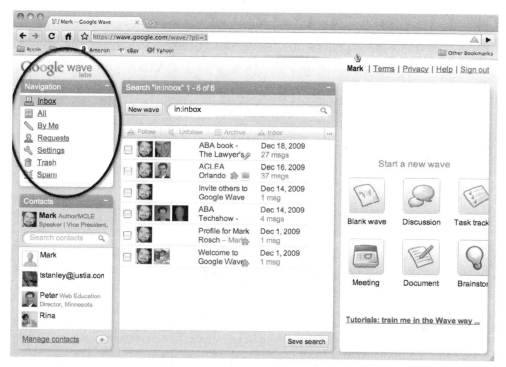

FIGURE 18.92 The links in Wave's **Navigation** panel are similar to Gmail's **Folder** and **Label** links (located in about the same place in the Gmail Web-based interface). Clicking the **Inbox** link displays your current waves in the center section. Clicking the **By Me** link displays only those waves that you have initiated. Clicking the **Spam** link displays messages that you have designated as spam or that Wave suspects of being spam. Clicking the **Settings** link displays Google-created waves that include gadgets you can add on to your account to extend its features (similar to the Gmail **Labs** settings tab discussed in Section 18.1.3.8). Clicking the **All** link displays all of your waves.

The center section of the screen is the Search panel.

FIGURE 18.93 In addition to displaying waves by category (as described in the preceding illustration), you can use the search box at the top of this section to keyword search for information in your waves. (Searching is by keyword or phrase only. Wave does not recognize Boolean connectors. Google Wave does a good job of locating your search terms in different waves. Unfortunately, keywords/phrases are only highlighted in the snippet that appears in the Search panel and not in the wave itself.)

In the lower left-hand corner is the **Contacts** panel.

FIGURE 18.94   In Wave's **Contacts** panel, you can search for new contacts by name, or add contacts from your existing Google Contacts list (as described in Section 18.1.2.5).

The right-hand panel is the Wave panel, where the wave you're currently working on is displayed.

18.5.2   Creating and Editing a Wave

To create a new wave, click the **New wave** button to the left of the search box in the Search panel. A new blank wave will appear in the right-hand panel.

Collaborators in a particular wave are displayed at the top of the Wave panel. You can add participants at any point by clicking the plus sign next to the existing participants in this section. (See Figure 18.98 for a view of this section of the Wave panel.) Clicking this button opens a new window from which you can select additional participants from your existing contacts list or you can add collaborators using their e-mail address. In turn, existing collaborators can be adding information at the same time.

Each post or comment in a wave is known as a "blip."

You can type information directly into the panel or copy and paste text from another document into the wave. When adding new text to a wave, any other collaborators you've added, who are online at the same time, will see what you're typing in real-time. (This can be a bit distracting, if not downright unnerving.)

Note that there is currently no way to formally name your waves. The first line of text in the first blip automatically serves as a *de facto* name for any wave. So be sure to always make that line descriptive.

FIGURE 18.95

When you are working on a new blip (or editing an existing one), this specialized toolbar appears, which allows you to format information in the blip. You can do the following:

1. Format text.
2. Highlight selected text.
3. Clear formatting from selected text.
4. Format paragraph headings.
5. Format selected paragraphs.
6. Create/add Web links to selected text.
7. Attach documents and/or images to the blip you're editing.
8. Conduct a Google Web search and add selected results to the blip you're working on.
9. Add a gadget to Wave if you know the URL.
10. Add a **Yes, No, Maybe** gadget to poll your collaborators.
11. Add a Google Map to the blip you're working on.

You can also drag and drop files from your own computer directly into a blip. If you drag multiple images into a wave, the **Images** button at the bottom of the Wave panel will allow you to **View as a slide show** or to **Copy to a new wave** (not pictured).

Double-clicking into any existing blip in a wave allows you to **Edit** that blip or to **Reply** to it. Editing an existing blip places your text directly into the blip you're editing (although your user icon is added to indicate you've made an addition). Replying to an existing blip places a new blip indented beneath the one on which you are commenting.

You can also **Edit** or **Reply** to a blip by using a (somewhat) hidden drop-down menu to the right of the blip's timestamp.

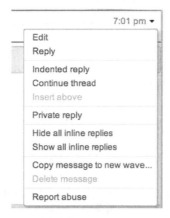

FIGURE 18.96 Clicking the downward-facing arrow next to a blip's timestamp reveals a drop-down menu that allows you to **Edit**, **Reply to**, add an **Indented reply** to the blip you're viewing, or just **Continue** (the) **thread** and add more content to the blip. You can also choose to send a **Private reply** to the sender of that particular blip. Additionally, you can **Copy to [a] new wave** or **Delete** the blip (even if you are not the author of that particular blip), among other options.

The upward- and downward-facing arrows on the right-hand side of the Wave panel (not pictured) scroll up and down through the wave.

You can use the **Tags** button in the lower left-hand corner of Wave Panel to add descriptive category identifiers (similar to the tags discussed when creating blog posts in Section 9.3).

18.5.3 Tracking Changes in a Wave

Wave includes a Playback feature that allows you to review each change/addition made to the wave.

FIGURE 18.97 Clicking the **Playback** button at the top of the active wave allows you to see how the wave was built over time with the additions and edits of the various users.

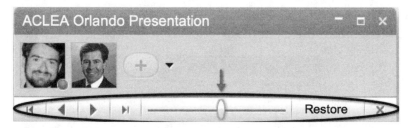

FIGURE 18.98 Once the Playback begins, a progress bar at the top of the wave shows each new edit or addition to the conversation. Clicking the right-arrow button advances through the wave one blip at a time. Clicking the left-arrow moves backward through the wave one blip at a time. You can left-click and hold down the slider in the progress bar and "fast-forward" or "reverse" to any portion of the conversation by dragging the slider to the right or left, respectively.

When the Playback feature shows an edit that has been made to a previously posted blip, it is noted in the yellow bar at the top of the wave (identifying the editor and the time the edit was made). The edit itself is highlighted within the blip in yellow.

18.6 Google Talk

Google Talk is a free text, voice, and video chat instant messaging service offered by Google. You can access the service in three ways: through a stand-alone application that you download and install on your computer; through a Web-based Google Talk gadget interface (at https://talkgadget. google.com/talkgadget/popout); and through a browser plug-in that integrates Google Talk into Gmail, iGoogle, and some other Google services.

> **Practice Tip**
>
> Google Talk can be useful for quick real-time video conferencing between members of your firm, clients, co-counsel, etc.

The stand-alone application is available only for Windows operating systems (Windows XP through Windows 7). Both the stand-alone application and the browser plug-in can be downloaded at http://www.google.com/talk/.

Usage Tip You must have a microphone and/ or a camera either built into or connected to your computer in order to use Google Talk.	Since this book has primarily covered accessing Google services through the Web browser, in this section we will focus on the third method of using Google Talk—

through the Web browser plug-in in conjunction with other Google services. This method is also available to a wider range of users.

18.6.1   Starting a Google Talk Video or Voice Chat

To begin a chat session, click on any of your chat contact names.

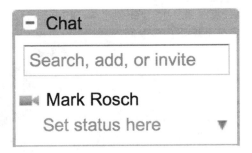

FIGURE 18.99   After you install the browser plug-in on your computer, a small green camera icon will appear next to your name in your Google Chat gadget when you're looking at your Gmail Inbox (as discussed and illustrated in Section 18.1.2.7). Contacts from whom you have previously accepted invitations to chat (or vice versa) will see this icon next to your name, indicating that you're Google Talk–enabled. Similarly, you would see the same icon next to the names of any chat contacts who have installed the Google Talk plug-in.

18.6.2   Google Talk Settings

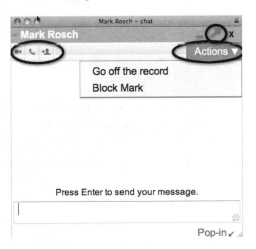

FIGURE 18.100   After clicking on a contact name from the list, begin a video or voice chat by clicking the corresponding icon/button (respectively), in the upper left-hand corner of the active chat window. The third button in the upper left-hand corner gives you the option to invite additional contacts to the chat. The upward-pointing arrow (in the upper-right hand corner of the chat window) invokes the **Pop-out** option that moves the chat to its own browser window. See Figure 18.27 in Section 18.1.3.6 for more information about the **Go off the record** option found behind the **Actions** drop-down menu.

After you install the Google Talk plug-in, locate its settings by clicking the **Settings** link in the upper right-hand corner of the Gmail Inbox and then clicking the **Chat** tab.

The **Report quality statistics to help improve Internet for Lawyers**

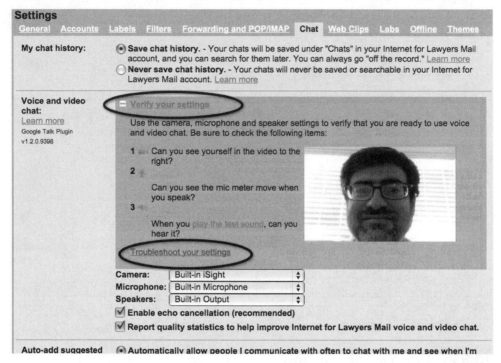

FIGURE 18.101 The Google Talk settings are added to the Chat settings (discussed in Section 18.1.3.6). Use the **Camera, Microphone,** and **Speakers** drop-down menus to select the devices on your computer to use for the audio and video chat. Links and tools in the **Verify your settings** section help you determine whether your devices are working with the Google Talk plug-in. If you're having hardware issues, click the **Troubleshoot your settings** link to try to diagnose the problem.

Mail voice and video chat option, seen at the bottom of the preceding illustration, sends non-identifiable information about connection quality, etc. back to Google. Many security advocates prefer not to allow this outbound flow of information from their networks. It is probably a good idea to uncheck this box.

18.7 Picasa

Picasa is an online image storage and sharing service. Attorneys can use Picasa Web Albums to share photos or other images (e.g., X-rays, diagrams) with clients, insurance adjusters, other members of their firm, co-counsel, or anyone else who needs to see the images. You can store up to 1 GB of photos in your Web Album. More storage is available for purchase, with prices starting at $5.00 per year for 20 GB of storage.

As with Google Talk, Picasa comes in both stand-alone and Web-based versions (Picasa Web Albums).

The stand-alone version is available for the Windows (Windows XP through Windows 7) and Mac operating systems (10.4.9 or newer; also requires a Mac with an Intel processor). It can be downloaded at http://www.Picasa.com.

Since the majority of this book deals with Google services available through your Web browser, we will focus on Picasa Web Albums. That service is located at http://picasaweb.google.com.

Picasa Web Albums are tied to your Google Account, so if you already have your Google Account, you will already have a Picasa Web Albums account. No additional set-up is required.

Usage Tip

Picasa Web Albums accounts do not seem to come by default with Google Apps Standard accounts like the one we use for our netforlawyers.com e-mail. For example, if Mark is logged into his netforlawyers.com Google Apps account, he cannot access Picasa Web Albums. However, if he is logged into his gmail.com e-mail account (the default e-mail address associated with his Google Account), he can access Picasa Web Albums.

You can tie the two accounts together by logging into the Gmail.com account, and then visiting the Google Account Dashboard at https://www.google.com/accounts/ManageAccount. (See Section 2.4.3 for more details.) **Edit** the **Email addresses** section to include your Google Apps Standard e-mail address (mrosch@netforlawyers.com in Mark's case) as an **alternate email address.** This will allow you to access Picasa Web Albums with either account login information.

FIGURE 18.102 The default view of Picasa Web Albums shows the "cover" image of each of the existing albums. Albums can be public or private. (The lock icon beneath the first two albums indicates that these are private.) Photos in public albums could turn up in Google Image Search results.

18.7.1 Creating New Picasa Web Albums and Uploading Photos

To create a new Picasa Web Album, click the **Upload** button (seen in the preceding illustration).

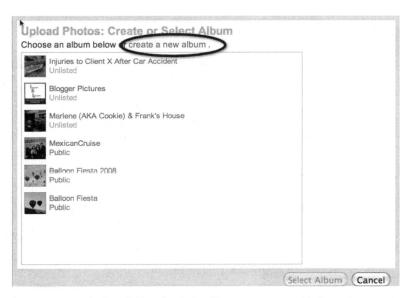

FIGURE 18.103   After clicking the **Upload** button, you can add photos to an existing album or **create a new album**.

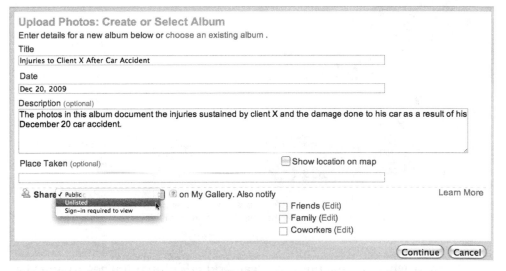

FIGURE 18.104   If you opt to **create a new album**, you're prompted to enter a **Title**, **Date**, **Description**, and **Place taken**. Use the **Share** drop-down menu to indicate whether you want the album to be **Public**, **Unlisted**, or **Sign-in required to view**. Note that Picasa Web Albums allows you to access your Google Contacts groups (lower right-hand corner) to easily share your albums.

Usage Tip

Sign-in required to view is the highest level of privacy. Using it, you can indicate specific people who can access the album—but they must have a Google Account to access the album. If they do not have a Google Account, they will be prompted to create one when they click on the link inviting them to view the album.

   Public albums are visible by anyone on the Internet. Photos in Public albums may show up in Google Image Search results.

   See Section 18.7.2 for information about **Unlisted** albums.

FIGURE 18.105   After you select the images to include, your new album will appear in your collection. Double-clicking any album opens it to display the collection of images it contains.

   As the owner of an album, you can add additional images to an existing album at any time using the **Add photos** link when viewing the album's contents (see the next illustration).

18.7.2 Sharing Picasa Web Albums

After you add images to the album, you can decide who else, if anyone, can access them.

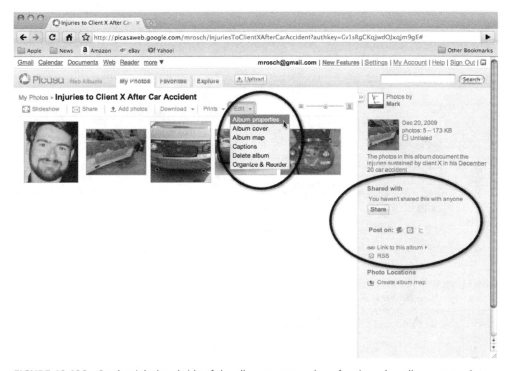

FIGURE 18.106 On the right-hand side of the album are a number of options that allow you to share the album with others. Clicking **Link to this album** displays a coded link that you can paste into an e-mail (in Gmail, Outlook, or other e-mail software) to send to those who you want to have access to the album.

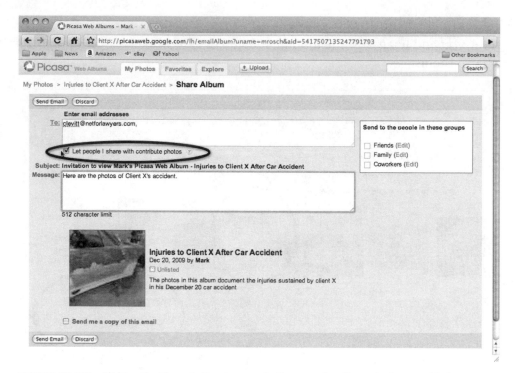

FIGURE 18.107 Clicking the **Share** button (as seen in the preceding illustration) opens this form, where you can generate an e-mail message (which includes an invitation and link) to send to those with whom you want to share the album. Note that you can allow others to add images to the album by checking the **Let people I share with contribute photos** box.

Ethics Alert

Take care to share client-related photos only with those people who need to have access to them. For example, you would not want to use the **Paste HTML to embed in website** or **Embed Slideshow** options to post client-related images to a public Web site.

If you **Paste HTML to embed in website** or **Embed Slideshow** from an Unlisted album into your Web site and Google's robot finds that photo (or slideshow) and follows the link back to the album, then photos in that album could turn up in Google Image Search results. See sections 2.2 and 2.3 for more information on how Google's robot (Googlebot) locates information on the Internet.

Note that Unlisted albums are not completely private. They only require a long URL (that includes an authentication code) to access them. For example, if you send the link to your client, he could forward the e-mail to others who would also be able to view the album. Two remedies would be (1) click **Reset unlisted link** to create a new unpublished URL for the album, or (2) set the **Share** option to the more stringent **Sign-in required to view** as described in the preceding section.

You can change an album's Share properties at any time by selecting the **Album Properties** option from the **Edit** drop-down menu as seen near the top of Figure 18.109.

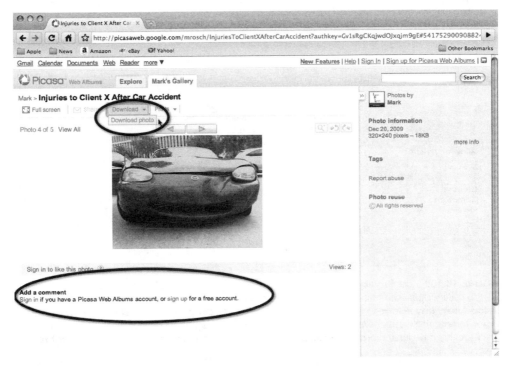

FIGURE 18.108   Anyone to whom you give access can view an album's images. They can also download them individually, as seen in this illustration. (See the next section for information on how to disable this capability.) A Google Account is required for viewers to add comments to a photo.

18.7.3   Customizing Picasa Web Albums Settings

Like most of the Google services discussed in this chapter, Picasa Web Albums can be customized by clicking the **Settings** link in the upper right-hand corner of any screen. The two most important **Settings** tabs are **Privacy and Permissions** and **Email notification**.

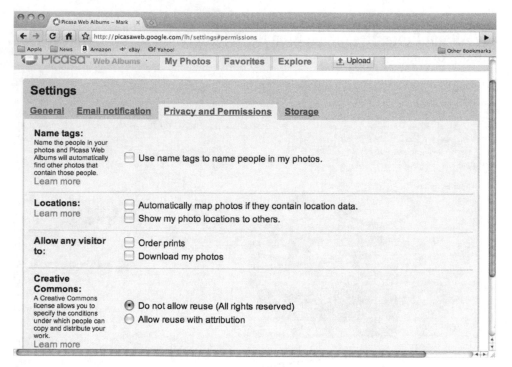

FIGURE 18.109 The **Privacy and Permissions** tab allows you to control more aspects of how your invited collaborators can manipulate the album and how much information is included with the images. In the **Allow any visitor to** section, you can uncheck the **Order prints** and/or **Download my photos** boxes to take these options away from collaborators. Even though most of your work-related albums will probably have limited access, it's still a good idea to select the **Do not allow reuse (All rights reserved)** option.

Additionally, the **Name tags** setting in the preceding illustration enables a feature that makes it easier to locate photos of particular individuals by running your images through an automated facial recognition process. The process allows you to add names to those faces—then Picasa can identify the same face in different photos and assign the appropriate name tag to photos it recognizes. Future images uploaded are also run through the facial recognition process and those new images are matched to your previously identified faces and names. This feature probably has less application in professional uses of Picasa Web Albums because many images do not include faces (e.g., accident scenes, defective products, improper construction).

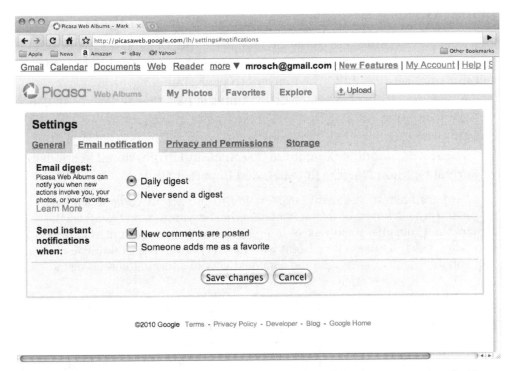

FIGURE 18.110   When your collaborators add a comment to one of the photos you've shared with them, Picasa Web Albums will send you an e-mail notification. On the **Email notification** tab, you can control whether you will receive a **Daily digest** message or if you prefer Picasa to **Send instant notifications when**... **New comments are posted**. If your albums aren't public, you won't have to worry about notifications when **Someone adds me as a favorite**.

18.8   Security and Privacy of Information Stored in Your Google Apps

When we discuss Gmail and Google Docs in our live seminars, one of the first questions we're asked is, "What about the security of the information stored in those documents and e-mails?"

The answer to that question depends on who you ask. No system is perfect. In the end, you will have to decide if you are comfortable enough with the security and privacy measures Google (or any other online storage provider) provide for the data you store.

18.8.1   What Does the Bar Say About Online Services?

The Rules of Conduct are generally silent on the specific question of out-sourced storage of documents. It is clear that lawyers have a duty to protect information related to the matters they are handling.

ABA Model Rule of Conduct 1.6 (a) states in part that "A lawyer shall not reveal information relating to the representation of a client unless the client gives informed consent" (http://www.abanet.org/cpr/mrpc/rule_1_6.html).

The ABA's Standing Committee on Ethics and Professional Responsibility Formal Opinion No. 99-413 concluded in part that:

> Lawyers have a reasonable expectation of privacy in communications made by all forms of e-mail, including unencrypted e-mail sent on the Internet, despite some risk of interception and disclosure. It therefore follows that its use is consistent with the duty under Rule 1.6 to use reasonable means to maintain the confidentiality of information relating to a client's representation.

The New York State Bar Association's Committee on Professional Ethics Opinion 820 – 2/8/08 (*available at* http://www.nysba.org/AM/Template.cfm?Section=Ethics_Opinions&TEMPLATE=/CM/ContentDisplay.cfm&CONTENTID=13652) concluded that "A lawyer may use an e-mail service provider that conducts computer scans of e-mails to generate computer advertising, where the e-mails are not reviewed by or provided to other individuals." While not named in the opinion, the question's description of an "e-mail service provider that scans e-mails for advertising purposes" clearly describes Gmail.

The State Bar of Nevada's Committee on Ethics and Professional Responsibility Formal Opinion Number 33 (*available at* http://linkon.in/aUDHqh) concluded that

> The lawyer's duty to protect client confidentiality under Supreme Court Rule 156 is not absolute. In order to comply with the rule, the lawyer must act competently and reasonably to safeguard confidential client information and communications from inadvertent and unauthorized disclosure. This may be accomplished while storing client information electronically with a third party to the same extent and subject to the same standards as with storing confidential paper files in a third party warehouse. If the lawyer acts competently and reasonably to ensure the confidentiality of the information, then he or she does not violate SCR 156 simply by contracting with a third party to store the information, even if an unauthorized or inadvertent disclosure should occur.

Be sure to check for the exact wording of rules and Ethics Opinions on-point in all jurisdictions where you are licensed to practice.

18.8.2   What Does Google Say About Its Security?

Google lists many examples of the security measures in place to keep your documents from prying eyes.

As part of the marketing materials for Google Apps (http://www.google.com/apps/intl/en/business/infrastructure_security.html), Google states the following:

> Google operates one of the largest networks of distributed datacenters in the world, and we go to great lengths to protect the data and intellectual property on these servers. These facilities are protected around the clock and we have a dedicated security operations team who focuses specifically on maintaining the security of our environment. The controls, processes and policies that protect these data have successfully completed a SAS 70 Type II audit. There are three main components to our security practices:
>
> - People—Google employs a full-time information security team including some of the world's foremost experts in information, application, and network security. This team is responsible for the company's perimeter defense systems, security review processes, and customized security infrastructure, as well as for developing, documenting, and implementing Google's security policies and standards.
> - Process—Security is part of the Google DNA. Each application is built from the ground up with security in mind. Google applications go through multiple security reviews as part of the Secure Code development process. The application development environment is closely restricted and carefully monitored to maximize security. External security audits are also regularly conducted to provide additional assurance.
> - Technology—Google Apps data is fractured and obfuscated across multiple servers and disks, making it human-unreadable. Data is replicated in multiple data centers for redundancy and consistent availability. To reduce exploit risks, each Google server is custom-built with only the necessary software components, and the homogeneous server architecture enables rapid updates and configuration changes across the entire network when necessary.

▼▼▼▼▼

WHAT IS A SAS 70 TYPE II AUDIT?

The term "SAS 70" refers to the Statement on Auditing Standards (SAS) No. 70 as issued by the American Institute of Certified Public Accountants. It provides guidelines for audits of service organizations' processes and controls. They are meant to determine, in part, whether companies were living up to claims made about the services they provide. Originally developed for financial services companies and their service providers, the audits have, more recently, been utilized by other types of service providers.

The SAS Type II audit includes a "[r]eport on policies and procedures placed in operation and tests of operating effectiveness," which is

> [a] service auditor's report on a service organization's description of its control structure policies and procedures that may be relevant to a user organization's internal control structure, on whether such policies and procedures were suitably designed to achieve specified control objectives, on whether they had been placed in operation as of a specific date, and on whether the policies and procedures that were tested were operating with sufficient effectiveness to provide reasonable, but not absolute, assurance that the related control objectives were achieved during the period specified.

SAS Type II audits are performed by independent Certified Public Accountants.

According to Google (http://www.google.com/support/a/bin/answer.py?answer=138340), as part of the SAS 70 Type II audit, "The independent third party auditor verified that Google Apps has the following controls and protocols in place":

- Logical security: Controls provide reasonable assurance that logical access to Google Apps production systems and data is restricted to authorized individuals
- Privacy: Controls provide reasonable assurance that Google has implemented policies and procedures addressing the privacy of customer data related to Google Apps
- Data center physical security: Controls provide reasonable assurance that data centers that house Google Apps data and corporate offices are protected

- Incident management and availability: Controls provide reasonable assurance that Google Apps systems are redundant and incidents are properly reported, responded to, and recorded
- Change management: Controls provide reasonable assurance that development of and changes to Google Apps undergo testing and independent code review prior to release into production
- Organization and administration: Controls provide reasonable assurance that management provides the infrastructure and mechanisms to track and communicate initiatives within the company that impact Google Apps

You may also want to review the white paper Google has published detailing the security steps it takes to protect Google Apps (and other) data it stores (http:www.google.com/a/help/intl/en/admins/pdf/ds_gsa_apps_whitepaper_0207.pdf).

18.8.3 Security Good Enough for Some Entities But Not Others

Dozens of state and local governments have "gone Google"—meaning that they have moved from hosting their own e-mail servers (and in some cases documents) to using the Premiere or Government versions of the Google Apps discussed in this chapter. This shift even extends to governmental legal departments.

In 2009, the New Mexico Attorney General's office switched the e-mail accounts of its 120 lawyers and 200 full-time employees (in three geographically distant offices) from Microsoft Exchange servers the agency managed in-house to Gmail. While one driver for the change was an estimated $300,000 (over five years) savings, the AG's office performed its due diligence on the security issues before making the change.

In a November 10, 2009 guest post on the "Official Google Enterprise Blog" (http://googleenterprise.blogspot.com/2009/11/microsoft-exchange-or-google-apps-one.html), James Ferreira, chief information officer for the Office of the New Mexico Attorney General, indicated that

> We began searching for something with ample inbox storage, easy backup and data redundancy and perhaps most importantly, a system that offered high security and reliability. Google Apps Premier Edition emerged as the clear alternative. To put it in perspective, Google Apps and Gmail can support any attorney over the course of a whole career, storing and backing up every email he or she ever sends. Google Apps Premier Edition also passed muster with well-known third-party security auditing organizations.

He went on to say that

> Google Apps Premier Edition was a good fit for the Attorney General's Office. It provides secure, available, and searchable access to documents and emails, while reducing costs and lessening workloads for our busy IT staff. It has reduced the "paper chase" across the board, from attorneys to our busy communications staff.

Additionally, in a November 12, 2009 Google-sponsored webinar discussing the shift (*available at* http://linkon.in/9HGACX—free registration required for viewing), Ferreira said, "Security was the number one thing we wanted to look at" when evaluating a new e-mail system. At first he was skeptical because "this is Gmail and anybody can have a Gmail account." As he investigated further, he realized the differences between the "consumer grade" Gmail and "enterprise grade" Apps. "Google data centers are so well protected they may be some of the safest places on Earth, from what we've seen from the documentation," he added later when specifically discussing security issues. "We knew we were actually looking at a security upgrade going with Google Apps over what we could build or provide ourselves." In a June 24, 2010 guest post on the "Official Google Enterprise Blog" discussing how his office had added document management components to its Google Apps implementation (*available at* http://linkon.in/cbc1zn), Ferreira once again singled out the security of the system, posting, "And since the entire data chain runs on Google servers through secure SSL connections, the risk of in-transit data attacks is minimized—a significant benefit given the sensitive nature of the legal documents in our data set."

In October 2009, the City of Los Angeles decided to switch all 34,000 of its employees from its existing GroupWise e-mail to Google Apps. This switch included the more than 500 lawyers and 1,000 employees over all of the Los Angeles City Attorney's Office. In a December 14, 2009 guest post on the "Official Google Enterprise Blog" (http://googleenterprise.blogspot.com/2009/12/why-city-of-los-angeles-chose-google.html), Randi Levin, chief technology officer for the City of Los Angeles and general manager of the city's Information Technology Agency (ITA), wrote that the decision was made "after a rigorous evaluation process to select the best email solution for the city." She added that "the decision to move to Google Apps was not taken lightly. The city issued a request for proposals and received 15 proposals, which were evaluated by city officials. The top four proposals were invited to give oral presentations, with [the] proposal for Google Apps receiving the highest marks."

The City of Los Angeles apparently also considered the security issues. In a video accompanying the post, Levin also noted that "[the city] will have more security. Our data is going to be much safer with the new system."

In the same video, Kevin Crawford, the Los Angeles ITA's assistant general manager, concurred, noting in a video that accompanies the post that "there are departments within the city that have specific legal requirements for how their data is managed. The data will never change ownership. It's always owned by the City of LA."

By mid-May 2010, The City of Los Angeles had migrated more than 10,000 users to Google Apps. The scheduled completion date for migrating all 30,000 employees to Google Apps was June 2010, according to the official Los Angeles Google Enterprise E-mail & Collaboration System blog (https://sites.google.com/a/lageecs.lacity.org/la-geecs-blog/home).

The City of Los Angeles also posted its contract for the Google Apps implementation, appendices to the contract, and its relevant e-mail retention policy on the blog.

While Google claims that 25 million people at companies around the world have "gone Google" (as of March 17, 2010—see http://googleblog.blogspot.com/2010/03/25-million-people-have-gone-google.html), assurances of the security and privacy of the data stored by Google have not been enough to convince everybody.

While numerous universities like Notre Dame and Brown have made the switch to Google Apps, in two widely reported instances, major universities have chosen to postpone or cancel their implementation of Google Apps over privacy concerns.

In May 2010, UC Davis ended a pilot program implementing Google Apps for all 30,000 plus of its students and faculty. The announcement was made in a letter to university employees that cited concern over Google's ability to keep the faculty's correspondences private as the primary reason for the halt, according to a report by Information Week magazine (http://www.informationweek.com/news/windows/security/showArticle.jhtml?articleID=224700847). However, the Information Week report continued that the letter also went on to state that "outsourcing e-mail may not be in compliance with the University of California Electronic Communications Policy. The policy forbids the university from disclosing or examining the contents of e-mails without the account holder's consent, and from distributing e-mails to third parties."

From this report, it seems as if some university leaders interpreted the outsourcing of e-mail storage via Google Apps to constitute "distributing e-mails to third parties." If that is the case, then it's not the originally stated privacy concerns that would have halted the program, but a violation of existing university policy.

In March 2010, Yale University cited different concerns for postponing the implementation of Google Apps. The Yale Daily News (http://www.yaledailynews.com/news/university-news/2010/03/30/its-delays-switch-gmail-community-input/) quoted computer science professor Michael Fischer as saying that, "People were mainly interested in technical questions like the mechanics of moving, wondering 'Could we do it?'" The article continued to quote Fischer as saying, "But nobody asked the question of 'Should we do it?'" In the article, Fischer also estimated that once the concerns were addressed, the shift to Google Apps would be implemented by the Spring of 2011.

Google Voice 19

Google Voice (http://www.google.com/voice) is Google's free telephone service offering a wide range of calling and voice-mail features. The service was born with Google's 2007 acquisition of telephone management start-up GrandCentral. It was relaunched as Google Voice in March 2009.

Once you have signed up for your Google Voice account (a free Google Account ID is also required; see Section 2.4.1), you can opt to use one of your own existing phone numbers (e.g., mobile, home, office) or receive a new phone number from Google. Google plans to have phone numbers available on all area codes. They reportedly reserved one million phone numbers (through a third-party telecommunications provider) in June 2009.

Google Voice's best-known feature is probably the ability to simultaneously forward incoming calls to multiple phone numbers like a switchboard. You can configure your Google Voice number to ring your home phone, office phone, and mobile phone all at the same time. This way, wherever you are, you can get the call or choose to let it go to voicemail. Once you answer an incoming Google Voice call on one of these phones, it is no longer available for pickup on the other phones.

However, Google Voice does allow you to switch from one phone to another during a call. This could come in handy, for example, if you're working from home when a client calls your Google Voice number, which is automatically sent to your cell phone, but partway through the call your cell phone battery starts to die. You can press the star key

(*) while you're talking and your other phones will ring. Then you can pick up the call from your house phone and not worry about losing the call.

Google Voice gives you an easy way to conduct conference calls. You can have multiple individuals call your Google Voice number at a prescribed time and then use the service's call-waiting feature to add each caller to the call.

You can create customized voicemail messages for specific people or have specific callers routed to specific phones (e.g., your clients' numbers can be set to ring only your office number, and your wife's number can be set to ring all your numbers). You can screen calls based on their caller ID information, listen in as someone leaves you a voicemail message (just as you would on a home answering machine)—and pick up the call while they're leaving the message (if you choose)—or block specific numbers entirely.

Voicemail messages can be accessed from any of your phones, or via the Web. Google Voice can even transcribe your voicemail messages to be read online using Google Voice's Web interface or e-mailed to you.

Because the service has a Web interface and offers many advanced features, it is often mistakenly referred to as a voice over Internet protocol (VOIP) phone service. Strictly speaking, however, Google Voice is actually a novel way of routing calls through standard phone services. In November 2009, Google did purchase VOIP provider Gizmo5. The reported intention was to integrate some of Gizmo5's features and functions into Google Voice.

19.1   Selecting Your Google Voice Number

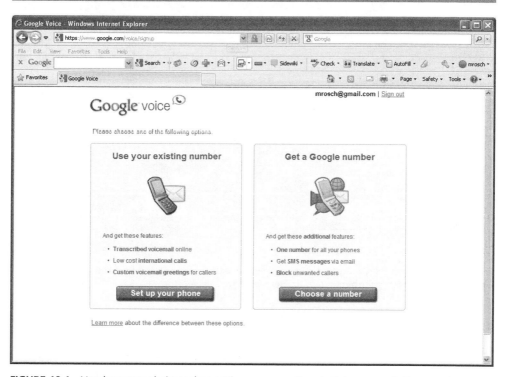

FIGURE 19.1   You have two choices when setting up a new Google Voice account. You can choose to either **Use your existing number** or **Get a Google number**. More features are available to accounts that **Get a Google number**. It's important to know that, once you make this selection, you cannot change your mind.

Throughout this chapter, we'll look at a Google Voice account that opts for an additional phone number from Google's pool of numbers. These are the most popular type of accounts because they have access to more features and functions than if you just add Google Voice to your existing phone number.

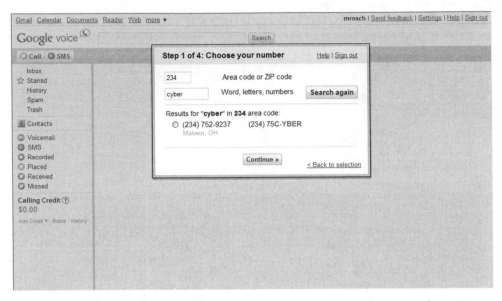

FIGURE 19.2 When selecting your Google Voice number, you can search by **Area code or ZIP code**; **Words**, **letters**, **numbers**; or both. Here we have selected the easy-to-remember Google Voice number 234-75-CYBER (29237).

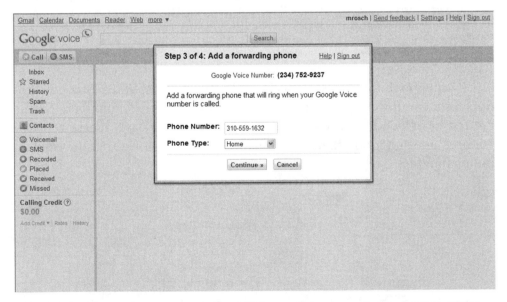

FIGURE 19.3 When setting up your new Google Voice number, you are asked to designate existing phone numbers that Google Voice should ring when calls come in to your Google Voice number. You can add home, work, or mobile numbers. You can even add a temporary number if you're working out of a remote office location or your vacation home phone number and then delete the number when you've returned.

▼▼▼▼▼

Google Voice Allows Low Cost Client Centered Legal and Mediation Services

Jennifer Bernstein, a partner in the Boston, MA-based general practice legal services and conflict resolution firm Bernstein & Yang, LLP (http://www.bernsteinyang.com), has put Google's Voice to work in her practice.

Two of Bernstein & Yang's main concerns are supplying our clients with affordable services and being accessible to clients. My philosophy for addressing the first concern is simple . . . keep your overhead and other operating costs down. This gives clients the assurance that their costs are going directly to legal and/or mediation services (not to paying the rent or the phone bill). To address the second concern, we strive to be available to our clients and to answer the phone when they call (or call them back within a reasonable amount of time). Google Voice helps my firm achieve both of those goals.

I have a virtual office with a live receptionist but I am personally not a permanent fixture in the office. Therefore, if a client calls the office directly, they will more than likely go directly to my voicemail. Google Voice allows me to hand my client a local phone number where they can almost always reach me since my Google Voice number rings directly on my personal cell phone. Google Voice supplies the name of the caller and prompts me to either take the call, or to send it to Google Voice's voicemail.

In addition to affordability, our Firm strives to ensure that each client feels that their individual needs are addressed. We are available to clients when they need us. So, outside of normal business hours I can forward my office phone to my Google Voice number and those calls are routed to my cell phone—where I can immediately pick up the call. If I am unable to answer the phone, callers will get my law firm message from Google Voice's voicemail box where they can leave a message. Once a client leaves a voicemail, the message is then transcribed and sent to me via text message (and saved online). This way I can immediately determine the priority level of the client call and determine how quickly I need to respond. By using Google Voice I can provide the accessibility that my clients deserve.

So, how does all this save money? IT'S FREE. There are absolutely no sign up, monthly or annual fees. Also, I can make outgoing domestic calls using Google Voice at no charge and international calls at an extremely reduced rate. By giving clients my Google Voice number (or forwarding my office phone to it) I can take work and personal calls on one cell phone, and not waste money every month on a second line, but still have separate voicemail boxes.

Google Voice allows Bernstein & Yang, LLP to provide lower cost legal and mediation services to our clients and allows our clients easier access to our people. It's a service that I highly recommend in a small firm environment.

Ethics Alert

THE ETHICS OF YOUR GOOGLE PHONE NUMBER

If you opt to use a new phone number from Google as your Google Voice, the number does not have to be in the area code where you are located. Note that we selected an easy-to-remember number that includes a sequential area code (**234**) and a word associated with our live MCLE seminars—**CYBER** (short for "cybersleuth").

Note that we are not located in the city covered by that 234 area code—Malvern, Ohio. That's okay for us, because we are not practicing law.

Could a lawyer's Google Voice number, with an area code in a state other than where the lawyer is licensed to practice, mislead a consumer into thinking that the lawyer is soliciting business, or otherwise willing to take clients in that jurisdiction? Would this constitute the unauthorized practice of law?

Similarly, lawyers must beware of making "false or misleading statements about . . . the lawyer's services." Could a Google Voice number containing the word(s) NUM1LAW, IWINLAW, or BESTLAW be considered a misrepresentation or create an "unreasonable expectation as to the outcome" of a lawyer's case?

Lawyers must be cognizant of the ethics rules in all of the jurisdictions in which they are licensed to practice.

19.2 The Google Voice Web Interface: A Unified Inbox

The Google Voice Web interface is reminiscent of the Gmail inbox discussed in Section 18.1.

The Google Voice Inbox contains all the voicemail, SMS text messages, and recorded calls received by your Google Voice number. Because messages are arranged in an e-mail inbox format, you can listen to them in any order you'd like—or even delete messages you're not interested in without listening to them.

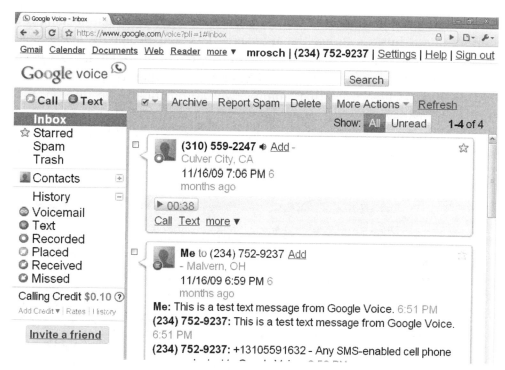

FIGURE 19.4   Similar to Gmail, you can mark favorite messages by clicking the star icon on the right-hand side of any message. Clicking the **Starred** link on the left-hand side of the Google Voice page displays only those Starred messages. Clicking the **History** link displays a list of **Received** and **Recorded** calls, **Voicemail** or **SMS** text messages. Further down the left-hand section are links to view only calls that you have **Placed** using the **Call** button, **Received** on your Google Voice number from outside callers, and **Missed** (although we have not had any missed calls—they all went to voicemail).

Clicking the checkbox to the left of any message and then clicking **Archive** moves the chosen message(s) out of the main **Inbox** and into their respective **Voicemail**, **SMS**, **Recorded**, **Placed**, **Received**, or **Missed** folders (depending on the type of message(s) selected). Clicking the **Voicemail**, **SMS**, **Recorded**, **Placed**, **Received**, or **Missed** links in the left-hand section displays only those individual types of archived messages.

Clicking the checkbox to the left of any message and then clicking the **Report spam** button above the messages lets you designate a message or caller as unwanted. This is useful to dispense of unsolicited calls from salespeople, etc. Once you've marked a message or caller as spam, all future voicemail messages from that number will automatically be filtered into the Spam mailbox. You can click the **Spam** link on the left-hand side of the screen to see messages that get sent to the Spam mailbox. You still have the option of clicking the **Play** button in any of those messages to listen to them.

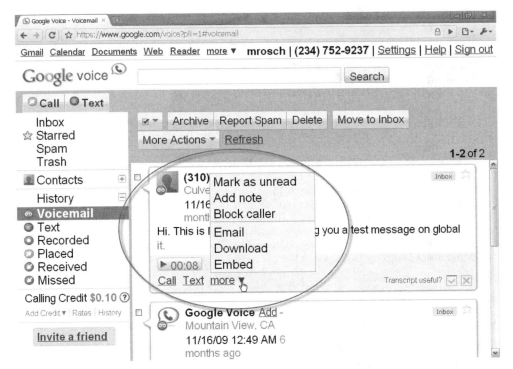

FIGURE 19.5 This screenshot illustrates the voicemail messages as displayed after clicking the **Voicemail** link on the left-hand side of the screen. You can click the **Call** or **SMS** links that accompany each message to call the person back or send them a text message (respectively). (See Section 19.3 for more information on placing calls via Google Voice.) Clicking the down arrow, next to the **more** link, gives you the ability to add a note to the message for your future reference, block this particular caller, **Email** the audio of the voicemail to someone else, **Download** the audio to your own computer, or generate HTML code that (when pasted into a page on your Web site) will **Embed** the audio into a page on your Web site. (See Section 19.8 regarding privacy issues.)

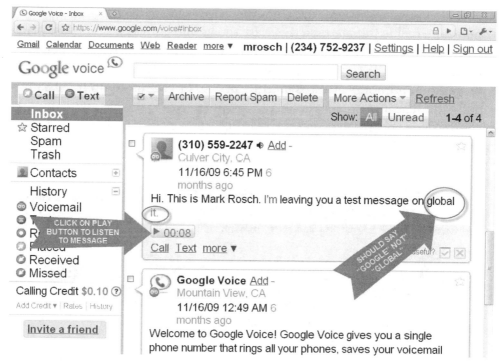

FIGURE 19.6   Google Voice not only links to the recorded voicemail messages received by your Google Voice number, it also transcribes those messages. The transcription is displayed underneath the date and time the message was left. A play button and a progress bar are underneath that. Clicking the play button not only replays the recorded voicemail message, but also highlights the text of the messages, following the audio in a "follow-the-bouncing-ball style" until the audio stops. You can opt to have the transcripts sent to your mobile phone as text messages. Note that because of the 160-character limit of text messages, you will receive only the beginning portions of transcripts sent as text messages. Also, the transcripts are not precise. The last two words of the message in this illustration should be "Google Voice" and not "global it."

19.3   Placing Calls Using Google Voice (Using a Phone or via the Web)

You can place calls from your Google Voice account by dialing your Google Voice number from any of your registered phones and pressing *2* when prompted. You will then be prompted to enter the number you wish to call.

Calls can also be initiated from the Google Voice Web interface. Even though the call is initiated via the Web, the actual conversation takes place on one of your registered phones. Calls can be placed to any U.S. (including Alaska and Hawaii) or Canadian phone number for free. You can also call international numbers at rates starting at $0.02 per minute up to $0.55 per minute depending on the country. See http://www.google.com/support/voice/bin/answer.py?hl=en&answer=141925 for an alphabetical list of rates by country.

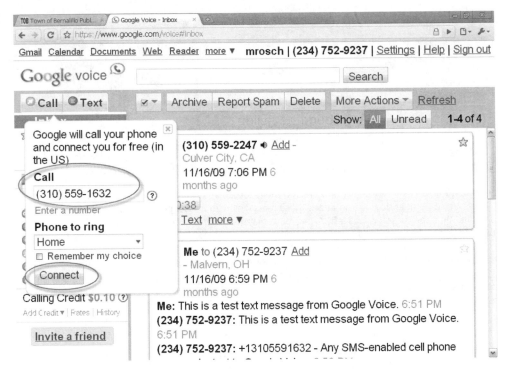

FIGURE 19.7   Click the **Call** button on the upper left-hand side of the Google Voice page to initiate a phone call to any phone number anywhere in the world. Calls to U.S. and Canadian phone numbers are free. Enter the number you want to call, select which of your registered phones you want Google Voice to use, and click the **Connect** button. Google Voice will call you on the phone you've chosen and then dial the number you've entered in the **Call** box. Sound quality in our test calls (to U.S. numbers) was as good as a direct connection.

A $0.10 calling credit is added to your new account when you first con-figure it. This will buy a five-minute call to Denmark or a one-minute call to Jamaica. To add calling credits, click **Settings** and then **Billing**. Credits can be added only in $10 increments (and you can only purchase them $10 at a time). Payments are made online via credit card.

19.4   Recording Incoming Calls

Google Voice allows you to record any incoming call you receive to your Google Voice number. (Recording is not possible for outgoing calls you initiate using the Call button described earlier.) You can initiate call recording by pressing the number *4* on your phone anytime during the call. Google Voice will announce to both parties that "recording has commenced." Recording will continue until you press *4* again or hang up the phone.

Ethics Note

RECORDING PHONE CALLS

Even though Google Voice clearly announces the fact that a call is being recorded, lawyers should be aware of the laws regarding recording phone calls in their state. Additionally, keep in mind that if you're talking to someone located in another state, different laws may apply.

19.5 Customizing Google Voice

Google Voice also gives you the ability to customize many aspects of how calls are treated when they come into your Google Voice number. These features are accessed by clicking the **Settings** link in the upper right-hand side of the Google Voice screen. Be sure to click the **Save changes** button before leaving any of the Settings screens.

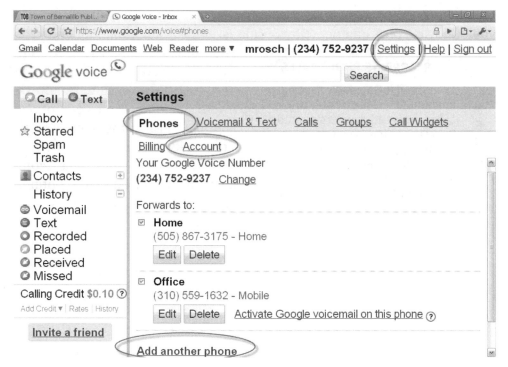

FIGURE 19.8 There are seven tabs (**Phones** through **Account**) available on which to customize and manage your Google Voice account after you've clicked on the **Settings** link. This screenshot illustrates the **Phones** tab, where you can add new/additional numbers to be rung when calls come into your Google Voice number.

19.5.1   Voicemail & SMS Settings

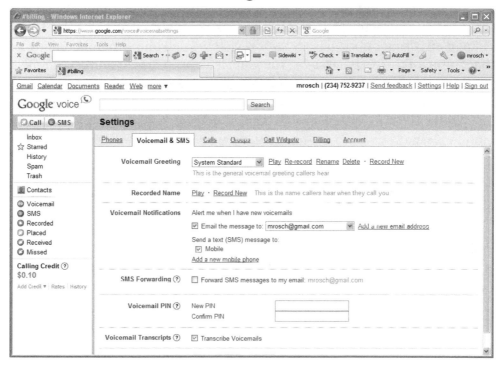

FIGURE 19.9   After clicking the **Settings** link and then the **Voicemail & SMS** tab, you can record multiple **Voicemail Greetings** (and play them back to review them), select your default greeting, decide whether you want to receive e-mails or text messages when you get a voicemail on your Google Voice number, whether you want text messages received on your Google Voice number forwarded to your existing cellular phone, and whether you want **Voicemail Transcripts** automatically generated from voicemails.

19.5.2   Calls Settings

Google Voice gives you the ability to receive a large amount of information about your callers before you even pick up a call. Google Voice's Call Screening feature can be configured to ask callers not already in your address book to say their names before the call is rung through to the phones you've designated. Enabling Call Screening gives you the ability to screen calls using the Call Presentation feature.

Call Presentation allows you to hear the name when you first pick up the call—giving you the opportunity to take the call or send it to voicemail (while you hear the name, the caller still hears the phone ringing). Callers only have to announce themselves the first time they call your Google Voice number; Google Voice remembers their names by associating the name to the incoming phone number. (Call Presentation is turned on by default in all new Google Voice accounts.)

The **Caller ID (out)** feature allows you to dictate what caller ID number will be passed along when you send a text message from your registered cell phone to a recipient's own Google Voice number. Selecting the **Don't change anything** option passes your registered cell phone number along as the source of the text message. You can also opt to mask your cell phone's number and pass along only your Google Voice number by selecting the **Display my Google Voice number** option.

Caller ID (in) works very much like it does on your existing landline or mobile phone.

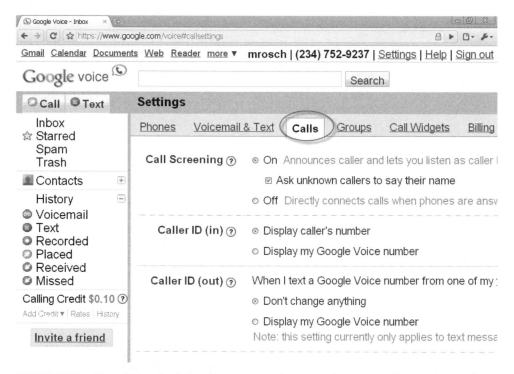

FIGURE 19.10 After clicking the **Calls** tab, you can configure Google Voice's **Call Screening**, **Call Presentation**, **Caller ID (in)**, and **Caller ID (out)** settings. **Do Not Disturb** sends all incoming calls directly to voicemail.

Google Voice's Call Presentation feature gives you the option of accepting an incoming call (after you've heard the name the caller has provided) by pressing the number *1*, sending it to voicemail by pressing the number *2*, or sending it to voicemail and listening in as the caller leaves the voicemail message by pressing number *3*. Pressing *1* at any point while listening to the message connects you to the caller.

Usage Tip

CALL PRESENTATION AND
HANDS-FREE MOBILE PHONES

The Call Presentation feature is excellent if you're sitting at your desk or have access to your mobile phone's keypad, but the feature is not at all convenient if you're using a Bluetooth headset (or some other hands-free device) with your mobile while you're driving, for example, and have no access to the keypad.

If you set up Groups (or individual callers) that ring only to your mobile phone, and you often use a hands-free device, it might be a good idea to turn off Call Presentation.

19.5.3   Creating Groups to Identify Callers

You can set up groups of contacts who are treated differently from one another. For example, you can create a group of coworkers (that could also include clients) whose calls are rung through to your office and mobile phones, friends whose calls are rung through to your home and mobile phones, and family whose calls are rung through to all your numbers.

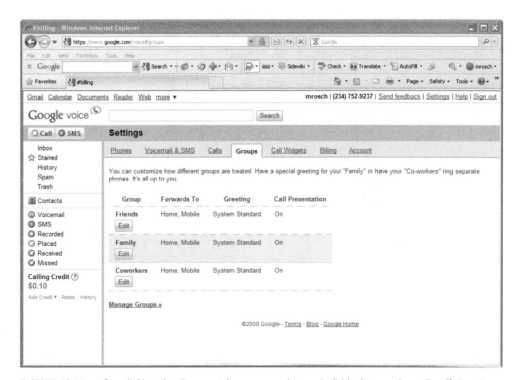

FIGURE 19.11 After clicking the **Groups** tab, you can select an individual group (e.g., **Family**) and add contacts to the group, decide which phones those contacts' calls will get rung through to, decide what greeting the members of this group will hear when they call (you can even record a separate greeting just for these callers), and decide whether you want **Call Presentation** turned on for these contacts. Click **Manage Groups** and then the **New Groups** button (closest to the **Search contacts** box) to create additional groups beyond the three default groups illustrated here.

19.5.4 Let Visitors to Your Web Site Call You on the Phone (for Free)

Google Voice's Call Widgets give potential clients a way to immediately contact you by phone directly from your Web site.

FIGURE 19.12 When a visitor to your Web site clicks on a Google Voice Call Widget, they are connected to your phone(s) similar to the way you can place calls by clicking the **Call** button (as described in Section 19.3). Clicking the **Call Widgets** tab and then the **Add a new Call Widget** link gives you the ability to generate HTML code that (when pasted into a page on your Web site) installs this feature. You can create more than one widget with different settings, such as which of your phones you want these calls rung through to, what greeting these callers will hear when they call (you can even record a separate message just for these callers or choose to have all the calls automatically go to voicemail), and whether you want Call Presentation turned on for these contacts.

19.5.5   Checking Your Bill

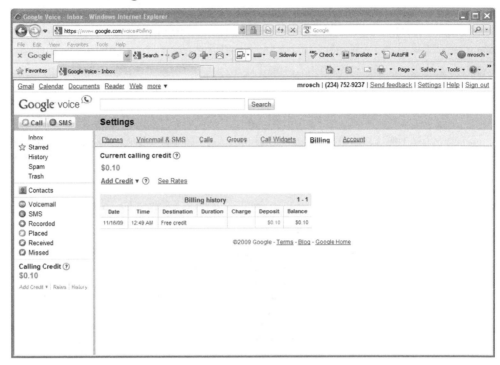

FIGURE 19.13   As described, most of Google Voice's features are free—only international calling currently carries a charge. Clicking the **Billing** tab displays the **Billing history** for your account (if any), including calling credits purchased, calling credits used (calls made), and remaining balance. If you don't use Google Voice to make international calls, this will be of no interest to you.

19.6   Importing Contacts from Other Sources

You can import the names, e-mail addresses, postal addresses, phone numbers, etc. for your contacts into Google Voice from your Outlook, Outlook Express, Yahoo! Mail, Hotmail, and Eudora (among others) e-mail applications. You can also import contacts from your existing Gmail account.

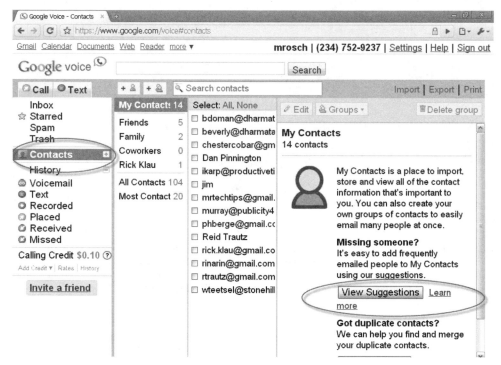

FIGURE 19.14   Clicking the **Contacts** link on the left-hand side of the screen and then the **View Suggestions** button displays contacts already stored in your Gmail account. Clicking the checkbox next to any name adds it to your Google Voice contact list.

19.7   Searching for Messages

Google Voice also allows you to keyword search through all of the messages contained in your Archive and Inbox folders. To keyword search, simply enter your keywords (or numbers) into the **Google Voice** search box at the top of the page. Google Voice recognizes the Boolean connector, word stemming, and phrase-searching strategies used in Google Web search discussed in sections 3.1–3.3, but not the proximity search capabilities discussed in Section 3.4.

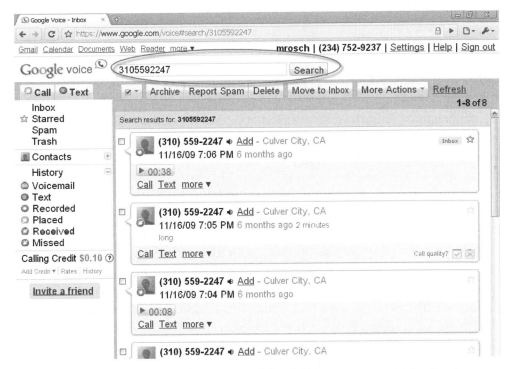

FIGURE 19.15 This screenshot illustrates a search of Google Voice messages containing the phone number *3105592247*. The search returns **Voicemail** and **SMS** messages, **Recorded**, **Placed**, **Received**, and **Missed** calls.

19.8 Privacy Concerns

There are many who have expressed concerns over the volume and type of information that Google Voice stores. They argue that Google Voice stores too much information about your placed and received phone calls, voice-mails, and text messages.

The first concern that comes to mind for many is that recorded voice-mails or transcripts of messages could become public despite the fact that Google Voice accounts are protected by a username and password to thwart unauthorized access. In fact, in October 2009, there was a flurry of reports that Google Voice voicemail messages were not only public, but were turning up in search engine searches. (See http://bit.ly/7Qk2d9 for an example.) After clarification by Google, it was revealed that those messages that were turning up in search engine searches had been made public by their owners and embedded in publicly available Web pages, where they were found and returned in search results. (See http://bit.ly/8ugecg and http://googlevoiceblog.blogspot.com/2009/10/about-voicemail-and-privacy.html for more details.)

Although Google's explanation of events in the scenario above relieves the concerns of some, another concern of many privacy advocates deals with how Google will handle the information it has gathered and for what purposes it will use it.

The Google Voice Privacy Policy reads, in part:

> When you use Google Voice, Google's servers automatically record certain information about your use of Google Voice. Similar to other web services, Google Voice records information *such as* [emphasis added] account activity (including storage usage, number of log-ins), data displayed or clicked on (including UI elements, links); and other log information (including browser type, IP-address, date and time of access, cookie ID, and referrer URL). Google's servers also automatically collect telephony log information (including calling-party number, forwarding numbers, time and date of calls, duration of calls, SMS routing information, and types of calls).

(The entire Google Voice Privacy Policy is located at http://www.google.com/googlevoice/privacy-policy.html.)

To one degree or another, however, all phone companies keep records of the calls placed and received through the numbers they control. Similarly, cell phone companies keep records, and in some instances copies, of the voicemail and text messages their customers receive and the text messages they send. However, some suggest that Google Voice's storage capacity gives individual Google Voice accounts archival potential unlike any available to traditional telephone companies for all Google Voice accounts.

They argue that Google could use this information in combination with other information gathered by Google about your online surfing habits and information you've turned over freely to Google as part of other services discussed in this book to create a sizable dossier about individual users. This would be a clear violation of Google's overall privacy policy.

Additionally, some privacy advocates argue that discovery of the large amount of calling, messages, etc. history potentially available in a Google Voice account could constitute a *de facto* "retroactive wiretap."

Note too that the policy uses the phrase *records information such as* rather than something more definite like *records the following information*. This makes it unclear whether the types of information listed in the privacy policy represent all of the information that Google Voice is retaining.

Some of those concerned over Google's trove of phone call, voicemail, and text message data express concern that government agencies could request access to

Practice Tip

DISCOVERY REQUESTS FOR DATA IN GOOGLE VOICE ACCOUNTS

An important question that so far remains unanswered is how courts will treat the information stored in Google Voice accounts for the purposes of discovery under the Federal Rules of Civil Procedure (specifically Rule 26, dealing with Electronically Stored Information [ESI]).

In your request to produce during discovery, you might try including language like "data including, but not limited to, time and date of placed, received, and missed calls; calling-party numbers; forwarding numbers, duration of time and date of placed, received, and missed calls; voicemail messages; SMS text messages; and SMS text message routing information contained in a Google Voice account," in addition to requests for retained voicemail, e-mail, etc. from other sources.

While a cottage industry has already grown up around processing the recorded audio content of voicemails and other recorded calls for discovery and compliance purposes, those recordings retained by corporations or other companies don't usually include the level of additional data (e.g., calling history) that is contained in a Google Voice account.

all of this data stored in individual personal accounts under the guise of the USA PATRIOT Act or similar legislation. The fact that the National Security Agency carried out warrantless wiretaps with the cooperation of traditional telephone companies during George W. Bush's presidency makes this argument a nonstarter.

For lawyers, the information stored about their calls, voicemails, etc. in a Google Voice account (e.g., call history, transcripts of messages, text of text messages) used in the course of their practice would, most likely, fall under the protections of work product and attorney-client privilege.

An added element that concerns many privacy advocates is how this information could be combined with other information Google has stored about its users from other services. For this there is no corollary. We can only rely on Google's unofficial mantra, "Don't be evil."

While the security of data in a lawyer's Google Voice account seems analogous to the protections surrounding data stored in Google Apps and Gmail, we hesitate to make a definitive "yes" or "no" recommendation that lawyers use Google Voice in their practice. You have to be comfortable with the hypothetical potential uses for the information stored in these accounts.

It should be noted that the ABA does not have similar privacy concerns related to the third-party storage of voicemail messages and phone call information. In November 2009, as a member benefit, the ABA began offering a 15 percent discount to a similar service called RingCentral. (See http://new.abanet.org/centers/ltrc/Pages/techez_dir.aspx for details.)

Google Search Shortcuts 20

Google has also created a number of different shortcuts to access many of the search features we discussed in the preceding chapters.

20.1 Google Toolbar

Google has created a specialized toolbar that allows you to perform a search no matter what Web page you're looking at. You don't have to visit Google.com. The toolbar seamlessly integrates with your Web browser. This free tool is easily downloaded and installed (http://toolbar.google.com).

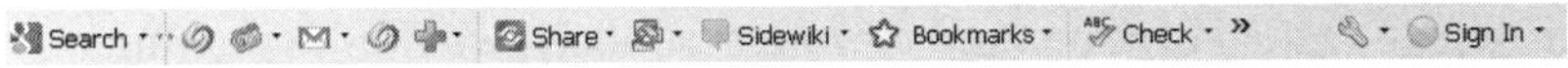

Search · ⋅ ⊘ ⚙ · M · ⊘ ♣ · | ⊠ Share · ▦ · ▮ Sidewiki · ☆ Bookmarks · ᴬᴮᶜ Check · »   ✎ · ◉ Sign In ·

FIGURE 20.1

Upon installation, Google Toolbar includes the following features (from left to right in the above illustration, but they may appear in a different order in your browser):

- Google Web Search: Access Google Search from any Web page. Clicking the down arrow on the right-hand side of this button gives you access to a drop-down list of more specialized search options—e.g., Google Groups (Chapter 7), Google Images (Chapter 8), Google Blog Search (Chapter 9).
- Google News Search: Conduct a search only through news resources (as discussed in Chapter 6).
- Google Desktop Search: Search for information on your own computer's hard drive (as discussed in Chapter 16).

Practice Tip

PRIVACY

Google does a good job of explicitly laying out what information they collect about users of its tools and how it treats that information. Most of the features offered as part of the toolbar do not require storing any readily identifiable information about your search activity. However, enhanced features such as Sidewiki and PageRank do send information about your searches (Sidewiki) and sites visited (PageRank) to Google.

Welcome to
Google Toolbar

Introducing Sidewiki, an enhanced Toolbar feature

Add helpful information beside any webpage

Read insights from other users

Sidewiki, PageRank, and future page-related services are part of the enhanced Toolbar. For enhanced Toolbar features to work, Toolbar has to tell us what site you're visiting by sending Google the URL (Privacy Policy).

| No thanks | Enable enhanced features |

FIGURE 20.2

Sidewiki offers users the ability to make notes or to add comments about the sites they have visited. It acts almost like an annotated bookmark system allowing for the addition of notations about why the site was useful or to call attention to particular information about functions found there. This information is sent back to Google and stored as part of the user's Google Account. These notations are then visible to anyone on the Web who subsequently visits that same page (and has the Sidewiki feature enabled in their own browser's toolbar). A user's Sidewiki comments are also visible through the user's Google Profile (see Section 2.4.2).

Sidewiki could be a useful knowledge-management tool for lawyers; however, because the notations are viewable publicly, we don't recommend clicking on the **Enable Enhanced Features** option.

- Button Gallery: Add more functions to the toolbar, such as Google Maps (see Chapter 14).
- Gmail: Once you have logged into your Gmail account, click the down arrow to the right of this button to display your most recent, unread e-mail messages.
- Pop-up Blocker: Block new pages and/or ads that are set to automatically pop up while you're viewing a Web page. Click this button to toggle between **Always allow pop-ups from [the site you're viewing]** and **Disallow pop-ups from [the site you're viewing]**.
- Sidewiki: Make notes or add comments about the sites you've visited. (See the Practice Tip ("Privacy") earlier in this chapter for more information.)

- Spell Check: Check the spelling entries in search boxes, contact forms, (Web-based) e-mails, etc. Clicking a misspelled word (which shows up in red) displays a list of suggested spellings from which to choose. Once corrected, the previously misspelled word turns green.
- Google Translate: Translate the page you're reading, either to or from any of 52 available languages. (See Chapter 12 for more information.)
- AutoFill: Automatically fill in forms that appear on Web sites (e.g., shopping sites) with your name, address, etc. To do so, you must input this information into the toolbar's settings (click the **Options** button, then **AutoFill**, then **Add new profile**). You can also opt to include credit card information to be autofilled from this profile.
- Highlight: Highlight search terms as they appear on the page—each word in its own color. Clicking this button also adds a new button for each keyword. Clicking a keyword's button automatically takes you to the first place that word appears on the Web page; clicking it again takes you to the next instance, and so on. (These buttons may also be hidden behind right-pointing chevrons to the right of the highlight button.) Clicking the highlight button again turns off the highlighting. (Highlighting your keywords makes them easy to spot in a long Web page. Turning the highlighting off is a good idea before printing out a Web page.)
- Options: Further customize the tools, buttons, and features available in your toolbar by clicking this button. (Note that on the **General** tab, there is an option to **Send usage statistics to Google**. For privacy reasons, discussed in Chapter 16, we recommend that lawyers uncheck this option.)
- Google Account Sign In: Access your free Google Account (as described in Section 2.4.1) by clicking this button.

The newest version of the Google Toolbar requires Microsoft Windows XP or Vista operating system and the Microsoft Internet Explorer browser (version 6.0 or newer). A version of the toolbar is also available for the Firefox browser (version 2 or newer) running on Windows 2000/XP/Vista or Mac OS X 10.4 and above. As of our publication deadline, no version of the toolbar was available for the Windows 7 operating system.

Usage Tip

TOOLBARS FOR OLD SYSTEMS STILL AVAILABLE

Users of older Windows or Mac operating systems (or older browsers) can still download previous versions of the toolbar for their use by clicking the **Previous Version** link on the Toolbar home page (http://toolbar.google.com)

20.2   iGoogle

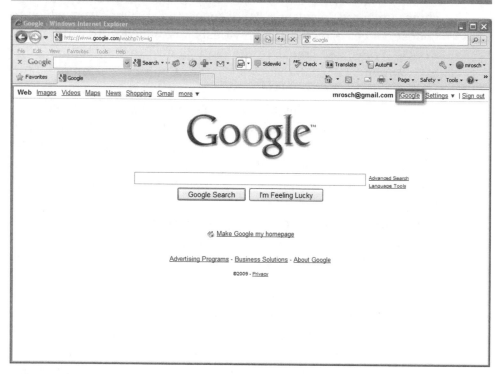

FIGURE 20.3   To access your iGoogle home page (once signed into your free Google Account), click the **iGoogle** link near the upper right-hand corner of the Google Web search page.

Those with a free Google Account (see Section 2.4.1) also have the ability to create a customized iGoogle home page that can display numerous types of information from a variety of sources, each in a separate module. The information is automatically drawn from the sources you select and then displayed on the iGoogle home page.

FIGURE 20.4   This iGoogle home page includes information from our Google Calendar, weather (in various cities we've defined), and current Google News headlines, among other information we've added. We can rearrange the placement of any of this information by holding down our left mouse button and dragging any of the modules to a new location. We could add more information by clicking the **Add stuff** link and choosing new modules. We can also click the **Classic Home** link in the upper right-hand corner of the page to return to standard view of the Google home page.

You can also set up specialized, custom tabs in iGoogle.

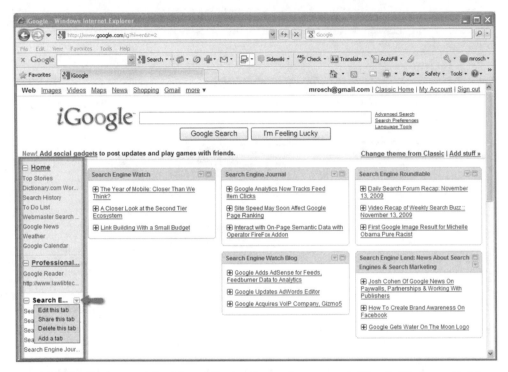

FIGURE 20.5 This is a specialized **Search Engine News** tab we set up in iGoogle. We have added the RSS feeds from various search engines to the tab so that they are all displayed together for easy reading and clicking. (See Section 9.2.1 for more information on using RSS feeds to keep up with information.) Click the down arrow next to the tab's name (on the left-hand side) to **Edit this tab**, **Delete this tab**, or **Share this tab** (via e-mail). You can use the same drop-down arrow to **Add a tab** containing completely different information.

Returning to the clean Google Web search interface is as simple as clicking the **Classic Home** link near the upper right-hand corner of the Google Web search home page.

Google SMS (Short Message Service): Retrieve Information via Text Messaging

21

Many "smartphone" users access Google's Web search using their phone's Internet connection. For people who have not yet made the leap to a phone that can connect to the Internet, or if you need information when your phone's Internet connection is down, Google offers its Google SMS service for text-message-enabled cellular phones.

Google SMS allows you to send your query to Google as a text message (to 466453) and then sends your results back to you as a text message. Google SMS is not case sensitive, so capitalization does not matter.

Results are text-only. They do not include images, or links to Web pages like Google Web search results. Information available includes directions, maps, definitions, language translations, currency converters, restaurant locations and phone numbers, movie showtimes, flight statuses, stock quotes, and more. All queries and responses are subject to the 160-character limit of SMS messages.

Google SMS will send three results per query (usually contained in one to two text messages, depending on the number of characters required to answer the query). There are exceptions. For example, nearby movie showtimes require more than one or two text messages to deliver all the available times. When responses require an additional text message, you will be instructed to respond to the first text with *Next* to receive the remaining responses for your query. In these instances, Google SMS will send a maximum of seven text messages for any particular query.

Adding a city or ZIP code to other types of text queries will bring you localized results near the location you've indicated. For example, texting *Hotels 33139* to Google SMS retrieves responses including the names, addresses, and phone numbers for hotels in Miami Beach, Florida. Because there are so many hotels in the vicinity, this query gen-

FIGURE 21.1   An interactive demonstration of Google SMS is available online at http://www.google.com/mobile/products/sms.html. This demonstration allows you to send simulated text queries to Google SMS and receive the same results as if you were sending those queries via your cellular phone. This example illustrates the service's response to the query *Hotels 33139*.

erates the maximum seven text messages in response. You can also type in a person's name and city (or ZIP code) and receive their listed residential phone number in the return text message from Google.

Google does not charge for this service, but your cellular phone carrier's regular text-messaging charges will apply to both the queries you send and the incoming text-message results. If your cellular service plan requires you to pay per message, charges could be an issue. If you have an unlimited text-message plan, you will see no additional charges for using this service.

Practice Tip

Google SMS offers a number of shortcuts to save characters in your query. For example:

- To define a word: Precede your query with a *D*, so texting *D fibromyalgia* to Google SMS will return three separate definitions for this medical term. Unfortunately, most Google SMS definitions do not include their sources, but they are usually good enough when you need to define an unfamiliar term in a pinch.
- To translate: Precede your query with a *T*, so you could text *T où est le palais de justice?* and Google SMS would respond *Translation: 'où est le palais de justice?' in French means 'where is the courthouse?' in English.* Or text *T Where is the courthouse? in French* to Google SMS to receive *Translation: 'where is the courthouse?' in English means 'où est le palais de justice?' in French.*
- To get current weather information: Precede the name of the city in which you want the current weather conditions with *WX*, so texting *WX Chicago IL* would return the current weather conditions in Chicago, Illinois.

Google Earth—
Now You Can Fly Under
the Surface of Oceans

22

Google Earth is a virtual searchable globe. It combines satellite imagery, street level photos, maps, live traffic data, and more into a database searchable by address, longitude and latitude, or business type and location. It displays its results in a graphical manner—showing images of the places you've searched for rather than just providing textual descriptions.

Google Earth was originally developed by Keyhole, Inc. under the product name Earth Viewer. Keyhole was acquired by Google in 2004 and Earth Viewer was relaunched as Google Earth in 2005. Over the years there have been many changes

---

Usage Tip

WHY USE GOOGLE EARTH INSTEAD OF GOOGLE MAPS (WHICH DOESN'T REQUIRE INSTALLATION)?

1. It's more interactive.
2. Street level images in Earth may be in 3-D.
3. Many images include an approximate date on which they were captured.
4. They draw user-generated content from different sources. For example when you add a **Photo** layer to a map, Earth draws from more sources (and has more photos) than Maps.
5. **Traffic** data is displayed differently. In test searches we ran, we found traffic data for more roads (on the same mapped area) in Maps than in Earth.
6. Earth searches more than street addresses; it searches under the surface of oceans and travels to Mars.
7. Earth flies (while Maps only travels by car, foot, and public transportation).

and additions to Google Earth, as well as integration with other Google products. For example, Google Maps' Street View function was integrated into Google Earth in 2008. Currently, Google Earth and Google Maps share many of the same search and viewing capabilities. (See Chapter 14.)

Navigating through the Street View images is a little different in Earth than it is in Maps.

Practice Tip

The additional data, options and views in Google Earth can be very useful, but if you're actually trying to practice law, beware, Google Earth can also be a huge time suck!

To virtually "walk down the street" in Earth, you have to double-click the camera icons in the street rather than grabbing Maps' Pegman icon and clicking the arrows overlaid on the roads. Once inside the Street View image in Earth, you can navigate through it using the same tools described in Section 22.2.

There are four ways to access Google Earth. Two are free and two are not. The first free version is a plug-in that displays Google Earth data in your Web browser. Then there are two standalone application versions of Google Earth: the free version (Google Earth) and the pay version (Google Earth Pro at $400.00). The fourth way to access Google Earth is through the on-site "Enterprise Solution" meant for the large "business, public agency, or organization" that needs to manage its own geographic information (price varies).

FIGURE 22.1 This is the Google Earth search result for *321 N. Clark Chicago*. We can instruct Earth to display additional information to the map by selecting options in the **Layers** section (in the lower left-hand corner). We can add **Businesses** (e.g., Sheraton Hotels, Billy Goat Tavern, Walgreens), **Places** (e.g., Merchandise Mart, N. Dearborn St. bridge), and more. The large camera icons dotting the map indicate that **Street View** street level imagery can also be added in the **Layers** section. If you compare this illustration with the Google Maps Search result for the same address in Chapter 14 you will see many similarities between the two services.

Usage Tip

DO LAWYERS NEED GOOGLE EARTH PRO?

The free Google Earth and Pro versions both use the same image database. Pro images are not more enhanced than the free version (the resolution of the image is the same in both versions). Nor are Pro images more up-to-date than the free version (note: neither is in real-time). However, you can print images at higher resolution using Pro, and there are other professional tools (see http://www.google.com/enterprise/earthmaps/pro_features.html).

Note however, that Google states the free version of the Google Earth stand-alone application is "[I]ntended for personal, non-commercial use . . . [It] sends you on an interactive, 3D exploration of the planet through terabytes of aerial and satellite imagery."

Additionally, on the Pro features page, Google poses this question and answer:

Do I need the Pro version?
If your business is looking to use Google Earth for any external purpose, you will need to license Google Earth Pro. Examples of external use include creating and distributing KML/KMZ files or movies, using imagery from Google Earth in reports and presentations, and developing information that will be displayed or distributed outside your organization.

Note the inclusion of the phrase "external purpose" and "displayed or distributed outside your organization."

Whether either of these preclude lawyers from using the free version of the software in their practices (e.g., using Google Earth to show a client locations of buldings on commercial property the client is considering for purchase) is unclear.

The purpose of this book is to inform you about some of the tools and services Google makes available and not to offer legal advice. You should read the End User License Agreements for both applications and decide for yourself which is appropriate for you.

- End User License Agreement for Google Earth Free
  http://earth.google.com/intl/en-US/license.html

- End User License Agreement for Google Earth Pro
  http://earth.google.com/intl/en-US/licensepro.html

The most widely-used of the three is the free stand-alone application, so that is the version we will focus on in this chapter.

According to Google, using the free version, you can:

- Zoom in on locations
- View 3D terrain and buildings
- Search for hotels and dining locations
- View dozens of other point-of-interest data layers

Usage Tip

Add Your Own Photos to Google Earth

Use the **Add** drop down menu at the top of the Earth Window and select **Photo** to add a photo of your own to your map. These photos are not seen by other Earth users unless you e-mail your added information to them (as described in Section 22.2.1).

- Layer multiple searches, save results to folders, and share with others
- Import GPS data, which allows you to read tracks and waypoints from select GPS devices

22.1 Installing Google Earth

To download and install Google Earth, you will need to visit http://earth. google.com/intl/en and click **Download Google Earth 5** (as of May 2010, version 5 is the latest). After you've installed it, a corresponding icon will appear on your desktop. Double click it to launch Google Earth.

Google Earth is available for Windows Operating System versions 2000, XP and Vista (as of May 2010 it is not available for Windows 7), Mac Operating System versions 10.4.11 or newer, Linux Ubuntu Operating System version 6.06 (and possibly others). For systems requirements, see http://earth.google.com/intl/en/userguide/v5/#systemreqs.

22.2 Anatomy of Google Earth Search Results

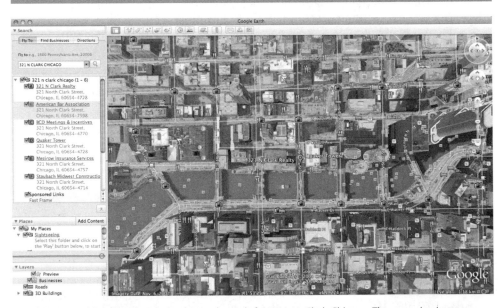

FIGURE 22.2 This is the Google Earth search result for *321 N. Clark Chicago*. The map viewing area dominates the application window. On the right-hand side of the map are the navigation tools. The top control orients you directionally (clicking the **N** automatically orients you facing North); click and hold your left mouse button and drag the outer ring to rotate your view. Below that is the "joystick;" click any of the directional arrows to move in that direction on the map. Below that is the zoom slider; click the **+** to zoom in, click the **−** to zoom out. Also notice the Status Bar along the bottom of the window. For this satellite and aerial view, Google Earth includes the **imagery date** on which the image was captured (sometimes exact, sometimes a date range; imagery date information is not included with Street View images), the latitude and longitude coordinates, and the elevation of your viewpoint (**Eye alt**).

CONTROLLING WHEN AND HOW YOU TILT THE VIEW OF YOUR MAP

For whatever reason, the Google Earth developers thought it would be useful to automatically tilt the orientation of the map from overhead to more of a street level view as you zoomed in. While this is in keeping with Earth's flying metaphor, it's a bit unsettling when trying to focus on a particular building or other landmark on the map. Luckily, we can turn this off. In Windows it is located in **Tools > Options > Navigation > Navigation controls**. On the Mac it's located in **Google Earth > Preferences > Navigation > Navigation controls**.

You can still use your mouse or trackpad to manually tilt your view of the map. The easiest way to do this is to click and hold down your left mouse button, press the **Shift** key on your keyboard, and move your mouse to tilt. On a trackpad, move your finger forward or backward on the pad in place of the mouse movements.

Usage Tip

FIGURE 22.3   The left-hand sidebar of the Earth window includes the **Search** panel where you can search for locations by address or latitude and longitude coordinates, types of businesses near a particular location (e.g., **What:** *Indian restaurant* **Where:** *321 N Michigan Chicago*), or get directions from one address to another. Below that is the **Places** panel where you can annotate, organize, and save information about places that you visit (e.g., add a client's name to the address shown on the map; your **Places** information is only available to you and not other Earth users). Beneath that is the **Layers** panel where you can select from a list of preset information to add on top of the map display (e.g., **Businesses**, **Roads**, **Street View**, **3D Building**, **Places of Interest**).

Usage Tip

GETTING DIRECTIONS TO NEARBY LOCATIONS IN UNFAMILIAR SURROUNDINGS

In Section 14.1, we discussed using Google Maps to get directions to and from locations. Google Maps offers more options for types of directions (e.g., **Driving**, **Walking**, or **Public Transit**) than Google Earth does. Google Earth, however, does engage its flying metaphor (one more time) to present an aerial tour of your trip from point A to point B.

FIGURE 22.4   After entering the beginning and ending points for which you want directions and clicking the magnifying glass icon, Google Earth retrieves a Google-standard set of directions and plots a route on the map to get from your beginning point to your ending point. To invoke Earth's flying carpet ride, click the small button (with the three diamonds) beneath the directions list. This **Play Tour** button will pop up the small controller in the lower left-hand corner of the map (it has play, fast forward, and reverse buttons like an MP3 or VCR controller). Clicking that play button "flies" you through the satellite image along the route noted in the directions, pointing out turns along the way.

Usage Tip

KEYBOARD CONTROLS

Google has posted a list of all of the keyboard control shortcuts recognized by Earth. It is located at http://earth.google.com/userguide/v5/ug_keyboard.html.

22.2.1 Using the Toolbar to Manipulate Your Map

At the top of the map display section is a toolbar that allows you to customize, manipulate, and otherwise manage information on and about the map you're viewing.

The toolbar buttons' functions are:

1. Conceal (or display) the left sidebar
2. Add a placemark to annotate a location (as discussed in the previous section; saved in your **My Places** folder)
3. Draw a 3D shape (polygon) onto the map (saved in your **My Places** folder like one of Google Earth's pre-assigned locations)
4. Draw a path or line as part of a 3D object you're adding to your map
5. Overlay an image or 3D model onto the map
6. Create tours of locations you define (flying between locations, viewing the surroundings, etc.) for later playback and sharing with other Google Earth users to whom you e-mail the tour (see button *11* below)
7. Display historical imagery for the location you're viewing (when available; coverage dates vary from location to location)
8. Display the effects of the sun (light, shadows, etc.) on the location you're viewing at the current time, or use the slider to simulate the passage of the sun overhead over time
9. Choose alternate bodies to view—**Sky**, **Mars**, **Moon**—from this drop-down menu
10. Measure a distance on the map of a line or path (along points you define on the map; e.g., along streets you select), in Earth Pro you can also measure the radius of a circle or the perimeter of a polygon; does not work to measure the height of buildings (or other features) only the distance between them

11. Share information from your map with others via e-mail; you can send a copy of the map you're viewing, along with any annotations or placemarkers you've added as a special file that other Google Earth users can open; you can also send a static image version of the map you're viewing to people who are not Earth users

12. Prints the map you're looking at

13. Opens the map you're looking at in Google Maps

Google has created an in-depth user's guide for Google Earth at http:// earth.google.com/userguide/v5/.

Google's Uncle Sam Search: A Specialized Search for Federal Government– Related Resources

23

Google maintains a separate U.S. Government Search (http://www.google.com/unclesam) that only returns results from official government sources. Despite its name, however, in addition to U.S. federal agencies, search results are also returned from state and local government agencies.

FIGURE 23.1 Google's U.S. Government Search (a.k.a. Uncle Sam Search) returns results from government agencies at all levels.

For example, a recent search for *"air pollution"* included results from the U.S. Department of Energy's Lawrence Berkeley Lab, the U.S. Environmental Protection Agency, the National Institutes of Health, the State of Minnesota Pollution Control Agency, and the Louisville (Kentucky) Air Pollution Control District, among numerous others.

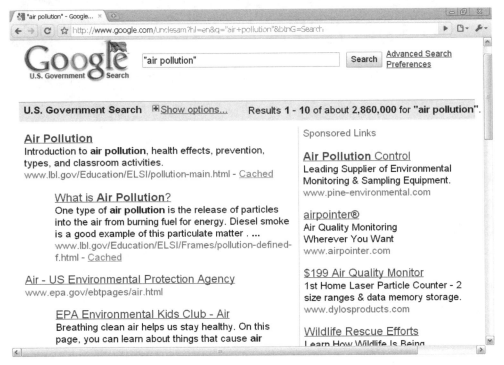

FIGURE 23.2

The Google Uncle Sam Search recognizes all of the Boolean connectors and search strategies applicable to the Google Web search discussed in Chapter 3 (with the exception of the inclusion of an **I'm Feeling Lucky** button).

23.1 Advanced Search

The Advanced Search page of Google's Uncle Sam Search (http://www.google.com/advanced_search?hl=en&lr=&as_qdr=all&site=unclesam&output=unclesam&restrict=unclesam) offers all of the same search limiters as Google's Web search described in Chapter 4.

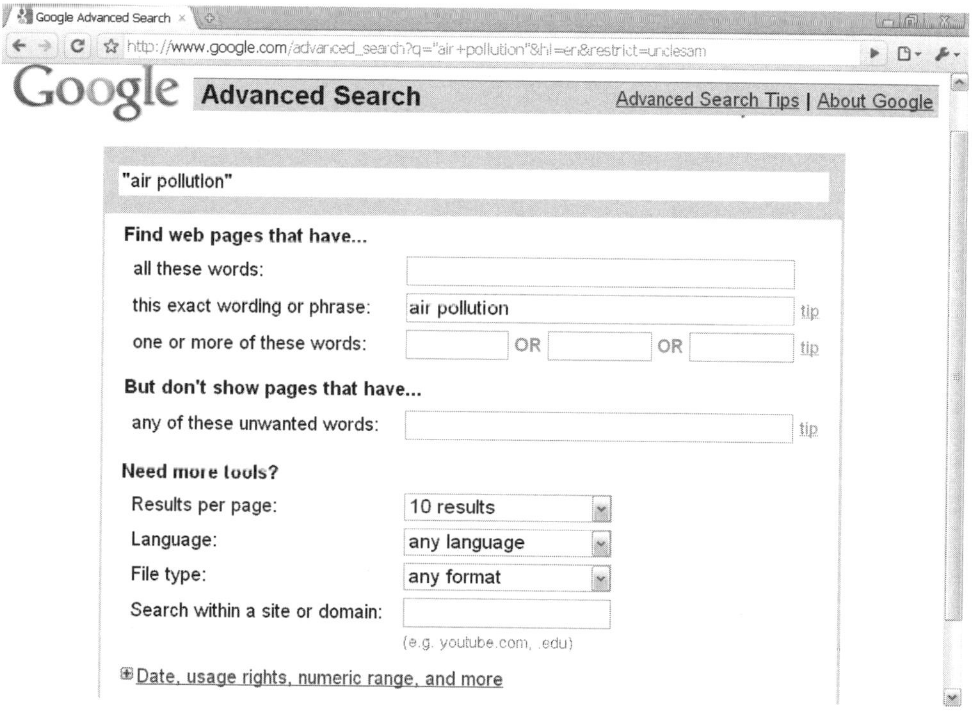

FIGURE 23.3

Practice Tip

The Advanced Search page of Google's Uncle Sam Search gives you the ability to limit your search results to resources located by Google during the **past 24 hours, past week, past month,** or **past year** (located behind the link labeled **Date, usage rights, numeric range, and more**).

However, you can specify an even more precise date limit (such as **past 3 days**) by altering the *qdr* parameter in the URL of the search results as explained in the Practice Tip in Section 5.5.

Google Analytics: Free Traffic Statistics for Your Web Site (You Do Have a Web Site, Don't You?)

24

The first challenge to marketing your practice online is creating an effective Web site that can attract potential clients and inform them about your experience and ability to help them solve the legal problems they are facing. We won't be covering these issues in this book. For information in this area, see the ABA Law Practice Management Section's excellent book on the subject, *The Lawyer's Guide to Marketing on the Internet* (http://www.abanet.org/abastore/index. cfm?section=main&fm=Product.AddToCart&pid=5110585).

The second challenge is tracking the visits that those potential clients make to your site to learn how those visitors got to your site and what pages they looked at while they were there. These are useful facts to help determine how your site should be managed. Google's free Analytics service (http:// www.google.com/analytics) gives you the ability to gather information about the visitors to your Web site. You can use it to learn what search engines they used to locate your site, what keyword searches led them to your site, whether they linked from another Web site to get to yours, how many pages they looked at, what pages they looked at, how much time they spent looking at those pages, and much more.

For example, a lawyer in Chicago might post articles on her Web site about child custody issues she has handled in her family law practice. Looking at her Google Analytics report, the lawyer might find that numerous visitors to her site arrived there after conducting search-engine searches for *"child custody" lawyer Chicago* and which pages of her site were most popular with visitors.

Google is able to gather and track this data because we have

Practice Tip

If there are important keyword/phrase combinations that you are not seeing in your Analytics report (or you are only seeing a low number of clicks for those keywords/phrases), you might want to consider running Google AdWords ads tied to those keywords/phrases. Running keyword/phrase-related ads can increase the possibility that Google Web searchers who use those keywords/phrases in their searches might find your site. See Chapter 25 for more information on AdWords.

added a few lines of code (supplied by Google Analytics when we created our account) to each page of our Web site. Adding the code requires little technical expertise. It is mostly a matter of cutting and pasting—although it does require the ability to edit and upload pages of your Web site.

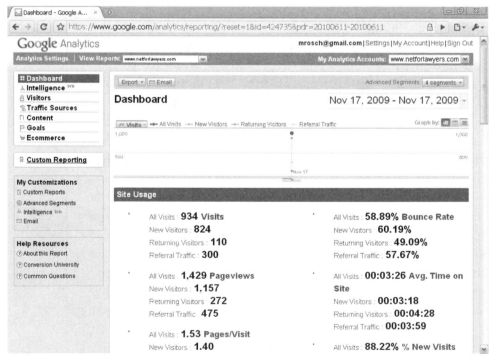

FIGURE 24.1 This illustration shows the Google Analytics Dashboard display for a single day's traffic to our www.netforlawyers.com Web site. Information available includes the total of **All Visits**, the number of **New Visitors**, the number of visits generated by search-engine searches (**Search Traffic**), the number of visits generated by links to our site from other sites (**Referral Traffic**), and much more. Significantly more information is available using the links in the left-hand column.

24.1   Find Out How Many People Are Visiting Your Web Site and How They Got There

As mentioned in the previous illustration, the links in the left-hand column lead to specialized reports about the numbers of visitors to your site and how they got there.

We'll take a look at the reports dealing with how many people are looking at your site and what pages they're viewing. We will not examine the reports primarily related to selling products online (the **Goals** and **Ecommerce** options).

24.1.1   Trends About Your Site Visitors

The Intelligence report spots trends in your Web-site traffic and alerts you to unusual developments related to that site's traffic in a variety of different categories. For example, if you experience a sudden spike in total traffic, or traffic sent to your site via a search engine, it will be noted in the Intelligence report.

FIGURE 24.2   The line graph near the top of the Analytics Intelligence report shows total visits to our www.netforlawyers.com Web site for the periods of November 1, 2009 through December 1, 2009 (the date range is customizable using the date boxes above and to the right of the graph). Each bar on the graph below that indicates a day on which Analytics spotted trends covered in the Intelligence report. In this illustration, we've clicked on the bar corresponding to November 17, 2009 to see the Intelligence report Alerts generated for our site's traffic on that day.

On November 17, 2009, Google announced the availability of case law in its Scholar database (see Section 17.4). We had posted one of the first comprehensive reviews of the service on our Web site. Because of that article, we saw a spike in traffic on that particular day. The Intelligence report gave a quick overview of how the day's traffic compared to average traffic in 14 different Alert categories. (See the following illustration for more details.)

The Alert categories seen in the preceding and following illustrations are default categories set by Google Analytics. You can also create your own Alert categories by clicking the **Create a Custom Alert** link seen in the middle right-hand portion of the preceding illustration.

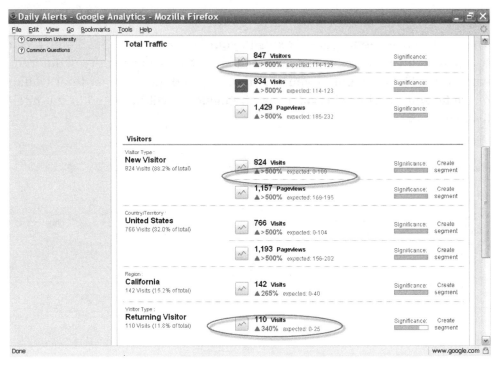

FIGURE 24.3 On November 17, 2009, Google Analytics detected a spike in traffic to our Web site. The Intelligence report for that day shows a greater than 500 percent increase in **Total Traffic** and **New Visitors**, as well as a 340 percent increase in **Returning Visitors**.

You can slice and dice this data even further by clicking the **Create segment** link to the right of any Alert (see the preceding illustration) to create more narrow segments (discussed in greater detail in the next section).

24.1.2 How Many People Are Visiting Your Web Site?

This Visitors report collects a lot more information about the visitors to your site than just raw numbers. Overall, Analytics tracks numerous characteristics about your site's visitors, such as what Web browser they used to visit your site, the language preferences they set in those browsers, and more.

Analytics uses cookies (a small piece of information that can be written to the visitor's hard drive) to "identify" visitors. On subsequent visits to your site, Analytics can read this cookie to determine that a prior visitor is returning, how long it's been between visits, and so on. Analytics does not store personally identifiable information about visitors to the sites it tracks. Analytics cannot tell you the names of people visiting your site.

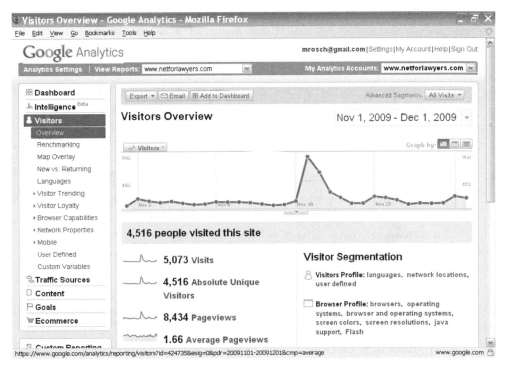

FIGURE 24.4 This illustration shows Analytics' Visitors Overview report. It includes the total number of **Visits** for the period (**5,073**) vs. the **Absolute Unique Visitors** (**4,516**, this number may be smaller if visitors to the site returned for a second or third visit. The subsequent visits are counted in the **Visits** because they are not **Unique**). Other information includes the number of pages those visitors looked at (**Pageviews**), the **Average Pageviews** per visitor, the average amount of time each visitor spent on the site, etc. You can access additional information about these visitors by clicking the links in the **Visitor Segmentation** section on the right-hand side of the report, or clicking the sub-report segmentation links beneath the **Visitors** link in the left-hand column.

Using the sub-report segmentation links beneath the **Visitors** link in the left-hand column, you can further segment the Visitors report data. The segmented sub-reports are:

- **Benchmarking**: allows you to compare your site's statistics to other similar Web sites (also utilizing Google Analytics)
- **Map Overlay**: shows the countries from which you drew visitors, as well as the numbers from each country, and other data

- **New vs. Returning**: breaks out your visitor numbers between new visitors and returning visitors
- **Languages**: shows the language preferences your visitors set in their Web browsers
- **Visitor Trending**: shows how your site is performing day to day, measuring:
  - **Visits**: whether total visits are trending up or down and how those visits compare to your site's average
  - **Absolute Unique Visitors**: whether absolute unique visits are trending up or down and how those visits compare to your site's average
  - **Pageviews**: whether daily pageviews are trending up or down and how those visits compare to your site's average
  - **Average Pageviews**: whether the average number of pages viewed per visitor is trending up or down and how those visits compare to your site's average
  - **Time on Site:** whether the average amount of time each visitor spends on the site is trending up or down and how those visits compare to your site's average
  - **Bounce Rate**: whether the percentage of visitors who leave your site after viewing only one page is trending up or down and how those visits compare to your site's average
- **Visitor Loyalty**
  - **Loyalty**: counts the number of times each visitor has visited your site
  - **Recency**: calculates how long it has been since a visitor's[**Edit correct?**] last visit
  - **Length of Visit**: graphs the duration of visits in seconds/minutes; does not calculate an average
  - **Depth of Visit**: graphs the number of pages viewed per visitor during each visit; does not calculate an average
- **Browser Capabilities**
  - **Browsers**: charts which browsers (e.g., Internet Explorer, Firefox, Chrome) visitors used to visit your site; calculates a percentage of usage for each browser listed
  - **Operating Systems**: charts which operating system (e.g., Windows, Mac, iPhone) visitors used to visit your site; calculates a percentage of usage for each operating system listed

- **Browsers and OS**: cross-references the previous two segmented sub-reports to chart which browser/operating system combinations (e.g., Internet Explorer/Windows, Firefox/Mac) visitors used to visit your site; calculates a percentage of usage for each combination listed
- **Screen Colors**: charts the capability of visitors' computers to display colors (expressed in bit depth; e.g., 8-bit, 12-bit); calculates a percentage of usage for each bit-depth listed
- **Screen Resolutions**. charts the display size of visitors' computers (expressed in pixels—width x height; e.g., 1,024 x 768, 1,920 x 1,200); calculates a percentage of usage for each resolution listed
- **Flash Versions**: charts which version (if any) of the Flash program visitors have installed on their computers (expressed by version and revision number; e.g., 9.0 r115, 10.0 r32); calculates a percentage of usage for each version listed
- **Java Support**: charts whether or not visitors have installed/enabled the program Java on their computers (expressed simply as **Yes** or **No**); calculates a percentage for each statement

- **Network Properties**
  - **Network Location**: charts the names of Internet service providers (ISPs) from which visitors accessed your Web site (e.g., Comcast Cable, Cox Communications); includes number of visitors per ISP, average time on the site per ISP, and more
  - **Hostnames**: lists which of your domains visitors are viewing (useful if you have the same Web page content hosted at multiple domains; e.g., www.FictitiousLawFirmWebSite.com, www.FictitiousChicagolawFirmWebSite.com)
  - **Connection Speeds**: charts the speed of your visitors' Web connections (e.g., cable, DSL, dial-up); includes number of visitors, average time on the site per connection type, and more

- **User Defined**: displays titles or other designations entered by the visitors (useful only if you have visitors log in or otherwise identify themselves during their visit; e.g., a *UserName*, *Existing Client*, *Potential Client*)

- **Custom Variables**: allows you to track variable visitor identities similar to the **User Defined** labels; generating information for both of these sub-reports requires a bit more sophisticated Web development expertise

24.1.3 Where Are Your Site's Visitors Coming From? (How Did They Find Your Site?)

Analytics' Traffic sources report charts the different kinds of sources that send traffic to your site—search engines, referring Web sites, direct traffic, and more. These charts give you an idea of how visitors found your site.

FIGURE 24.5 This illustration shows Analytics' Traffic Sources Overview report. It includes the number and percentage of visitors who came to your site via **Search Engines**, **Referring Sites** (visitors linked from some other site to get to yours), and **Direct Traffic** (visitors used a bookmark or typed your site's URL directly into their browser to get to your site). It also lists the **Sources** of the search engine and direct traffic, as well as the **Keywords** used in the search-engine searches that led visitors to your Web site.

One of the recurrent statistics in this section is the Bounce Rate. The Bounce Rate is the percentage of people who enter and leave your site on the same page (without visiting other pages). If you see a high Bounce Rate in your reports, then your Web pages could do more to entice visitors to click to read other pages on the site, rather than leaving after viewing just one page.

Using the sub-report segmentation links beneath the **Traffic** link in the left-hand column, you can further segment the Traffic report data. The segmented sub-reports are:

- **Direct Traffic**: charts only the visitors who used a bookmark or typed your site's URL directly into their browser to get to your site; calculates the number and percentage of visits utilizing this method, average time on the site, Bounce Rate, and more

- **Referring Sites**: charts only the visitors who reached your site by following a link from another Web site; lists each site from which visitors linked, calculates the number of referrals, average time on the site, Bounce Rate, and more for each referral source
- **Search Engines**: charts only the visitors who reached your site by first conducting a search-engine search and then following a link on the results list to get to your site; lists each search engine from which visitors linked, calculates the number of referrals, average time on the site, Bounce Rate, and more for each referral source
- **All Traffic Sources**: combines the data from the Direct Traffic, Referring Sites, and Search Engines sub-reports
- **AdWords** (see Chapter 25 for more details on AdWords)
  - **AdWords Campaigns**: tracks visitors who reach your site by linking on your Google AdWords ad; calculates the number and percentage of visits per ad campaign, average time on the site, Bounce Rate, and more

FIGURE 24.6

  - **Keyword Positions**: tracks the number of visitors based on the keywords they searched and your AdWords ads that were displayed alongside those search results. On the lower left-hand side of this illustration we see that our ads displayed alongside searches for the keywords *California MCLE* generated **141** total visits. On the lower right-hand side we see that **8** of these visits came from ads in the first position, **32** from ads in the second position on top, **10** from ads in the first position on the side, **14** from ads in the second position on the side, etc. The **Position breakdown** drop-down menu on the right, which currently displays data by **Visits** in this illustration can also display data by pages per visit, percentage of new visitors, average time on the site, and other criteria, while cross-referencing that criteria with the AdWords keywords/phrases and the position of your ads in relation to the search results.

– **TV Campaigns**: tracks visitors to your site generated by TV ads purchased through AdWords (Yes, you can bid to run your video ads on TV through the AdWords interface; however, you cannot target the ads geographically, so they would be of limited use to attorneys.)

• **Keywords**: charts the keywords/phrases used by visitors who reached your site by first conducting a search-engine search and then following a link on the results list to get to your site; lists each keyword/phrase used in the search-engine search, calculates the number of referrals, average time on the site, Bounce Rate, and more for each referral source

• **Campaigns**: provides the same data and analysis as the AdWords Campaign sub-report (described above)

• **Ad Versions**: tracks the number of visitors based on which of your AdWords ads they clicked on to reach your site; charts number of visits, pages per visit, percentage of new visitors, average time on the site, and other criteria, for each ad version

24.1.4 What Are They Looking At?

Analytics' Content report charts the individual pages that visitors are viewing on your Web site. It shows you not only which pages are most popular on your site, it can also tell you which pages visitors are entering your site on and which ones they're leaving from.

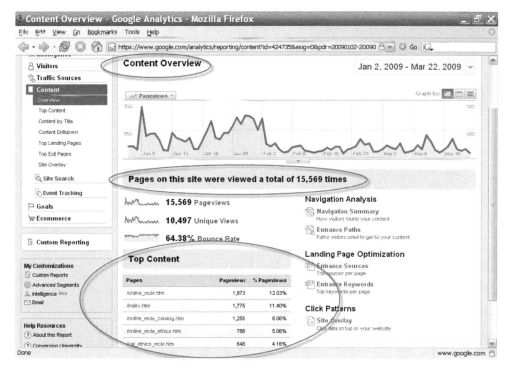

FIGURE 24.7 This illustration shows Analytics' Content Overview report. It includes the number of views per page, as well as the **Top Content** (percentage of total views each page represents for the top five pages of your site). Clicking the view full report link under the list of Pages displays all of the pages viewed during the period in descending order of popularity.

On the right-hand side of the Content Overview report page are a number of interesting reports—the **Navigation Summary**, **Entrance Paths**, **Entrance Sources**, **Entrance Keywords**, and **Site Overlay**.

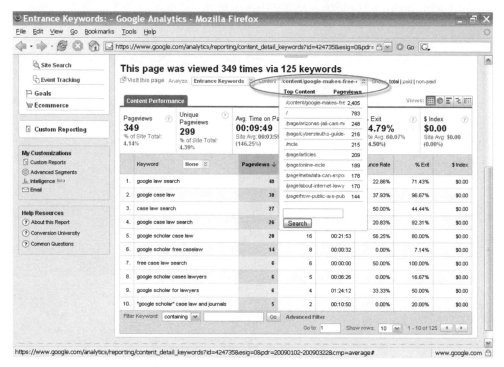

FIGURE 24.8   This illustration shows Analytics' Content Entrance Keywords report. You can select any page (from your Web site) from the drop-down menu to display the keywords that your visitors used to perform the searches that led them to your site. The chart includes Unique Pageviews, Avg. Time on Page, Bounce Rate, and percentage of visitors who also exit from that page for each of the keywords used to reach that particular page.

Using the sub-report segmentation links beneath the **Content** link in the left-hand column, you can further segment the Content report data. The segmented sub-reports are:

- **Top Content**: tracks the most popular pages on your site (by URL) while **Content by Title** tracks the most popular pages on your site (by title); both chart **Unique Pageviews**, **Avg. Time on Page**, **Bounce Rate**, and percentage of visitors who also exit from that page for each of the pages listed

- **Content Drilldown**: tracks the most popular categories of content on your site (e.g., MCLE) and allows you to narrow down to the most popular pages in those categories (e.g., MCLE/elimination-of-bias); charts **Unique Pageviews**, **Avg. Time on Page**, **Bounce Rate**, and percentage of visitors who also exit from that page for each of the pages listed; the charting in this report may vary depending on how your Web site is organized

- **Top Landing Pages**: tracks the most popular pages on which visitors to your site first land; charts the number of **Entrances**, **Bounces** (those who leave your site after viewing just one page), and **Bounce Rate** (ratio of **Bounces** to **Entrances**) for each particular page listed

- **Top Exit Pages**: tracks the most popular pages from which visitors leave your site; charts the number of **Exits**, **Pageviews**, and **% Exit** (the percentage of viewers who leave the site from that page) for each particular page listed

- **Site Overlay**: shows where on your site visitors are clicking by superimposing click data over your actual Web page(s) for specific links on your page(s); shows number and percentage of clicks on each link on a particular page (e.g., 590 clicks on the **About Us** link, 7.5% of the page's total clicks; 240 clicks on the **Articles** link, 3.1% of the page's total clicks)

Advertising Services from Google 25

Google has created a series of advertising services that allows Web site owners to market their own Web sites and services (AdWords) and earn money by placing advertisements from others on their own sites (AdSense).

25.1 AdWords

You've probably noticed the sponsored links that accompany Google Web search results. Those are paid ads generated through Google's AdWords service. Google AdWords enables you to create ads for your practice that appear alongside related Google Web searches or on Google's network of partner Web sites. The service can be found online at http://adwords.google.com. You must have a Google Account to utilize this service.

As an advertiser, you can select the search terms alongside which you want your ads to appear and set the amount that you are willing to pay each time someone clicks on your ad to follow the link to your Web site. The minimum bid for a click on your ad is $0.01. However, a low bid will usually leave you at the bottom of the list of other advertisers interested in the same keywords. AdWords offers guidelines and suggestions for maximum bid amounts for particular keywords (based on their popularity and the bids of other advertisers for the same keywords).

The ads are charged to you on a "pay-per-click" basis—meaning that you do not pay for the displayed ad until someone clicks on it. You can set a daily and monthly spending limit so you won't be surprised by a bill bigger than you're prepared to pay.

A valid credit card is required when creating your AdWords account. The ad costs are charged (automatically) to your credit card at the end of the month.

There is a one-time $5.00 charge to establish your new AdWords account.

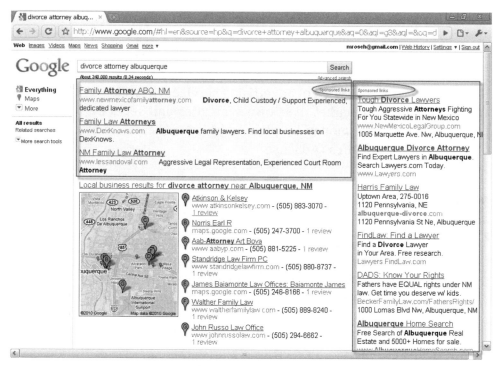

FIGURE 25.1 This illustration shows Google AdWords advertisements accompanying a search for *divorce attorney albuquerque*. They are segregated in the areas labeled **Sponsored Links**. (Note that we added the boxes surrounding the ads for emphasis.) Generally, the more an advertiser bids to pay per click on their ad, the higher on this list their ad will appear.

These ads can be an effective part of a lawyer's marketing plan. Remember, though, these ads can only entice people to visit your Web site. To get them to actually contact you and/or hire you, you'll need an effective Web site.

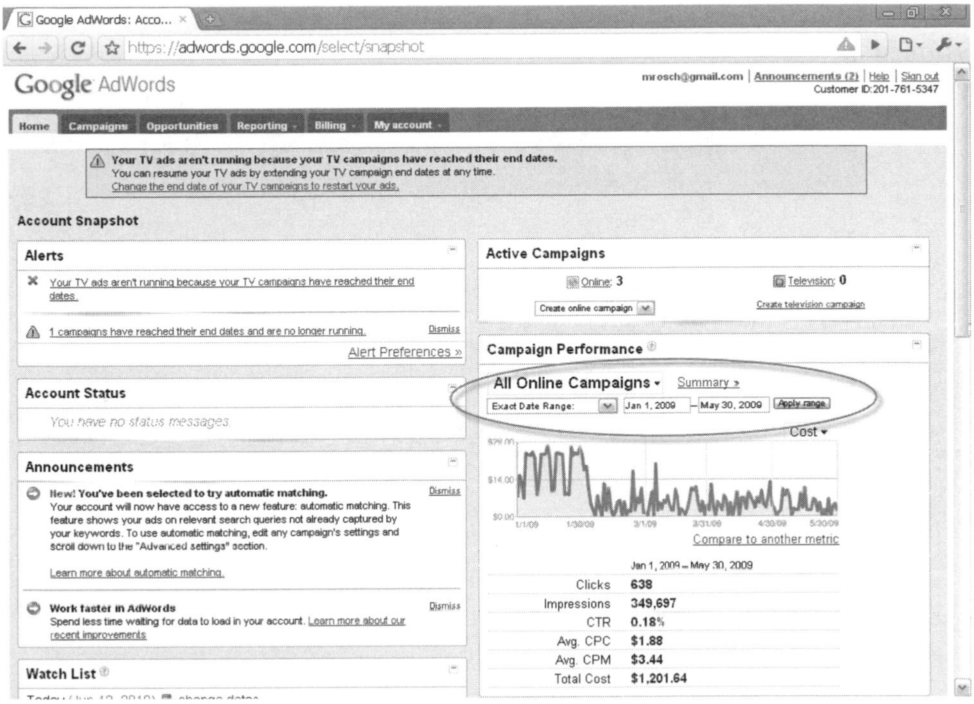

FIGURE 25.2 The AdWords **Home** tab graphs your AdWords **Campaign Performance** over time—you can see data for an individual campaign, or all your campaigns if you have more than one. **Alerts**, **Account Status**, and **Announcements** are also available.

TV ADS

Usage Tip

You might have noticed a link for **Television** campaigns in the previous illustration. Yes, you can bid on the purchase of TV advertising time through the AdWords interface. To run TV ads, you do have to produce a traditional commercial on video, which you can upload to Google or send via postal mail.

You can target your ad purchases by keyword (names or topics related to the programs available); audience interest or demographic characteristics; or even by the available TV networks (mostly cable), days, and times.

One of the things that you cannot do, however, is target the ads geographically. The vast majority of ad placements run nationally. There are some exceptions, with a few regional sports networks on the list of available networks (e.g, Comcast Sports Net West, Mid-Atlantic Sports Network, and Madison Square Garden network).

Since most lawyers have no need for this type of national advertising, we're not going to provide details on creating TV ad campaigns via AdWords.

For those who might be interested in exploring advertising on the regional sports networks, Google has created an informative site at http://www.google.com/adwords/tvads/.

Further down the **Home** tab is additional useful information about your ads.

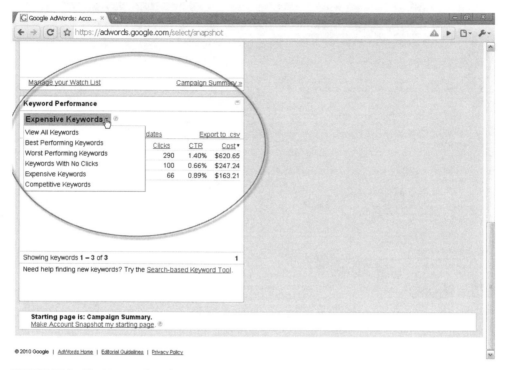

FIGURE 25.3 The **Keyword Performance** section, near the bottom of the AdWords **Home** tab, allows you to see costs associated with your **Best Performing Keywords**, **Worst Performing Keywords**, and **Expensive Keywords**, among other criteria.

There are hundreds (if not thousands) of individuals and companies marketing their services as AdWords consultants. In fact, Google has a Google Advertising Professionals Program for individual consultants and companies. The information in this chapter is not meant to prepare you for Google's certification exam (yes, there is one); it is meant to give you an overview of the AdWords process—and enough information to get started on your own.

25.1.1 Creating Ads

The first step to creating a new ad (or a campaign made up of multiple ads) is to click the **Campaigns** tab near the top of the screen (see the following illustration) and then click the **New campaign** button.

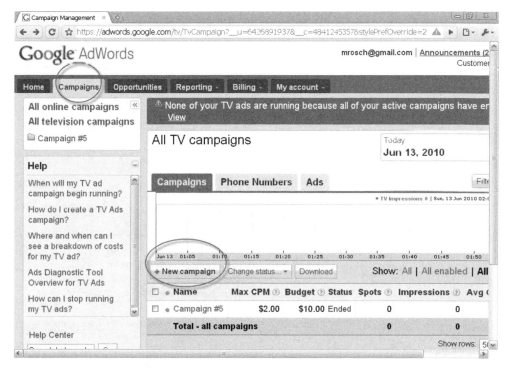

FIGURE 25.4 Once you're on the **Campaigns** tab, clicking the **New campaign** button starts the process of creating new ads.

25.1.1.1 Campaign Settings

AdWords gives you control of many aspects of your ads during the creation process.

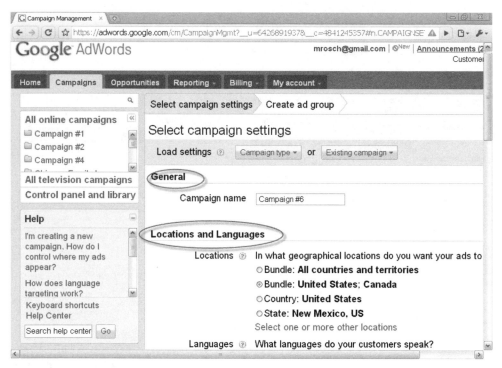

FIGURE 25.5 After clicking the **New campaign** button on the **Campaigns** tab, this is the first screen you see. In the **General** section you can assign a name to your ad campaign. In the **Locations and Languages** section you can limit the regions in which your ads will appear (Google is generally able to determine a rough geographical location from a user's IP address) and age ranges of Web users who will see your ads, and the languages of users who will see your ads.

You will probably want to limit ads for your law practice to jurisdictions in which you are licensed. In some states, you can also target down to a major metropolitan area.

Further down this first screen you can dictate on what sites your ad(s) will appear and how much you are willing to pay each time someone clicks on your ad.

In the **Position preference, delivery method (advanced)** section, the default options (shown in the preceding illustration) are probably best for new advertisers.

Clicking the **Continue** button at the bottom of the page takes you to the next step.

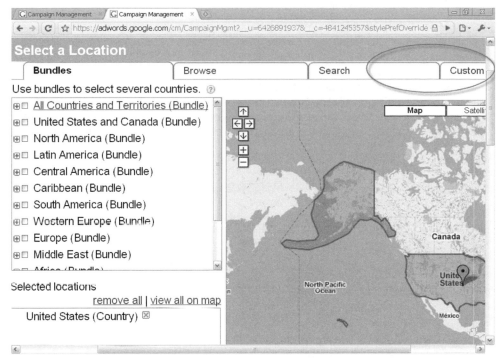

FIGURE 25.6 If you are a lawyer based in Chicago who's willing to travel within a 50-mile radius of your office to handle cases, AdWords allows you to limit the delivery of your ads to that radius. First, look at Figure 25.5's **Locations** option and click the radio button to the left of **Country: United States**. Second, click the **Select one or more other locations** link (see Figure 25.5). Third, click the **Custom** tab displayed in this illustration and then see Figure 25.7.

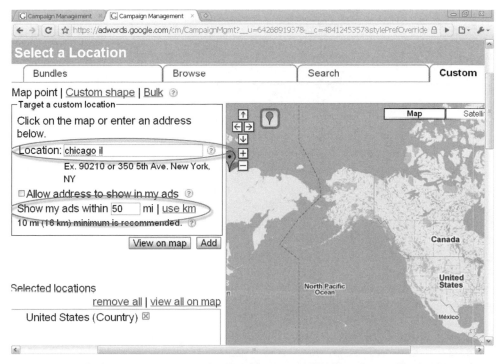

FIGURE 25.7 The last two steps to targeting your ad to a 50-mile radius of your office in Chicago are to enter *Chicago, IL* into the **location** box and enter *50 miles* into the **Show my ads within X mi** box.

Practice Tip

Similarly, a lawyer who works with clients who speak other languages should click the Edit link next to the Languages option and opt to deliver their ads to Web users who have set their language preferences to the languages the lawyer speaks. (Note that Google does not translate the ads from English into any selected language.)

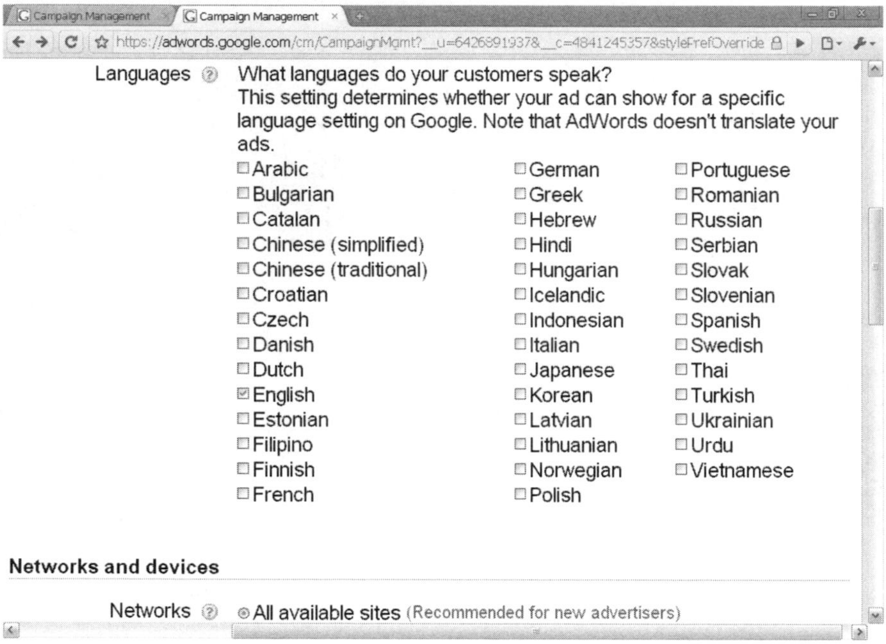

FIGURE 25.8 To display your ad to those who have chosen a specific language setting on Google, click into one box (or multiple boxes) to the left of the listed languages.

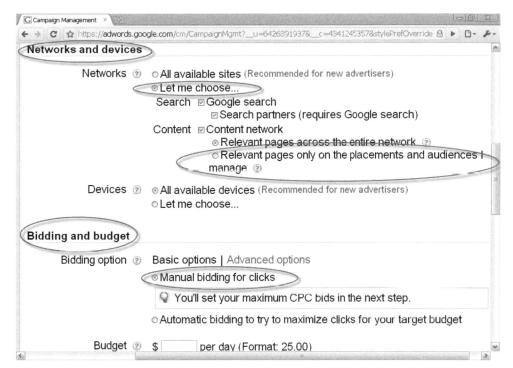

FIGURE 25.9   In the **Networks** and **devices** section you can determine whether you want your ads to appear alongside search results (as seen in the first illustration in this chapter), on relevant third-party Web sites, or both. You can also let Google automatically (keyword) match your ad(s) to appear on pages on participating Web sites or you can cherry-pick the participating sites on which your ads will appear by clicking into the **Let me choose radio** button and then selecting the **Relevant pages only on the placements and audiences I manage** option. In the **Bidding option** (in the **Bidding and budget** section), selecting **Manual bidding for clicks** gives you the most control over your ad spending—setting a maximum amount per click that you will pay. In the **Budget** section, you can set the amount of your maximum (average) daily budget for clicks.

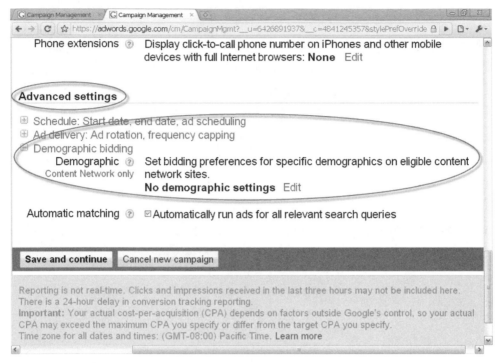

FIGURE 25.10   In the **Advanced Settings**, you can target your ads to specific demographics (or exclude specific demographics). To select specific genders and age ranges who will view your ad (or to exclude specific genders or demographics), click on **Edit**. Not all Web sites are eligible for demographic targeting, however.

25.1.1.2   Creating the Ad Content

The Create Ad Group page is where you enter the actual text for the ad(s) you want to run. We will focus on creating a **Text ad,** because they are the most commonly run ads on the AdWords network.

In the **Ad group default bids (Max. CPC)** section you can specify a set amount that you will pay for each click on your ad for the various types of ad placement. The more you bid, generally, the higher your ad will appear. You can also leave the **automatic placements** option blank and AdWords will adjust your bid amount automatically, to maximize your placement in the ad list, the number of clicks you (might expect to) receive per day, or

---

Practice Tip

You can add additional instructions to your keywords to more precisely target your ads' placement:

- *keyword* = broad match
- *"key phrase"* = match exact phrase
- *[keyword]* = match exact term only
- *-keyword* = don't match this term

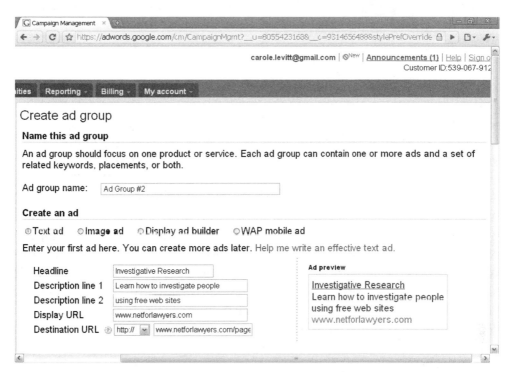

FIGURE 25.11 In the **Create an ad** section you can enter your **Headline** (25 characters), two lines of description in **Description line 1** and **Description line 2** (70 characters each), the **Display URL** (that will be seen in the ad; 35 characters), and the actual **Destination URL** where Web visitors will be taken when they click on your ad (1,024 characters; this can be different from the **Display URL**).

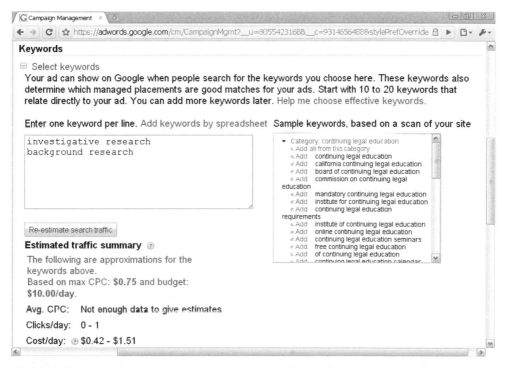

FIGURE 25.12 In the **Keywords** section you can enter the keywords you want to associate your ad with, by either selecting from the suggested list on the right, or typing keywords/phrases (one per line) in the box on the left.

your budget, depending on your Bidding and Budget settings (as discussed in the preceding section).

Click the **Save ad group** button to save your new ad.

25.1.2 Advertising on Sites Other Than Google

As discussed in Section 25.1.1.1, when you create your ad(s) on the Campaign Settings page, you can dictate whether you want your ad(s) to appear only in conjunction with Google search results or to also appear on the pages of Google's network of participating (third-party) Web sites. Any Web site owner can participate in Google's ad network (http://adsense.google.com). The main restrictions against participation are for Web sites with "content that is adult, violent or advocating racial intolerance." (See https://www.google.com/adsense/support/bin/answer.py?hl=en&answer=48182.)

FIGURE 25.13 Farther down the Create Ad Group page, the **Estimated traffic summary** section automatically generates an estimate of the number of clicks you might expect for the ad based on the keywords you entered above and the budget you set (as discussed in the preceding section). In the **Placements** section you can specify particular Web sites (or even specific pages on those sites) that are part of Google's network of participating (third-party) Web sites on which to display your ad. You can also exclude sites from running your ad(s). It can be difficult to build this list when first creating an ad campaign. Using the AdWords Placement Tool described in the next section, or revising the campaign after a few days to include this level of detail after you've had a chance to review the sites included in **automatic placements,** can be more useful.

The preceding illustration showed where on the Create Ad Group page you can specify particular Web sites (or even specific pages on those sites) on which to display your ad. As mentioned in Figure 25.13's caption, it can be difficult to know what sites to

Practice Tip

It's okay to advertise on national topic-related Web sites as long as you've set a limited geographic region in which to display your ad (as discussed in Section 25.1.1.1).

advertise on when first creating an ad campaign so it might be more useful to use the **Placement Tool** to locate appropriate sites on which to display your ad(s). The **Placement Tool** (shown in Figures 25.15 and 25.16) allows you to **Browse categories**, **Describe topics**, **List URLs**, or **Select demographics** to locate appropriate sites on which to display your ad(s). To access the **Placement Tool**, you must first click into the **Campaign** tab as illustrated in Figure 25.4.

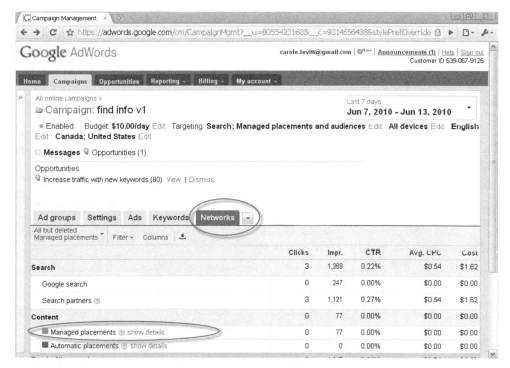

FIGURE 25.14   From the Campaigns page, select the Networks Tab. Then, you can access AdWords' list of participating sites by clicking the **show details** link next to **Managed placements** in the **Content** section (of the Campaigns management page) and the **Add placements** button that appears below it (not pictured).

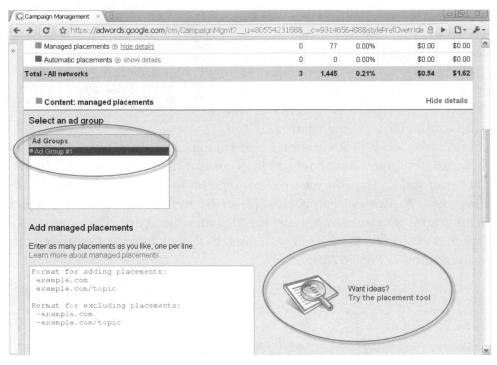

FIGURE 25.15 Select an Ad Group from the box on the left and then click the **Try the placement tool** link for help locating appropriate sites on which to run your ad(s).

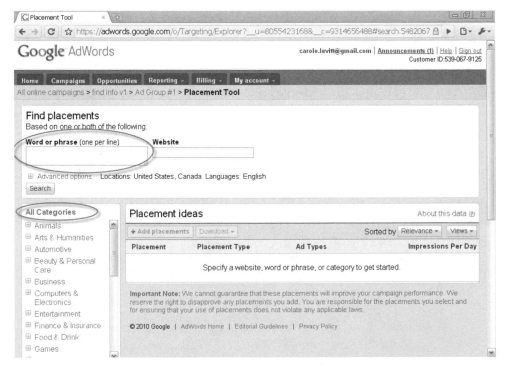

FIGURE 25.16 Use the **Word or Phrase** box to enter topical keywords or phrases (one per line) to return a list of related sites that participate in Google's AdWords ad network—on which you might display your ad(s). You can also locate appropriate sites by browsing the list of categories on the left-hand side.

25.1.3 Tracking Your Ads' Performance

AdWords gives you the ability to view and track the performance of your ads and compare the performance of your individual ads to one another.

FIGURE 25.17 Clicking the **Ads** tab on the Campaigns management page allows you to see the performance of each ad in a group. The **% Served** column lists the percentage of time a particular ad was displayed. The **Clicks** column indicates the number of times a particular ad was clicked. The **Impr.** column indicates how many times a particular ad was displayed. The **CTR** column indicates the Clickthrough Rate (the ratio of clicks to impressions). The **Avg. CPC** indicates the average cost per click (The average amount you pay each time someone clicks your ad). The **Cost** column is self-explanatory. The **Avg. Pos.** column indicates the average position of each particular ad when displayed in a list that also includes ads from other advertisers. You can re-sort the chart by any of the column criteria by clicking on the column label. You can define the date range you want to review using the date boxes near the upper right-hand corner of the page.

In addition to tracking the performance of individual ads, you can track the performance of the various keywords you selected for your ads (as discussed in Section 25.1.1.2).

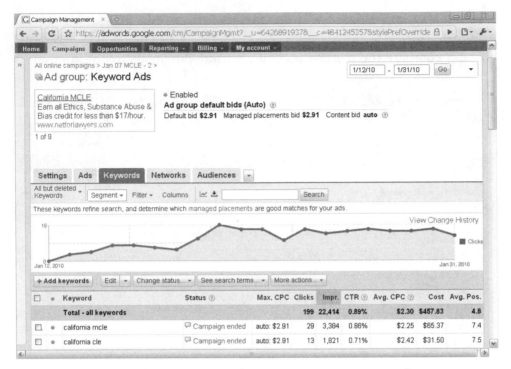

FIGURE 25.18 Clicking the **Keywords** tab on the Campaigns management page allows you to see the performance of each keyword or phrase you selected for your ad(s). The **Max. CPC** column lists the maximum amount we set to pay per click. The **Clicks** column indicates the number of times that ads were clicked (displayed in relation to a particular keyword). The **Impr.** column indicates the number of times ads were displayed in association with particular keywords. The **CTR** column indicates the Clickthrough Rate (the ratio of clicks to impressions). The **Avg. CPC** column lists the average cost per click charged to my account for a particular keyword. The **Avg. Pos.** column indicates the average position of ads triggered by a particular keyword (number 1 would be the highest position). The **Cost** column is self-explanatory.

25.2 AdSense

Google AdSense is a program that allows Web site owners to include the kinds of ads described throughout Section 25.1 in their own Web sites. As a Web site owner who includes these ads, you get a share of the money Google collects from the advertisers each time visitors click on an ad that appears on your site. AdSense can be found online at http://adsense.google.com.

Because the integration of third-party ads, based on the content of your site's Web pages could include ads for competitors, and generally would look unprofessional for a law-practice Web site, we do not recommend including AdSense ads in your site.

Google's Web Browser: Chrome | **26**

While most of you probably use the Microsoft Internet Explorer or Firefox browser to locate and view Web pages, some of you may be using Google's browser, Chrome, which was launched in September 2008. It was originally available only for computers running the Windows operating system, but on December 8, 2009, the Chrome betas for Mac and Linux were launched. In addition, "extensions" (customized features that can be added onto Chrome) were announced, but only for Windows and Linux. This chapter will focus only on the Windows version of Chrome, as the Mac and Linux versions are still in beta (and have a different look than the Windows version).

According to W3schools.com, Chrome's market share was reportedly 8.5 percent by November 2009 (http://www.w3schools.com/browsers/browsers_stats.asp), but October 2009 statistics from NetApplications placed Chrome's market share at 3.58 percent while StatCounter placed it at 4.52 percent (Thomas Claburn, *Firefox, Chrome, Safari Erode Internet Explorer Usage,* INFORMATIONWEEK, Nov. 2, 2009, http://www.informationweek.com/news/internet/browsers/showArticle.jhtml?articleID=221400283).

Usage Tip

WHY USE GOOGLE CHROME INSTEAD OF ANOTHER WEB BROWSER?

Google cites the following features as some of the reasons for using Google Chrome as your primary Web browser:

1. Launches quickly
2. Loads web pages quickly
3. Allows you to search the web from the address bar (which means that you search and navigate from the same box—sometimes referred to as the "Omnibox")
4. Runs Web applications fast (e.g., Gmail)
5. Allows you to visit your favorite Web sites by clicking thumbnails

Note: Some of these features are also available in current versions of Firefox and Internet Explorer.

See some "creative interpretations of Google Chrome's key features" at http://www.google.com/chrome/intl/en/features_mac.html.

26.1   Installing and Customizing Chrome

Like other browsers, you will need to download and install Chrome (http://www.google.com/chrome). And, like other browsers, Chrome is a free application.

After you've installed Google Chrome, a corresponding icon will appear on your desktop. Double-click it to launch Chrome.

Before you begin using Chrome, you should take time to set your browser preferences to import data from your former browser, such as your bookmarks/favorites, passwords, search settings, browsing history, and your default search engine. For details on how to set your preferences, see http://tinyurl.com/chromeprefs and see the "Wrench Icon" portion of Section 26.03.

FIGURE 26.1   This illustration shows the Chrome home page after I imported my bookmarks from Internet Explorer. They will now be found in the folder labeled by Chrome as **Other bookmarks** (on the right-hand side of this illustration, just under the address bar). Although a URL appears in the address box, you can also enter your keyword search here (see the next illustration). By default, the results are returned from Google's Web search.

26.2   The Omnibox: How to Use the Address Box as a Search Box

FIGURE 26.2   Instead of entering your keyword search into the usual search-engine search box, this illustration shows that you can enter your keyword search into the address box, thus turning the address box into an "Omnibox."

26.3   Other Features Located on the Address/Omnibox Bar

Throughout this section, we'll take a look at the various features on the address/Omnibox bar, by explaining the icons (from left to right).

Back-and-Forth Arrow Icons

The first icon is the back arrow, which has two uses. The first (and obvious) use is go back to the preceding page (click the arrow once) while the second (and not-so-obvious use) is to view your history and choose which Web page to go back to. (Hold your left mouse button down on the arrow to view the various pages you have recently viewed and then choose the one you want to go back to from the drop-down menu.) The forward arrow has the same two uses as the back arrow, but will take you forward instead of backward.

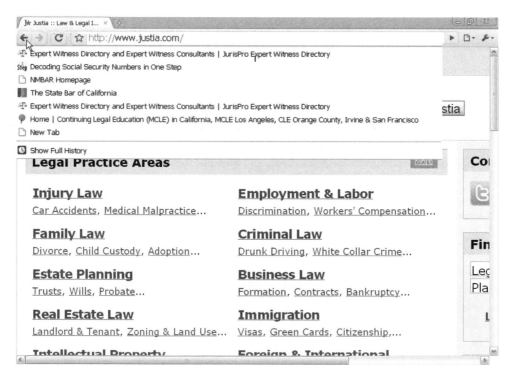

FIGURE 26.3   In this illustration of Justia.com, we have held down the back arrow to view a drop-down list of the various pages we have already viewed. From this list, we can then select one of the sites to go back to.

Circular Arrow Icon

When you hover over the circular arrow icon, the following message appears: **Reload this page**. Click this icon if you need to refresh the page.

House Icon

When you hover over the house icon, the following message appears: **Open the homepage**. Click this icon if you need to return to the Web page that you have set as your default home page.

Star Icon

When you hover over the star icon, the following message appears: **Bookmark this page**. Click this icon to bookmark the Web page that you are viewing. A pop-up box will appear, offering you an opportunity to rename the bookmark and to place it into a specific folder. The pop-up also offers you the opportunity to remove the bookmark if the page had previously been set as one.

Page Menu Icon

When you hover over the page icon (to the right of the address/Omnibox search box, which we discussed and illustrated previously in Section 26.2), the following message appears: **Control the current page**. Google refers to this as the Page Menu (while Explorer refers to it as the File Menu). The Page pull-down menu provides you with the following tools to use with the Web page that you're currently viewing: **Cut**, **Copy**, or **Paste** [text on the Web page]; **Find in page; Save page as; Print**. Most of these tools are self-explanatory. See the next illustration for a further explanation of **Find in page** and **Zoom**.

FIGURE 26.4 **Find in page** is one of the most useful functions because it opens a Find box into which you can enter a word (or phrase) to quickly locate that word (or phrase) in a long Web page. It will highlight the word (or phrase). Clicking the down arrow will take you to the next place on the page where the word (or phrase) appears. Clicking the up arrow takes you to the previous place it appears. The **Zoom** tool allows you to change the font size of text on your current Web page.

Another feature on the Page pull-down menu, **Create application short-cuts**, allows you to create a shortcut to the page you are viewing. The short-cut can be placed onto your desktop, Start menu, or Quick Launch Bar. For example, while reading my Gmail (in the Chrome browser), I clicked on the **Create application shortcuts** and created a shortcut to Gmail on my desktop.

Wrench Icon

When you hover over the wrench icon, the following message appears: **Customize and control Google Chrome**. Click this icon to open the Wrench pull-down menu.

FIGURE 26.5 Notice that there are shortcuts for the various tools, such as **Ctrl+T** to open a new tab or **Ctrl+N** to open a new window.

Using the Wrench pull-down menu, you can accomplish the following:

- Open a **New Tab**: Tabs allow you to quickly switch between different Web pages that you've visited. (See Section 26.04 for more about tabs.)
- Open a **New window**: If you wish to begin a new search, but also want to retain your former search (and all of the tabs) to return to later, you can open a new window.
- Open a **New incognito window**: While this feature does not protect you from leaving a trail at the sites you visit, it does protect anyone who uses your computer from knowing what sites you visited because they will not show up in your browsing history.

- **Always show bookmarks bar**: Use this tool if you want your folder of bookmarks to be readily accessible. You can also drag specific bookmarked sites onto this bar so you can quickly visit them.
- Change to a **Full screen**: This tool is useful for viewing videos on the Web.
- View your browsing **History**.
- Open your **Bookmark manager**: You will be able to move favorites/bookmarks into existing folders, rename bookmarks or folders, create new (or delete old) folders or bookmarks, re-sort bookmarks alphabetically by title, and import or export bookmarks.
- View your **Downloads**.
- **Clear browsing data** (history).
- **Import bookmarks & settings:** See the discussion about importing bookmarks/favorites in Section 26.01.
- Set **Options** (or the **Preferences** dialog on a Mac): This is where you can set your home page, save passwords (or not), invoke (or reject) AutoFill, choose privacy options, etc. See the illustration below to learn about the three different menus on the Options page and some specific privacy/security settings.
- Click **Help** from the Wrench pull-down menu for step-by-step guidance in how to use Chrome.

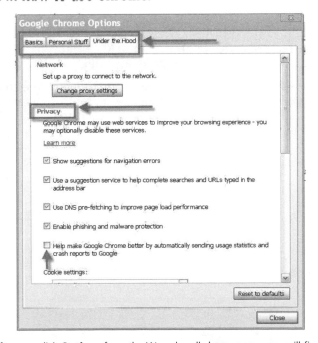

FIGURE 26.6   After you click **Options** from the Wrench pull-down menu, you will find three different menus (**Basics**, **Personal Stuff**, and **Under the Hood**). You should open each one to set your various options. The **Under the Hood** menu is displayed in this illustration. Under **Privacy**, we recommend that you uncheck the box to the left of this setting: **Help make Google Chrome better by automatically sending usage statistics and crash reports to Google**. For security reasons, it is best to not allow this type of outbound stream of communication from your computer.

26.4   How to Quickly Revisit Web Pages Using Tabs or Thumbnails

At the top of the browser window (where Internet Explorer's Title Bar is located), Chrome has placed a Tab strip. Each time you navigate to a new Web page, Chrome places the Web page's title into the tab. You can open a new, blank tab to place each Web page that you visit into its own discrete tab either by clicking the plus sign to the right of the last tab or right-clicking on any link on a Web page that you want to visit. Clicking on any one of the displayed tabs allows you to quickly revisit that particular Web page. (Newer versions of Explorer and Firefox also have tabs.)

FIGURE 26.7   In this illustration, we can return to any of our recently visited Web pages by clicking on its tab, such as the tab labeled **Mark Rosch | Googl...** (if you hover over this title, the rest of the Web page's title appears—**Google Search**...). In the alternative, for those who prefer a graphical interface, you can click the plus sign to the right of the last tab (even if the tab is not still open) to view thumbnails of the Web pages you recently visited. Click on any one of the thumbnails to return to the page. See the next illustration to view the thumbnail page.

Research Tip

HOW TABS CAN HELP YOU KEEP ORGANIZED WHEN RESEARCHING MULTIPLE TOPICS

Opening a new tab for each topic (or sub-topic) you are researching online can help you jump back and forth from one matter to another. When you have completed a matter, you can close it by clicking the **x** on the far right side of the tab.

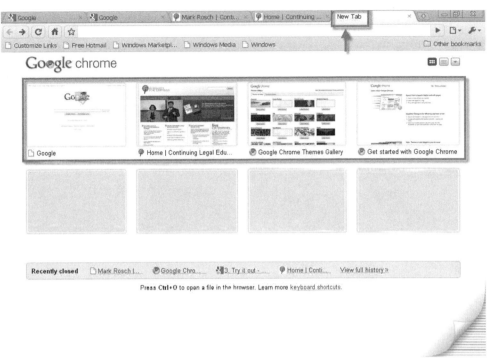

FIGURE 26.8   After we clicked the plus sign noted in the prior illustration, a new tab opened (labeled **New Tab**) and thumbnails of the four Web pages we recently visited were displayed in the browser window. You can click on any thumbnail to revisit that site.

CHROME AND TABS HELP STABILIZE YOUR WEB SEARCHING

Research Tip

If a Web page suddenly freezes, you generally need to close your browser and then restart it. However, with Chrome, if a particular Web page freezes, you simply close that tab and continue using the Chrome browser. So one Web page that gives you a problem should not affect your other tabs and your ability to view those Web pages. (Newer versions of Firefox and Explorer also have this feature.)

Google Knol: Experts Sharing Their Knowledge, One Unit at a Time

27

In late December 2007, in what looked like a bid to develop a rival to the near-ubiquitous online encyclopedia Wikipedia, Google announced a new project called Knol. According to a post on Google's official blog by Udi Manber, Google's Vice President of Engineering, "the goal is for knols to cover all topics, from scientific concepts, to medical information, from geographical and historical, to entertainment, from product information, to how-to-fix-it instructions" (http://googleblog. blogspot.com/2007/12/encouraging-people-to-contribute. html).

A "knol" is described as "a unit of knowledge" and is meant to apply to both the whole project and each individual entry in the collection. For clarity's sake, we'll refer to the entire collection as "Knol" and to the individual entries as "knols."

By May 2010, more than two years after the launch of Knol, it was still labeled as a beta project.

WHY SEARCH WITH GOOGLE KNOL INSTEAD OF GOOGLE.COM?

Although Knol results will be displayed in Google.com results, they may be buried so far down the results list that you will miss them. For example, we searched for *college degree mills* at Google.com and received over 79,000 results. None of the first five pages of results linked to a knol on that subject. The same search at Knol, however, returned 74 results, and the first result on the first results page ("Fraud Alert - How to Protect Yourself from College Diploma Mills & Degree Mills") was quite relevant and was authored by someone who seemed credible (Vicky Phillips, who "designed and directed America's first online counseling center for distance learners for America Online").

Another reason to search at Knol instead of Google.com is the ability to use some Knol features (not available on a non-Knol Web page) that could help you establish the credibility of a particular Knol author, such as reading online Knol reviews about a particular author's knol (Section 27.5).

27.1   Who Can Author a Google Knol?

Participation in Knol is completely open. Udi Manber explained (in his original blog post about Knol) that "Google will not serve as an editor in any way, and will not bless any content. All editorial responsibilities and control will rest with the authors. We hope that knols will include the opinions and points of view of the authors who will put their reputation on the line. Anyone will be free to write." He also acknowledged that, "we cannot expect that all of them will be of high quality."

27.2   Are Knol Authors Verified?

Based on Manber's blog assertion that "We believe that knowing who wrote what will significantly help users make better use of web content," we thought that one primary difference between Knol and Wikipedia would be Knol's focus on the credibility of Knol authors. However, while some of the knols include a photo and affiliation information for the author, as well as an indication that "peer review" of individual entries is possible (in addition to ratings and comments offered by general readers), we found some knols to be written anonymously.

Although you may see the word "Verified" beneath an author's name, this doesn't actually verify the author's credibility or expertise. This simply verifies that the author's name is as they have stated because Google has compared it against a credit bureau's data. (Authors who agree to Google's "verification" submit their name and credit card number (or Social Security number) to Google. Authors are not required to be verified.) Verification is available only for U.S. accounts.

27.3   How to Access Google Knol

You can access Google Knol by clicking the **more** link on Google's home page and then clicking **even more**. On the right-hand column, you would then click **Knol** (or go directly to Knol at http://knol.google.com/k).

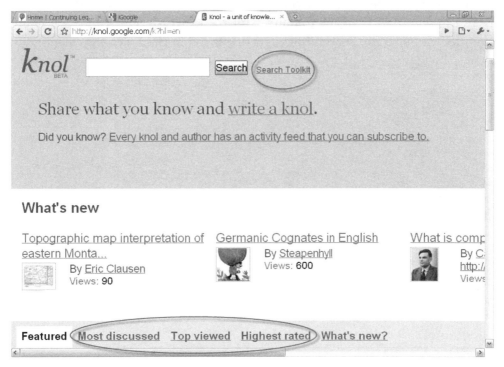

FIGURE 27.1   You can enter your search into the Knol search box or scroll down to view the **Most discussed**, **Top viewed**, or **Highest rated** knols. Notice the **Search Toolkit** to the right of the search box. This **Search Toolkit** link, while not labeled as such, provides you with an advanced search page.

Usage Tip

LOG INTO YOUR GOOGLE ACCOUNT BEFORE USING KNOL

If you are logged into your Google Account (see Section 2.4.1) when using Knol, you can access more Knol features (see Section 27.5) and you can also create your own knols (see Section 27.6).

27.4 How to "Advance" Search Google Knol by Using the Search Toolkit

You can deploy various advanced searches by clicking **Search Toolkit** (located to the right of the search box on the Knol home page). Alternatively, you can go directly to the Search Toolkit page at http://tinyurl.com/knoladvanced.

The Search Toolkit helps you search through knols and their accompanying reviews and comments as narrowly or as broadly as you choose. You can limit your search by entering information into one (or multiple) search fields. Some of the search fields are identical to (or similar to) the search fields found on non-Knol Google advanced search pages (described in Section 4.1), such as **Find documents with these words,** but there are many unique Knol-specific search fields, as displayed in the following image.

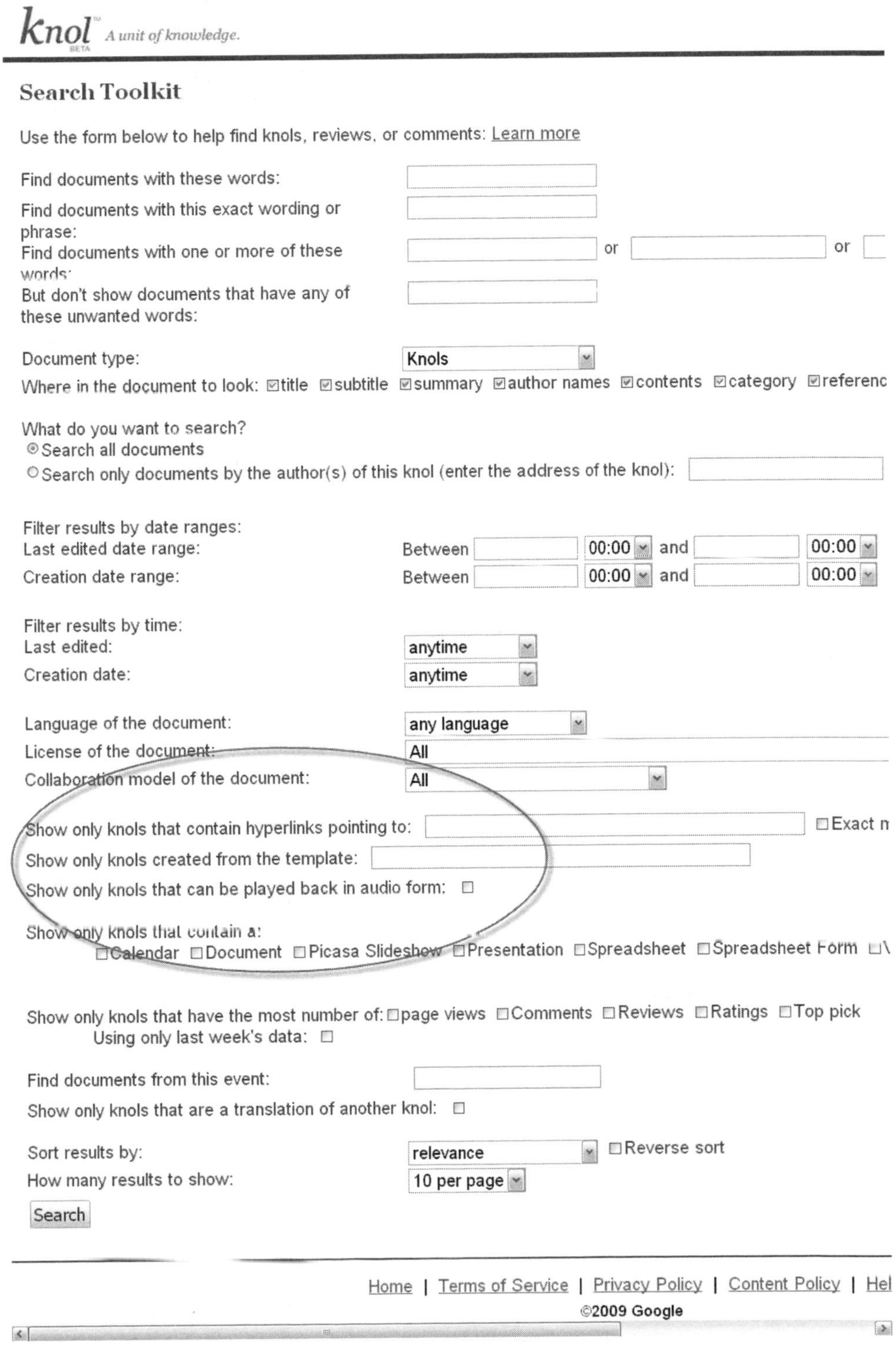

knol ™ _A unit of knowledge._

Search Toolkit

Use the form below to help find knols, reviews, or comments: Learn more

Find documents with these words:

Find documents with this exact wording or phrase:

Find documents with one or more of these words: or   or

But don't show documents that have any of these unwanted words:

Document type: Knols

Where in the document to look: ☑title ☑subtitle ☑summary ☑author names ☑contents ☑category ☑referenc

What do you want to search?
⦿ Search all documents
○ Search only documents by the author(s) of this knol (enter the address of the knol):

Filter results by date ranges:
Last edited date range: Between   00:00 ⌄ and   00:00 ⌄
Creation date range: Between   00:00 ⌄ and   00:00 ⌄

Filter results by time:
Last edited: anytime ⌄
Creation date: anytime ⌄

Language of the document: any language ⌄
License of the document: All
Collaboration model of the document: All

Show only knols that contain hyperlinks pointing to: ☐ Exact n
Show only knols created from the template:
Show only knols that can be played back in audio form: ☐

Show only knols that contain a:
☐ Calendar ☐ Document ☐ Picasa Slideshow ☑ Presentation ☐ Spreadsheet ☐ Spreadsheet Form ☐ \

Show only knols that have the most number of: ☐ page views ☐ Comments ☐ Reviews ☐ Ratings ☐ Top pick
Using only last week's data: ☐

Find documents from this event:

Show only knols that are a translation of another knol: ☐

Sort results by: relevance ⌄   ☐ Reverse sort
How many results to show: 10 per page ⌄

Search

FIGURE 27.2 Some of the Knol-specific search fields are **Show only knols that contain hyperlinks pointing to**, **Show only knols that can be played back in audio form**, and **Show only knols created from the template**.

<table>
<tr><td>

Practice Tip

</td><td>

LOCATE KNOLS AUTHORED BY EXPERT WITNESSES

To find out whether an expert has authored a knol, you can enter the expert's name into the **Find documents with these words** search box, select **knols** from the **Document type** search field's drop-down menu, and then click into the **author names** box in the **Where in the document to look** search field. You may be able to surmise how credible certain experts are by reading reviews about their knols or learning how many times their knols were viewed by others (see Section 27.5).

</td></tr>
</table>

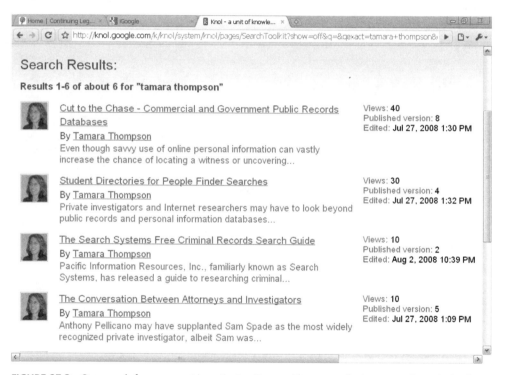

FIGURE 27.3 Our search for an expert investigator, Tamara Thompson, by her name, brought back a list of six knols by Thompson. Also displayed was the number of times each knol was viewed and the date each was last edited.

27.5   The Anatomy of a Knol

In addition to the knol, each knol will typically include a Table of Contents (automatically generated by Google). Beneath that are the following links:

- **Link**: the permanent URL of the specific knol
- **Citation**: author name, title of article, and date of the article
- **Listen**: an audio clip from the article
- **mp3**: an audio download of the article
- **Print**

> **Usage Tip**
>
> **SOME KNOLS DON'T CONTAIN ARTICLES**
>
> Some authors' knols lack an actual article and instead either provide a list of links to Web sites (on the knol's specific topic) or link you to their personal Web site to read the article there.

If you are logged into your Google Account, you can also access these links:

- **Email**: Use this to email someone a link to the knol that you are viewing.
- **Favorite**: You can star a knol as a favorite (which you will see next time you visit the same knol).
- **Collect this page**: Use this to add a knol to your own collection of knols.
- **Edit this knol**: This is a bit of a misnomer because authors can disable editing by choosing a closed collaboration (where only pre-selected co-authors can edit) or limit editing by choosing a moderated collaboration (where any edits you wish to make are actually sent to the author as "suggestions" and the author can accept or reject them).
- **Write a knol**
- **Comment**
- **Add a category**: You can add a category to better describe the knol.

In the right-hand column of a knol, you can rate, review, or translate it. You can also see a list of other knols also written by the author of the knol you are reading and learn how many times it was viewed this week (and in total). At the end of the column are any Google ads.

27.6 How to Author a Google Knol

To author a knol, log into your Google Account and then visit Knol at http://knol.google.com/k. Beneath the search box, click **write a knol**. You are presented with four choices:

- **Create a new knol:** This is the default.
- **Copy an existing knol:** You're not actually copying someone else's knol; you are using their knol as a template to create your knol.
- **Create a new collection of knols:** This really has nothing to do with authoring a knol. Instead it allows you to collect a list of existing knols (authored by others and/or by you).
- **Import a file as a new knol:** This allows you to import an article from your computer that you have already written and now want to turn into a knol.

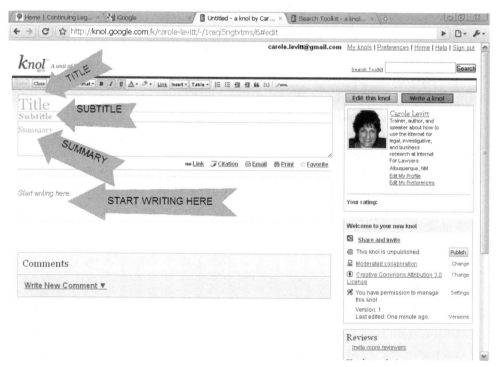

FIGURE 27.4 In this illustration, Carole selected **Create a new knol**. Information from her Google Profile (see Section 2.4.2 for information about Google Profile) was automatically inserted on the right-hand side of her knol. She can add a **Title**, **Subtitle**, and a **Summary** and then she can begin writing her knol in the space labeled **Start writing here**.

▼▼▼▼▼

Should Lawyers Create Knols?

We found many knol authors who are lawyers. Authoring knols could be a good way to market your practice. However, don't be too blatant about advertising yourself. Try to share enough knowledge to satisfy someone who wants some basic information. If they want more in-depth information, they may contact you and eventually be converted to a client.

▼▼▼▼▼

Ethics Alert for Lawyers Creating Knols

Consider adding a disclaimer to your knol, such as one we found on some of lawyer Chris Lemens's knols: "I AM NOT YOUR LAWYER. None of [the] information in this article is legal or professional advice. You should not rely solely on the information contained on knol.google. com. You should consult with a lawyer for specific advice tailored to your situation."

27.7   AdSense Participation at Google Knol

Knol allows its authors to publish Google's Adsense for Content ads alongside their knols. Google's Adsense for Content ad program automatically displays targeted ads based on the topic (or keywords) within your knol. As an author, you share in a portion of the fees Google collects from the advertisers who place these ads. You can apply to participate in the AdSense program by selecting this option in your Administrative Settings.

For more information on Google AdSense, see Chapter 25.

Appendices

Appendix A: Case Study 1

John Davis, Appellant v. Department of Justice, Appellee
United States Court of Appeals,
District of Columbia Circuit. - 460 F.3d 92
Argued February 13, 2006
Decided August 22, 2006

James H. Lesar argued the cause and filed the briefs
for appellant.

Heather Graham-Oliver, Assistant U.S. Attorney, argued the
cause for appellee. With her on the brief were *Kenneth L.
Wainstein,* U.S. Attorney, and *Michael J. Ryan,* Assistant U.S.
Attorney. *R. Craig Lawrence,* Assistant U.S. Attorney, entered
an appearance.

Before: RANDOLPH and GARLAND, *Circuit Judges,* and
WILLIAMS, *Senior Circuit Judge.*

Opinion for the Court filed by *Circuit Judge* GARLAND.

GARLAND, *Circuit Judge:* This case involves four audiotapes
recorded more than twenty-five years ago during an FBI corruption investigation in Louisiana. The plaintiff, an author,

seeks release of the tapes under the Freedom of Information Act (FOIA), 5 U.S.C. § 552. There are two speakers on the tapes, one a "prominent individual" who was a subject of the FBI's investigation, and the other an "undercover informant" in that investigation. The only question on this appeal is whether the FBI has undertaken reasonable steps to determine whether the speakers are now dead, in which event the privacy interests weighing against release would be diminished.

The FBI has not been able to determine whether either speaker is dead or alive. It says it cannot determine whether the speakers are over 100 years old (and thus presumed dead under FBI practice), because neither mentioned his birth date during the conversations that were surreptitiously recorded. It says it cannot determine whether the speakers are dead by referring to a Social Security database, because neither announced his social security number during the conversations. And it declines to search its own files for the speakers' birth dates or social security numbers, because that is not its practice. The Bureau does not appear to have contemplated other ways of determining whether the speakers are dead, such as Googling them.[1]

We conclude that the FBI has not "made a reasonable effort to ascertain" whether the two speakers, on whose behalf it has invoked a privacy exemption from FOIA, are living or dead. *Schrecker v. Dep't of Justice*, 349 F.3d 657, 662 (D.C. Cir. 2003) ("*Schrecker II*"). As a consequence, there is a serious "'question whether the Bureau's invocation of the privacy interest represented a reasonable response to the FOIA request.'" *Id.* (quoting *Summers v. Dep't of Justice,* 140 F.3d 1077, 1085 (D.C. Cir. 1998) (Williams, J., concurring)). We therefore reverse the district court's dismissal of the plaintiff's FOIA complaint and remand for further proceedings.

I

This is the fourth time we have considered an appeal arising out of the FOIA dispute between Davis and the FBI. In 1986, Davis submitted a FOIA request for all audiotapes recorded during an FBI criminal investigation known as "BRILAB." That investigation, conducted during 1979–80, concerned bribery and racketeering activities among organized crime figures, politicians, and labor unions in Louisiana. The investigation led to the indictment of five individuals, two of whom were ultimately convicted—including reputed Mafia boss Carlos Marcello.[2] Portions of more than 130 BRILAB tape record-

---

[1]*See* Oxford English Dictionary Online, http://www.oed.com (defining "Google" as "to use the Google search engine to find information on the Internet").

[2]The convictions were later overturned on collateral review. *See United States v. Marcello,* 876 F.2d 1147 (5th Cir.1989).

ings were played at the defendants' 1981 trial. Davis sought the tapes as background for a book he subsequently published in 1989. *See* JOHN H. DAVIS, MAFIA KINGFISH: CARLOS MARCELLO AND THE ASSASSINATION OF JOHN F. KENNEDY (McGraw-Hill 1989).

After the government refused to release the tapes, Davis brought suit pursuant to FOIA. *See* 5 U.S.C. § 552(a)(4)(B). The government contended that each tape was properly withheld under one or more statutory exemptions, but the district court concluded that material "unconditionally revealed in open court . . . enter[s] the public domain beyond recall for all time" and therefore cannot be withheld under FOIA. *Davis v. Dep't of Justice,* No. 88-0130, Order at 3 (D.D.C. May 6, 1991). Although the government argued that it was no longer possible to determine which of a "play list" of 163 taped excerpts had actually been played in the courtroom, the district court held that the government bore the burden of showing that the tapes had not entered the public record and must "suffer the consequences of the impasse." *Id.* at 4. The court ordered release of all the tapes.

On appeal, this court reversed. See *Davis v. Dep't of Justice,* 968 F.2d 1276, 1282 (D.C. Cir. 1992) ("*Davis I*"). We held that, while the ultimate burden of persuasion remains on the government, "a party who asserts that material is publicly available carries the burden of production on that issue." *Davis I,* 968 F.2d at 1279 (emphasis omitted). We then remanded to give Davis an opportunity to show that the tapes he sought, or portions of them, were played at the trial. *Id.* at 1282.

In an effort to meet his burden under *Davis I*, Davis produced docket entries and transcripts from the Marcello trial. In response, the FBI released 157 of the 163 tapes and said it would have released another tape but could not find it. The FBI continued to withhold the five remaining tapes on the basis of FOIA Exemption 7(C), which permits an agency to withhold otherwise disclosable records if they were "compiled for law enforcement purposes" and their release "could reasonably be expected to constitute an unwarranted invasion of personal privacy." *See* 5 U.S.C. § 552(b)(7)(C). The district court sustained the FBI's actions. See *Davis v. Dep't of Justice,* No. 88-0130, Order at 15 (D.D.C. Oct. 16, 1997).

Davis appealed a second time. In *Davis II,* we upheld the district court's determination that the FBI's search for the missing tape was adequate. See *Davis v. Dep't of Justice,* 1998 WL 545422, at *1 (D.C. Cir. July 31, 1998) ("*Davis II*"). We again remanded, however, this time for the court to determine "whether any of the five tapes withheld in their entirety . . . contains material that can be segregated and disclosed without unwarrantably impinging upon anyone's privacy." *Id.*

On remand, the FBI determined that it could release one of the five tapes because the principal speaker on the tape had died. But the Bureau concluded that the remaining four tapes were wholly subject to Exemption 7(C), because it could not determine whether the speakers on those tapes were living or dead. *See* Decl. of Scott A. Hodes ¶¶ 5, 7 (Nov. 24, 1998). Citing an FBI affidavit, *see id.* ¶ 7, the district court held that the "defendant has made adequate efforts to establish that the speakers on these tapes are not deceased." *Davis v. Dep't of Justice,* No. 88-0130, Order at 2 (D.D.C. Sept. 15, 2000).

Once again, Davis appealed. In *Davis III,* we summarily reversed the district court and again remanded the case. *See Davis v. Dep't of Justice,* 2001 WL 1488882, at *1 (D.C. Cir. Oct.17, 2001) ("*Davis III*"). "The FBI's affidavit," we held, was "insufficient to determine the extent of the Bureau's efforts to ascertain whether putative beneficiaries of Exemption 7(C) are alive or dead." *Id.* As a consequence, we were "unable to say 'whether the Government reasonably balanced the interests in personal privacy against the public interest in release of the information at issue.'" *Id.* (quoting *Schrecker v. Dep't of Justice,* 254 F.3d 162, 167 (D.C. Cir. 2001) ("*Schrecker I*")). Citing our recent opinion in *Schrecker v. Department of Justice,* we remanded so that "the FBI may document what sources it consulted, and the district court can decide in the first instance whether the government 'did all it should have done, and whether it may withhold the disputed information pursuant to Exemption 7(C).'" *Id.* (quoting *Schrecker I,* 254 F.3d at 167).

Following our remand order, the FBI filed two more affidavits, spelling out the steps it took to determine whether the speakers were dead or alive, and declaring that those steps did not establish that the speakers on the tapes were deceased. *See* Second Decl. of Scott A. Hodes (Feb. 26, 2002); Third Decl. of Scott A. Hodes (July 11, 2002). We detail those steps in Part II.A below. The FBI's filings make clear that there are only "two speakers on the audiotapes at issue." Def.'s Mot. for Recons. at 3 (citing Fourth Decl. of Scott A. Hodes ¶ 4 (Aug. 7, 2002)). According to the government, the four tapes come from the FBI's undercover investigation of a "prominent individual," and the speakers are that "prominent individual and the undercover informant." Appellee's Br. 11 (citing affidavits).

In July 2002, unsatisfied with the government's efforts, the district court ordered the FBI to advise each of the two speakers, "by first class mail[,] . . . of defendant's obligation pursuant to this Order to [release the tapes] unless the speaker objects thereto in writing within 30 days." *Davis v. Dep't of Justice,* No. 88-0130, Order at 1 (D.D.C. July 23, 2002). More than a year later, after this court issued a subsequent opinion in the *Schrecker* case, see *Schrecker II,* 349 F.3d at 657, the government asked the district court to reconsider that order. On August 31, 2004, the court granted the motion to reconsider, "relieve[d] the government from undertaking the additional tasks mandated" in its July 2002 order, and granted summary judgment in favor of the FBI. *Davis v. Dep't of Justice,* No. 88-0130, Order at 1 (D.D.C. Aug 31, 2004).

Davis then filed his fourth notice of appeal, challenging both the district court's grant of summary judgment dismissing his FOIA complaint, and an earlier order denying his motion for an award of attorney's fees. We consider the former in Part II and the latter in Part III. We "review de novo a decision granting summary judgment to an agency claiming to have complied with FOIA." *Schrecker II,* 349 F.3d at 661-62. We also review de novo a district court's attorney's fees determination, like the one at issue here, that "rests on an interpretation of the statutory terms that define eligibility for an award." *Edmonds v. FBI,* 417 F.3d 1319, 1322 (D.C. Cir. 2005) (internal quotation marks omitted).

II

FOIA Exemption 7(C) exempts law enforcement records from release "to the extent that" release "could reasonably be expected to constitute an unwarranted invasion of personal privacy." 5 U.S.C. § 552(b)(7)(C). In deciding whether the release of particular information constitutes an "unwarranted" invasion of privacy, an agency must balance the privacy interest at stake against the public interest in disclosure. *See Department of Justice v. Reporters Comm. for Freedom of the Press,* 489 U.S. 749, 777, 109 S.Ct. 1468, 103 L.Ed.2d 774 (1989); *Schrecker I,* 254 F.3d at 166. We have recognized "that the privacy interest in nondisclosure of identifying information may be diminished where the individual is deceased." *Schrecker II,* 349 F.3d at 661. Indeed, the "fact of death, . . . while not requiring the release of information, is a relevant factor to be taken into account in the balancing decision whether to release information." *Id.* (quoting *Schrecker I,* 254 F.3d at 166). Consequently, "without confirmation that the Government took certain basic steps to ascertain whether an individual was dead or alive, we are unable to say whether the Government reasonably balanced the interests in personal privacy against the public interest in release of the information at issue." *Schrecker I,* 254 F.3d at 167.

The government's obligation in this regard is to "ma[k]e a reasonable effort to ascertain life status." *Schrecker II,* 349 F.3d at 662. Its "efforts must be assessed in light of the accessibility of the relevant information." *Id.* As we said in *Schrecker II,* there "'would be a question whether the Bureau's invocation of the privacy interest represented a reasonable response to the FOIA request . . . *if the Bureau has, or has ready access to, data bases that could resolve the issue.'" Id.* (quoting *Summers,* 140 F.3d at 1085 (Williams, J., concurring)) (emphasis added in *Schrecker II*). In short, "the proper inquiry is whether the Government has made reasonable use of the information readily available to it, and whether there exist reasonable alternative methods that the Government failed to employ." *Schrecker II,* 349 F.3d at 662.

A

The government's affidavits and pleadings declare that the FBI took three steps to determine whether the two speakers on the tapes were deceased. The Bureau reports that, because those individuals' deaths could not "be ascertained" by these methods, "the four tapes were withheld in full pursuant to exemption b(7)(C)." Second Hodes Decl. ¶ 8. Of course, "[t]he failure to discover the information sought is not conclusive evidence that the agency has failed to make a reasonable effort." *Schrecker II,* 349 F.3d at 662. Here, however, the government's own declarations provide that evidence.[3]

1. The government describes the first method it employed in the following paragraph from its principal affidavit:

> The FBI has institutional knowledge of the death of certain individuals from the processing of prior FOIA requests or internal records. The FBI relies on this institutional knowledge, as well as *Who Was Who*, a book of famous individuals [who have died].

Second Hodes Decl ¶ 5. From this description, it appears that the government's first step involved resort to two different sources: institutional knowledge and *Who Was Who.*

If the FBI truly used its "institutional knowledge" to determine whether the speakers were dead or alive, this first step might well be reasonable. But the Bureau's method of accessing that knowledge is so constrained as to render it effectively useless. Although the affidavit could be read as suggesting that the FBI uses its "internal records" to determine an individual's status, the same affidavit indicates that the Bureau did *not* search any records that were not themselves "responsive" to Davis' FOIA request—that is, it did not search any records other than the audiotapes themselves. *See* Second Hodes Decl. ¶¶ 6, 7.[4] Needless to say, the tapes themselves disclose nothing on this point, other than that the speakers were alive when they were speaking sometime during 1979–80.

---

[3]We measure the reasonable sufficiency of the government's effort on the basis of the aggregate of the steps it took, not on the basis of any individual step alone.

[4]Subsequently, the FBI did conduct one search of its internal records. According to another affidavit, the FBI searched a specific index in its Criminal Justice Information Service Division for the names of the speakers. However, "the only individuals . . . within the index[] are those whose fingerprints are taken from corpses by law enforcement personnel." Third Hodes Decl. ¶ 4. There was no reason—or at least none has been offered—to suggest that a search of this index was likely to be productive, and apparently it was not.

The only other piece of "institutional knowledge" mentioned in the FBI's description is knowledge gained from "the processing of prior FOIA requests." Second Hodes Decl. ¶ 5. We have no idea what that means. On its face, however, its utility must depend upon there having been a prior FOIA request involving the same individuals. The FBI does not suggest that there had ever been such a request.

If the FBI's reference to its institutional knowledge means anything more than what we have just described, we cannot determine that from the affidavit the Bureau filed. What we said of an earlier affidavit in this case, one that made a similar reference to the FBI's "institutional knowledge," remains equally true regarding this affidavit's treatment of that subject: "The FBI's affidavit is insufficient to determine the extent of the Bureau's efforts to ascertain whether putative beneficiaries of Exemption 7(C) are alive or dead." *Davis III*, 2001 WL 1488882, at *1. Indeed, with respect to the FBI's reliance on its institutional knowledge, it appears that the Bureau has "been completely passive on the issue, taking death into account only if the fact has happened to swim into [its agents'] line of vision." *Summers*, 140 F.3d at 1085 (Williams, J., concurring); *see also Schrecker I*, 254 F.3d at 167 (reversing and remanding the district court's judgment regarding the applicability of Exemption 7(C) because the FBI's affidavit was too vague to determine if the agency had taken "certain basic steps to ascertain whether an individual was dead or alive").

The other source mentioned in the FBI's affidavit is *Who Was Who*, a multi-volume set of books published periodically by Marquis Who's Who, LLC. Each new volume "includes the biographies of the most prominent and noteworthy people who have died since the publication of the previous edition."[5] It is a select company: of the more than 7.2 million Americans who died during 2000–02,[6] for example, no more than 4000 are portrayed in the *Who Was Who* volume covering that period. See 14 WHO WAS WHO IN AMERICA, 2000–02 (2002). How one earns a place in it is unclear, although Marquis reports that most of the entries were originally listed with the subjects' permission in its sister *Who's Who in America* publication, and that many of the biographies "have been scrutinized and revised by relatives or legal representatives of the deceased Biographee." *Id.* at vi. All of this suggests both considerable self-selection and considerable lag time.

---

[5]Marquis Who's Who, LLC, Home Page, http://www. marquiswhoswho.com.
[6]Centers for Disease Control and Prevention (CDC), *Deaths: Final Data for 2002,* NAT'L VITAL STAT. REP., Oct. 12, 2004, at 1; CDC, *Deaths: Final Data for 2001,* NAT'L VITAL STAT. REP., Sept. 18, 2003, at 1; CDC, *Deaths: Final Data for 2000,* NAT'L VITAL STAT. REP., Sept. 16, 2002, at 1.

The government describes one of the two speakers at issue here as a "prominent individual" and the other as an "undercover informant." Appellee's Br. 11. The latter seems unlikely to qualify for the distinction of a *Who Was Who* entry, and we have no way of knowing whether the former was prominent enough to qualify. Accordingly, we cannot conclude that the FBI's first method—reference to its institutional knowledge and to *Who Was Who*—was reasonably calculated to determine whether the speakers on the tapes were living or dead.

2. The government describes the second method it employed as follows:

> *When birth dates are provided in responsive records,* and these dates indicate the individual would be over 100 years of age, the name and/or any other identifiers will be released. Although the FBI is aware that many individuals live to be older than 100 years of age, . . . the FBI has consistently relied upon the 100-year rule in all of its FOIA processing.

Second Hodes Decl. ¶ 6 (emphasis added). The key to the utility of the FBI's 100-year rule is the clause that we have italicized. As explained above, when the FBI refers to "responsive records," it means those records—and only those records—actually sought in the FOIA request. In this case, the only responsive records were the audiotapes, and "there were no birth dates on these tapes." Second Hodes Decl. ¶ 6. Therefore, the affidavit concludes, since "no birth dates were provided in the responsive records, the FBI did not assume death of the individuals speaking on these tapes." *Id.*

The reasonableness of this second method obviously depends upon the probability that the responsive records will contain the individual's birth date—as might well be the case if the records sought by the FOIA requester were FBI investigative reports or personnel files. But unless the FBI has tape recorded a birthday party, it seems highly unlikely that the participants in an audiotaped conversation would have announced their ages or dates of birth.[7] Accordingly, this second method was also destined to fail, as it did.

3. The third method the FBI used was the following:

> *If a social security number is revealed on the responsive records,* the FBI, in its administrative discretion, may check the Social Security Death Index (SSDI)—a database maintained by a third party on the Internet. This website is maintained by a private individual, and the FBI cannot verify or vouch for the accuracy of this index, which the website purchases from the Social Security Administration.

---

[7]Although a tape might also reveal a speaker's birth date if that date were inscribed on the outside of the cassette that holds the tape, the government provides no information as to whether that is ever the case.

Second Hodes Decl. ¶ 7 (emphasis added). Once again, the rub is that the FBI will not even check the Social Security Death Index unless the speaker's social security number is revealed on responsive records. *See id.* (declaring that the "FBI does not research third-party names internally to discover social security" numbers). As expected, the FBI reports that, because "[t]his case concerns audio tapes," and "[a]s no social security numbers are on the tapes at issue, this website [the SSDI] was not checked." Needless to say, no one announces his or her social security number in ordinary conversation—not even at a birthday party. Accordingly, the Bureau again utilized a method that could not help but fail in the circumstances of this case.

4. As we have discussed, none of the three methods used by the FBI had any likelihood of discovering whether the two individuals, whose conversations were captured by the audiotapes in question, were living or dead. Indeed, if the FBI limits itself to those methods in the future, it is doubtful that it will ever be able to discover the status of a speaker on an audiotape. Although futility alone may not render the FBI's efforts unreasonable, it surely is an important factor in the equation.

The other factor we must consider is "whether the Government has made reasonable use of the information readily available to it, and whether there exist reasonable alternative methods that the Government failed to employ." *Schrecker II,* 349 F.3d at 662. As we have said, the question is whether *"the Bureau has, or has ready access to, data bases that could resolve the issue." Id.* (internal quotation marks omitted). We now consider some of the alternatives the FBI failed to employ.

Turning first to the FBI's internal records, we cannot conclude that the government "made reasonable use" of its own information in this case. The flaw in the government's 100-year rule and Social Security Death Index methodologies—at least as far as audiotapes are concerned—is that the Bureau refused to look anywhere but in the tapes themselves to discover the speakers' birth dates or social security numbers. This meant that, even if those personal identifiers were present in other FBI records, the FBI would not have found them. In this case, it is not unlikely that such other records do exist. In an FBI undercover operation like BRILAB, for example, one would expect to find investigative reports that list the various players (witnesses, informants, subjects, targets) and identifying information about them.[8] The FBI's Electronic Surveillance (ELSUR) indices also may

---

[8] *See, e.g., Blanton v. Dep't of Justice,* 64 Fed. Appx. 787, 788 (D.C. Cir. 2003) (noting that the FBI maintained "informant files" relating to an investigation); *Perri v. United States,* 53 Fed. Cl. 381, 395-96 (2002) (noting that the FBI maintained a "137 (Confidential Informant) File" and a "270 (Cooperative Witness) File" in an undercover operation); *Meeropol v. Meese,* 790 F.2d 942, 947 (D.C. Cir. 1986) (noting that the FBI maintained "subject files" regarding eleven named principals).

well contain the necessary personal identifiers for the two individuals, whose voices were captured by electronic surveillance.[9]

The FBI has neither denied that it has such records nor suggested that it would be difficult to access them in this case. To the contrary, yet another FBI affidavit explains that the Bureau's Central Records System (CRS) contains "all pertinent information which it has acquired in the course of fulfilling its mandated law enforcement responsibilities," and makes clear that much of that system can be searched by an individual's name. Fourth Hodes Decl. ¶ 7. For example, with respect to FBI Headquarters:

> Communications directed to FBIHQ from the various field offices . . . are filed in the pertinent case files and *indexed to the names of individuals,* groups, or organizations *which are listed* in the case caption(s) or title(s) *as a subject(s),* a suspect(s), or as a victim(s). Therefore, for example, *a search made in this index to locate records concerning a particular individual would be made by searching the name of that individual* in the index.

Id. ¶ 8 (emphasis added). And similarly, with respect to FBI field offices:

> Access to the CRS files at FBI field divisions is also afforded by the General Indices (automated and manual), which are likewise arranged in alphabetical order, and consist of an index on various subjects, including the names of individuals and organizations. *Searches made in the General Indices to locate records concerning a particular subject, such as John Doe, are made by searching the subject requested* in the index. Indexing functions have been automated by field divisions.

Id. ¶ 9 (emphasis added).

It is plain, then, that the FBI could have searched its files by the names of the two speakers—one the subject of a criminal investigation, the other an informant—to determine whether records in those files disclose their dates of birth or social security numbers (or even their deaths). But the FBI did not do so. *See* Second Hodes Decl. ¶¶ 6, 7. The Bureau gave no reason at all for not searching its records for the speakers' birth dates, and only one reason for not searching for their social security numbers:

> The FBI does not research third-party names internally to discover social security [numbers] because to do so would violate these third parties' privacy rights. The records that may possess these individual[s'] social security numbers were created for law enforcement purposes; they were not created for the purpose of ascertaining whether individuals contained in FBI records are still alive.

---

[9]*See Wheeler v. Dep't of Justice,* 403 F.Supp.2d 1, 4 (D.D.C. 2005) (noting that, through ELSUR, "the FBI maintains information on all subjects whose electronic and/or voice communications have been intercepted by the FBI since January 1, 1960," and that ELSUR can be searched by name, "date of birth, place of birth and social security number"); *see also Campbell v. Dep't of Justice,* 164 F.3d 20, 29 (D.C. Cir. 1998) (remanding with instructions that the FBI search its ELSUR records).

Second Hodes Decl. ¶ 7. We expressly rejected this precise rationale (asserted by the same FBI declarant) in *Schrecker II,* saying: "We fail to see how the purpose for which an internal record was created bears on whether searching the record for an individual's social security number would violate that individual's privacy." 349 F.3d at 664.

Turning from the FBI's own databases to those it "*has ready access to,*" *id.* at 662 (internal quotation marks omitted), we have to ask why the FBI limited itself to *Who Was Who.* The fact that the Bureau uses such an outside source indicates that there is no bar to its doing so. And apparently the biographies of the decedents contained in those books make it possible to determine that the "John Doe" for whom the FBI is searching is the same John Doe whose death is there reported. *See infra* Part II.B.

But if that is so, one has to ask why—in the age of the Internet—the FBI restricts itself to a dead-tree source with a considerable time lag between death and publication, with limited utility for the FBI's purpose, and with entries restricted to a small fraction of even the "prominent and noteworthy"? Why, in short, doesn't the FBI just Google the two names? Surely, in the Internet age, a "reasonable alternative" for finding out whether a prominent person is dead is to use Google (or any other search engine) to find a report of that person's death.[10] Moreover, while finding a death notice for the second speaker—the informant—may be harder (assuming that he was not prominent), Googling also provides ready access to hundreds of websites collecting obituaries from all over the country, any one of which might resolve that speaker's status as well. *See, e.g.,* http://www.legacy.com (hosting the obituary sites of more than 275 newspapers, including three Louisiana papers); http://www.obituarycentral.com (containing a directory of links to online obituaries and death notices in every state).

We do not suggest that the FBI must use one, or any, of the search methods outlined above. But when the only search methods the FBI did employ were plainly fated to reach a dead end (in a manner of speaking), and when there appear to be reasonable alternatives that the government failed to consider, there is a serious "question whether the Bureau's invocation of the privacy interest represented a reasonable response to the FOIA request." *Schrecker II,* 349 F.3d at 662 (internal quotation marks omitted). This a question that has not yet been answered, and that the district court must address on remand.

---

[10]That is particularly so here, since an FBI affidavit declared that the Bureau knew the "prominent individual" at issue was alive as recently as 1994. Decl. of Robert A. Moran ¶ 19 (Oct. 21, 1994). (How the FBI knew the individual was living in 1994, but could not determine whether he was living or dead by 1998, remains a mystery.)

B

The government does not dispute that the steps the FBI took to determine whether the speakers on the audiotapes were dead could not reasonably be expected to answer that question. Nor does it contend that resort to any of the alternatives identified above would be burdensome on the facts of this case. Instead, its argument is simply that "the steps taken by the FBI here were the same taken by the FBI in *Schrecker II*," and that because we affirmed the grant of summary judgment for the government there, we must do so here as well. Appellee's Br. 9; *see* Oral Arg. Tape at 29:15-34:12 (confirming the government's view that the FBI does not have to search for the speakers' birth dates or social security numbers, even if it knows they can quickly be found by a name search, because "there is no obligation under Schrecker to conduct additional searches" of nonresponsive records). That is a serious misreading of *Schrecker II.*

It is true that the three methods the FBI employed to determine whether individuals mentioned in responsive records in *Schrecker II* were dead are the same as those it employed in this case. See *Schrecker II*, 349 F.3d at 660. It is also true that we affirmed summary judgment in that case, holding, in particular, that the Bureau did not have to examine nonresponsive internal records for the mentioned individuals' birth dates or social security numbers. *Id.* at 663-65. But *Schrecker II* did not purport to affirm a set of search methodologies as per se sufficient to satisfy the "reasonable efforts" standard. *Id.* at 662. To the contrary, we noted that the "'adequacy of an agency's search is measured by a standard of reasonableness, and is dependent upon the circumstances of the case.'" *Id.* at 663 (quoting *Truitt v. Dep't of State,* 897 F.2d 540, 542 (D.C. Cir. 1990)) (additional quotation marks omitted). And we expressly "cautioned . . . that it would be inappropriate for the court to mandate 'a bright-line set of steps for an agency to take in this situation,'" because FOIA requires "'both systemic and case-specific exercises of discretion and administrative judgment and expertise.'" *Id.* at 662 (quoting *Johnson v. Executive Office for U.S. Attorneys,* 310 F.3d 771, 776 (D.C. Cir. 2002)).

Our determination in *Schrecker II*, that in that case the FBI had reasonably decided to examine only responsive records for birth dates and social security numbers, is distinguishable from this case in two important respects. First, *Schrecker* involved a FOIA request not for audiotapes, but for documents. Although there is virtually no chance that a speaker will announce those personal identifiers during an oral conversation, there is a reasonable probability that they will be contained in responsive documents. Indeed, in *Schrecker II* itself, the FBI found the birth dates and social security numbers of at least some of the mentioned individuals in a search of responsive pages. 349 F.3d at 663, 664.

Second, at issue in *Schrecker II* were 113 names appearing in over 24,000 responsive documents, making a search of nonresponsive documents for personal identifiers "unduly burdensome." *Id.* at 664. That burden was magnified by the fact that the 113 names were not those of the subjects of an FBI investigation, but rather were merely mentioned in documents relating to that investigation. This meant that "any name-based search would likely encounter . . . duplication" of common names, "making verification difficult or impossible." *Id.* It also meant that the prospects of success were "dubious." *Id.* Under those circumstances, we held that to "require the Government to shoulder such a potentially onerous task . . . goes well beyond the 'reasonable effort' demanded in this context." *Id.*

But Davis' FOIA request entails no such burden. Here, there are only two names and only four responsive records. Those two names belong to the prominent subject of a major FBI investigation, and to the FBI's own undercover informant. Given the Bureau's knowledge of their biographies, even if those individuals have common names, verification that a name-based search has produced records that relate to them would be neither "difficult [n]or impossible." *Id.* While there may be thousands of John Does, there are unlikely to be thousands connected with the BRILAB investigation. And given the fact that the FBI maintains name-specific records regarding its subjects and informants, *see* Fourth Hodes Decl. ¶¶ 8, 9 (quoted *supra* Part II.A.4); cases cited *supra* notes 8 & 9, here a name-based search would not have "dubious prospects of success." *Schrecker II,* 349 F.3d at 664.

Indeed, the request in this case looks less like the one at issue in *Schrecker II* and more like one that *Schrecker II* expressly distinguished. The latter involved another FOIA request by Ellen Schrecker, for documents relating to Joseph Fischetti, a Chicago-based organized-crime figure. As we explained, "Fischetti was the *sole subject* of that FOIA request, not one of a *multitude of third parties* appearing in responsive documents." *Id.* at 664 (emphasis in original). The request in *Schrecker II* was different, we said, because "[w]hile it may be reasonable to pursue internal research to determine whether a single subject is the same individual shown by the [Social Security Death Index] to be deceased, . . . it would be unduly burdensome to require the Government [to] do so for the large number of third parties appearing in documents responsive to Schrecker's request." *Id.* Davis' request, involving only two names in four audiotapes, is far closer to the Fischetti request than to the one we dismissed in *Schrecker II.*[11]

---

[11]We note the possibility that a FOIA requester could attempt to circumvent this distinction by slicing a single request for many names into multiple requests of one name each. We are confident, however, that a district court would be able to see through such a ruse.

To repeat what we said at the beginning of this subpart, there is no "bright-line set of steps for an agency to take in this situation." *Id.* at 662 (internal quotation marks omitted). Rather, the "adequacy of an agency's search is measured by a standard of reasonableness, and is dependent upon the circumstances of the case." *Id.* at 663 (internal quotation marks omitted). In determining whether an agency's search is reasonable, a court must consider the likelihood that it will yield the sought-after information, the existence of readily available alternatives, and the burden of employing those alternatives. In this case, the methodology employed by the agency was extremely unlikely to produce the needed information, and it appears—although we do not know for certain—that there are readily available alternatives that would not impose an undue burden on the government. We remand to permit the agency an opportunity to evaluate the alternatives, and either to conduct a further search or to explain satisfactorily why it should not be required to do so.

III

Finally, we address Davis' request for an award of attorney's fees, which the district court denied on the authority of this circuit's decision in *Oil, Chemical & Atomic Workers International Union, AFL-CIO v. Department of Energy,* 288 F.3d 452 (D.C. Cir. 2002) ("*OCAW*"). *See Davis*, Order at 2 (July 23, 2002). The district court's denial was correct. *OCAW* forecloses a decision in Davis' favor.

FOIA provides that a district court "may assess against the United States reasonable attorney fees . . . reasonably incurred in any case under this section in which the complainant has *substantially prevailed*." 5 U.S.C. § 552(a)(4)(E) (emphasis added). In *Buckhannon Board & Care Home, Inc. v. West Virginia Department of Health & Human Resources,* 532 U.S. 598, 121 S.Ct. 1835, 149 L.Ed.2d 855 (2001), the Supreme Court construed the attorney's fees provision of two other statutes that permit courts to award fees to a "prevailing party."[12] The Court rejected the plaintiffs' contention, which it characterized as the "catalyst theory," that "a plaintiff is a 'prevailing party' if it achieves the desired result because the lawsuit brought about a voluntary change in the defendant's conduct." *Buckhannon*, 532 U.S. at 601, 121 S.Ct. 1835. Rather, the Court ruled that, for a litigant to be a "prevailing party," there must have been a "judicially sanctioned change in the legal

---

[12] At issue in *Buckhannon* were provisions of the Fair Housing Amendments Act, 42 U.S.C. § 3613(c)(2), and the Americans with Disabilities Act, 42 U.S.C. § 12205.

relationship of the parties." *Id.* at 605, 121 S.Ct. 1835. "[E]nforceable judgments on the merits and court-ordered consent decrees," the Court said, suffice to create such a change. *Id.* at 604, 121 S.Ct. 1835.

In *OCAW*, this circuit extended the holding of *Buckhannon* to the fee-shifting provision of FOIA. 288 F.3d at 454-57. The *OCAW* court concluded that "the 'substantially prevail' language in FOIA [is] the functional equivalent of the 'prevailing party' language found in" the statutes interpreted in *Buckhannon*. *Id.* at 455-56. It "therefore h[e]ld that in order for plaintiffs in FOIA actions to become eligible for an award of attorney's fees, *they must have 'been awarded some relief by [a] court,' either in a judgment on the merits or in a court-ordered consent decree.*" *Id.* at 456-57 (quoting *Buckhannon*, 532 U.S. at 603, 121 S.Ct. 1835) (emphasis added).

Davis' problem is that, although to date he has received a total of 158 tapes from the government, none were produced as the result of a "judgment on the merits" or a "court-ordered consent decree." *Id.* at 457. It is true that, in 1991, he did secure such a judgment from the district court, directing the FBI to release 163 tapes. But that judgment was reversed by this court in *Davis I,* and the government's subsequent release of 157 of those tapes—after the FBI determined that they had been played at the trial—was not made pursuant to any judgment or order. Similarly, although *Davis II* remanded for the district court to determine whether any of the remaining tapes contained material that could be segregated, *Davis II,* 1998 WL 545422, at *1, such a remand is insufficient to satisfy the *OCAW* test.[13] The FBI's subsequent release of an additional tape (after determining that the speaker was dead) similarly was not pursuant to a judgment or order.

Davis appears to recognize the futility of his effort to distinguish *OCAW*, as his brief devotes considerably more pages to arguing that *OCAW* was wrongly decided than to arguing that it can be distinguished. *See* Appellant's Br. 24-28. The former is an argument that we cannot entertain, because "[o]ne three-judge panel . . . does not have the authority to overrule another three-judge panel of the court." *LaShawn A. v. Barry,* 87 F.3d 1389, 1395 (D.C. Cir. 1996) (en banc). We therefore conclude that the district court correctly determined that it could not grant Davis' request for attorney's fees.

---

[13]*See OCAW,* 288 F.3d at 458 (holding that an order directing the government to review documents by a specified date did not qualify the plaintiffs as "prevailing," because it did "not order[] the [agency] to turn over any documents" or "disallow any of the [agency's] justifications for exempting documents, or portions of documents, from disclosure").

IV

For the foregoing reasons, we affirm the district court's denial of attorney's fees, but we reverse its grant of summary judgment dismissing Davis' FOIA complaint. The case is remanded with directions that the FBI evaluate alternative methods for determining whether the speakers on the requested audiotapes are dead, and that thereafter the district court determine whether the FBI's chosen course is reasonable.

So ordered.

Appendix B: Case Study 2

SRI Intern., Inc. v. Internet Sec. Systems, Inc., 511 F.3d 1186 - Court of Appeals, Federal Circuit 2008511 F.3d 1186 (2008)

SRI INTERNATIONAL, INC., Plaintiff-Appellant,

v.

INTERNET SECURITY SYSTEMS, INC. (a Delaware Corporation) and INTERNET SECURITY SYSTEMS, INC. (a Georgia Corporation), Defendants-Appellees,

and

SYMANTEC CORPORATION, Defendant-Appellee.

No. 2007-1065. United States Court of Appeals, Federal Circuit.

January 8, 2008.

Frank E. Scherkenbach, Fish & Richardson, P.C., of Boston, MA, argued for plaintiff-appellant. With him on the brief was Robert E. Hillman. Also on the brief were Joshua Bleet, of Minneapolis, MN; Howard G. Pollack, of Redwood City, CA; Todd G. Miller and Michael M. Rosen, of San Diego, CA.

Bradley A. Slutsky, King & Spalding LLP, of Atlanta, GA, argued for defendants-appellees Internet Security Systems, Inc., et al. With him on the brief were Holmes J. Hawkins, III, Bradley A. Slutsky, and Charles A. Pannell, III. Also on the brief were Theresa A. Moehlman, Bhavana Joneja, and Ryan J. Stempniewicz, of New York, NY.

Paul S. Grewal, Day Casebeer Madrid & Batchelder LLP, of Cupertino, CA, argued for defendant-appellee, Symantec Corporation. With him on the brief were Robert M. Galvin, Renee DuBord Brown, and Geoffrey M. Godfrey. Of counsel on the brief was Joseph FitzGerald, Symantec Corporation, of Cupertino, CA.

Before MAYER, RADER, and MOORE, Circuit Judges.

Opinion for the court filed by Circuit Judge RADER. Opinion dissenting in part filed by Circuit Judge MOORE.

RADER, Circuit Judge.

On summary judgment, the United States District Court for the District of Delaware held U.S. Patent Nos. 6,484,203 ("the '203 patent"), 6,708,212 ("the '212 patent"), 6,321,338 ("the '338 patent"), and 6,711,615 ("the '615 patent") invalid as anticipated by SRI International, Inc.'s ("SRI's") own prior art publication "Live Traffic Analysis of TCP/IP Gateways" ("Live Traffic"). SRI Int'l, Inc. v. Internet Sec. Sys., Inc., 456 F.Supp.2d 623 (D. Del. 2006). The district court also granted summary judgment of invalidity of the '212 patent as anticipated by a paper entitled "EMERALD: Event Monitoring Enabling Responses To Anomalous Live Disturbances" ("EMERALD 1997"). Id. Because the district court correctly determined that the EMERALD 1997 paper anticipated the '212 patent, this court affirms that decision. However, due to genuine issues of material fact about the public accessibility of the Live Traffic paper, this court vacates and remands the district court's other determination.

I

SRI owns the '203, the '212, the '338, and the '615 patents. The SRI patents relate to cyber security and intrusion detection. Specifically, the patents describe "[a] computer-automated method of hierarchical event monitoring and analysis within an enterprise network including deploying network monitors in the enterprise network, detecting, by the network monitors, suspicious network activity based on analysis of network traffic data." '203 Patent Abstract. All four patents originated from a November 9, 1998 application by inventors Phillip Porras and Alfonso Valdes.

A. EMERALD 1997

SRI had done considerable research on network intrusion detection. In fact, SRI's Event Monitoring Enabling Responses to Anomalous Live Disturbances ("EMERALD") project attracted considerable attention in this art field. SRI first received funding for the EMERALD project in August 1996 and almost immediately began publicizing EMERALD at a workshop in November 1996. In June 1997, SRI posted an EMERALD 1997 paper on its SRI file transfer protocol[1] ("FTP") server. In October 1997, SRI presented EMERALD 1997 at the 20th National Information Systems Security Conference. The conference published the peer-reviewed article.

The EMERALD 1997 paper contains a detailed description of a tool for tracking malicious activity across large networks. Furthermore, the EMERALD 1997 paper discusses SRI's early research in Intrusion Detection Expert System ("IDES") technology. The paper then explains the development of the Next Generation IDES ("NIDES"). This technology uses a wide range of multivariate statistical measures to profile user behavior and detect anomalies in network traffic. The EMERALD 1997 paper describes the use of NIDES to detect network anomalies. EMERALD 1997 also teaches signature analysis,

---

[1]"FTP is a protocol for exchanging files over any computer network that supports the TCP/IP protocol [such as the internet]". SRI Int'l, Inc., 456 F.Supp.2d at 626 n.7.

among other analysis engines. The EMERALD 1997 paper and the '212 specification contain some overlapping material. For instance, both the '212 patent specification and the EMERALD 1997 article feature two nearly identical figures. Figures 1 and 2 in the EMERALD 1997 paper are nearly identical to Figures 2 and 3 from the '212 patent, shown below.

The EMERALD 1997 paper and the '212 patent specification also share overlapping text. The paper and the specification contain similar descriptions of the NIDES algorithm for statistical detection. The paper also discusses changes to the algorithm to accommodate network traffic. SRI Int'l, Inc., 456 F.Supp.2d at 633. Specifically, EMERALD 1997 and the '212 patent both state:

> Profiles are provided to the computational engine as classes defined in the resource object 32. The mathematical functions for anomaly scoring, profile maintenance, and updating do not require knowledge of the data being analyzed beyond what is encoded in the profile class. Event collection interoperability supports translation of the event stream to the profile and measure classes. At that point, analysis for different types of monitored entities is mathematically similar. This approach imparts great flexibility to the analysis in that fading memory constants, update frequency, measure type, and so on are tailored to the network entity being monitored.

> SRI Int'l, Inc., 456 F.Supp.2d at 633 fn.22; '212 Patent col.7 ll. 13-24.

During prosecution of the '212 patent, SRI disclosed the EMERALD 1997 paper in its Information Disclosure Statement, listing the paper in the patent's Other Publications section. The trial court found that "[SRI] does not argue that the EMERALD 1997 paper fails to disclose each of the limitations of the asserted claims of the '212 patent." Id. at 632. Instead, SRI contends that the EMERALD 1997 paper is not an enabling disclosure with respect to the '212 patent. On this basis, SRI challenges the district court's grant of summary judgment.

B. The Live Traffic Paper

The inventors drafted the Live Traffic paper based on the EMERALD project. Mr. Porras and Mr. Valdes authored the paper in 1997. SRI displayed the paper on its web site on November 10, 1997. The four patents in this case incorporate the paper by reference. Furthermore, SRI listed the Live Traffic paper in its information disclosure to the government agency that funded some of SRI's cyber security research.

SRI filed its patent application on November 9, 1998, one day before the critical date of November 10. The Live Traffic paper, as published in the December 12, 1997 proceedings of the 1998 Symposium on Network and Distributed Systems Security ("SNDSS"), was cited in the Information Disclosure Statement of the patents-in-suit.

The Internet Society ("ISOC") posted the 1998 SNDSS call for papers on its web site. The call for papers stated that all submissions were to be made via electronic mail by August 1, 1997 with a backup submission sent by postal mail. The call for papers announcement did not include any information on confidentiality of paper submissions. On August 1, 1997, Mr. Porras sent an email to Dr. Bishop, the Program Chair for SNDSS, in response to the SNDSS call for papers. Mr. Porras attached the Live Traffic paper to his email. Mr. Porras stated that SRI would make a copy of the Live Traffic paper available on the SRI FTP server as a backup. He included the specific FTP address, ftp://ftp.csl.sri.com/pub/emerald/ndss98.ps, in the email.

The record reflects seven instances in which Mr. Porras previously directed people to the EMERALD subdirectory to find other papers related to the EMERALD project. In four instances, Mr. Porras provided the full path and filename of the paper. In every instance, Mr. Porras directed the people to a specific paper, which included the term "emerald" in the filename. SRI brought an action against defendants Internet Security Systems, Inc.[2] ("ISS") and Symantec Corporation ("Symantec") for infringement of the '203, the '212, the '338, and the '615 patents. Defendants moved for summary judgment that each of the four patents-in-suit is invalid under 35 U.S.C. § 102(b). The Live Traffic paper served as the prior art for the summary judgment motion. Defendants also moved for partial summary judgment that the EMERALD 1997 paper was enabling and thus constituted anticipatory prior art.

SRI countered with a motion for partial summary judgment that the Live Traffic paper did not qualify as a printed publication under 35 U.S.C. § 102(b). SRI also moved for partial summary judgment that the EMERALD paper did not anticipate.

The district court ruled that the Live Traffic paper was a printed publication that anticipated all asserted claims of the four patents-in-suit. The trial court also determined that the EMERALD 1997 paper was enabling and anticipated the '212 patent. SRI appeals the district court's grant of summary judgment of invalidity as to the Live Traffic paper and the EMERALD 1997 paper. This court has jurisdiction under 28 U.S.C. § 1295(a)(1).

II

This court reviews a district court's grant of summary judgment without deference, reapplying the same standard as the district court. <u>Bruckelmyer v. Ground Heaters, Inc.</u>, 445 F.3d 1374, 1377 (Fed. Cir. 2006). "Summary judg-

---

[2]Two defendants have the name "Internet Security Systems, Inc.," one a Delaware corporation and one a Georgia corporation. For purposes of this opinion, they shall collectively be referred to as "ISS".

ment is appropriate if there is no genuine issue as to any material fact and the moving party is entitled to a judgment as a matter of law. Fed.R.Civ.P. 56(c)." Id. "Whether an anticipatory document qualifies as a 'printed publication' under § 102 is a legal conclusion based on underlying factual determinations." Cooper Cameron Corp. v. Kvaerner Oilfield Prods., 291 F.3d 1317, 1321 (Fed. Cir. 2002).

A. EMERALD 1997

As a matter of law, this court must review the decision that the EMERALD 1997 publication disclosed sufficient information to enable use of this prior art to invalidate the '212 patent. The trial court determined that the EMERALD 1997 paper anticipated the '212 patent, rendering the patent invalid under 35 U.S.C. § 102(b). "A [patent] claim is anticipated only if each and every element as set forth in the claim is found, either expressly or inherently described, in a single prior art reference." Verdegaal Bros. v. Union Oil Co. of Cal., 814 F.2d 628, 631 (Fed. Cir. 1987).

"[SRI] does not argue that the EMERALD 1997 paper fails to disclose each of the limitations of the asserted claims of the '212 patent. Rather, [SRI] asserts that EMERALD 1997 cannot anticipate claim 1 of the '212 patent because it does not provide an enabling disclosure of the claimed invention." SRI Int'l, Inc., 456 F.Supp.2d at 632. "The standard for enablement of a prior art reference for purposes of anticipation under section 102 differs from the enablement standard under 35 U.S.C. § 112." Novo Nordisk Pharm., Inc. v. BioTechnology Gen. Corp., 424 F.3d 1347, 1355 (Fed. Cir. 2005). "Significantly, [this court has] stated that 'anticipation does not require actual performance of suggestions in a disclosure. Rather, anticipation only requires that those suggestions be enabled to one of skill in the art.'" Id. (internal quote from Bristol-Myers Squibb Co. v. Ben Venue Labs. Inc., 246 F.3d 1368, 1379 (Fed. Cir. 2001)).

On summary judgment, the district court found that no reasonable jury could conclude that the EMERALD 1997 paper was a non-enabled "proposal" or an "intent to try" statistical profiling of network traffic. SRI Int'l, Inc., 456 F.Supp.2d at 635. The district court "finds the similarity in disclosure between EMERALD 1997 and the specification of the '212 patent convincing with respect to enablement." Id. at 634. Thus, "if the specification of the '212 patent was sufficient to enable the claims of that patent, so, too, is the description of EMERALD 1997." Id. (citing In re Epstein, 32 F.3d 1559, 1568 (Fed. Cir. 1994)). Besides the similarities between the disclosures, the district court accepted SRI's broad construction of "statistical detection method" to "encompass [] any method of detecting suspicious activity by 'applying one or more statistical functions' to analyze network traffic data." SRI Int'l, Inc., 456 F.Supp.2d at 634. Because SRI asserted that a variety of statistical functions fall within the scope of the '212 patent, the district court found that a person of ordinary skill in the art would find the EMERALD 1997 paper enabling with respect to the invention. Id. The district court clarified that a person of ordinary skill in this art field would have a background in computer science, electrical engineering, or computer engineering as well as knowledge of cyber and internet security. Id. at 630.

SRI asserts that the EMERALD 1997 paper is not an enabling disclosure and does not anticipate the claims of the '212 patent because implementing the EMERALD 1997 concepts required extensive and undue experimentation. In particular, SRI points to the declaration of one of the '212 inventors, Mr. Porras, that the 1997 paper was completed just at the outset of the EMERALD project. After the 1997 paper, SRI itself engaged in a great deal of time, effort, and research before achieving a workable system. Dr. Kesidis, SRI's expert, also explained that the EMERALD 1997 paper was a mere statement of intent to try several prior art techniques and would not have enabled one of ordinary skill in the art to make a functional system.

The Defendants respond that one of ordinary skill in the art, without undue experimentation, could have combined the teachings in EMERALD 1997 with general knowledge in the art to practice the invention using any species of the statistical detection method. See Elan Pharm., Inc. v. Mayo Found., 346 F.3d 1051, 1054-55 (Fed. Cir. 2003). Furthermore, the Defendants contend that substantial evidence from a number of different sources, including references in the '212 patent, confirmed that statistical detection methods were known in the art and used to analyze network traffic data. See, e.g., Valdes, et al., "Statistical Methods for Computer Usage Anomaly Detection using NIDES (Next-Generation Intrusion Detection Expert System)," 3rd International Workshop on Rough Sets and Soft Computing, San Jose, CA 1995, 306-11 as listed in the Other Publications section of the '212 patent. In sum, the Defendants contend that a person of ordinary skill in the art was capable of applying a statistical methodology in the analysis of network traffic data before the date of the '212 claimed invention.

This court discerns that the district court correctly determined that the EMERALD 1997 paper enabled one of ordinary skill in the art to practice the claimed invention. Based on the '212 patent specification, the EMERALD 1997 paper, and the record before the district court, no reasonable jury could conclude that the EMERALD 1997 paper did not enable statistical profiling of network traffic.

Both the '212 patent specification and the EMERALD 1997 paper contain similar sections explaining statistical detection. For example, both the specification and the publication contain similar descriptions of the use of NIDES algorithms for statistical detection. Furthermore, the identical figures are a graphical depiction of a network monitor to scrutinize an event stream and a diagram of a resource object that configure the network monitor. These figures show an architecture for network monitoring based on a profile engine and configurable event structures sufficient to enable one skilled in the art.

Indeed, these disclosures helped the inventors obtain issuance of the '212 patent. The issuance itself shows that the specification satisfied the enablement requirements of 35 U.S.C. § 112, ¶ 1. With the 1997 paper providing similar, or even a partially identical, disclosure to the '212 patent specification, the record meets the lower enablement standard for prior art under 35 U.S.C. § 102(b). Thus, the 1997 publication with its similarities in technical scope and description to the specification of the '212 patent meets the enabling hurdle for a prior art reference. See Constant v. Advanced Micro-Devices, Inc., 848 F.2d 1560, 1569 (Fed. Cir. 1988) ("The disclosure in Exhibit 5 is at least at the same level of technical detail as the disclosure in the '491 patent. If disclosure of a computer program is essential for an anticipating reference, then the disclosure in the '491 patent would fail to satisfy the enablement requirement of 35 U.S.C. § 112, First ¶.")

Dr. Kesidis's testimony is not sufficient to overcome the weight of evidence that the EMERALD 1997 paper offers an enabling disclosure for § 102(b). His testimony contains only generalized conclusions without any analysis regarding the alleged differences between the '212 patent disclosure and the EMERALD 1997 paper. In short, Dr. Kesidis just restated SRI's position. As such, SRI's only semblance of possible evidence to show a lack of an enabling disclosure in the EMERALD 1997 paper was not sufficient to create a genuine issue of material fact. Therefore, this court affirms the district court's ruling, as a matter of law, of invalidity of the '212 patent as anticipated by the EMERALD 1997 paper.

B. The Live Traffic Paper

This court must determine the accessibility to the public of the Live Traffic paper before the critical date. If this paper qualifies as prior art, the parties agree that its disclosure renders the asserted patents ('203, '338, '212, and '615) invalid under 35 U.S.C. § 102(b). The 35 U.S.C. § 102 printed publication bar states: "A person shall be entitled to a patent unless—(b) the invention was patented or described in a printed publication in this or a foreign country or in public use or on sale in this country, more than one year prior to the date of the application for patent in the United States. . . ." 35 U.S.C. § 102(b)(emphasis added). "The bar is grounded on the principle that once an invention is in the public domain, it is no longer patentable by anyone." Application of Bayer, 568 F.2d 1357, 1361 (C.C.P.A. 1978).

"Because there are many ways in which a reference may be disseminated to the interested public, 'public accessibility' has been called the touchstone in determining whether a reference constitutes a 'printed publication' bar under 35 U.S.C. § 102(b)." In re Hall, 781 F.2d 897, 898-99 (Fed. Cir. 1986) (emphasis added). "A given reference is 'publicly accessible' upon a satisfactory showing that such document has been disseminated or otherwise made available to the extent that persons interested and ordinarily skilled in the subject matter or art exercising reasonable diligence, can locate it." Bruckelmyer v. Ground Heaters, Inc., 445 F.3d 1374, 1378 (Fed. Cir. 2006). "The decision whether a particular reference is a printed publication 'must be approached on a case-by-case basis.'" In re Cronyn, 890 F.2d 1158, 1161 (Fed. Cir. 1989) (internal quote from In re Hall, 781 F.2d 897, 899 (Fed. Cir. 1986)); see also In re Wyer, 655 F.2d 221, 227 (C.C.P.A. 1981) ("Decision in this field of statutory construction and application must proceed on a case-by-case basis.").

The district court granted summary judgment of invalidity under § 102(b) as to all four patents-in-suit. The district court based its summary judgment ruling on its interpretation of the evidentiary record. According to the district court, the evidentiary record "indicates that the ftp://ftp.csl.sri.com site was publicly accessible." SRI Int'l, Inc., 456 F.Supp.2d at 629. Furthermore, the district court determined that the evidence clearly showed "Mr. Porras provided this [aforementioned] FTP site to other members of the intrusion detection community both in presentations and via email." Id. The district court thus determined that SRI's FTP server's directory structure gave access to the article to a person of ordinary skill in the art. Id. In the district court's view, one of ordinary skill would know that the SRI FTP server contained information on the EMERALD 1997 project and therefore would navigate through the folders to find the Live Traffic paper. Id.

SRI asserted that, as a matter of law, the file on SRI's FTP server containing the Live Traffic paper fell short of a publication under § 102(b). SRI contends that the Live Traffic paper sent to Dr. Bishop via email and placed on the FTP server for seven-days as a backup to this email was a private pre-publication communication. SRI also asserts that the district court misread this court's jurisprudence with respect to the ability of a person of ordinary skill to navigate the FTP server's directory structure to find the Live Traffic paper. SRI contends that the ndss98.ps file name of the Live Traffic paper was not indexed or catalogued in any meaningful way to enable a person of ordinary skill to locate the paper.

The Defendants assert that the district court properly applied this court's printed publication case law in finding that the Live Traffic paper was publicly accessible before the critical date. The Defendants point out that posting the Live Traffic paper to a publicly accessible FTP server made the paper publicly available to persons interested and skilled in the art. Furthermore, posting to a publicly accessible FTP server could not constitute a private transmission as alleged by SRI.

After review of the record, this court perceives factual issues that prevent entry of summary judgment of invalidity based on the Live Traffic paper. Specifically, this court does not find enough evidence in the record to show that the Live Traffic paper was publicly accessible and thus a printed publication under 35 U.S.C § 102(b).

This court's case law has discussed public accessibility under § 102(b), in one line of cases illustrating a lack of public accessibility and in another line of cases pointing out public accessibility. For instance, Application of Bayer and In re Cronyn illustrate situations that do not warrant a finding of public accessibility. In re Wyer, In re Klopfenstein and the recently decided Bruckelmyer v. Ground Heaters, on the other hand, illustrate situations that found public accessibility.

From the perspective of cases lacking public accessibility, Bayer featured a graduate thesis in a university library. The library had not catalogued or placed the thesis on the shelves. Only three faculty members even knew about the thesis. Application of Bayer, 568 F.2d 1357, 1358-59 (C.C.P.A. 1978). Under these circumstances, this court's predecessor found that the thesis did not constitute a printed publication because a customary search would not have rendered the work reasonably accessible even to a person informed of its existence. Id. at 1361-62. Similarly, in In re Cronyn, the thesis document was in a library with an alphabetical index by the author's name. This court found no public accessibility because "the only research aid in finding the theses was the student's name, which of course, bears no relationship to the subject of the student's thesis." In re Cronyn, 890 F.2d 1158, 1161 (Fed. Cir. 1989).

Several cases have also illustrated situations that rendered documents available to the public. For example, in Wyer, an Australian patent application was laid open to the public and "properly classified, indexed or abstracted" to enable public access to the application. In re Wyer, 655 F.2d 221, 226-27 (C.C.P.A. 1981). Wyer explained various factors involved in the public accessibility determination, including intent to publicize and disseminating activities. Still the court emphasized: "Each [printed publication] case must be decided on the basis of its own facts." Id. at 227. In Klopfenstein, two professional conferences displayed posters. These posters were printed publications because their entire purpose was public communication of the relevant information. In re Klopfenstein, 380 F.3d 1345, 1347-50 (Fed. Cir. 2004). And, most recently, in Bruckelmyer, this court found that a Canadian patent application, properly abstracted, indexed and catalogued, was a printed publication under § 102(b). This court explained:

"[T]he [Canadian] patent was classified and indexed, similar to the abstract in <u>Wyer</u>, further providing a road map that would have allowed one skilled in the art to locate the [patent] application." <u>Bruckelmyer v. Ground Heaters, Inc.</u>, 445 F.3d 1374, 1379 (Fed. Cir. 2006).

Based on this appeal record, this case falls somewhere between <u>Bayer</u> and <u>Klopfenstein</u>. Like the uncatalogued thesis placed "in" the library in the <u>Bayer</u> case, the Live Traffic paper was placed "on" the FTP server. Yet, the FTP server did not contain an index or catalogue or other tools for customary and meaningful research. Neither the directory structure nor the README file in the PUB subdirectory identifies the location of papers or explains the mnemonic structure for files in the EMERALD subdirectory, or any subdirectory for that matter. In fact, the EMERALD subdirectory does not contain a README file. Further, the summary judgment record shows that only one non-SRI person, Dr. Bishop, specifically knew about the availability of the Live Traffic paper, similar to the knowledge of the thesis's availability by the three professors in <u>Bayer</u>.

The record on summary judgment does not show that an anonymous user skilled in the art in 1997 would have gained access to the FTP server and would have freely navigated through the directory structure to find the Live Traffic paper. To the contrary, the paper's author, Mr. Porras, thought it necessary to provide Dr. Bishop with the full FTP address for the file. Surely Dr. Bishop, the Program Chair for SNDSS, would have qualified as one of ordinary skill in the art in 1997. Yet, despite his knowledge of the field, FTP servers, and the paper, Dr. Bishop apparently would not have found the reference without Mr. Porras's precise directions. It is doubtful that anyone outside the review committee looking for papers submitted to the Internet Society's Symposium would search a subfolder of an SRI FTP server. These are separate entities. It is also doubtful that anyone outside the review committee would have been aware of the paper or looked for it at all in early August 1997. These facts seem to militate against a finding of public accessibility. At least they warrant examination upon remand.

In one respect, the public accessibility factors are less compelling for the Live Traffic paper than they were for the thesis in <u>Bayer</u>. In <u>Bayer</u>, the thesis was complete and ready for public consumption, while the Live Traffic paper was still subject to pre-publication review. The Live Traffic paper was not a finished thesis, but was posted on the FTP server solely to facilitate peer review in preparation for later publication.

On the other hand, similar to the posters in <u>Klopfenstein</u>, the Live Traffic paper was "posted" on an open FTP server and might have been available to anyone with FTP know-how and knowledge of the EMERALD subdirectory. Unlike the posters hung at a conference in <u>Klopfenstein</u>, the Live Traffic paper was not publicized or placed in front of the interested public. In effect, the Live Traffic paper on the FTP server was most closely analogous to placing posters at an unpublicized conference with no attendees. The Live Traffic paper, like posters at a vacant and unpublicized conference, was available by being "posted," but available only to a person who may have wandered into the conference by happenstance or knew about the conference via unpublicized means. Indeed the record does not show that anyone accessed the Live Traffic paper via the FTP server during the seven days in which it was posted. While actual retrieval of a publication is not a requirement for public accessibility, this record does not evince that the Live Traffic paper was accessible to anyone other than the peer-review committee, thus further suggesting an absence of actual public accessibility. See Constant v. Advanced Micro-Devices, Inc., 848 F.2d 1560, 1569 (Fed. Cir. 1988).

The record reflects seven instances in which Mr. Porras previously directed people to the /pub/emerald subdirectory to find other papers related to the EMERALD project. In four instances, Mr. Porras provided the full path and filename of the paper, presumably to provide an adequate research aid for a user to locate the paper. In every instance, Mr. Porras directed the people to a specific paper, which included the term "emerald" in the filename. In this case, there was no such specific direction, and the filename did not mimic the subdirectory or publicized project name. Thus, the record offers no suggestion that because people had been told that they could find other papers in the past in the /pub/emerald subdirectory, they would—unprompted—look there for an unpublicized paper with a relatively obscure filename.

The current record leaves the Live Traffic paper on the Bayer nonaccessible side of this principle, not on the Klopfenstein side of public accessibility. Therefore, on summary judgment, this court finds that the prepublication Live Traffic paper, though on the FTP server, was not catalogued or indexed in a meaningful way and not intended for dissemination to the public. See In re Wyer, 655 F.2d 221 (C.C.P.A. 1981); Application of Bayer, 568 F.2d 1357 (C.C.P.A. 1978); In re Klopfenstein, 380 F.3d 1345, 1347-50 (Fed. Cir. 2004).

The FTP server directory structure (/pub/emerald/) of a well-known institution in the intrusion detection community and the acronym of "ndss98.ps" might have hinted at the path to the Live Traffic paper; however, an unpublicized paper with an acronym file name posted on an FTP server resembles a poster at an unpublicized conference without a conference index of the location of the various poster presentations. As noted, the peer-review feature also suggests no intent to publicize. Without additional evidence as to the details of the 1997 SRI FTP server accessibility, this court vacates and remands for a more thorough determination of the publicity accessibility of the Live Traffic paper based on additional evidence and in concert with this opinion.

III
CONCLUSION

This court affirms the district court's grant of summary judgment as to the invalidity of the '212 patent based on the EMERALD 1997 paper. However, this court vacates and remands the district court's summary judgment ruling of invalidity based on the Live Traffic paper because of genuine issues of fact about public accessibility.

AFFIRMED-IN-PART, VACATED AND REMANDED-IN-PART.

Costs

Each party shall bear its own costs.

MOORE, Circuit Judge, dissenting-in-part.

The majority finds that the district court erred in granting summary judgment that the Live Traffic paper invalidates SRI's four patents under 35 U.S.C. § 102(b). The majority concludes that there are genuine issues of material fact about the public accessibility of the Live Traffic paper. As the district court found, the evidentiary record "indicates that the ftp://ftp.csi.sri.com site was publicly accessible." SRI Int'l, Inc. v. Internet Sec. Sys., Inc., 456 F.Supp.2d 623, 629 (D. Del. 2006). The defendants presented evidence that the Live Traffic paper was posted on the Internet on a public FTP server for seven days and was available to anyone. In contrast, SRI failed to introduce any evidence showing a genuine issue of material fact as to the public accessibility of the Live Traffic paper, and attorney argument, no matter how good, simply cannot fill this void. Therefore, I respectfully dissent.

DISCUSSION
I.

In this case, the defendants supported their summary judgment motion with evidence as required by Rule 56, and SRI presented no evidence to establish that there is a genuine issue of material fact as to whether the publication at issue constitutes a "printed publication" under 35 U.S.C. § 102(b). A party may not overcome a grant of summary judgment by merely offering conclusory statements. Moore U.S.A., Inc. v. Standard Register Co., 229 F.3d 1091, 1112 (Fed. Cir. 2000).

Rule 56(e) provides, in relevant part:

When a motion for summary judgment is made and supported as provided in this rule, an adverse party may not rest upon the mere allegations or denials of his pleading, but his response, by affidavits or as otherwise provided in this rule, must set forth specific facts showing

<u>that there is a genuine issue for trial</u>. If he does not so respond, summary judgment, if appropriate, shall be entered against him.

Fed. R. Civ. P. 56(e) (emphasis added). When the moving party has carried its burden under Rule 56(c), its opponent "must do more than simply show that there is some metaphysical doubt as to the material facts." <u>Matsushita Elec. Indus. Co. v. Zenith Radio Corp.</u>, 475 U.S. 574, 586, 106 S.Ct. 1348, 89 L.Ed.2d 538 (1986).

II.

A.

The majority concludes without any evidence or support in the record that the FTP server "did not contain an index or catalogue or other tools for customary and meaningful research."[3] <u>Maj. op.</u> at 1196. I agree with the district court that all of the evidence of record supports the conclusion that the navigable directory structure of the FTP server rendered the Live Traffic paper publicly accessible. The subject matter of this publication is complex computer software technology on computer security/intrusion detection. There is no dispute that the ordinarily skilled artisan is quite computer savvy. <u>SRI</u>, 456 F.Supp.2d at 630. The defendants introduced evidence indicating that the 1997 version of the FTP server had navigable directories and subdirectories exactly the same as the 2006 version of the FTP server.

The evidence showed that the inventor, Mr. Porras, repeatedly directed

---

[3]The majority bases this conclusion on a number of "facts" not supported by the record or even argued by the parties. First, the majority implies that a sophisticated computer security researcher would need a "README" file to find a file in an FTP server. <u>Maj. op.</u> at 1196. There is no support in the record for this suggestion and the parties never argued it. The majority also states, without record support, that "[i]t is doubtful that anyone outside the review committee looking for papers submitted to the Internet Society's Symposium would search a subfolder of an SRI server" and "[i]t is also doubtful that anyone outside the review committee would have been aware of the paper or looked for it at all in early August 1997." <u>Id.</u> at 1196-97. <u>Neither of these</u> "doubts" are supported by any record evidence. Moreover, the relevant inquiry for public accessibility is not whether a reference is available to people looking specifically for that reference, but rather whether the reference is publicly available to someone looking for information relevant to the subject matter. <u>Bruckelmyer v. Ground Heaters, Inc.</u>, 445 F.3d 1374, 1378 (Fed. Cir. 2006) (reference is publicly accessible upon a showing that reference "has been disseminated or otherwise made available to the extent that persons interested and ordinarily skilled in the subject matter or art exercising reasonable diligence, can locate it"). Given that the EMERALD subdirectory was publicized to the cyber security community as a source of information related to projects on intrusion detection, this paper, like everything else in the EMERALD subdirectory, was publicly accessible to anyone interested in material on intrusion detection.

people of ordinary skill in the art to the SRI FTP server prior to the critical date as a place to find materials on EMERALD in presentations and emails:

- Dec. 17, 1996 11:35 AM email: "Bill, a copy of our paper can be found on ftp.csl.sri.com under pub/emerald-oakland97.ps."

- Dec. 17, 1996 3:45 PM email: "By the way, a postscript version of the paper is also available via anonymous ftp from ftp.csl.sri.com. You can find the file under /pub/emerald-oakland97.ps."

- Dec. 31, 1996 email: "FYI, we've placed an update of our paper and a 1-page executive summary of EMERALD on ftp.csl.sri.com in the pub directory."

- Jan. 6, 1997 email: "FYI: I mentioned to you that I'd send you a paper on our Intrusion Detection research when it was available. You can find that paper (and an executive summary) at ftp.csl.sri.com under /pub/emerald*.ps."

- Jan. 8, 1997 email: "ps: I realize folks may not be able to review our paper before the meeting. We have, however, made available on ftp.csl.sri.com (/pub/emerald-position1.ps) a concise executive summary of our research."

- Jan. 14, 1997 email: "By the way, this exec summary and a more lengthy paper on EMERALD are available for anonymous ftp at ftp.csl.sri.com under /pub/emerald*.ps."

- DARPA Presentation slides dated Feb. 5, 1997: This presentation repeatedly directed participants to the EMERALD sub-folder and materials contained therein: "Executive Summary: ftp://ftp.csl.sri.com/pub/emerald-position 1.ps"[4]

This record evidence supports the district court's conclusion that the FTP server was widely known and easily navigable. SRI presents <u>no</u> evidence to the contrary. In fact, SRI's primary argument on appeal was:

> But most importantly, there was no evidence that in 1997, at the time the draft was supposedly placed on the server for one week, SRI's FTP server was structured to allow an anonymous user to navigate through

---

[4]The majority repeatedly relies for support upon its claims that "[i]n every instance, Mr. Porras directed the people to a specific paper, which included the term 'emerald' in the file name." <u>Maj. op.</u> at 1191, 1197. With all due respect to the majority, that simply is <u>not</u> accurate. In a presentation Mr. Porras gave on EMERALD, he presented slides with at least six references to SRI's FTP server and the EMERALD subdirectory. In two such references, the slides directed people to the EMERALD subdirectory and to materials in that subdirectory that did not contain the 'emerald' name in the title, but nonetheless related to the EMERALD project.

directories and subdirectories to find a specific file without knowing its specific, complete address.

In fact, as the defendants point out, SRI presents no evidence that any FTP server was not navigable in 1997. See Oral Arg. at 22:42-23:38, available at http://www.cafc.uscourts.gov/oralarguments/mp3/XXXX-XXXX.mp3. In contrast, the defendants presented evidence that the FTP server was navigable in 2006 (which SRI does not dispute), and the emails and presentations indicate that the FTP server was similarly navigable in 1997. In fact in the December 31, 1996 email, Mr. Porras directed Ms. Lunt to ftp.csl.sri. com and told her to go to the "pub directory." If this FTP server was not navigable, this email would be meaningless. Moreover, SRI never responds to the evidence indicating widespread use of the FTP server by the cyber security community at the relevant time including citations, and evidence that the FTP server was referenced seventy times by individuals on Google Groups and other on-line newsgroup forums. SRI, 456 F.Supp.2d at 629. SRI does not respond to the fact that many of the USENET references from 1997 just cite the FTP server leaving individuals to navigate to the material of interest.[5] See Oral Arg. at 20:44-21:25, available at http://www.cafc.uscourts. gov/oralarguments/mp3/XXXX-XXXX.mp3. In the face of all this evidence, SRI offers nothing other than a hollow claim that defendants did not prove it navigable in 1997. It must also be acknowledged that this FTP server was at all times within SRI's control. Hence, if contrary to all the evidence, it was not navigable in 1997, SRI should be able to proffer some proof.

In light of the mountain of evidence presented by the defendants and the complete absence of any contrary evidence presented by SRI, the district court's determination that the FTP server was publicly accessible by virtue of the navigable directory structure must be affirmed.

B.

I agree with the majority that this case, placing a paper on an FTP server, is not clearly governed by either our library cases, such as In re Bayer, 568 F.2d 1357 (Fed. Cir. 1978), In re Hall, 781 F.2d 897 (Fed. Cir. 1986), or In re Cronyn, 890 F.2d 1158 (Fed. Cir. 1989), or our dissemination cases, such as In re Klopfenstein, 380 F.3d 1345, 1350 (Fed. Cir. 2004).

---

[5]Without addressing most of this evidence, the majority claims that Mr. Porras provided Dr. Bishop with the full FTP address for the file because "Dr. Bishop apparently would not have found the reference without Mr. Porras's precise directions." Maj. op. at 1196 [18?]. There is no support in the record for this determination by the majority. And again the parties do not argue this. Of course, it is easier to locate something with a precise address, rather than general instructions.

1. Library Cases

Like a thesis in a library, the Live Traffic paper was placed on the FTP server. However, unlike the library cases, the Live Traffic paper was in a navigable directory structure. As the district court held, once at the FTP server, to get to the Live Traffic paper, one only needed to enter the directory entitled PUBS (there were only two directories to choose from PUBS and DEV) and once in PUBS enter the subdirectory EMERALD. SRI, 456 F.Supp.2d at 629-30. It was undisputed that people of skill in the art were aware of the EMERALD project to which the Live Traffic paper pertained prior to the critical date. Id. at 630. The district court concluded from the extensive record evidence that "a person of ordinary skill in this art, having the FTP host address available to him/her, could readily navigate through two subfolders on a simple website and access the Live Traffic paper." Id.

The Live Traffic paper was in the EMERALD subdirectory under the name "ndss98.ps." The majority refers to the filename as "relatively obscure." Maj. op. at 1197. There is no evidence to suggest that the filename was obscure—it is the acronym for a conference (1998 Network and Distributed System Security Symposium) sponsored by the Internet Society. By 1997, the NDSS Symposium was in its fifth year and the record evidence demonstrated that its program committee included representatives from important government, corporate and academic institutions in the intrusion detection field, such as the National Security Agency, DARPA, AT&T Labs, Bellcore, 3Com, Purdue University, and Cambridge University. The Internet Society website's "call for papers" referred to the 1998 conference as "NDSS" and the link to the website's call for papers used "ndss" in its file path ("http://www.isoc.org/conferences/ndss/98/cfp.shtml."). Further, even if the filename were obscure and did not convey the nature of the subject matter, the file existed in the EMERALD subdirectory. In this case, members of the relevant cyber community had been repeatedly directed to the EMERALD subdirectory to find files related to computer intrusion detection and the cyber community had repeatedly cited the EMERALD subdirectory in USENET and other articles as a source for intrusion detection materials. If a librarian directed a researcher to a particular shelf of books on intrusion detection, even if a book on that shelf had an obscure title, the fact that the librarian referred to the shelf as containing books on intrusion detection would provide enough direction for the researcher to know that the book was related to intrusion detection. The standard enunciated in our caselaw is "research aid" or "customary research tool." Cronyn, 890 F.2d at 1161; In re Howarth, 654 F.2d 103, 105 (CCPA 1981). The navigable directory meets this standard. The paper "ndss98.ps" was located in a subdirectory, EMERALD, which was known to be a source for materials related to intrusion detection.

This case is quite unlike the uncatalogued, unshelved thesis in a general university library in <u>Application of Bayer</u>, 568 F.2d 1357 (CCPA 1978). In this case, the Live Traffic paper existed on an FTP server that was used for cyber security work, in a subdirectory named for a specific, well-known cyber security project (EMERALD). As the district court pointed out, it is ironic that SRI, which is in the intrusion detection business, argues that those skilled in the art of intrusion detection could not detect information purposefully posted on the internet by a member of the cyber security community.

This case is also unlike <u>Cronyn</u>, where the court held that three theses in a shoebox in the chemistry department library filed by author's name did not make them readily accessible to the public. 890 F.2d at 1161. The court held that "the only research aid was the student's name, which, of course, bears no relationship to the subject matter of the student's thesis." <u>Id.</u> In contrast to <u>Cronyn</u>, the Live Traffic paper was located in a navigable directory in a subdirectory entitled EMERALD, which the record evidence indisputably shows people in the industry understood as a project related to computer software for intrusion detection—the same subject matter as the Live Traffic paper. <u>SRI</u>, 456 F.Supp.2d at 630-31. Under the library cases, it is my view that the district court properly ruled on summary judgment because the navigable directory was a research aid which rendered the Live Traffic paper readily accessible to the computer security community (the relevant public).

2. Dissemination Cases

"[D]istribution and indexing are not the only factors to be considered in a § 102(b) 'printed publication' inquiry." <u>Klopfenstein</u>, 380 F.3d at 1350; see also <u>Bruckelmyer</u>, 445 F.3d at 1378 (reference is publicly accessible if it has been "disseminated or otherwise made available to the extent that persons interested and ordinarily skilled in the subject matter or art exercising reasonable diligence, can locate it and recognize and comprehend therefrom the essentials of the claimed invention"). As the majority recognizes, the determination of whether a reference is a "printed publication" under 35 U.S.C. § 102(b) involves a case-by-case inquiry into the facts and circumstances surrounding the reference's disclosure to the public.

<u>Klopfenstein</u> articulates several factors that guide our case-by-case inquiry. See <u>Klopfenstein</u>, 380 F.3d at 1350. The factors to consider include: (1) the length of time the reference was available; (2) the expertise of the target audience; (3) the existence (or lack) of reasonable expectations that the reference would not be copied; and (4) the simplicity with which the reference could have been copied. <u>See id.</u> at 1350-51.

a. Length of Time the Live Traffic Paper was Available

The more transient the display, the less likely it is to be considered a "printed publication." Klopfenstein, 380 F.3d at 1350. Conversely, the longer a reference is displayed, the more likely it is to be considered a printed publication. Id.

It is undisputed that the Live Traffic paper was available on the FTP server for seven days. This is more than double the amount of time found sufficient in Klopfenstein. Further, the paper was available twenty-four hours a day, as opposed to the poster in Klopfenstein, which was only available during conference hours. Moreover, because the Live Traffic paper was available on an FTP server, it could be accessed from anywhere, as opposed to Klopfenstein where the display was at a conference in a single physical location. SRI failed to introduce any evidence that seven days was not sufficient time to give the public the opportunity to capture information conveyed by the Live Traffic paper.

b. Expertise of the Target Audience of the Live Traffic Paper

The expertise of the target audience "can help determine how easily those who viewed it could retain the displayed material." Klopfenstein, 380 F.3d at 1351. In this case, the defendants introduced evidence to show that the target audience of the Live Traffic paper is persons interested and skilled in cyber security. Counsel for SRI conceded at oral argument that the target audience included sophisticated members of the internet security community. See Oral Arg. at 6:12-32, available at http://www.cafc.uscourts.gov/oral-arguments/mp3/XXXX-XXXX.mp3; SRI, 456 F.Supp.2d at 630. The defendants presented evidence showing that in 1996 and 1997, the inventor advertised the FTP server to let people of ordinary skill in the art locate his research in the field of cyber security, using both emails to colleagues in the field and presentations to the cyber security community. The defendants presented evidence showing the cyber security community included sophisticated computer scientists who knew how to use the FTP server, and who in fact often used the FTP server to share information. SRI presented no evidence to the contrary.

c. Expectation That the Live Traffic Paper Would Not Be Copied

If "professional and behavioral norms entitle a party to a reasonable expectation that the information displayed will not be copied, we are more reluctant to find something a 'printed publication.'" Klopfenstein, 380 F.3d at 1351. When parties have taken protective measures, such as license agreements, non-disclosure agreements, anti-copying software, or even simple disclaimers, those protective measures may be considered to the extent they create a reasonable expectation on the part of the inventor that the information will not be copied. Id.

The defendants introduced evidence that the public FTP server where the Live Traffic paper was posted was widely known in the cyber security community and accessible to any member of the public. The defendants even introduced evidence that the inventor had specifically advertised the FTP server to persons particularly interested in his research and skilled in the art, using emails and presentations. Moreover, the evidence is undisputed that the inventor took absolutely no protective measures with regard to the FTP server or the Live Traffic paper, such as license agreements, non-disclosu re agreements, anti-copying software, or even simple disclaimers. Id. As counsel for SRI conceded during oral argument, the Live Traffic paper was not even labeled confidential. See Oral Arg. at 9:40-46, available at http://www.cafc.uscourts.gov/oralarguments/mp3/XXXX-XXXX.mp3.

The majority analogizes the Live Traffic paper to "posters at an unpublicized conference with no attendees." Maj. op. at 1197. This analogy is incorrect. The evidence showed that: (1) the inventor publicized the FTP server to the cyber security community (hence the conference was publicized), and (2) the FTP server was widely known and frequently used in the cyber security community (there were lots of attendees), in direct contrast to an "unpublicized conference with no attendees."[6]

The majority accepts SRI's argument that "this record does not evince that the Live Traffic paper was accessible to anyone other than the peer-review committee." Maj. op. at 1197. But the record shows the Live Traffic paper was available to any member of the general public, and not just the peer-review committee. There are two different disclosures of the Live Traffic paper.[7] The first, via email to the peer-review committee, and the

---

[6]The majority's focus on whether the paper was publicized or whether the existence of the paper was known beyond the peer-review committee for the conference ignores the fact that the FTP server and the particular subdirectory where the paper was located, EMERALD, were well known as a source for information related to intrusion detection. There has never been a requirement that the publication itself be publicized. Unpublicized books, articles, or theses have always been printed publications provided they were publicly accessible. Bruckelmyer, 445 F.3d at 1378; In re Wyer, 655 F.2d 221, 226 (CCPA 1981).

[7]The majority contends that the Live Traffic paper, unlike the thesis in Bayer, was incomplete and not "ready for public consumption." Maj. op. at 1196 [17?]. Virtually no changes (other than the removal of references to SRI and the EMERALD project name to facilitate blind review) exist between the version of the Live Traffic paper posted on the FTP server and the final version of the Live Traffic paper. Further, this issue is irrelevant to our inquiry of whether the paper as posted on the FTP server was publicly accessible for all that it disclosed.

second, posted to the public FTP server. While the inventor may have had a reasonable expectation the copy of the Live Traffic paper that he sent to the peer-review committee would not be copied, the record does not indicate the inventor could have any expectation of confidentiality with respect to the copy of the Live Traffic paper he posted on the publicly accessible FTP server, which was the same FTP server the cyber security community frequently used. The inventor took no precautions to restrict access to the Live Traffic paper on the FTP server, and based on the record, no reasonable person would expect something posted on the FTP server to be confidential. The record even shows that in December of 1996 and January of 1997, the inventor directed multiple members of the cyber security community (outside the peer-review committee) to the EMERALD subdirectory of the FTP server to read about his intrusion detection research—the same subdirectory where the inventor posted the Live Traffic paper.

d. Simplicity of Copying the Live Traffic Paper

"The more complex a display, the more difficult it will be for members of the public to effectively capture its information." Klopfenstein, 380 F.3d at 1351. The defendants introduced evidence that the FTP server existed for the sole purpose of allowing members of the cyber security community to post and retrieve information relevant to their research. FTP—which stands for "File Transfer Protocol"—is an Internet tool which exists for the purpose of moving files from one computer to another—copying. The inventor "stuck a copy" of the Live Traffic paper on the FTP server for seven days where others could view and copy the paper with great ease.

SRI does not contend that papers on an FTP server are difficult for a user to copy or print. It is undisputed that at the touch of a button, the entire Live Traffic paper could be downloaded or printed. Copying could not be simpler. Unlike Klopfenstein, where members of the public would have to quickly transcribe the text or graphics of the poster during a conference, members of the public could download or print the Live Traffic paper immediately upon accessing the paper, and at any time of the day or night during the seven days it was posted on the FTP server.

Whether the case is analyzed under the rubric of the library thesis cases or the temporary dissemination cases, the result is the same. The defendants carried their burden under Rule 56(c). Because SRI presented no evidence showing genuine issues of material fact for trial, I would affirm the district court's ruling of invalidity based on the Live Traffic paper.

Appendix C: Case Study 3

Whirlpool Financial Corp. v. GN Holdings, Inc., 67 F. 3d 605 (7th Cir. 1995)

WHIRLPOOL FINANCIAL CORPORATION, Plaintiff-Appellant,

v.

GN HOLDINGS, INC., f/k/a CCHP Delaware, Inc., W.R. Grace & Company-Connecticut, Kevin Clark, Michelle Clark, Robert Bok, and Diane Bok, Defendants-Appellees.

No. 95-1292.

United States Court of Appeals, Seventh Circuit.

Argued June 6, 1995.
Decided September 28, 1995.
Rehearing and Suggestions for Rehearing Denied October 31, 1995.

Jonathan G. Bunge, John F. Young, Roy M. Van Cleave (argued), Keck, Mahin & Cate, Chicago, IL, for plaintiff-appellant Whirlpool Financial Corporation, a Delaware corporation.

Mark E. Ferguson (argued), Mark L. Levine, Bartlit, Beck, Herman, Palenchar & Scott, Chicago, IL, for defendants-appellees GN Holdings, Incorporated, a Delaware corporation fka CCHP Delaware, Incorporated, W.R. Grace & Company-Connecticut, a Connecticut corporation.

Matthew F. Kennelly, Cotsirilos, Stephenson, Tighe & Streicker, Chicago, IL, for defendants-appellees Kevin Clark, Michelle Clark, Robert Bok, Diane Bok.

Before ESCHBACH, KANNE, and ROVNER, Circuit Judges.

Rehearing and Suggestions for Rehearing In Banc Denied October 31, 1995.

KANNE, Circuit Judge.

Whirlpool Financial Corporation filed this securities action on July 11, 1994, against GN Holdings, Inc., W.R. Grace & Co.-Connecticut, Kevin and Michelle Clark, and Robert and Diane Bok seeking rescission of Whirlpool's

$10 million loan to GN. In its complaint, Whirlpool alleged: (Count 1) violation of Section 10(b) of the Securities Exchange Act of 1934 and Rule 10b-5 thereunder; (Count 2) violation of Section 13 of the Illinois Securities Law of 1953; and (Count 3) violation of Section 12(2) of the Securities Act of 1933. In response to a motion filed by the defendants pursuant to Fed.R.Civ.P. 12(b)(6), the district court dismissed Whirlpool's federal claims with prejudice because they were filed beyond their respective statutes of limitation. The court also dismissed the state claim without prejudice. The end result was that the action was dismissed in its entirety. For our review of the district court's Rule 12(b)(6) dismissal of this action, we summarize and take as true the facts alleged by Whirlpool in its complaint and supporting documents.

In July 1991, Whirlpool Financial Corporation made a $10 million loan to GN Holdings, Inc., to partially finance GN's purchase of Cross Country Healthcare Personnel, Inc. ("CCHP"). CCHP provided hospitals across the United States with temporary health care personnel such as nurses, physical therapists, and occupational therapists. GN, which W.R. Grace had created as the vehicle through which it would purchase CCHP, executed a promissory note in favor of Whirlpool for the loan. Under the terms of the note, Whirlpool was to receive 15.5% annual interest (payable in quarterly installments) with a balloon payment of the principal in 1998. GN also borrowed $44.8 million from Heller Financial, Inc., and W.R. Grace invested $25.2 million through the purchase of stock.

To solicit financing for the purchase, the defendants, with the help of Shearson Lehman Brothers, circulated a Private Placement Memorandum, which provided narrative information,[1] historical financial data, and projections for future performance. These projections were later, before Whirlpool purchased the note, "revised and made significantly less optimistic." The Private Placement Memorandum and the subsequent amendment set out projections for, among other things, net sales, operating profit, pretax profit and net income during the remainder of 1991 and fiscal years 1992 and 1993. To allow Whirlpool to monitor GN's performance, the loan agreement required GN to send to Whirlpool monthly, quarterly, and yearly financial statements accompanied by management reports. GN complied with these requirements and Whirlpool received the financial statements as scheduled.

---

[1]The Private Placement Memorandum included several optimistic and self-laudatory statements, such as describing CCHP as "the largest, most respected and most imitated firm in the travel nurse industry"; stating that the travel nurse industry was "one of the 25 hottest careers for the 1990s"; and citing "one industry expert" as estimating "the size of the industry at approximately $350 million in 1990 and growing in excess of 20% per year."

As often happens with new ventures, the projections painted a much rosier picture than what actually unfolded. In fact, in the years 1991 through 1993, net sales were 32 to 48% lower than projected, operating profit was 50 to 73% lower than projected, pretax profit was 95 to 257% lower than projected, and net income was 104 to 283% lower than projected. On September 12, 1991, shortly after receiving the first financial statement, Whirlpool account executive Steven Furman first traveled to Boca Raton, Florida (GN's headquarters) to question GN executives about the discrepancies between the financial projections and actual performance. Furman made similar trips on February 5, 1992; July 24, 1992; October 16, 1992; and June 23, 1993. At these meetings, GN executives explained that the general economic recession was softening the demand for traveling nurse services but that better times were just around the corner. Happy days did not arrive, and GN defaulted on the interest payment due Whirlpool on April 1, 1994. Whirlpool filed this suit in July of 1994.

We review de novo the district court's Rule 12(b)(6) dismissal of this action and take, as we have, Whirlpool's factual allegations as true, giving Whirlpool the benefit of all reasonable inferences drawn therefrom. Murphy v. Walker, 51 F.3d 714, 717 (7th Cir. 1995). However, as we have observed in the context of securities litigation, if a plaintiff pleads facts that show its suit barred by a statute of limitations, it may plead itself out of court under a Rule 12(b)(6) analysis. Tregenza v. Great Am. Communications Co., 12 F.3d 717, 718-19 (7th Cir. 1993), cert. denied, ___ U.S. ___, 114 S.Ct. 1837, 128 L.Ed.2d 465 (1994).

Before reviewing the dismissal of its action for failing to meet the statutes of limitation for Rule 10b-5 and Section 12(2), we make note of the major thrust of Whirlpool's complaint. Whirlpool's brief summarizes what it views as the highly significant factual underpinnings as follows:

> The Revised Projections were unreasonable when made because they were based on GN's historical performance while defendants knew, but did not disclose, that the industry was subject to material adverse trends including proposed and enacted state and federal legislative and regulatory actions which would limit GN's revenue, increased competition to recruit nurses, trends toward reduced usage of temporary nurses, trends toward increased compensation and benefits for traveling nurses, shifts from inpatient to ambulatory care and trends toward hospital closings and a decrease in licensed beds.

(Whirlpool brief at 8) (emphasis added). The highlighted portion of the foregoing quote could be read to mean that Whirlpool asserts that the defendants had a duty to disclose this information—apart from a duty to make reasonable projections.

If the failure to disclose the above information formed the sole basis for Whirlpool's Rule 10b-5 claim, the matter would be at an end. The information Whirlpool states that the defendants failed to disclose is widely available public information and, therefore, by definition is available to any and all who take the time to discover it.

For example, Whirlpool says that the defendants failed to disclose the existence of state and federal legislation and regulations which exemplified a negative trend that affected the viability of GN's projections. Specifically, Whirlpool in its complaint cites legislation adopted prior to 1991 in California, Connecticut, Florida, Massachusetts, New Jersey, and New York regulating the fees charged by traveling nurse agencies, as well as attempts to take similar action in Kentucky, Louisiana, Michigan, and Rhode Island. Moreover, the information regarding adverse industry trends, which Whirlpool alleges defendants failed to disclose, is public information and was available at the time Whirlpool purchased the note. See, e.g., Emily Friedman, Nursing: Breaking the Bonds?, 264 JAMA 3117 (1990) ("In spite of nursing's historic ability to beat the odds and its recent record of accomplishment and growing power, the profession's future is uncertain. It is, like most of health care, facing restricted funding, work force shortages, rationing, and political upheavals.")

The nondisclosure of enacted or pending legislation and industry-wide trends is not a basis for a securities fraud claim. See Wielgos v. Commonwealth Edison Co., 892 F.2d 509, 515 (7th Cir. 1989) ("Securities laws require issuers to disclose firm-specific information; investors and analysts combine that information with knowledge about the competition, regulatory conditions, and the economy as a whole to produce a value for stock."); Acme Propane, Inc. v. Tenexco, Inc., 844 F.2d 1317, 1323-24 (7th Cir. 1988) ("The securities laws require the disclosure of information that is otherwise not in the public domain. Sellers of securities need not 'disclose' the statutes at large of the states in which they operate. . . .") (citation omitted).

However, we discern that it is not the failure of the defendants to disclose adverse legislation and industry trends that forms the basis of Whirlpool's Rule 10b-5 claim. Rather the thrust of its argument is that the defendants' revised projections were made without a reasonable basis. In other words, there was no reasonable basis for the defendants' revised projections in light of the adverse legislative, regulatory, and industry trends known to them. Such a Rule 10b-5 claim based on projections made in bad faith or without a reasonable basis is cognizable under the securities laws. Stransky v. Cummins Engine Co., Inc., 51 F.3d 1329, 1333 (7th Cir. 1995). With this clarification of the appropriate nature of Whirlpool's claim, we examine the district court's rationale for the dismissal of Whirlpool's action—its failure to comply with the applicable statutes of limitation.

As alluded to above, in both Section 12(2)[2] and Rule 10b-5 actions, a plaintiff must file its claim for relief within one year from the time that its action accrues. 15 U.S.C. §§ 77m, 78i(e); see Lampf, Pleva, Lipkind, Prupis & Petigrow v. Gilbertson, 501 U.S. 350, 361-62, 111 S.Ct. 2773, 2781, 115 L.Ed.2d 321 (1991). Moreover, inquiry notice is sufficient to begin the limitations clock. See 15 U.S.C. § 77m; Tregenza, 12 F.3d at 722. Inquiry notice starts the running of the statute of limitations "when the victim of the alleged fraud became aware of facts that would have led a reasonable person to investigate whether he might have a claim." Id. at 718. Thus, to determine if inquiry notice has been triggered an objective "reasonable" diligence standard must be applied to the facts.

The defendants argue that, assuming they committed any fraud, reasonable diligence by Whirlpool would have suggested the possibility of fraud before July 11, 1993 (one year prior to the date Whirlpool filed its complaint). They point to the dramatic discrepancies (Whirlpool's own description) between the projections and the actual results, which the defendants argue would have led a reasonable investor to suspect fraud.

In Tregenza, Great American Communications Company, with the help of Shearson Lehman Brothers, sold several million shares of common stock to the public in order to retire debt it incurred from purchasing Taft Broadcasting Company for $1.5 billion. Potential purchasers were told "that the stock was greatly undervalued and within two years its price should be well above $20 [and] that the stock's downside risk at its current price level of $12 to $12.50 was less than 10 percent." Tregenza, 12 F.3d at 719-20. Within one year, the price of the stock had fallen to $1.50. The complaint alleged that at the time of these statements the stock was grossly overvalued and the downside risk was immense because Great American was so debt ridden. We held that the precipitous fall in the price of Great American's stock was sufficient to put the plaintiffs on inquiry notice. We reasoned that "an investor would have become suspicious and investigated when Lehman's emphatic and precise prediction was so swiftly and dramatically falsified." Id. at 720.

Likewise, in this case, the dramatic discrepancies between the very precise projections made by the defendants and the actual results, which Whirlpool learned through the financial statements, were sufficient to give notice to Whirlpool and spur them to investigate—inquiry notice which

---

[2]After the district court dismissed Whirlpool's complaint, the Supreme Court held that a "prospectus" for § 12(2) purposes includes only public offerings by issuers or their controlling shareholders. Gustafson v. Alloyd Co., ___ U.S. ___, ___, 115 S.Ct. 1061, 1073-1074, 131 L.Ed.2d 1 (1995). As this case does not concern a public offering, § 12(2) is inapplicable, and this serves as an alternative ground for affirming the district court's dismissal of Whirlpool's § 12(2) claim.

started the limitations clock.[3] This is not to say that the discrepancies proved fraud, but simply that a reasonable investor would have believed that fraud was a possible explanation.

Moreover, once the significant discrepancies between the projections and actual results placed Whirlpool on notice regarding the possibility of fraud, the information Whirlpool says it needed to "uncover" the alleged fraud was in the public domain. In today's society, with the advent of the "information superhighway," federal and state legislation and regulations, as well as information regarding industry trends, are easily accessed. A reasonable investor is presumed to have information available in the public domain, and therefore Whirlpool is imputed with constructive knowledge of this information. See Eckstein v. Balcor Film Investors, 58 F.3d 1162, 1169 (7th Cir. 1995).

When examined consistent with an objective reasonable diligence standard, the only reasonable inference that could be drawn from the facts as alleged by Whirlpool was that it was put on inquiry notice before July 11, 1993. Thus, the district court properly determined that Whirlpool's federal claims, not asserted until its complaint was filed on July 11, 1994, were time barred.

Whirlpool finally argues that even if it were put on inquiry notice before July 11, 1993, the defendants should be equitably estopped from arguing the statute of limitations because they "lulled" Whirlpool into missing the statute of limitations. Whirlpool contends that the explanations Furman received for GN's poor performance—primarily the general economic recession—concealed the defendants' alleged fraud. Equitable estoppel may apply where a defendant took active steps to conceal evidence from the plaintiff that the plaintiff needed in order to determine it had a claim. Singletary v. Continental Ill. Nat'l Bank, 9 F.3d 1236, 1241 (7th Cir. 1993). However, in light of our determination that the information Whirlpool needed to uncover the fraud was in the public domain, GN's continued attempts to explain away the discrepancies between the revised projections and the actual earnings could not have prevented Whirlpool from filing its complaint on time.

AFFIRMED.

---

[3]Whirlpool maintains that the limitations clock should not have run because, notwithstanding its investigation of the discrepancies (Furman's trips to Boca Raton), it could not uncover the fraud. In essence, Whirlpool is arguing that the statute of limitations should be equitably tolled—in spite of reasonable diligence, it could not discover the facts underlying the defendants' fraud. See Tregenza, 12 F.3d at 721. However, as we noted in Tregenza, the plain import of the Supreme Court's decision in Lampf, Pleva, Lipkind, Prupis & Petigrow v. Gilbertson, 501 U.S. 350, 111 S.Ct. 2773, 115 L.Ed.2d 321 (1991), is that "when knowledge or notice is required to start the statute of limitations running, there is no room for equitable tolling." Tregenza, 12 F.3d at 721. Therefore, consistent with our determination that Whirlpool was on notice of the facts that would have led a reasonable person to investigate whether he had a claim, the one-year statute of limitations was not subject to equitable tolling.

Appendix D: Case Study 4

76 F.Supp.2d 773 St. Clair v. Johnny's Oyster & Shrimp, Inc.,
> S.D.Tex.
> F.Supp.2d
> 76 F.Supp.2d 773
> 2000 A.M.C. 769, 53 Fed. R. Evid. Serv. 1
> United States District Court, S.D. Texas, Galveston Division.
> Teddy ST. CLAIR, Plaintiff,
> v. JOHNNY'S OYSTER & SHRIMP, INC., Defendant. No. Civ.A. G-99-594.
December 17, 1999.

Seaman brought action for personal injuries sustained aboard a vessel. Upon defendant's motion to dismiss, the District Court, Kent, J., held that information taken off the internet was insufficient to establish that defendant was owner of vessel aboard which seaman sustained an injury.

Motion conditionally denied.

774

Kenneth Ross Citti, Citti & Crinion, Houston, TX, for Ross Citti, mediator.

Paul G. Ash, Jr, Attorney at Law, Galveston, TX, David Alan Slaughter, Attorney at Law, Houston, TX, for Teddy St. Clair, plaintiff.

James Richard Watkins, Royston Rayzor et al, Galveston, TX, Marc H. Schneider, Waldron Schneider et al, Houston, TX, for Johnny's Oyster & Shrimp, Inc., defendant.

James Richard Watkins, Royston Rayzor et al, Galveston, TX, Marc H. Schneider, Waldron Schneider et al, Houston, TX, for Shrimps R US, Inc., defendant.

ORDER DENYING DEFENDANT'S MOTION TO DISMISS

KENT, District Judge.

Plaintiff St. Clair brings claims for personal injuries allegedly sustained while employed as a seaman for Defendant Johnny's Oyster & Shrimp, Inc. aboard the vessel CAPT. LE'BRADO. Now before the Court is Defendant's Motion to Dismiss. For the reasons stated below, Defendant's Motion is conditionally DENIED for the time being.

The Federal Rules of Civil Procedure authorize a court, upon suitable showing, to dismiss any action or any claim within an action for failure to state a claim upon which relief can be granted. See FED.R.CIV.P. 12(b)(6). When considering a motion to dismiss, the Court accepts as true all well-pleaded allegations in the complaint, and views them in a light most favorable to the plaintiff. See *Malina v. Gonzales*, 994 F.2d 1121, 1125 (5th

Cir.1993). Unlike a motion for summary judgment, a motion to dismiss should be granted only when it appears without a doubt that the plaintiff can prove no set of facts in support of her claims that would entitle her to relief. See *Conley v. Gibson*, 355 U.S. 41, 45-46, 78 S.Ct. 99, 102, 2 L.Ed.2d 80 (1957); Tuchman v. DSC Communications Corp., 14 F.3d 1061, 1067 (5th Cir.1994).

The basis for Defendant's Motion to Dismiss surrounds the ownership of CAPT. LE'BRADO at the time of Plaintiff's accident, which occurred on August 26, 1999. Defendant alleges that it "does not now, and did not at the time the alleged incident own or operate the vessel CAPT. LE'BRADO." Def.'s Am. Mot. to Dismiss at 1. Defendant notes that on July 1, 1999, ownership was transferred to Oysters R Us, Inc., and on August 1, 1999, Oysters R Us, Inc. transferred ownership of the vessel to Shrimps R Us, Inc. Therefore, because Defendant is not the owner of the vessel, it seeks dismissal under FED.R.CIV.P. 12(b)(6). Plaintiff responds that he has discovered "evidence"—taken off the Worldwide Web on December 1, 1999—revealing that Defendant does "in fact" own CAPT. LE'BRADO. See Pl.'s Resp. to Def.'s Am. Mot. to Dismiss Ex. A at 1-2 (citing data from the United States Coast Guard's on-line vessel data base).

Plaintiff's electronic "evidence" is totally insufficient to withstand Defendant's Motion to Dismiss. While some look to the Internet as an innovative vehicle for communication, the Court continues to warily and wearily view it largely as one large catalyst for rumor, innuendo, and misinformation. So as to not mince words, the Court reiterates that this so-called Web provides no way of verifying the authenticity of the alleged contentions that Plaintiff wishes to rely upon in his Response to Defendant's Motion. There is no way Plaintiff can overcome the presumption that the information he discovered on the Internet is inherently untrustworthy.

775

Anyone can put anything on the Internet. No Web site is monitored for accuracy and nothing contained therein is under oath or even subject to independent verification absent underlying documentation. Moreover, the Court holds no illusions that hackers can adulterate the content on any Web site from any location at any time. For these reasons, any evidence procured off the Internet is adequate for almost nothing, even under the most liberal interpretation of the hearsay exception rules found in FED.R.CIV.P. 807.

Instead of relying on the voodoo information taken from the Internet, Plaintiff must hunt for hard copy back-up documentation in admissible form from the United States Coast Guard or discover alternative information verifying what Plaintiff alleges. Accordingly, Plaintiff has until February 1, 2000 to garner legitimate documents showing that Defendant owns the CAPT. LE'BRADO. If Plaintiff cannot provide the Court with credible, legitimate information supporting its position by February 1, 2000, the Court will be inclined to grant Defendant dispositive relief.

IT IS SO ORDERED.

Appendix E: Case Study 5

829 N.E.2d 52 Munster v. Groce
FOR PUBLICATION

ATTORNEYS FOR APPELLANT:
THOMAS D. BLACKBURN
Blackburn & Green
Fort Wayne, Indiana

KARL L. MULVANEY
NANA QUAY-SMITH
CANDACE L. SAGE
Bingham McHale, LLP
Indianapolis, Indiana

ATTORNEY FOR APPELLEES:
MICHAEL D. CONNER
Spitzer Herriman Stephenson
Holderead Musser & Conner, LLP
Marion, Indiana

IN THE
COURT OF APPEALS OF INDIANA

DAVID MUNSTER,	)	
	)	
Appellant-Plaintiff,	)	
	)	
vs.	)	No. 18A02-0409-CV-738
	)	
JOE GROCE and	)	
BUSINESS WORLD, INC.,	)	
	)	
Appellees-Defendants.	)	

APPEAL FROM THE DELAWARE CIRCUIT COURT
The Honorable Marianne L. Vorhees, Judge
Cause No. 18C01-0401-CT-1

June 8, 2005
OPINION—FOR PUBLICATION

BARNES, Judge

Case Summary

David Munster appeals the dismissal of his complaint against Joe Groce and
Business World, Inc. ("BWI"). We affirm in part, reverse in part, and remand.

Issues

The restated issues before us are:
I. whether Munster properly effected service of process on Groce; and
II. whether Munster properly effected service of process on BWI.

Facts

On February 25, 2000, Munster and Groce were involved in an automobile accident. At the time, Groce was an employee of BWI, a corporation that later was dissolved in July 2001. On February 15, 2002, Munster filed a complaint against Groce and BWI. Munster attempted to serve both Groce and BWI by certified mail. Both mailings were returned undelivered on March 1, 2002; the mailing to Groce was marked "attempted not known" and the mailing to BWI was marked with a new address. App. p. 2.

No further action was taken in the case until December 2003, when Munster obtained new counsel. Second attempts to serve BWI and Groce by certified mail were again returned undelivered, with the marking on each "forwarding order expired." *Id.* Munster then attempted to serve BWI and Groce through the Indiana Secretary of State, as provided by Indiana Trial Rule 4.10. Munster did not file a praecipe for summons with the trial court, but instead delivered copies of the summons and complaint directly to the Secretary of State. Munster provided the Secretary of State with addresses for BWI and Groce, the Secretary of State mailed copies of the summons and complaint to those addresses, and they were returned undelivered as before.

At least by December 2003, BWI's former insurer learned of Munster's lawsuit and filed an answer on behalf of BWI and Groce, which among other things asserted the affirmative defenses of lack of personal jurisdiction, insufficiency of process, and insufficiency of service of process. On January 22, 2004, counsel also filed a motion to dismiss on behalf of BWI and Groce under Indiana Trial Rules 12(B)(2), (4), and (5), alleging a lack of personal jurisdiction due to insufficiency of process and service of process. The motion also sought dismissal due to failure to prosecute pursuant to Indiana Trial Rule 41(E).

On January 26, 2004, Steve Harris, an investigator hired by Munster's counsel, delivered a copy of the summons and complaint to the residence of George Mikesell, who was listed as a director of BWI in its articles of incorporation. Mikesell was not home at the time, but his wife Lois personally received the summons and complaint. Harris phoned Mikesell the next day and confirmed that he received the summons and complaint. Also on January 26 and January 31, 2004, Harris attempted personal delivery of the summons and complaint at Groce's alleged former places of residence and employment, but could not locate him.

On May 17, 2004, the trial court dismissed Munster's complaint pursuant to Trial Rules 12(B)(2), (4), and (5); it did not dismiss under Trial Rule 41(E). It stated in its order that Munster had not complied with Trial Rule 4.10 allowing for service through the Secretary of State because he had not filed a praecipe for summons with the trial court first. As for the January 26, 2004 delivery of the summons and complaint to Lois Mike-sell, the trial court struck the acknowledgment of service she had signed and concluded that she had no actual or apparent authority to accept service on BWI's behalf.

On June 14, 2004, Munster filed a motion to correct error. On the same date, Munster also filed, with the trial court this time, a praecipe for summons for service upon BWI and Groce through the Secretary of State. Using the same addresses as before, the Secretary of State again sent certified mail addressed to BWI and Groce, and the mailings again were returned undelivered. On August 24, 2004, the trial court denied the motion to correct error. Munster now appeals.

Analysis

I. Standard of Review

Technically, Munster is appealing from the denial of a motion to correct error. We generally review a trial court's denial of a motion to correct error for an abuse of discretion. *Principal Life Ins. Co. v. Needler*, 816 N.E.2d 499, 502 (Ind. Ct. App. 2004). Except for pointing out Munster's reattempt to effect service through the Secretary of State, however, the motion to correct error in this case merely asked the trial court to reconsider its earlier ruling on the motion to dismiss.

BWI and Groce have not claimed that they lacked insufficient contacts with Indiana for the trial court to exercise jurisdiction over them and base their arguments solely on insufficient service of process. Indiana Trial Rule 12(B)(5) allows for dismissal of a complaint if there is insufficient service of process; Trial Rule 12(B)(2) similarly allows for a dismissal of a complaint if there is a lack of personal jurisdiction. A trial court does not acquire personal jurisdiction over a party if service of process is inadequate. *King v. United Leasing, Inc.*, 765 N.E.2d 1287, 1290 (Ind. Ct. App. 2002).

When a defendant argues a lack of personal jurisdiction, the plaintiff must present evidence to show that there is personal jurisdiction over the defendant. *Anthem Ins. Companies, Inc. v. Tenet Healthcare Corp.*, 730 N.E.2d 1227, 1231 (Ind. 2000). The defendant ultimately bears the burden of proving the lack of personal jurisdiction by a preponderance of the evidence, unless the lack of jurisdiction is apparent on the face of the complaint. *Id.* The existence of personal jurisdiction over a defendant is a question of law and a constitutional requirement to rendering a valid judgment, mandated by the Due Process Clause of the Fourteenth Amendment to the United

States Constitution. *Id.* at 1237. Thus, we review a trial court's determination regarding personal jurisdiction de novo. *Id.* at 1238. To the extent a trial court may make findings of jurisdictional facts, these findings are reviewed for clear error if they were based on in-court testimony. *Id.* at 1238. If, however, only a paper record has been presented to the trial court, we are in as good a position as the trial court to determine the existence of jurisdictional facts and will employ de novo review as to those facts. *Id.* at n.12.

Here, the trial court ruled on the motion to dismiss based entirely on a paper record, consisting of records of Munster's attempts at service and affidavits of Harris and Lois Mikesell. No testimony was presented at the hearings conducted on the motion to dismiss and motion to correct error. Thus, our review of the trial court's personal jurisdiction ruling is entirely de novo. Additionally, we note that although the trial court in dismissing Munster's complaint provided an explanation as to why it was doing so, we will affirm a trial court's grant of a motion to dismiss if it is sustainable on any theory or basis found in the record. See *Minks v. Pina*, 709 N.E.2d 379, 381 (Ind. Ct. App. 1999), *trans. denied.*

II. Service as to Groce

Groce argues that Munster's attempts to serve him with process were insufficient to permit the trial court to exercise jurisdiction over him.[1] This question has two aspects: whether there was compliance with the Indiana Trial Rules regarding service, and whether such attempts at service comported with the Due Process Clause of the Fourteenth Amendment. We conclude that due process required more than was attempted here with respect to service on Groce.

In the seminal case regarding due process and notice, the Supreme Court held that the Due Process Clause requires at a minimum "that deprivation of life, liberty or property by adjudication be preceded by notice and opportunity for hearing appropriate to the nature of the case." *Mullane v. Central Hanover Bank & Trust Co.*, 339 U.S. 306, 313, 70 S. Ct. 652, 656-57 (1950). "This right to be heard has little reality or worth unless one is informed that the matter is pending and can choose for himself whether to appear or default, acquiesce or contest." *Id.* at 314, 70 S. Ct. at 657. "An elementary and fundamental requirement of due process in any proceeding which is to be accorded finality is notice reasonably calculated, under all the circumstances, to apprise interested parties of the pendency of the action and afford

---

[1]For the sake of clarity, we are referring to Groce as if he has actual knowledge of and has participated in this lawsuit. In fact, there is no indication in the record that he personally has any knowledge of it. Likewise, although we refer to BWI throughout the opinion, it no longer exists as a functioning company.

them an opportunity to present their objections." *Id.* "[W]hen notice is a person's due, process which is a mere gesture is not due process. The means employed must be such as one desirous of actually informing the absentee might reasonably adopt to accomplish it." *Id.* at 315, 70 S. Ct. at 657. The Court held that alternatives to personal service and actual notice of a suit, such as publication, are permissible

> where it is not reasonably possible or practicable to give more adequate warning. Thus it has been recognized that, in the case of persons missing or unknown, employment of an indirect and even a probably futile means of notification is all that the situation permits and creates no constitutional bar to a final decree foreclosing their rights. . . . [Parties] whose interests or whereabouts could not *with due diligence* be ascertained come clearly within this category.

Id. at 317, 70 S. Ct. at 658-59 (emphasis added). *Mullane* thus clearly indicates that although it is acceptable in some instances to proceed with a lawsuit by using a service method that it is unlikely to give actual notice to an interested party, this is only the case if that party's whereabouts cannot reasonably, and in the exercise of due diligence, be ascertained.

The textbook example of constructive service and notice of a lawsuit is service by publication, as exemplified by *Mullane*. Indiana Trial Rule 4.13 allows the use of this form of "service" or notice, but only if the party seeking publication files with the trial court "supporting affidavits [showing] that diligent search has been made that the defendant cannot be found, has concealed his whereabouts, or has left the state." This rule, therefore, preemptively requires a party to swear to "due diligence" in attempting to locate an interested party before he or she may seek service by publication.

In the present case, Munster never sought service by publication on Groce. Instead, before turning to the Secretary of State, the CCS indicates that he attempted two certified mailings to Groce, once in February 2002 and once in December 2003. The first mailing was to an apartment address in Muncie, and there is no evidence in the record as to what address was used for the second mailing; the address provided to the Secretary of State was for a street address in Muncie. There is also no evidence in the record as to what information was used to determine Groce's possible whereabouts. In any event, none of these mailings resulted in actual service to Groce, as both mailings were returned to sender. This court has held, "Unclaimed service is insufficient to establish a reasonable probability that the defendant received adequate notice and to confer personal jurisdiction." *King*, 765 N.E.2d at 1290. We have also held, "Service upon a defendant's former residence is insufficient to confer personal jurisdiction." *Mills v. Coil*, 647 N.E.2d 679, 681 (Ind. Ct. App. 1995), *trans. denied.* Additionally, Indiana Trial Rule

4.1(A)(1), which allows for service by certified mail, requires that a return receipt must show receipt of the letter in order for service to be effective.

After the December 2003 failed mailing to Groce, Munster attempted to perfect service through the Secretary of State. Indiana Trial Rule 4.4(A)(2) states:

> Any person or organization that is a nonresident of this state, a resident of this state who has left the state, or a person whose residence is unknown, submits to the jurisdiction of the courts of this state as to any action arising from the following acts committed by him or her or his or her agent: . . . causing personal injury or property damage by an act or omission done within this state. . . .

Trial Rule 4.4(B) goes on to state:

> A person subject to the jurisdiction of the courts of this state under this rule may be served with summons:
>
> (1) As provided by Rules 4.1 (service on individuals), 4.5 (service upon resident who cannot be found or served within the state), 4.6 (service upon organizations), 4.9 (in rem actions); or
> (2) The person shall be deemed to have appointed the Secretary of State as his agent upon whom service of summons may be made as provided in Rule 4.10.

Finally, Trial Rule 4.10 provides:

> Whenever, under these rules or any statute, service is made upon the Secretary of State or any other governmental organization or officer, as agent for the person being served, service may be made upon such agent as provided in this rule.
>
> (1) The person seeking service or his attorney shall:
>   (a) submit his request for service upon the agent in the praecipe for summons, and state that the governmental organization or officer is the agent of the person being served;
>   (b) state the address of the person being served as filed and recorded pursuant to a statute or valid agreement, or if no such address is known, then his last known mailing address, and, if no such address is known, then such shall be stated;
>   (c) pay any fee prescribed by statute to be forwarded together with sufficient copies of the summons, affidavit and complaint, to the agent by the clerk of the court.
>
> (2) Upon receipt thereof the agent shall promptly:
>   (a) send to the person being served a copy of the summons and complaint by registered or certified mail or by other public means by which a written acknowledgment of receipt may be obtained;
>   (b) complete and deliver to the clerk an affidavit showing the date of the mailing, or if there was no mailing, the reason therefor;

    (c) send to the clerk a copy of the return receipt along with a copy of
        the summons;

    (d) file and retain a copy of the return receipt.

Initially, the parties spent much time arguing as to whether Rule 4.10 required Munster to file a praecipe for summons with the trial court, instead of directly with the Secretary of State, before service could be effected under this rule; the trial court also based its ruling on Munster's not first filing a praceipe for summons with it. It would appear to us that the rule contemplates filing the praecipe with the trial court, which would then forward the necessary materials to the Secretary of State for service. Most tellingly, subsection 1(c) of the rule requires the person seeking service to "pay any fee prescribed by statute to be forwarded together with sufficient copies of the summons, affidavit and complaint, to the agent *by the clerk of the court*." (Emphasis added.) This seems to say that the clerk of court forwards the summons, affidavit, complaint, and any required fee to the Secretary of State or other government officer, which necessarily means the clerk was provided with those materials in the first place by the party seeking service. We also reject Munster's argument that a party seeking service through the Secretary of State does not have to follow Rule 4.10 to the letter. Subsection (1) clearly states that the party seeking such service "shall" do so as delineated.

Even assuming, however, that it was not fatal to Munster's service attempt that he initially filed a praecipe for summons directly with the Secretary of State instead of with the trial court, there is a fundamental problem in this case. It is evident that attempting to serve Groce through the Secretary of State would, at best, amount only to constructive service and constructive notice of the pending lawsuit. Munster had already twice attempted to mail summons to Groce unsuccessfully. Having the Secretary of State make the mailing instead was not going to somehow give Groce actual notice of the lawsuit.

As noted, the Due Process Clause requires that in order for constructive notice of a lawsuit to be sufficient, a party must exercise due diligence in attempting to locate a litigant's whereabouts. See *Mullane*, 339 U.S. at 317, 70 S. Ct. at 659. A party must provide "notice reasonably calculated, under all the circumstances, to apprise interested parties of the pendency of the action and afford them an opportunity to present their objections." *Id.* at 314, 70 S. Ct. at 657. Rule 4.4(B)(2) does allow for service through the Secretary of State with respect to a defendant "whose residence is unknown," and presumably such service is effective even if the defendant does not receive actual notice of the lawsuit; Rule 4.10 does not expressly require actual notice. We conclude, however, that in order for such service to be constitutionally effective there must be a showing by the plaintiff or party who sought such service that due diligence to ascertain the defendant's current whereabouts was exercised and service through the Secretary of State was reasonable under the circumstances.

We are also aware that neither Rule 4.4(B)(2) nor Rule 4.10 requires a party seeking service through the Secretary of State to provide an affidavit asserting that due diligence to locate the defendant was unsuccessfully attempted, in contrast to service by publication under Rule 4.13. If such service is subsequently challenged by a motion to dismiss or motion to set aside a default judgment, however, we conclude that a plaintiff is required to present evidence of unsuccessful due diligence in locating the defendant, which in turn necessitated the use of constructive notice and service. Otherwise, parties who wished to serve opposing parties whose whereabouts they did not know could always sidestep the due diligence requirements of notice by publication and simply ask for service through the Secretary of State, which is not a proper reading of the Indiana Trial Rules and the Due Process Clause.

With issues as important as due process, notice of a lawsuit, and personal jurisdiction, we will not presume from the scant evidence in this record that Munster used due diligence in attempting to ascertain Groce's current whereabouts. Harris provided the following affidavit describing his efforts to serve Groce: "I duly pursued and exhausted all known information to perfect service upon Joe Groce by attempting to deliver to his possession a true copy of the Summons and Complaint in the above-captioned manner at his former places of residence and employment." App. p. 46. Harris also swore elsewhere that he asked the Mikesells if they were aware of Groce's *current* whereabouts. There is no evidence in the record as to what information was used to ascertain Groce's alleged former places of residence and employment. There is no evidence in the record as to any attempts to locate his current whereabouts, aside from asking the Mikesells.[2] There is no evidence in the record that Groce was or is attempting to hide his whereabouts.

Harris' bare-bones affidavit does not permit the conclusion that due diligence was used to locate Groce's current whereabouts, or that service via the Secretary of State, using an address that apparently was known to be invalid, was reasonably calculated to provide Groce notice of this lawsuit. *Cf. Bays v. Bays*, 489 N.E.2d 555, 557-59 (Ind. Ct. App. 1986) (finding sufficient due diligence to justify service by publication where a husband had spoken

---

[2]At the hearing on the motion to dismiss, counsel for Munster asserted that other steps were taken to ascertain Groce's whereabouts that were not recounted in Harris' affidavit. Arguments of counsel, however, are not evidence that courts may consider in making factual determinations. *El v. Beard*, 795 N.E.2d 462, 467 (Ind. Ct. App. 2003).

to his wife's parents eleven times in three years and her parents stated they did not know his wife's whereabouts, and where husband employed private investigator who searched for wife for three years and provided letter to trial court detailing efforts to locate wife).[3] As such, the trial court never obtained personal jurisdiction over Groce in a manner consistent with the Due Process Clause. Dismissal of Munster's lawsuit as to him for lack of personal jurisdiction and insufficient service of process was proper.

III. Service as to BWI

Next, we address whether Munster effectively served BWI with process. We decline to address Munster's attempts to serve BWI by certified mail and through the Secretary of State, and solely address service at the Mikesell's household. The question of how to serve a defunct corporation like BWI has not previously been addressed by Indiana case law. The trial rules and Indiana Business Corporation Law, however, provide sufficient guidance for how to resolve this issue.

Indiana Code Section 23-1-45-5(b)(5), which governs voluntary dissolution of a corporation and which apparently is what occurred to BWI, expressly provides that dissolution "does not . . . prevent commencement of a proceeding by or against the corporation in its corporate name. . . ." As far as how to serve a defunct corporation with process, BWI points out that subsection (7) of Section 23-1-45-5(b) provides that the authority of the registered agent of a corporation does not terminate with the corporation's dissolution. BWI also notes that Indiana Code Section 23-1-24-4(a) states, "A corporation's registered agent is the corporation's agent for service of process, notice, or demand required or permitted by law to be served on the corporation." BWI essentially argues that pursuant to this statute, Munster was required to attempt to serve BWI's registered agent, Robert Compton, instead of Mikesell, and such attempt never occurred.

Subsection (c) of Section 23-1-24-4, however, plainly states, "This section does not prescribe the only means, or necessarily the required means, of serving a corporation." The Official Comment to this statutory provision of the Indiana Business Corporation Law confirms that methods of service permitted by the Indiana Trial Rules, but not expressly mentioned by Section 23-1-24-4, should be viewed as supplementary to the statute, not

---

[3]*Bays* does not necessarily establish the minimum that should be required for a showing of due diligence in locating a missing litigant. We do note that there is no evidence in this case of a public records or Internet search for Groce or the use of a skip-trace service to find him. In fact, we discovered, upon entering "Joe Groce Indiana" into the Google™ search engine, an address for Groce that differed from either address used in this case, as well as an apparent obituary for Groce's mother that listed numerous surviving relatives who might have known his whereabouts.

inconsistent with it. The Official Comment further cites *Burger Man, Inc. v. Jordan Paper Products, Inc.*, 170 Ind. App. 295, 352 N.E.2d 821 (1976) as an "illustrative" case where this court approved service upon a corporation's "executive officer" rather than the corporation's registered agent, much like what happened in this case. The Indiana Trial Rules and the Indiana Business Corporation Law permitted Munster to attempt service upon someone other than BWI's registered agent.

Indiana Trial Rule 4.6(A) provides that service upon a domestic organization may be made "upon an executive officer thereof. . . ." Trial Rule 83 states, " 'Executive officer' of an organization includes the president, vice president, secretary, treasurer, cashier, *director*, chairman of the board of directors or trustees, office manager, plant manager, or subdivision manager, partner, or majority shareholder." (Emphasis added.) Munster provided BWI's 1986 articles of incorporation to the trial court, which listed George Mikesell as one of its three directors. BWI presented no evidence that Mikesell was not still a director of this closely-held corporation at the time of its dissolution in 2001. As the party seeking dismissal of a complaint on personal jurisdiction grounds, we conclude it was BWI's burden to prove by a preponderance of the evidence that Mikesell was not a director of BWI at the time of its dissolution and to demonstrate that the articles of incorporation's listing of directors was not accurate as of 2001. See *Anthem Ins. Companies*, 730 N.E.2d at 1231. Also, although Trial Rules 4.6(A) and 83 are not crystal clear on this point, we also hold that in the case of a dissolved corporation, it is appropriate to serve process upon a former director of the corporation at the time of its dissolution. See *Warren v. Dixon Ranch Co.*, 260 P.2d 741, 743 (Utah 1953) (holding that service upon former director of defunct corporation was effective service upon the corporation under trial rules similar to Indiana's).

We now address whether Mikesell was adequately served so as to confer jurisdiction upon BWI. Trial Rule 4.6(B) provides that service shall be made upon a proper representative of the corporation, as listed by Rule 4.6(A), in a manner provided for service upon individuals elsewhere in the Trial Rules. Rule 4.6(B) also states that generally such service cannot knowingly be made at the person's dwelling house or place of abode. This restriction, however, clearly is inapplicable in the case of a corporation such as BWI that is no longer functioning and, a fortiori, no longer has a business address. We conclude it was proper to attempt service at Mikesell's dwelling house or place of abode.

Next, we address the effect of leaving the summons and complaint with Lois Mikesell at the Mikesell residence. We find it unnecessary to address whether Lois had the authority to accept service of process on behalf of her husband. Even assuming that she did not, Trial Rule 4.1(A)(3) allows for service by leaving a copy of the summons and complaint at a person's dwelling house or usual place of abode. Thus, even if Lois had not personally been handed the summons and complaint by Harris and he had merely left the documents at the house, this would have constituted service upon Mikesell.[4]

We do observe that there is nothing in the record to indicate that a copy of the summons only was subsequently mailed to the Mikesell residence, which is required as a second step in effective service by Trial Rule 4.1(B) when the complaint and summons has been left at a person's dwelling under Trial Rule 4.1(A)(3). This omission is not fatal to Munster's attempt to serve Mikesell and, hence, BWI, in light of Harris' affidavit recounting that he spoke to Mikesell over the phone the day after delivery of the summons and complaint and Mikesell confirmed that he received them. BWI presented no evidence to refute Harris' memory of events. We have previously held that failure to follow-up delivery of a complaint and summons under Trial Rule 4.1(A)(3) with mailing of a summons under Trial Rule 4.1(B) does not constitute ineffective service of process if the subject of the summons does not dispute actually having received the complaint and summons. See *Boczar v. Reuben*, 742 N.E.2d 1010, 1016 (Ind. Ct. App. 2001).

Finally, BWI argues that service upon it via service upon Mikesell was ineffective because the summons was directed only to BWI, not to Mikesell or any other person, such as a "director" or "officer" of BWI. BWI relies upon *Volunteers of America v. Premier Auto*, 755 N.E.2d 656 (Ind. Ct. App. 2001). There, we held that service upon Volunteers of America ("VOA") was ineffective because none of the initial attempts were directed to a person; instead, the summonses were simply addressed to "Volunteers of America." *Id.* at 660. We also held that this defect in service was not saved by Trial Rule 4.15(F), which provides: "No summons or the service thereof shall be set aside or be adjudged insufficient when either is reasonably calculated to inform the person to be served that an action has been instituted against him, the name of the court, and the time within which he is required to respond." *Id.* We additionally noted that the first time Premier sent a garnishment proceeding notice to VOA addressed to the "Highest Ranking Officer" was also the first time a "proper person" for corporate service received notice of the lawsuit and default judgment. *Id.*

Here, the record does seem to indicate that the summons for BWI was addressed only to BWI, and not to any specific individual or title. This case, however, clearly differs from *VOA* because that case concerned mailings to VOA's office that subsequently were never brought to the attention of a high-

---

[4]BWI has never asserted that Harris did not deliver the summons and complaint to Mikesell's dwelling house or usual place of abode.

ranking corporate officer. Here, by contrast, the summons and complaint were delivered directly to Mikesell's residence and he acknowledged receipt of them; there was no chance that the summons and complaint would fail to follow the proper internal corporate channels to a high-ranking officer or director because they were delivered directly to a director. As such, even if there was a technical defect in the summons to BWI, the method of service by delivery at Mikesell's residence still was reasonably calculated to inform BWI of the pending lawsuit and, in fact, did provide such notice. Trial Rule 4.15(F) excuses minor, technical defects in the method of service where actual service has been accomplished. See *Reed Sign Service, Inc. v. Reid*, 755 N.E.2d 690, 696 (Ind. Ct. App. 2001), *trans. denied.* In summary, Munster sufficiently complied with the Indiana Trial Rules so as to effect service upon BWI and give the trial court personal jurisdiction over it. Likewise, as we have indicated the method of service on BWI was reasonably calculated so as to provide it with notice of the lawsuit and, therefore, comports with the Due Process Clause. See *Mullane*, 339 U.S. at 314, 70 S. Ct. at 657. We reverse the trial court's grant of the motion to dismiss with respect to BWI.

Conclusion

Munster has failed to demonstrate that his attempts to serve Groce comported with the Due Process Clause and the trial court was correct to dismiss the lawsuit as to Groce for lack of personal jurisdiction. With respect to BWI, we find sufficient compliance with the Indiana Trial Rules and Due Process Clause regarding service of process to allow the lawsuit against it to proceed. We affirm in part, reverse in part, and remand for further proceedings.

Affirmed in part, reversed in part, and remanded.

KIRSCH, C.J., and BAKER, J., concur.

Appendix F: Case Study 6

IN THE DISTRICT COURT OF APPEAL OF THE STATE OF FLORIDA
FOURTH DISTRICT   JANUARY TERM 2005

SONIA DUBOIS and **9060-0677 QUEBEC, INC.,**
d/b/a **AUTOCARS SYMPOSIUM,**

Appellants,

v.

ASHLEY BUTLER, a minor, by and through her mother and natural
guardian **CHRISTINE BUTLER, CHRISTINE BUTLER,** individually, and
JAMES BUTLER, individually, **BTM TRAVEL GROUP, INC.,** and **QUALITY
TRANSPORTATION SERVICES, INC.,**

Appellees.

CASE NOS. 4D04-3559 and 4D04-3561

Opinion filed May 25, 2005

Consolidated appeals of non-final orders from the Circuit Court for the
Seventeenth Judicial Circuit, Broward County; J. Leonard Fleet, Judge; L.T.
Case No. 03-16918(03).

Richard M. Gomez of Law Offices of Roland Gomez, Miami Lakes, for
appellants.

Nancy Little Hoffmann of Nancy Little Hoffmann, P.A., Pompano Beach,
and Timothy P. Beavers of McFann & Beavers, P.A., Fort Lauderdale, for
appellees Ashley Butler, a minor, by and through her mother and natural
guardian, Christine Butler, Christine Butler, individually, and James Butler,
individually.

GROSS, J.

Sonia Dubois and Quebec, Inc., the defendants below, appeal an order
denying their motions to dismiss brought under Florida Rule of Civil Procedure 1.140(b)(2) for lack of jurisdiction over the person due to improper
service. *See* Fla. R. App. P. 9.130(a)(3)(C)(i) (authorizing appeals of non-final
orders that determine "the jurisdiction of the person"). We reverse, holding
that service was defective as to both defendants.

To serve Dubois, the plaintiffs used the substituted service procedures
of section 48.171, Florida Statutes (2003). "Because the statute allowing sub-

stituted service is an exception to the general rule requiring a defendant to be personally served, due process values require *strict compliance* with the statutory requirements." *Monaco v. Nealon*, 810 So. 2d 1084, 1085 (Fla. 4th DCA 2002) (emphasis in original). When using a substituted service statute, "to overcome the primary requirement of personal service, the plaintiff must demonstrate the exercise of due diligence in attempting to locate the defendant." *Wiggam v. Bamford*, 562 So. 2d 389, 391 (Fla. 4th DCA 1990). In *Wiggam*, we indicated what would satisfy the due diligence requirement:

> The test [for determining the sufficiency of substitute service] is not whether it was in fact possible to effect personal service in a given case, but whether the [plaintiff] reasonably employed knowledge at [her] command, made diligent inquiry, and exerted an honest and conscientious effort appropriate to the circumstances, to acquire the information necessary to enable [her] to effect personal service on the defendant.

Id. (quoting *Grammer v. Grammer*, 80 So. 2d 457, 460-61 (Fla. 1955) (quoting *McDaniel v. McElvey*, 108 So. 820, 831 (Fla. 1926))).

Numerous cases involve plaintiffs who fail to exercise "an honest and conscientious effort" to serve a defendant. A common theme of these cases is that the plaintiff fails to follow an "obvious" lead.

For example, in *Robinson v. Cornelius*, 377 So. 2d 776 (Fla. 4th DCA 1979), a plaintiff relied exclusively on an address for the defendant provided by the Department of Motor Vehicles; because the plaintiff did not check the telephone directory or investigate the address disclosed in interrogatories by the defendant's insurer, the court held that the plaintiff failed to exercise due diligence. See also *Cross v. Kalina*, 681 So. 2d 855, 856 (Fla. 5th DCA 1996) (while the plaintiff made an effort to serve the defendant through registered mail, plaintiff had failed to use due diligence: "Here, other than one mailing, there is no evidence that any effort was expended to locate [the defendant]."); *Torelli v. Travelers Indem. Co.*, 495 So. 2d 837 (Fla. 3d DCA 1986) (plaintiff did not demonstrate due diligence in attempting to locate the defendant where he failed to seek information from the defendant's attorney as to his client's whereabouts); *Knabb v. Morris*, 492 So. 2d 839 (Fla. 5th DCA 1986) (plaintiff failed to exercise due diligence when the private investigator, who the plaintiff hired to locate the defendant, failed to utilize obvious and available resources to actually find the defendant).

Here, the record does not demonstrate that the plaintiffs used due diligence to locate Dubois. Other than attempting to serve the defendant at the address listed on a nearly three year-old accident report [the accident happened in December 2000, while the complaint was filed in September 2003], the plaintiffs attested that "attempts were made through information in Canada to obtain a current telephone listing for the correct Sonia Dubois." However, the plaintiffs only tried one method of locating the defendant—calling "Directory Assistance in L'Epiphanie, Quebec, Canada, and request[ing] the telephone number for Sonia Dubois."

While prior case law has not drawn a bright line between efforts that show due diligence in locating a defendant and those that are insufficient, what was done here falls short of "an honest and conscientious effort." *Grammer*, 80 So. 2d at 461. The plaintiffs argue that their attempts were similar to those of the plaintiff in *Bodden v. Young*, 422 So. 2d 1055 (Fla. 4th DCA 1982). In *Bodden*, this court found that a plaintiff had made a good faith effort at serving a defendant where the plaintiff sought to locate a driver through United States Postal authorities, the telephone company, utility company, and other public agencies, and also took discovery from another potential defendant concerning the defendant's whereabouts. The plaintiff in this case utilized only *one* of the five methods used by the plaintiff in *Bodden*. We note that in the 23 years since *Bodden*, advances in modern technology and the widespread use of the Internet have sent the investigative technique of a call to directory assistance the way of the horse and buggy and the eight track stereo.

As to the corporate defendant, Quebec, Inc., the plaintiffs have conceded error. Pursuant to section 48.181, Florida Statutes (2003), the plaintiffs properly served Quebec, Inc. through the Secretary of State. However, the plaintiffs acknowledge that they "did not file a certified mail return receipt of the summons and complaint on Quebec, Inc., or the affidavit of compliance as required by section 48.161(1)."

We therefore reverse the orders denying the motions to dismiss, quash the service of process as to both defendants, and remand to the circuit court where the plaintiffs may seek to perfect proper service.

STEVENSON and SHAHOOD, JJ., concur.

NOT FINAL UNTIL DISPOSITION OF ANY TIMELY FILED MOTION FOR REHEARING.

Appendix G: Case Study 7

STATE OF LOUISIANA

COURT OF APPEAL

FIRST CIRCUIT

NUMBER 2004 CA 2734

MICKEY L. WEATHERLY

VERSUS

OPTIMUM ASSET MANAGEMENT, INC. AND
BARBARA F. B. BROYLES AND STEPHEN BROYLES

Judgment Rendered: December 22, 2005

* * * * * * * * * *

Appealed from the Nineteenth Judicial District Court
in and for the Parish of East Baton Rouge,
State of Louisiana
Suit Number 495,255

Honorable Curtis Calloway, Judge

* * * * * * * * * *

Thomas D. Fazio   Counsel for Plaintiff/Appellee
Baton Rouge, LA   Mickey L. Weatherly

Robert V. McAnelly   Counsel for Defendants/Appellants
Baton Rouge, LA   Stephen E. Broyles and
                         Barbara F. B. Broyles

* * * * * * * * * *

BEFORE: KUHN, GUIDRY, AND PETTIGREW, JJ.

PETTIGREW, J.
    This appeal challenges a trial court's invalidation of a tax sale.
We affirm.

BACKGROUND

Most of the facts forming the basis for this lawsuit to annul a tax sale have been stipulated by the parties, and thus are not in dispute. On March 29, 1988, Dr. Leonard A. Buckner, a dentist, purchased an office condominium on Old Hammond Highway in East Baton Rouge Parish ("the property"). The property was encumbered by a collateral mortgage and collateral mortgage note executed by Dr. Buckner in favor of Baton Rouge Bank and Trust Company. The sale and the mortgage were recorded in the mortgage records for East Baton Rouge Parish. The collateral mortgage and the note were later acquired by Whitney National Bank in its merger with Baton Rouge Bank and Trust Company.

In 1996, Dr. Buckner experienced financial difficulties and contacted an acquaintance, Dr. Mickey Weatherly, a Texas resident with a dental practice there for the past 25 years, for assistance. As an accommodation to Dr. Buckner, Dr. Weatherly agreed to pay off Dr. Buckner's debt to Whitney National Bank and accept an assignment of the bank's security interest in the property in return. On September 13, 1996, Whitney National Bank and Dr. Weatherly executed a document styled "Notarial Endorsement and Assignment of Notes and Other Related Security." Therein, Whitney National Bank assigned its security interest in the property to Dr. Weatherly. The document was recorded on February 20, 1997, in the East Baton Rouge Parish mortgage records. Dr. Weatherly is identified in the document by his name, Mickey L. Weatherly, as the holder of a mortgage on the property by virtue of the assignment. There is no other information pertaining to Dr. Weatherly in the document.

In April of 1997, the East Baton Rouge Parish Sheriff's Office sent two notices of an impending tax sale to Dr. Buckner at the mailing address for the property. Both notices were received and signed for by persons other than Dr. Buckner. The sheriff's office also ran two newspaper advertisements as required by law, the first on May 2, 1997, and the second on June 2, 1997. The sheriff's office did not send notice of the tax bills, tax delinquency, or the impending tax sale to Dr. Weatherly.

On June 27, 1997, the property was sold for nonpayment of 1996 property taxes to Optimum Asset Management, Inc., a foreign corporation. On December 21, 2001, Optimum Asset Management, Inc. executed a Quit Claim Deed, transferring whatever interest it had in the property to Barbara and Stephen Broyles.

Dr. Weatherly was not notified by the sheriff's office of the tax sale. In the spring of 2001, he discovered that the sale had occurred. On January 3, 2002, Dr. Buckner and Dr. Weatherly executed a *Dation En Paiement*, extinguishing the debt Dr. Buckner owed and transferring to Dr. Weatherly whatever ownership rights Dr. Buckner had in the property.

Thereafter, on May 13, 2002, Dr. Weatherly filed this suit to annul the tax sale against Optimum Asset Management, Inc. and Barbara and Stephen Broyles. He alleged that as a mortgagee, whose identity was ascertainable at the time of the tax sale, he was entitled to notice of the proceeding, and the failure of the authorities to provide him with such notice violated his procedural due process rights under the United States and Louisiana Constitutions.

In response, the Broyles filed a reconventional demand asking for a confirmation of their tax title. They urged that Dr. Weatherly was not entitled to actual notice of the tax sale because he was not "reasonably identifiable." The Broyles stressed that Dr. Weatherly never lived in East Baton Rouge Parish or maintained an office here, he did not list his name, address or telephone number in any East Baton Rouge Parish directory or registry, and he failed to include any identifying information in the act of assignment other than his name. They submitted that in the absence of additional identifying information in the recorded instrument, notice to Dr. Buckner by publication, was adequate.

Following a hearing, the trial court ran an Internet search on the name "Mickey Weatherly" and, based on the results of that search, found that Dr. Weatherly was "reasonably identifiable." Therefore, the court concluded, the jurisprudence required that the governmental authority make some effort to provide Dr. Weatherly with notice of the tax sale. Finding no evidence that any steps were undertaken to locate the named mortgagee, the court held that the tax sale violated Dr. Weatherly's due process rights. Accordingly, the court decreed the tax sale null and void and declared Dr. Weatherly to be the owner of the property.

This appeal, taken by the Broyles, followed.

DISCUSSION

The trial court correctly observed that the record is devoid of evidence that the sheriffs office made any attempt to notify Dr. Weatherly, whose name appears in the public record as the assignee of the mortgage on the property, of the impending tax sale. Ms. Brenda Edwards, the assistant tax director for the sheriff's tax office, attested that in 1997, the sheriff's office simply did not undertake to identify and send notices to mortgagees of property tax delinquencies. However, she stated, the office currently has a procedure in place for notifying mortgagees of the nonpayment of taxes on every tax sale. Ms. Edwards explained that the office does a public records search, and if it were to disclose the name of a mortgagee without an address, further steps would be taken to ascertain an address, including enlisting the aid of the Clerk of Court's research department, as well as a search of the Lexis/Nexis directory.

In their first assignment of error, the Broyles contend that the trial court erred by conducting an Internet search to determine whether Dr. Weatherly's identity was reasonably ascertainable. We agree. A finder of fact may not consider evidence outside the record in making its findings. *Burdis v. Lafourche Parish Police Jury*, 618 So.2d 971, 976 (La. App. 1st Cir.), *writ denied*, 620 So.2d 843 (La. 1993). More particularly, it is well settled that the resolution of disputed issues by judicial notice is improper. *Id.* Nevertheless, we find any error the trial court may have committed by conducting the Internet search is harmless, because the trial court's ultimate conclusion that the tax sale violated Dr. Weatherly's due process rights is legally correct.

The due process clause of the Fourteenth Amendment to the United States Constitution requires that deprivation of property by adjudication be preceded by notice and opportunity for hearing appropriate to the nature of the case. *Mullane v. Central Hanover Bank & Trust Company*, 339 U.S. 306, 313, 70 S.Ct. 652, 656-657, 94 L.Ed. 865 (1950). Thus, an elementary requirement of due process in any proceeding which is to be accorded finality is notice, reasonably calculated, under all of the circumstances, to apprise interested parties of the pendency of the action and afford them an opportunity to present their objections. *Mullane*, 339 U.S. at 314, 70 S.Ct. at 657.

In *Mennonite Board of Missions v. Adams*, 462 U.S. 791, 798, 103 S.Ct. 2706, 2711, 77 L.Ed.2d 180 (1983), the United States Supreme Court recognized that a mortgagee possesses a substantial property interest that is significantly affected by a tax sale, and therefore, the Court held, a mortgagee is entitled to notice reasonably calculated to apprise him of a pending tax sale. In *Mennonite*, the Court ruled that when a mortgagee is identified in a mortgage that is publicly recorded, constructive notice by publication must be supplemented by notice mailed to the mortgagee's last known available address, or by personal service. *Mennonite*, 462 U.S. at 798, 103 S.Ct. at 2711. Constructive notice suffices, the court stressed, only when the mortgagee is not "reasonably identifiable."

Appellants contend that Dr. Weatherly was not entitled to notice of the tax sale because he was not "reasonably identifiable." They submit that it was Dr. Weatherly's inaction, in failing to give identifying information in the assignment, such as an address or Social Security number, and in failing to request written notice of a tax delinquency pursuant to La. R.S. 47:2180.1, that resulted in his lack of notice of the tax sale. Appellants insist that without the proper identifying information in the act of assignment itself, any investigation by the sheriff's office to identify Dr. Weatherly would have been a "vain and useless endeavor," and therefore, the lack of any attempt by the sheriff's office to identify or provide notice to Dr. Weatherly should not serve to invalidate the tax sale.

We disagree. Dr. Weatherly's failure to include identifying information in the assignment, or his failure to request a notice of the tax delinquency under La. R.S. 47:2180.1, did not constitute a waiver of his right to notice under the due process clause. It has long been held that a party's ability to take steps to safeguard his interests does not relieve the state of its constitutional obligation to give notice. *Mennonite*, 462 U.S. at 799, 103 S.Ct at 2712; *Bank of West Baton Rouge v. Stewart*, 2000-0114 (La. App. 1st Cir. 2/16/01), 808 So.2d 464 (holding that a reasonably ascertainable mortgagee does not waive her constitutional due process right to notice of a tax sale by failing to request notice of a tax delinquency as provided for in La. R.S. 47:2180.1); *Parkview Oak Subdivision Corp. v. Tridico*, 95-0604 (La. App. 1st Cir. 11/9/95), 667 So.2d 1101, *writ denied*, 96-0622 (La. 5/10/96), 672 So.2d 921 (holding that the failure of a mortgagee to request notice of a property seizure under La. R.S. 13:3886 is not a waiver of due process notice and does not relieve a creditor of its constitutional obligation if it has reasonable means at its disposal to identify those parties whose interests will be adversely affected by the foreclosure).

Furthermore, the mere fact that the recorded instrument did not contain an address is not fatal to Dr. Weatherly's due process claim. In *Mennonite*, the name of the mortgagee was identified in the public records, but no address was listed. The Court assumed that the mortgagee's address could have been ascertained by "reasonably diligent efforts." The Court stressed, however, that a governmental body was not required to undertake "extraordinary efforts" to discover the identity and whereabouts of a mortgagee whose identity is not in the public record. *Mennonite*, 462 U.S. at 798, 103 S.Ct. at 2711 n.4. Thus, under *Mennonite*, the identification of a mortgagee by name in a publicly recorded instrument triggers a duty on the part of the governmental body to undertake reasonably diligent efforts to give notice of a tax sale to the mortgagee.

Because Dr. Weatherly was identified as a mortgagee in the mortgage records, *Mennonite* required that he be notified of the impending tax sale if his whereabouts could have been ascertained by reasonably diligent efforts. It is undisputed in this case that the sheriff's office made no attempt to identify Dr. Weatherly as an interested party or ascertain his whereabouts. Had the sheriff's office looked into the mortgage records, it would have learned that Mickey Weatherly had a mortgage on the property, and it could have contacted Whitney National Bank, the assignor, or Dr. Buckner, the owner of the property, to obtain an address. Where an interested party's name and address could have been found after a reasonably diligent search, that person is reasonably ascertainable. *Henderson v. Kingpin Development Co.*, 2001-2115, p. 10 (La. App. 1st Cir. 8/6/03), 859 So.2d 122, 130. Under the circumstances of this case, we can only conclude that the sheriff's office failed to undertake "reasonably diligent efforts" to identify and provide notice of the impending tax sale to Dr. Weatherly, and that failure rendered the tax sale an absolute nullity. See also *In re Raz*, 2003-0893 (La. App. 1st Cir. 2/23/04), 871 So.2d 363 (holding a tax sale absolutely null where, despite the presence of a mortgage in the public records, the sheriff's office made no attempt to notify the mortgagee).

CONCLUSION

For the above reasons, the judgment decreeing the tax sale to be a nullity is affirmed. All costs of this appeal are assessed to appellants.

AFFIRMED.

Appendix H: Case Study 8

IN THE COMMONWEALTH COURT OF PENNSYLVANIA

Charles Fernandez,	:	
	:	
Appellant	:	
	:	
v.	:	No. 1600 C.D. 2006
	:	
Tax Claim Bureau of Northampton	:	Argued: April 10, 2007
County	:	
	:	
v.	:	
	:	
John Heilman and Mary Ann Heilman	:	
a/k/a Mary Heilman	:	

BEFORE: HONORABLE DAN PELLEGRINI, Judge
HONORABLE RENÉE COHN JUBELIRER, Judge
HONORABLE JAMES R. KELLEY, Senior Judge

OPINION BY JUDGE COHN JUBELIRER   **FILED: May 31, 2007**

This case is an appeal from an Order and Adjudication of the Northampton County Court of Common Pleas (trial court) denying a petition to set aside a judicial sale. The case involves the notice provisions of the Real Estate Tax Sale Law (Law).[1] Prior to the tax sale, Charles Fernandez (Owner)

---

[1]Section 607.1 of the Act of July 7, 1947, P.L. 1368, added by Section 30 of the Act of July 3, 1986, P.L. 351, 72 P.S. § 5860.607a. This case involves interpretation and application of Section 607.1 of the Law, which provides:

When any notification of a pending tax sale or a tax sale subject to court confirmation is required to be mailed to any owner, mortgagee, lienholder or other person or entity whose property interests are likely to be significantly affected by such tax sale, and such mailed notification is either returned without the required receipted personal signature of the addressee or under other circumstances raising a significant doubt as to the actual receipt of such notification by the named addressee or is not returned or acknowledged at all, then, before the tax sale can be conducted or confirmed, *the bureau must exercise reasonable efforts to discover the whereabouts of such person or entity and notify him. The bureau's efforts shall include, but not necessarily be restricted to, a search of current telephone directories for the county and of the dockets and indices of the*

owned the property in question, a vacant lot in Easton, Northampton County (Subject Property). After Owner became delinquent by not paying taxes on the Subject Property, the Northampton County Tax Claim Bureau (Bureau) provided various forms of notice and then sold the Subject Property at judicial sale to John and Mary Ann Heilman (Purchasers). Owner avers that the Bureau did not take sufficient steps to discover his current address, resulting in his not receiving notice of the sale and, so, accordingly, the sale should be set aside. Before the Court are two primary issues: (1) whether the Bureau was required, under the plain language of the Law and in employing reasonable efforts to ascertain the Owner's address, to consult with local, municipal and school tax bureaus;[2] and (2) whether the posting of the Subject Property constitutes actual and sufficient notice to the Owner of the pending sale.

Owner owned both the Subject Property, which is a vacant lot at 204 West St. Joseph Street, Easton, and the single family house immediately adjacent to it at 210 West St. Joseph Street (210 Property). The Subject Property is on the corner of West St. Joseph Street, where it intersects with West St. John Street.[3] Owner used the Subject Property as a yard for the 210 Property. (Trial Ct. Tr. at 26, May 17, 2006.) The deeds to both properties contain a certification by Owner "that the precise residence of the within grantee, [Owner] is: 50 Kiernan Avenue, Hellertown, PA" (Hellertown

---

county tax assessment offices, recorder of deeds office and prothonotary's office, as well as contacts made to any apparent alternate address or telephone number which may have been written on or in the file pertinent to such property. When such reasonable efforts have been exhausted, regardless of whether or not the notification efforts have been successful, a notation shall be placed in the property file describing the efforts made and the results thereof, and the property may be rescheduled for sale or the sale may be confirmed as provided in this act.

72 P.S. § 5860.607a(a) (emphasis added).

[2] Owner frames this as two issues: (1) Did the trial court properly determine that the Bureau in this case made reasonable efforts to learn the correct address of Taxpayer; and (2) Do the reasonable efforts a tax claim bureau must engage in to find an owner's address include contacting local, municipal and school tax bureaus to learn where each mails its tax bill for the property subject to the sale?

[3] There is some discrepancy from Owner as to whether the Subject Property or 210 Property is on the corner. At the hearing, Owner's Counsel stated that "[Owner] lives at Saint Joseph, Your Honor. But it's on the corner of Saint Joseph and Saint John." (Trial Ct. Tr. at 13, May 17, 2006.) In Owner's Statement of Facts and Conclusions of Law filed with the trial court on May 25, 2006, Owner indicates that: "4. The premises of 204 W. St. Joseph Street, City of Easton, Northampton County, Pennsylvania, is on the corner of W. St. Joseph Street and St. John Street." ([Owner's] Statement of Facts and Conclusions of Law, Facts ¶ 4, May 25, 2006.)

Property). (Deed for Subject Property at 3, November 27, 2001; Deed for 210 Property at 3, November 27, 2001.) Owner did not own the Hellertown Property, but rented it from another person.

In May 2003, the Bureau sent notice by certified mail to the Hellertown Property that Owner had unpaid 2002 school real estate taxes on the Subject Property in the amount of $395.36.[4] Owner acknowledged his receipt of the notice by signing for it. The notice indicated that if he failed to pay the taxes the Subject Property could be sold to satisfy the outstanding taxes.

It is not clear exactly when, but at some point subsequent to the recording of these deeds, Owner switched his residence from the Hellertown Property to the 210 Property.[5]

In July 2004, the Northampton County Sheriff's Office (Sheriff) posted the Subject Property to put Owner on notice of the 2002 delinquent taxes. The Sheriff also posted the Subject Property in August 2004 with notice of the tax upset sale.

On August 2, 2004, the Bureau mailed notice of the tax upset sale to the Hellertown Property. The Postal Service returned the notification to the Bureau with a notation that it could not be forwarded.

On September 13, 2004, the Bureau exposed the Subject Property to a tax upset sale as a result of the 2002 delinquent taxes. At the tax upset sale, no one bid on the Subject Property. On November 22, 2004, the Northampton County Court of Common Pleas (trial court) issued a Rule to Show Cause as to why the Subject Property should not be sold at a judicial sale. The Sheriff posted the Subject Property in December 2004, with notice of the upcoming judicial sale.

The judicial sale was held on January 10, 2005, and Purchasers successfully bid on, and were sold, the Subject Property. Purchasers received title to the Subject Property by deed dated February 22, 2005.

In March 2005, Owner contacted the tax department about his 2004 taxes, at which time he learned of the judicial sale of the Subject Property

---

[4]The amount of the initial bill was $370.36. (*See* Trial Ct. Tr. at 34, May 17, 2006.) The amount in the certified notice seems to include an additional amount for fees and interest, bringing the total at the time of the notice to $395.36. With additional interest and fees that accrued during the time leading up to the sale, the amount the Bureau ended up paying to the District from the judicial sale was $425.56. (*See* Trial Ct. Tr. at 33, May 17, 2006.)

[5]Owner testified that he left the Hellertown Residence in 2001; however, assuming that to be the case, it is not clear why he was there to sign for the notice that was sent to the Hellertown Property in May 2003. It is unclear if he made the county aware of this change, although in 2004 and 2005, the City of Easton's 2004 and 2005 real estate tax bill and the Easton Area School District's real estate school tax bill for 2004/2005 for the Subject Property were sent to the 210 Property.

for the 2002 taxes. On May 13, 2005, Owner filed a Petition to Set Aside Judicial Sale Nunc Pro Tunc (Petition).[6]

The trial court conducted a hearing on Owner's Petition and heard the testimony of four witnesses: (1) Owner; (2) two representatives from different local taxing authorities; and (3) the Tax Claim Supervisor for Northampton County (Tax Claim Supervisor).

At the hearing, Owner testified that he did not receive notice of the tax upset sale or the judicial sale. He testified that he essentially used the Subject Property as a yard for his house, and that he regularly cut the Subject Property's grass. He also testified that he did not see any signs posted on the Subject Property prior to the judicial sale.

Representatives from two local taxing authorities, the City of Easton (City) and the Easton Area School District (District) testified that their respective tax bills for the Subject Property for the years 2004 and 2005 were sent to the 210 Property.[7]

In contrast, the Tax Claim Supervisor testified that the Bureau's records for the Subject Property *did not* indicate that mail for the Subject Property should be sent to the 210 Property. She indicated that the only information regarding his address was that Owner resided at the Hellertown Property. She testified in detail as to her ultimately unsuccessful efforts to try to obtain Owner's address, but also acknowledged that she did not contact either the City or the District to see what contact or forwarding information either might have had.

The Tax Claim Supervisor testified that she did not check the telephone book and that she was not sure if anyone else in her office checked the telephone book, but that it was standard practice within her office to check the telephone book.[8] She also testified that she conducted a "Google" computer-

---

[6]The parties engaged in settlement discussions and reached a settlement agreement that was approved by the trial court. (*See* Trial Ct. Tr. at 2-5, Aug. 30, 2005.) Under the terms, Owner agreed to compensate Purchasers approximately $2000.00 in exchange for the Subject Property. Owner was also to pay Northampton County $2000.00, and Northampton County was to return to Purchasers the excess money they paid at the sale, totaling approximately $1000.00. Owner failed to make the payments set forth in the agreement, and the trial court held him in contempt, fining him $500.00. The trial court also scheduled the case for a hearing on the merits of Owner's Petition.

[7]The first representative was from the Treasurer's Department for the City of Easton. He testified that the 2004 and 2005 tax bills were sent to the 210 Property. The second representative was from the collection agency used by the Easton Area School District (District). She testified that the tax bills for the Subject Property for the 2004/2005 school year were sent to the 210 Property.

[8]Two telephone books (both from calendar year 2004, but in different fiscal years) were introduced into evidence. The telephone books did not identify a Charles Fernandez, and did not list the 210 West St. *Joseph* Street address, but both telephone books did have a "Chuck Fernandez" at 210 West St. *John* Street.

based search for Owner's whereabouts, which produced a "Chuck Fernandez" living at the Hellertown Property. She dialed the telephone number the Google search provided, and found that the telephone had been disconnected.

The Tax Claim Supervisor checked the recorder of deeds office, which showed that Owner resided at the Hellertown Property. The Tax Claim Supervisor also testified that the Bureau does not change its records without notice from either the tax collector's office or from the owner and that, in this case, it had received no such notice from either that there was a change of address.

The Tax Claim Supervisor also testified that the Subject Property was posted on three occasions. She acknowledged, though, that she had no direct knowledge of the posting, and that "I cannot swear to a posting, no, sir, I cannot swear to that at all." (Trial Ct. Tr. at 36, May 17, 2006.)[9]

At the hearing, during Bureau's questioning of the Tax Claim Supervisor, the trial court asked if Owner's Counsel was going to require that the individuals who posted the Subject Property appear to testify; Owner's Counsel stipulated that the Subject Property was posted, but did not stipulate to the manner in which it was posted.[10]

---

[9]This testimony, placed in context, follows:

> A: . . . His property was posted after [the notice of the judicial sale was returned] because he did not sign for his notice.
> Q: I'm sorry?
> A: His property was posted by a sheriff.
> Q: But you didn't see the sheriff post it, did you?
> A: No, sir. We never see any of the postings personally. He was also posted for the upset sale.
> Q: Again, you did not see whether anyone posted that property for an upset sale?
> A: I cannot. I cannot say that I saw it no. But it is—he would have been posted three times in the year; once for the notice that was not signed for the 2003 [sic] taxes, that would have been in—most likely in July, then he was posted for the upset sale also in July, and then he would have been posted for the judicial sale in January.
> Q: But you didn't see any posting, you didn't drive by the property and see the posting?
> A: I cannot swear to a posting, no, sir, I cannot swear to that at all.

(Trial Ct. Tr. at 35-36, May 17, 2006.)

[10]The discussion surrounding this stipulation follows:

> Q: Okay. Then you've testified very briefly in reference to the property being posted, and that was posted on a number of occasions to your knowledge?
> A: Yes. It was posted on August 12th of 2004 for the upset sale. And that was bought by one gentleman, one person that we the county hires for—
> **[Owner's Counsel]**: Your Honor, I'm going to object to this, because she can't testify to any type of posting in that on direct examination.

The trial court denied the Petition, finding that the Bureau had engaged in reasonable efforts to contact Owner.[11] Additionally, the trial court found the evidence credible that the Subject Property was posted, but found the Owner "incredible" that he did not see the notices, particularly because he maintained the Subject Property and lived next to it. Relying on *In the Matter of Tax Sale of 2003 Upset*, 860 A.2d 1184, 1185 (Pa. Cmwlth. 2004), and based on its credibility determinations, the trial court concluded that Owner received actual notice of the sale. The trial court, alternatively, concluded that Owner received actual notice in May 2003 when he signed and received the certified mail notice indicating that he had delinquent school real estates taxes for 2002. The trial court concluded that since actual notice can cure defects in statutory notice requirements, the sale was not void.[12] Accordingly, the trial court set aside the Petition and Owner appeals that decision.

We first address whether the trial court properly determined that the Bureau made reasonable efforts to learn the correct address of Owner.

The law is well settled in Pennsylvania that a valid tax sale requires strict compliance with all three of the notice provisions of Section 602 of the

---

> They already said she didn't see it. The only way you can have the evidence.
>
> **[The Court]**: Do you really want the sheriff's or whoever it is to come in here and say that they actually posted it?
>
> **[Bureau Counsel]**: Judge, I was hoping that the Court would take this as a business record exception. We have given Mr. Coffin, [Owner's Counsel,] great leeway with [the Tax Claim Supervisor's] records. What I'm suggesting is that Mr. Coffin is correct, she did not see the posting, but her records would indicate when the posting was done. And I think the Court did rely upon—
>
> **[Owner's Counsel]**: I would stipulate to it within the records.
>
> **[The Court]**: Then a business record, very well. So it was posted 8/12 for the upset sale—for the upset sale, and it was posted on December 13th, '04 for the judicial sale.
>
> **[Tax Claim Supervisor]**: They are by two different people.

(Trial Ct. Tr. at 54-55, May 17, 2006.) We note that the original record does not contain the records of posting to which the trial judge and counsel referred during the hearing.

[11] In doing so, the trial court first found that the Petition was timely because it was brought within the six month statute of limitations under Section 5522(b)(5) of the Judicial Code, 42 Pa. C.S. § 5522(b)(5). This finding is not challenged on appeal.

[12] In tax sales cases, this Court's review is limited to determining whether the trial court abused its discretion, clearly erred as a matter of law or rendered a decision with a lack of supporting evidence. *Rice v. Compro Distributing, Inc.*, 901 A.2d 570, 574 (Pa. Cmwlth. 2006). The trial court is the finder of fact and has exclusive authority to weigh the evidence, make credibility determinations, and draw reasonable inferences from the evidence presented. *Id.*

Law, 72 P.S. § 5860.602: publication, certified mail, and posting. *In re Upset Price Tax Sale of September 25, 1989*, 615 A.2d 870, 872 (Pa. Cmwlth. 1992). If any of the notices are defective, the sale is void. *Id.* Owner's first argument addresses the certified mail notice requirement.[13]

Owner argues that the sale is null and void because Owner never received actual notice of either the upset or judicial sale. Owner argues that, if the Bureau's certified mailed notice is returned to the Bureau, the Bureau is required by statute to contact local tax collectors for contact information for the owner. Section 607.1(a) of the Law, 72 P.S. § 5860.607a(a). Owner argues the Bureau failed to abide by this requirement. Additionally, Owner argues that the due process clause of the Fourteenth Amendment of the United States Constitution requires additional steps to find a property owner when notice is returned that was sent to the owner to apprise him of an upcoming sale of his property. *Jones v. Flowers*, 547 U.S. 220, 126 S. Ct. 1708 (2006).

In response, the Bureau argues that its efforts, most notably the computer "Google" search and the telephoning of the telephone number the search obtained, was sufficient. Additionally, the Bureau argues that review of the local printed telephone directories would have been fruitless because none of these directories contained a listing for Charles Fernandez, but only had one for Chuck Fernandez. The Purchasers raised arguments similar to those of the Bureau.

In addressing these arguments we note that, under Section 607.1(a) of the Law, the focus of our analysis is on the reasonableness of the Bureau's efforts: "the bureau must exercise reasonable efforts to discover the whereabouts of such person or entity and notify him." 72 P.S. § 5860.607a(a). This section, while listing efforts that must be taken, does not provide an exhaustive list of efforts that could be taken.[14] Reasonable efforts are thus

---

[13]The certified mail notice requirement of Section 602 provides that:

> (1) At least thirty (30) days before the date of the sale, by United States certified mail, restricted delivery, return receipt requested, postage prepaid, to each owner as defined by this act.

72 P.S. § 5860.602(e)(1).

[14]Section 607.1(a) provides that:

> The bureau's efforts shall include, but not necessarily be restricted to, a search of current telephone directories for the county and of the dockets and indices of the county tax assessment offices, recorder of deeds office and prothonotary's office, as well as contacts made to any apparent alternate address or telephone number which may have been written on or in the file pertinent to such property.

72 P.S. § 5860.607a(a).

determined, in part, by the facts of the particular case. The Bureau has the burden of establishing that it has complied with the reasonable efforts requirements of Section 607.1 and the notice requirements of Section 602. *Rice v. Compro Distributing, Inc.*, 901 A.2d 570, 575 (Pa. Cmwlth. 2006). A reasonable investigation is one that "use[s] *ordinary common sense business practices to ascertain proper addresses. . . ." In re Tax Sale of Real Property Situated in Jefferson Township (Ruffner)*, 828 A.2d 475, 479 (Pa. Cmwlth. 2003) (emphasis added). This ordinary common sense "must go beyond the mere ceremonial act of notice by certified mail," but does not require "the equivalent of a title search. . . ." *Id.*[15] Additionally, the Bureau is required to strictly adhere to the notice provisions of the Law. *Rivera v. Carbon County Tax Claim Bureau*, 857 A.2d 208, 214 (Pa. Cmwlth. 2004).

Applied to the present case, we find that the Bureau failed to strictly adhere to the statutory requirements, and that this failure, by itself, is sufficient to sustain Owner's Petition. Owner focuses on the Bureau's failure to consult with the various county tax assessment offices. Section 607.1 specifies, using the directive, "shall" language, that "the dockets and indices of the county tax assessment offices" be consulted. 72 P.S. § 5860.607a(a). As evidence was presented that the 2004 and 2005 tax bills from the City of Easton and the 2004/2005 school tax bills were sent to the 210 Property, it seems that such a consultation with the tax assessment offices would have been fruitful. Worth noting is that the sale itself arose from a failure to pay school real estate taxes in 2002—yet the District knew to send 2004/2005 tax bills—issued within the same time frame as the upset sale and judicial sale notices—to the 210 Property. The Bureau seems to focus on the reasonableness of its actions, but does not squarely address whether it was actually required to contact the tax assessment offices. When questioned as to why she did not contact the tax collector for the District to find out where the Dis-

---

[15] *Jones* similarly holds that the mailing of notice by certified mail that is returned to the governmental body does not, by itself, satisfy due process requirements. In the two cases that this Court has issued since *Jones*, we have placed their holdings squarely within *Ruffner*. *See Miller v. Clinton County Tax Claim Bureau*, 909 A.2d 461 (Pa. Cmwlth. 2006); *Rice*. The focus of the Supreme Court's analysis is that the governmental body must "provide notice reasonably calculated, under all the circumstances, to apprise interested parties of the pendency of the action and afford them an opportunity to present their objections." *Jones*, 126 S. Ct. at 1713-14 (quoting *Mullane v. Central Hanover Bank & Trust Co.*, 339 U.S. 306, 314 (1950)) (quotations omitted). The Court explained that "the State should have taken additional reasonable steps to notify [owner], if practicable to do so" and that "[w]hat steps are reasonable in response to new information depends upon what the new information reveals." *Jones*, 126 S. Ct. at 1718.

trict sent the mail, the Tax Claim Supervisor testified that "I probably made an erroneous assumption because the taxes came from the school district for the following two years." (Trial Ct. Tr. at 49, May 17, 2006.) The Tax Claim Supervisor explained that the county maintains the addresses, which it provides to the various taxing authorities, so she assumed that the authorities would have the same addresses that she did. (Trial Ct. Tr. at 49-50, May 17, 2006.)[16] This failure to consult with these tax assessment offices provides sufficient basis on its own to require the judicial sale to be set aside.[17]

We have held that the primary purpose of the Law is not to strip away citizens' property rights but, rather, to ensure the collection of taxes.

---

[16]She testified that:

> the county is to be the main contact for all changes of mailing addresses. All things are suppose to be coming from our office. And the records that are present here with these addresses on were not provided by the county when they provided the tax downloads. And the county is the one that provides those—those disks. Those addresses were not on those disks that were presented to the school district nor the municipalities.

(Trial Ct. Tr. at 48, May 17, 2006.)

[17]It does not appear that Owner argues this point, but it does seem that the county failed to search the county-wide telephone book, which, by the Law, it was required to consult. The trial court made the following relevant finding: "[The Tax Claim Supervisor] personally did not search the telephone book for Fernandez and [it] is uncertain whether any staff members in her office did so. [The Tax Claim Supervisor] testified that it is standard practice to search the telephone book for information." (Trial Ct. Adj., Finding of Fact 25.) This finding is supported by the testimony and evidence. Among the specific actions required to be taken is that "current telephone directories for the county" be searched. 72 P.S. § 5860.607a(a). Section 607.1 does not contain the permissive, "may" be consulted, when referring to telephone books, but rather, contains the directive, "shall . . . search . . . current telephone directories." As there was no evidence that this was done, it appears the Bureau did not strictly adhere to the statutory terms.

Additionally, evidence presented before the trial court indicated that, had the telephone books been examined, it would have found a "Chuck Fernandez." The Bureau seeks to diminish this fact, by arguing that the listing contains a different first name, and by also noting that the address listed in the directory is different from the actual mailing address. This argument is undercut by the Tax Claim Supervisor's own testimony as to the computer search that she performed which specifically linked a "Chuck Fernandez" with the Hellertown Property to which the Bureau had sent the notices. Had the Bureau used the telephone number provided for "Chuck Fernandez" in the telephone book, it may have been able to reach him.

In addition, checking the telephone book seems to qualify as an ordinary common sense business practice when one is seeking to obtain an address. Nonetheless, it does not appear that this issue is directly argued before this Court.

Rivera, 857 A.2d at 214.[18] The United States Supreme Court has noted that "[p]eople must pay their taxes, and the government may hold citizens accountable for tax delinquency by taking their property. But before forcing a citizen to satisfy his debt by forfeiting his property, due process requires the government to provide adequate notice of the impending taking. U.S. Const., Amdt. 14." *Jones*, 126 S. Ct. at 1718. Consistent with these principles, we have explained that, in reviewing whether due process requirements have been met, "the focus is not on the alleged neglect of the owner, which is often present in some degree, but on whether the activities of the Bureau comply with the requirements of the statute." *Smith v. Tax Claim Bureau of Pike County*, 834 A.2d 1247, 1251 (Pa. Cmwlth. 2003).

The Bureau's representative identified the error in this case—a failure to perform statutorily required searches because of an assumption as to what the results of the search would be. Additionally, the assumption does not comport with ordinary common sense business practices. The statutory requirements protect the property rights of citizens and provide a minimum as to what must be accomplished to protect those rights. As noted in *Ruffner* and *Jones*, that minimum may not be sufficient under the facts of a particular case. That minimum was not accomplished here.[19] Accordingly, we conclude that the judicial sale must be set aside.[20]

---

[18]In contrast we must call attention to a statement made by the Tax Claim Supervisor that the Bureau's "*goal is to sell the property.*" (Trial Ct. Tr. at 40, May 17, 2006 (emphasis added).) Arguably, this statement can be characterized as a mere comment, or perhaps a misstatement. However, given what is at issue in this case, a deprivation of a person's property interest, and given that this deprivation occurred without following statutorily prescribed procedures, we use this statement to reemphasize the principle that the Law's purpose, and with it, the Bureau's primary purpose, is not to strip away citizen's property, but to ensure payment of taxes. Although selling of the property may end up being the ultimate means used toward achieving that end, it is not the end itself.

[19]It does not appear that Owner makes this argument, but it seems that the trial court erred in finding that actual notice of *tax delinquency* would suffice as actual notice of the *tax sale*. In *Jones*, the United States Supreme Court reiterated its rejection that notice of tax delinquency satisfied the notice requirements for the *actual sale* of property:

> [T]he common knowledge that property may become subject to government taking when taxes are not paid does not excuse the government from complying with its constitutional obligation of notice before taking private property. We have previously stated the opposite: **An interested party's knowledge of delinquency in the payment of taxes is not equivalent to notice that a tax sale is pending**.

126 S. Ct. at 1717 (quotations omitted) (emphasis added). Under this authority, to the extent the trial court found actual notice from the tax delinquency notice that Owner received, the trial court erred. However, as noted, Owner does not seem to squarely raise this argument.

[20]Based on our resolution of this first issue, we do not reach the issue of actual and sufficient notice.

For these reasons, the order of the trial court is reversed.

RENÉE COHN JUBELIRER, Judge

IN THE COMMONWEALTH COURT OF PENNSYLVANIA

Charles Fernandez,	:
	:
Appellant	:
	:
v.	: No. 1600 C.D. 2006
	:
Tax Claim Bureau of Northampton County	: Argued: April 10, 2007
	:
v.	:
	:
John Heilman and Mary Ann Heilman a/k/a Mary Heilman	:

O R D E R

NOW, May 31, 2007, the order of the Court of Common Pleas of Northampton County in the above-captioned matter is hereby **REVERSED.**

RENÉE COHN JUBELIRER, Judge

Appendix I: Web Site Credibility Checklist

1. Can you determine the site's owner, editor, or authors when you visit the site?
2. Determine the identity of the site's owner or sponsoring organization if it's not clear from the site itself.
3. Verify credentials by doing an independent search, not just by relying upon what is stated on the site.
4. Discover who else relies on a particular site by conducting a link search.
5. How fresh is the content?
6. What is the quality of the content?
7. Is the site missing any content? Is it as complete as its print version (if there is one)?
8. Verify all information by trying to find the same data at another site.
9. Ascertain the top-level domain (TLD) to help decide credibility.
10. Document your search.

Can you determine the site's owner, editor, or authors when you visit the site?

Look for a publication statement on the site to ascertain the owner, editor, and authors. Be suspicious if you don't easily find one. A credible site owner should post their name, professional affiliation (if any), and contact information in a readily visible place on the site so visitors can verify the owner's identity or contact them via e-mail or phone. We've contacted site owners countless times to ask about their credentials, the currency of their data, or even to let them know that links weren't working.

For example, when we went to the Jurist.law site (http://jurist.law.pitt. edu/about.htm#Masthead), it was easy to find out that it was hosted by the University of Pittsburgh. Also listed was its advisory board, made up of law professors from around the world (although when we noticed one of their names was "Lawless" we were momentarily concerned about credibility!).

Determine the identity of the site's owner or sponsoring organization if it's not clear from the site itself.

To try to discover who is behind a Web site, type the URL into a registry such as DomainTools (http://domaintools.com), Better-Whois (http://www. betterwhois.com), or Allwhois (http://www.allwhois.com). Allwhois also provides links to other countries' registries. The reason we emphasized "try" in the first sentence of this paragraph is because no registry, for a variety of reasons, seems to be "completely complete."

A registry may claim to be the "most complete 'who is' service on the Internet," but this doesn't mean complete as in "comprehensive"—just the most complete that it can be, given all the obstacles. It's difficult to create a comprehensive registry because registries may receive less-than-complete records when a domain is registered, and most registries only cover the most popular top-level domain (TLD) types such as .com, .net, or .org, thus leaving out many records from the less popular TLDs such as .biz or .museum.

Even if you do find the registration statement, it's hard to say whether you have found the site owner because anyone can list themselves as the contact person on the registration statement—the site owner, the company's IT manager, or the Web site's outside designer.

Verify credentials by doing an independent search, not just by relying upon what is stated on the site.

Don't just rely on the information about a site that is given on the site itself. If the site owner says he's a lawyer in California, run his name through the California State Bar Association's member records to verify his license and review his discipline record. If the site owner claims to be an author, run his name through the Library of Congress online catalog (http://catalog.loc.gov), its copyright database (http://www.copyright.gov/search), or even Amazon.com.

Discover who else relies on a particular site by conducting a link search.

Another way to determine the credibility of a Web site is to see who else thinks highly enough of the site to link to it from their own site. For example, to see if others rely upon a specific site (such as www.netforlawyers.com), conduct a link search using Google's Advanced Search page. Enter *www.netforlawyers.com* into the **Find pages that link to the page:** box and click the **Search** button. You'll get a list of Web sites that link to the pages of www.netforlawyers.com. Reviewing the sites that link to a site (and examining their credibility) can help you determine a site's credibility.

How fresh is the content?

Look for a statement saying when the site as a whole was last updated. Also look for publication dates for the individual articles or other material posted on the site. For example, on November 11, 2008, we visited the Jurist.law site (http://jurist.law.pitt.edu/) and found a 2008 copyright statement at the bottom of the home page. We were most interested in the content of the main article linked from the site's home page. At the very top of that article was the date and time on which the article had been posted (earlier that same day), as well as the name of the editor who posted it. Other stories linked from the home page (posted that same day) also listed the times at which they were posted. All of this information indicated that the site was being kept fresh.

What is the quality of the content?

Is the content one-sided or objective? One-sided information might be acceptable if it's being used to persuade. For example, the Electronic Privacy Information Center (EPIC) states that it is "a public interest research center . . . established . . . to focus public attention on emerging civil liberties issues and to protect privacy, the First Amendment, and constitutional values." Is this site biased? You bet. But, as noted above, it clearly states its bias on its home page by way of its mission statement. Is the information of high quality? Yes—it's just presented from a privacy advocate's viewpoint.

Is the site missing any content? Is it as complete as its print version (if there is one)?

Ever since the *Tasini* decision (*New York Times Co. v. Tasini*, 533 U.S. 483 [2001], *available at* http://supreme.justia.com/us/533/483/case.html), many publications have had to remove individual authors' articles from their Web sites. Additionally, some newspapers do not license the wire-service content that appears in their print editions for use on their Web sites. The result is the same in either case—many Web sites do not contain all of the content offered in their corresponding print versions. Content that is not licensed for use on a publication's own Web site is usually also not licensed for use in pay databases such as LexisNexis. However, the author/copyright holder might make separate arrangements with those outlets to archive/sell access to their works, so the material could be available online after all—just from a different source.

Conversely, a Web site may contain more content than the print publication. This is the case with sites that continually update throughout the day.

Verify all information by trying to find the same data at another site.

Just by reviewing your results, you can often tell that the information is being published at many sites. Does this make it any more credible? Not necessarily, but you can click on a few of the sites and apply the credibility test. We typically don't verify information if we've already run the site through a credibility test, or if someone else whose judgment we trust has done so. Whom do we trust? People who test sites before writing about them. These are some of the sites of authors who we know test sites before recommending them: SearchEngineLand, SearchEngineWatch, Search Engine Showdown, LLRX, and Netforlawyers (just add a .com to each to visit the sites), and the ABA's Site-tation (http://new.abanet.org/sitetation/Pages/home.aspx).

Ascertain the top-level domain (TLD) to help decide credibility.

Does the TLD indicate it's a government (.gov), educational (.edu), or commercial (.com) site?

Can you always trust a site with a .gov TLD? The U.S. General Services Administration Federal Technology Service (GSA FTS) validates each .gov TLD name before registering it. It's likely then that a site with the .gov TLD is actually sponsored by the government. We say "likely" because on January 24, 2003, the GSA was faced with the first known "hijacking" of a .gov TLD. CNET.com questioned AONN.gov's governmental status (http://news.cnet.com/2100-1023-983384.html). AONN.gov's Web site proclaimed that it was "a 24-hour data exchange system" whose "core mission is to defend America's streets and communities in areas where there has been little or no oversight, isolate and defeat terrorists domestic and foreign who are operating both in and out of cyberspace, expose corruption and extremely difficult to identify threats to the national security while implementing countermeasures to such, create new laws through legislation to protect citizens, penetrate what have traditionally been nearly impenetrable networks, and reform by means of altering previously criminal and anti-American ideologies." The GSA pulled AONN's .gov domain as a result.

Even when you're sure a .gov site is authentic, there are other aspects of credibility that must be considered, such as whether the information on the site is current. For example, the U.S. Code is published by two governmental entities—the House of Representatives and the Government Printing Office (GPO)—but the House site (http://uscode.house.gov/lawrevisioncounsel.shtml) is the more current of the two. On November 13, 2008, for example, Title 1, Section 1 on the GPO site (http://www.gpoaccess.gov/uscode/index.html) was current only up to laws that took effect on January 3, 2006, while the House site showed dates of January 3, 2007.

Another credibility issue to consider is whether the information on a government site is the "official" record. For example, many court sites warn that their site is for "informational purposes only" and that the information "is not the official record." This is especially true for courts that publish their slip opinions, since the court can later modify these opinions.

Can you trust the .edu TLD? Just because an academic institution sponsors a site doesn't mean an academician is writing the content. Case in point: we did a search using the words "lemon" and "law" and came up with a .edu site with a page written by an elementary school child, who liked lemonade and root beer and wanted to be a law professor when he grew up! Needless to say, even though the page contained all of our keywords, it didn't help us with our lemon-law questions. Not all such instances will be as obvious, unfortunately.

Therefore, as with all information sources, data retrieved from the Internet must be viewed with skepticism until its credibility has been verified. Any cybersleuth can access data sources. But the best cybersleuths know that if you are after genuine knowledge, you must establish the data's credibility before relying on it.

Can you trust well-known pay resources? Even pay resources can contain errors. While you don't have to go through the same credibility checklist to identify owners and sponsors of pay resources (such as Lexis-Nexis or Westlaw), their data is only as reliable as the source(s) from which they obtain it. Data can be entered incorrectly at a county clerk's office, for example, leading to misspelled names, incorrect dates of birth, etc. in the data sold to these pay resources. So, even though it's usually correct, you still need to verify the veracity and currency of the information you find there.

Document your search.

Take detailed notes throughout your research process, so you can document the steps you took (e.g., which sources yielded which information or led to other sources).

Print out a paper copy of the pages you will be relying on so you can prove credibility to others.

In addition to creating this paper record of the information as it appeared on the day you conducted your research, it can also be useful to create an electronic copy of the page(s) you're relying on. One way to do this is to capture the pages as PDF documents.

Appendix J: Google Scholar Alerts

Google has made it easier to keep up to date with topics, cases, patents, etc. searched via Google Scholar with the addition of e-mail alerts to the Scholar service.

FIGURE J.1 An envelope icon now appears at the top of each Scholar search results list. The Scholar Alerts feature functions similarly to the more-familiar Google Alerts (previously known as News Alerts) but with a few differences.

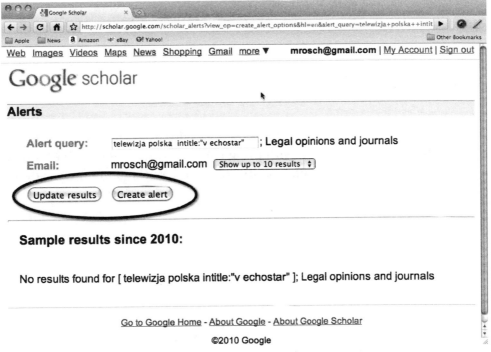

FIGURE J.2 Clicking the envelope icon creates this intermediate page that displays your original search query (you do have the ability to modify the original query), a box into which you can enter the e-mail address to which you want the Alert sent (this address is auto-filled if you are logged into your Google Account), and **Sample Results** showing what content would be included in the Alert.

You can click the **Update Results** button to generate a new **Sample Results** list if you have altered your original query. Clicking the **Create Alert** button completes the process.

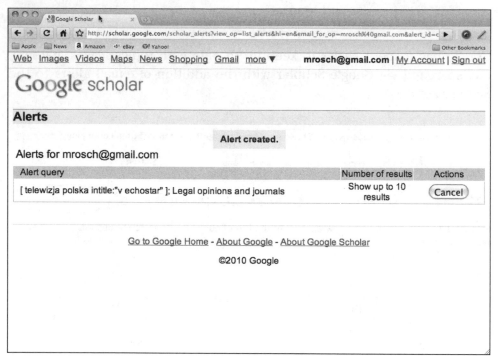

FIGURE J.3   Once the Alert is created, Scholar displays your list of existing Alerts. Interestingly, this is a separate list from any existing Google Alerts (News Alerts) that you had previously created.

Also, Scholar Alerts do not give you the ability to dictate how often you receive the Alerts, as you can with Google Alerts which offers **as-it-happens** and **once a day/once a week** update frequency options via a drop-down menu.

Appendix K: Google Drawings

In Spring 2010, Google launched a stand-alone drawing creation and editing tool known as Drawings. It allows you to create charts, diagrams, timelines, etc., (online) using standard shape, line, and text tools. Many of Drawing's features were first introduced in the Spring of 2009, but they were only accessible via the **Insert** menu in the existing Document, Spreadsheet, or Presentation files.

Along with the launch of the stand-alone editing tool, came the ability to share and collaborate on those drawings.

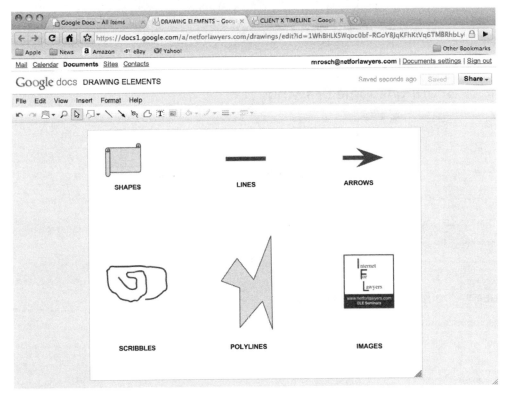

FIGURE K.1   Google allows you to add various elements to the Drawings you create. You can choose from a series of pre-determined shapes, lines, or arrows (top); or you can draw freehand curves/scribbles, multi-sided polyline drawings, or insert images from the Web or your own computer.

Once completed, Google Drawings can be inserted into a Google Document or Presentation. At the time of our publication deadline, you could only share drawings that were created using the Google Drawings editor. You could not import existing drawings to edit and share. Additionally, Drawings cannot be pasted into Spreadsheets.

Completed Drawings can also be downloaded to your own computer in the .JPEG, .PNG and .SVG image formats; or as a .PDF.

K.1 Adding Elements to Google Drawings

Adding any of the elements listed in Figure K.1 to a Google Drawing is a fairly straight-forward process using the toolbar icons.

FIGURE K.2 Clicking each of the annotated icons in this illustration allows you to add a specific type of elements to your Google Drawing: 1) Shapes. 2) Lines. 3) Arrows. 4) Curves. 5) Polylines. 6) Text Boxes. 7) Images.

K.2 Sharing Google Drawings

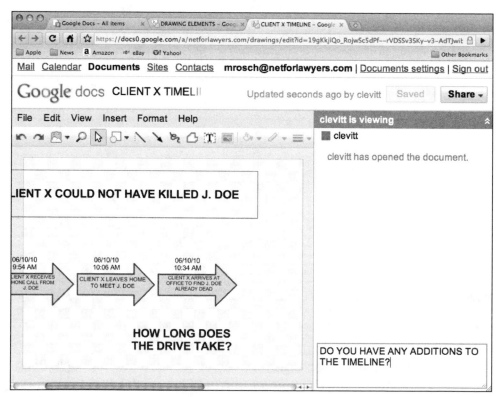

FIGURE K.3 Clicking the downward facing arrows to the right of **[collaborator name] is viewing** (seen on the right-hand side of Figure K.2) opens up this Chat window on the right-hand side of your screen. You can type back and forth with your collaborator(s) as you're editing the Drawing.

If you and a collaborator are both viewing and/or editing a Drawing at the same time, you can open up a Chat session to communicate in real time on the screen (as seen in Figure K.3).

K.3 Adding Drawings to Other Documents

Once a Google Drawing is completed, you can insert the entire Drawing into another document (e.g., a letter, brief, or report). How you insert the Drawing depends on the type of document into which you want to insert it.

K.3.1 Google Documents

Google has made it fairly easy to insert a Google Drawing into a Google Document or Presentation. At the time of our publication deadline, Drawings cannot be pasted into Spreadsheets.

Google has created a special "Web Clipboard" (also known as the "Server Clipboard") onto which you can copy the entire Drawing to paste into another Google Docs file (with the exception of Spreadsheets).

Note that this is different from the **Copy** and **Paste** options found on the **Edit** menu of the Drawing toolbar.

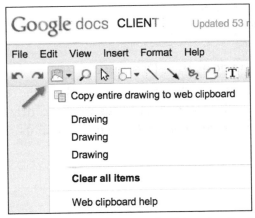

FIGURE K.4 Selecting the **Copy entire drawing to web clipboard** option from the Web Clipboard icon's drop-down menu allows you to save the drawing's elements (on Google's servers). Once you have opened the Google Document into which you want to paste the Drawing, click the Web Clipboard icon in that Document and select one of the items on the Web Clipboard list (all labeled **Drawing** in this illustration) to paste.

K.3.2 Traditional Offline Documents

You cannot copy the elements of a Google Drawing and then paste them into a non-Google document you're editing on your own computer.

You can add a Google Drawing to a document you're editing on your own computer by first downloading it to your computer as a static image file and then inserting that image into your document.

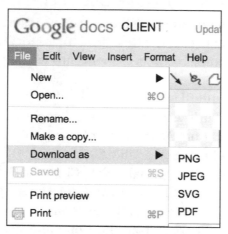

FIGURE K.5 Clicking the **File** drop-down menu (in the upper left-hand corner of your Drawing) and selecting **Download as** gives you the option of downloading your Drawing to your own computer in one of four formats. The **.JPEG** or **.PNG** formats would be the easiest for you to insert into a document you're editing on your own computer.

K.4 Tracking Changes in a Drawing

A major weakness of Google Drawings, at the time of our publication deadline, is the inability to track changes made to drawings over time by collaborators the way you can in Google Documents, Spreadsheets, and Presentations.

Index

The Lawyer's Guide to Collaboration Tools and Technologies: Smart Ways to Work Together
By Dennis Kennedy and Tom Mighell
This first-of-its-kind guide for the legal profession shows you how to use standard technology you already have and the latest "Web 2.0" resources and other tech tools, like Google Docs, Microsoft Office and Share-Point, and Adobe Acrobat, to work more effectively on projects with colleagues, clients, co-counsel and even opposing counsel. In *The Lawyer's Guide to Collaboration Tools and Technologies: Smart Ways to Work Together*, well-known legal technology authorities Dennis Kennedy and Tom Mighell provides a wealth of information useful to lawyers who are just beginning to try these tools, as well as tips and techniques for those lawyers with intermediate and advanced collaboration experience.

The Lawyer's Guide to Marketing on the Internet, Third Edition
By Gregory H. Siskind, Deborah McMurray, and Richard P. Klau
In today's competitive environment, it is critical to have a comprehensive online marketing strategy that uses all the tools possible to differentiate your firm and gain new clients. The Lawyer's Guide to Marketing on the Internet, in a completely updated and revised third edition, showcases practical online strategies and the latest innovations so that you can immediately participate in decisions about your firm's Web marketing effort. With advice that can be implemented by established and young practices alike, this comprehensive guide will be a crucial component to streamlining your marketing efforts.

The Lawyer's Guide to Adobe Acrobat, Third Edition
By David L. Masters
This book was written to help lawyers increase productivity, decrease costs, and improve client services by moving from paper-based files to digital records. This updated and revised edition focuses on the ways lawyers can benefit from using the most current software, Adobe® Acrobat 8, to create Portable Document Format (PDF) files.

PDF files are reliable, easy-to-use, electronic files for sharing, reviewing, filing, and archiving documents across diverse applications, business processes, and platforms. The format is so reliable that the federal courts' Case Management/Electronic Case Files (CM/ECF) program and state courts that use Lexis-Nexis File & Serve have settled on PDF as the standard.

You'll learn how to:

- Create PDF files from a number of programs, including Microsoft Office
- Use PDF files the smart way
- Markup text and add comments
- Digitally, and securely, sign documents
- Extract content from PDF files
- Create electronic briefs and forms

The Electronic Evidence and Discovery Handbook: Forms, Checklists, and Guidelines
By Sharon D. Nelson, Bruce A. Olson, and John W. Simek
The use of electronic evidence has increased dramatically over the past few years, but many lawyers still struggle with the complexities of electronic discovery. This substantial book provides lawyers with the templates they need to frame their discovery requests and provides helpful advice on what they can subpoena. In addition to the ready-made forms, the authors also supply explanations to bring you up to speed on the electronic discovery field. The accompanying CD-ROM features over 70 forms, including, Motions for Protective Orders, Preservation and Spoliation Documents, Motions to Compel, Electronic Evidence Protocol Agreements, Requests for Production, Internet Services Agreements, and more. Also included is a full electronic evidence case digest with over 300 cases detailed!

The 2010 Solo and Small Firm Legal Technology Guide
By Sharon D. Nelson, Esq., John W. Simek, and Michael C. Maschke
This annual guide is the only one of its kind written to help solo and small firm lawyers find the best technology for their dollar. You'll find the most current information and recommendations on computers, servers, networking equipment, legal software, printers, security products, smart phones, and anything else a law office might need. It's written in clear, easily understandable language to make implementation easier if you choose to do it yourself, or you can use it in conjunction with your IT consultant. Either way, you'll learn how to make technology work for you.

Social Media for Lawyers
By Carolyn Elefant and Nicole Black
The world of legal marketing has changed with the rise of social media sites such as Linkedin, Twitter, and Facebook. Law firms are seeking their companies attention with tweets, videos, blog posts, pictures, and online content. Social media is fast and delivers news at record pace. *Social Media for Lawyers: The Next Frontier* provides you with a practical, goal-centric approach to using social media in your law practice that will enable you to identify social media platforms and tools that fit your practice and implement them easily, efficiently, and ethically.

How to Start and Build a Law Practice, Fifth Edition
By Jay G Foonberg
This classic ABA bestseller has been used by tens of thousands of lawyers as the comprehensive guide to planning, launching, and growing a successful practice. It's packed with over 600 pages of guidance on identifying the right location, finding clients, setting fees, managing your office, maintaining an ethical and responsible practice, maximizing available resources, upholding your standards, and much more. If you're committed to starting your own practice, this book will give you the expert advice you need to make it succeed.

ABA **LAW PRACTICE MANAGEMENT SECTION**
MARKETING · MANAGEMENT · TECHNOLOGY · FINANCE

The Lawyer's Guide to Concordance
By Liz M. Weiman

In this age, when trial outcomes depend on the organization of electronic data discovery, *The Lawyer's Guide to Concordance* reveals how attorneys and staff can make Concordance the most powerful tool in their litigation arsenal. Using this easy-to-read hands-on reference guide, individuals who are new to Concordance can get up-to-speed quickly, by following its step-bystep instructions, exercises, and time-saving shortcuts. For those already working with Concordance, this comprehensive resource provides methods, strategies, and technical information to further their knowledge and success using this robust program.

Inside The Lawyer's Guide to Concordance readers will also find:

- Techniques to effectively search database records, create tags for the results, customize printed reports, redline and redact images, create production sets
- Strategies to create and work with transcript, e-document, and e-mail databases, load files from vendors, manage images, troubleshoot, and more
- Real-world case studies from law firms in the United States and England describing Concordance features that have improved case management

The Lawyer's Guide to CT Summation iBlaze, Second Edition
By Tom O'Connor

CT Summation iBlaze gives you complete control over litigation evidence by bringing all you need—transcripts, documents, issues, and events, to your fingertips in one easy-to-use software program. Working in close collaboration with CT Summation, author and noted technology speaker Tom O'Connor has developed this easy-to-understand guide designed to quickly get you up and running on CT Summation software. Fully up-to-date, covering the latest version of iBlaze, the book features step-by-step instructions on the functions of iBlaze and how to get the most from this powerful, yet easy-to-use program.

The Lawyer's Guide to Microsoft Word 2007
By Ben M. Schorr

Microsoft Word is one of the most used applications in the Microsoft Office suite—there are few applications more fundamental than putting words on paper. Most lawyers use Word and few of them get everything they can from it. Because the documents you create are complex and important—your law practice depends, to some degree, upon the quality of the documents you produce and the efficiency with which you can produce them. Focusing on the tools and features that are essential for lawyers in their everyday practice, *The Lawyer's Guide to Microsoft Word* explains in detail the key components to help make you more effective, more efficient and more successful.

The Lawyer's Guide to Microsoft Excel 2007
By John C. Tredennick

Did you know Excel can help you analyze and present your cases more effectively or help you better understand and manage complex business transactions? Designed as a hands-on manual for beginners as well as longtime spreadsheet users, you'll learn how to build spreadsheets from scratch, use them to analyze issues, and to create graphics presentation. Key lessons include:

- Spreadsheets 101: How to get started for beginners
- Advanced Spreadsheets: How to use formulas to calculate values for settlement offers, and damages, business deals
- Simple Graphics and Charts: How to make sophisticated charts for the court or to impress your clients
- Sorting and filtering data and more

Find Info Like a Pro, Volume 1: Mining the Internet's Publicly Available Resources for Investigative Research
By Carole A. Levitt and Mark E. Rosch

This complete hands-on guide shares the secrets, shortcuts, and realities of conducting investigative and background research using the sources of publicly available information available on the Internet. Written for legal professionals, this comprehensive desk book lists, categorizes, and describes hundreds of free and fee-based Internet sites. The resources and techniques in this book are useful for investigations; depositions; locating missing witnesses, clients, or heirs; and trial preparation, among other research challenges facing legal professionals. In addition, a CD-ROM is included, which features clickable links to all of the sites contained in the book.

The Lawyer's Guide to Microsoft Outlook 2007
By Ben M. Schorr

Outlook is the most used application in Microsoft Office, but are you using it to your greatest advantage? *The Lawyer's Guide to Microsoft Outlook 2007* is the only guide written specifically for lawyers to help you be more productive, more efficient and more successful. More than just email, Outlook is also a powerful task, contact, and scheduling manager that will improve your practice. From helping you log and track phone calls, meetings, and correspondence to archiving closed case material in one easy-to-store location, this book unlocks the secrets of "underappreciated" features that you will use every day. Written in plain language by a twenty-year veteran of law office technology and ABA member, you'll find:

- Tips and tricks to effectively transfer information between all components of the software
- The eight new features in Outlook 2007 that lawyers will love
- A tour of major product features and how lawyers can best use them
- Mistakes lawyers should avoid when using Outlook
- What to do when you're away from the office

30-Day Risk-Free Order Form
Call Today! 1-800-285-2221
Monday–Friday, 7:30 AM – 5:30 PM, Central Time

Qty	Title	LPM Price	Regular Price	Total
_____	The Lawyer's Guide to Collaboration Tools and Technologies: Smart Ways to Work Together (5110589)	$59.95	$ 89.95	$_____
_____	The Lawyer's Guide to Marketing on the Internet, Third Edition (5110585)	74.95	84.95	$_____
_____	The Lawyer's Guide to Adobe Acrobat, Third Edition (5110588)	49.95	79.95	$_____
_____	The Electronic Evidence and Discovery Handbook: Forms, Checklists, and Guidelines (5110569)	99.95	129.95	$_____
_____	The 2010 Solo and Small Firm Legal Technology Guide (5110701)	54.95	89.95	$_____
_____	Social Media for Lawyers (5110710)	47.95	79.95	$_____
_____	How to Start and Build a Law Practice, Fifth Edition (5110508)	57.95	69.95	$_____
_____	The Lawyer's Guide to CT Summation iBlaze, Second Edition (5110698)	49.95	69.95	$_____
_____	The Lawyer's Guide to Microsoft Word 2007 (5110697)	49.95	69.95	$_____
_____	The Lawyer's Guide to Microsoft Excel 2007 (5110665)	49.95	69.95	$_____
_____	Find Info Like a Pro, Volume 1: Mining the Internet's Publicly Available Resources for Investigative Research (5110708)	47.95	79.95	$_____
_____	The Lawyer's Guide to Microsoft Outlook 2007 (5110661)	49.99	69.99	$_____

*Postage and Handling	
$10.00 to $49.99	$5.95
$50.00 to $99.99	$7.95
$100.00 to $199.99	$9.95
$200.00+	$12.95

**Tax
DC residents add 5.75%
IL residents add 10.25%

*Postage and Handling	$_____
**Tax	$_____
TOTAL	$_____

PAYMENT

❑ Check enclosed (to the ABA)

❑ Visa   ❑ MasterCard   ❑ American Express

_____
Account Number   Exp. Date   Signature

Name _____ Firm _____

Address _____

City _____ State _____ Zip _____

Phone Number _____ E-Mail Address _____

Guarantee
If—for any reason—you are not satisfied with your purchase, you may return it within 30 days of receipt for a complete refund of the price of the book(s). No questions asked!

Mail: ABA Publication Orders, P.O. Box 10892, Chicago, Illinois 60610-0892
♦ Phone: 1-800-285-2221 ♦ FAX: 312-988-5568

E-Mail: abasvcctr@abanet.org ♦ Internet: http://www.lawpractice.org/catalog